OXFORD STUDIES IN THEOLOGICAL ETHICS

General Editor
Oliver O'Donovan

OXFORD STUDIES IN THEOLOGICAL ETHICS

The series presents discussions on topics of general concern to Christian Ethics, as it is currently taught in universities and colleges, at the level demanded by a serious student. The volumes will not be specialized monographs nor general introductions or surveys. They aim to make a contribution worthy of notice in its own right but also focused in such a way as to provide a suitable starting-point for orientation.

The titles include studies in important contributors to the Christian tradition of moral thought; explorations of current moral and social questions; and discussions of central concepts in Christian moral and political thought. Authors treat their topics in a way that will show the relevance of the Christian tradition, but with openness to neighbouring traditions of thought which have entered into dialogue with it.

Political Worship
■ ■ ■
Ethics for Christian Citizens

BERND WANNENWETSCH

Translated by
MARGARET KOHL

OXFORD
UNIVERSITY PRESS

OXFORD
UNIVERSITY PRESS

Great Clarendon Street, Oxford OX2 6DP

Oxford University Press is a department of the University of Oxford.
It furthers the University's objective of excellence in research, scholarship,
and education by publishing worldwide in

Oxford New York

Auckland Bangkok Buenos Aires Cape Town Chennai
Dar es Salaam Delhi Hong Kong Istanbul Karachi Kolkata
Kuala Lumpur Madrid Melbourne Mexico City Mumbai Nairobi
São Paulo Shanghai Taipei Tokyo Toronto

Oxford is a registered trade mark of Oxford University Press
in the UK and in certain other countries

Published in the United States
by Oxford University Press Inc., New York

Originally published in 1997 German as *Gottesdienst als Lebensform—Ethik für Christenbürger*,
by Verlag W. Kohlhammer, Stuttgart, Berlin, Cologne.
First published in English 2004

British Library Cataloguing in Publication Data

Data available

Library of Congress Cataloging in Publication Data

Data available

ISBN 0-19-925387-0

1 3 5 7 9 10 8 6 4 2

Typeset by Kolam Information Services Pvt. Ltd, Pondicherry, India
Printed in Great Britain
on acid-free paper by
Biddles Ltd,
King's Lynn.

PREFACE AND ACKNOWLEDGEMENTS

This book came into being on the banks of the Cam, the Wear, the Schwabach, and the Thames. Its first port of call was Cambridge, in 1991, where I began to take up questions left at the conclusion of a long-standing consultation between the theological faculties of Durham and Tübingen. During these discussions about the traditions of Anglican and Lutheran social ethics, the connection between worship and ethics proved to offer a serviceable bridge. But in the framework of the consultation, this could of course be no more than the indication of a programme—and the stimulus for a more thoroughgoing investigation of what ethics can learn from worship. It is that investigation to which I should like the present study to contribute.

The context in which the subject emerged made it clear to me from the outset that this was a theme which could be worked through only in awareness of its ecumenical bearings. It therefore seemed necessary to push forward the enquiry in conversation with theologians from a variety of traditions. Here a number of months spent in the USA and Great Britain on several occasions proved particularly helpful. These visits were made possible through the help of the Deutsche Forschungsgemeinschaft, which supported the project with a two-year research grant. Theological friendships with English-speaking theologians have contributed in no small part to the present form of the enquiry. Of course, at that time I could not guess that I would one day be writing the preface to the English edition of this book from my desk in Oxford.

The list of those to whom I should like to express my thanks is long, and must nevertheless remain incomplete. First I have to thank the participants in the Durham–Tübingen consultation, of whom I should like to name three. Oswald Bayer, Tübingen, provided me with the insight that it is always worthwhile to bring Reformation theology (and especially Luther's) face to face with present-day questions—and vice versa. During my time in Durham, England, Allan Suggate introduced me to the tradition of English social ethics. And the years of co-operation with Hans Ulrich in Erlangen made me happily aware of how much a good theology has to do with friendship, and how much a good friendship has to do with theology.

I have to thank another theological 'companion on the way', Reinhard Hütter, not only for a number of new impulses, but for an introduction to the theological scene in the United States. I recall with pleasure many helpful discussions with theologians from a wide range of denominational traditions, among whom Gregory Jones provided especially stimulating ideas. The hospitality of the Jones family is as unforgettable a memory as my time at Duke University, in the American Durham. Here I gained an insight into the way Stanley Hauerwas developed his course on ethics, following the pattern and progress of the liturgy, and thus already practising what I was trying to justify. From him I learnt a great deal, and was grateful for his encouragement. I profited as much from discussions with John Milbank as from his books.

Above all, however, I should like to express my gratitude to Oliver O'Donovan. The inspiring theological exchange with him helped to formulate the emphases of this study; but in addition I have to thank him for his role as editor of the series, and for the scrupulous and committed care of his editorial oversight. I should like to thank Margaret Kohl for intensive co-operation and for her endless patience in discussing detailed problems of translation.

For the present English version, I have shortened the book by about a quarter. A number of excursuses fell victim to this curtailment, above all an ecumenical survey of previous work on the connection between liturgy and ethics.

The German edition of the book appeared in 1997, and its reception showed a curious imbalance. The book was reviewed more often under the heading of liturgical studies or systematics than under the heading of ethics. This may perhaps tell us just as much about the framework in which ethics is perceived in the German discussion as it does about the difficulty of tilling the ground of this discussion. Several objections deserve consideration, and for these I should like to thank the reviewers. Here I should like to take up only one point. The study does not deal with worship in its full liturgical scope. It picks out only individual elements, as examples on the basis of which the ethical connection can be worked out. As some critics see it, one outcome of this eclecticism is a certain overemphasis on the audible over the visible, or of 'word' over 'sacrament'. Here I should like to make two comments.

First, from the perspective of Reformation theology, the Word has a sacramental quality, just as the other sacraments have their own specific quality as proclamation. The proclamation is a 'bodily Word', both in its sacramental character ('taste and see') and as an ethical turning to the world. Second, I am conscious of the need to extend the enquiry into 'worship and ethics' beyond my illustrative treatment of some individual elements of worship. Here I may draw attention to a working group of Lutheran and Anglican theologians organized by Dan Hardy and myself. This group has been working for a number of years on an investigation of the ethical significance of the individual elements of worship as a whole, with the aim of spelling out in detailed studies the programme to which the present book is committed.

I should like to add a final word of thanks to two very special readers. What greater satisfaction can a writer have than to encounter readers who have found in his work more than he himself was aware of having put into it? For this unexpected and undeserved pleasure I wish to thank the Romanian Orthodox theologian Picu Ocoleanu, and Brian Brock as a first congenial reader of the English version. May it find a few more.

The publication of this book was sponsored by Inter Nationes.

B.W.

TRANSLATOR'S NOTE

Biblical quotations in the translation follow the Revised Standard Version of the Bible, except where modifications were required in order to bring out the nuance of the German text.

Extended quotations from Luther's writings are taken from the English translation of his works edited by Jaroslav Pelikan and Helmut T. Lehman (54 vols., Philadelphia and St Louis, 1955–). Shorter quotations, cited in the German text only with a reference to the Weimar edition of Luther's works (WA), have been translated directly from the German.

Short titles have been used in the notes for contributions appearing in full in the bibliography. A date has been added for modern, generally secondary literature, in order that the reader may see at a glance how recent a contribution to the discussion is. Full journal information is also given in the notes, for the sake of clarity.

Both Dr Wannenwetsch and Professor Oliver O'Donovan have been unsparingly generous with their patient help in the preparation of the translation. To both of them I should like here to express my sincere thanks.

M.K.

CONTENTS

ABBREVIATIONS

AV	Authorized (King James) Version of the Bible, 1611
BevTh	Beiträge zur evangelischen Theologie
BSLK	*Die Bekenntnisschriften der evangelisch-lutherischen Kirche*
CA	Confessio Augustana (Augsburg Confession)
CD	Karl Barth, *Church Dogmatics*
DS	H. Denzinger and A. Schönmetzer, *Enchiridion Symbolorum*
EKD	Evangelische Kirche in Deutschland
EKK	Evangelisch-Katholischer Kommentar zum Neuen Testament
EvTh	*Evangelische Theologie*
EWNT	*Exegetisches Wörterbuch zum Neuen Testament*
FGLP	Forschungen zur Geschichte und Lehre des Protestantismus
HWPh	*Historisches Wörterbuch der Philosophie*
KuD	*Kerygma und Dogma*
LM	*Lutherische Monatshefte*
NTD	Das Neue Testament Deutsch
NZSTh	*Neue Zeitschrift für systematische Theologie und Religiousphilosophie*
PTh	*Praktische Theologie*
ThQ	*Theologische Quartalschrift*
ThTo	*Theology Today*
TRE	*Theologische Realenzyklopädie*
VELKD	Vereinigte evangelisch-lutherische Kirche Deutschlands
WA	Martin Luther, *Werke* (Weimar edn.)
WUNT	Wissenschaftliche Untersuchungen zum Neuen Testament
ZEE	*Zeitschrift für evangelische Ethik*
ZNW	*Zeitschrift für die neutestamentliche Wissenschaft*
ZThK	*Zeitschrift für Theologie und Kirche*

Introduction: Beyond Communitarianism and Liberalism

The most important shift in recent ethical theory might be termed the recontextualization of ethics. In the tradition determined by Kant, ethics was committed to as formal as possible a formulation of its content and methods, so that it could be universalized, generalized, and made communicable. But this tradition no longer reigns unchallenged. For the abstraction that was required brought with it a loss of sensibility for history, culture, and bodily life; and the consequent discomfort has led to a new thinking about the specific conditions in which an 'ethos' can emerge and develop, upon which 'ethics' as a reflective discipline can then ponder critically. The newly awakened concern for ethical theories which are embedded in forms of life (as in Aristotelian ethics) brought into the centre of the discussion themes and topics which had long been pushed out on to the fringe—virtue, the emotions, friendship, the role of tradition in shaping communities, and so forth. Subjects of this kind are once again being debated with an intellectual curiosity which is backed by the question of how a post-liberal ethic of this kind is related to the standards of liberal ethics in the Kantian tradition.

Kantian ethics drew its dynamic from the search for an ultimate rational foundation for moral conduct, and its methodic approach was in a sense backward-looking: starting from specific problems of the moral life, there was a systematic recourse to a series of rules of graduated conciseness which made as general as possible an appeal to reason, culminating in ideal principles, foundational propositions such as Kant's categorical imperative. The post-liberal alternative sets off in a different direction. It too asks what lies behind a moral proposition or a moral act, but it does not search for ideal principles. It looks for the specific, historical, socio-cultural conditions from which the particular moral competence to speak and act is drawn.

In the discussion as it has moved on, the connections are presented as follows: a moral proposition or act expresses the speaker's *conviction*, which—unlike a mere opinion, which can readily change—is intimately bound up with the person's *character*. This character is nourished by specific *traditions* (especially narrative ones); and conviction crystallizes in the individual during the process through which the traditions are received and handed on. These living traditions, for their part, have their site in specific tradition-formed communities of conviction, where they are cultivated and where, conversely, they shape the identity of these communities. For theological ethics, this change of direction in the ethical discussion finds a particular focus inasmuch as the connection between ecclesiology and ethics now enters the field in a new way. Do we not have to see the Church, it is now suggested, as the matrix out of which Christian ethics is born?

This question indicates the point where we can enter the discussion. By defining more precisely the parameters of this discussion, we can also determine its special character. I believe that the new trend I have mentioned is necessary, and to be welcomed. But in putting forward an 'ethic springing from worship', I should nevertheless like to take a further step which I believe is also required. The decisive question is *how*—in what respect—the Church has an essential importance for ethics. For there are theologically cogent reasons for *not* assuming that the Church provides the foundation for Christian ethics. My point in proposing an 'ethic springing from worship' instead of a 'church' ethics is that the Church does not have itself at its own disposal, in a sense which would permit it to deduce anything from that fact—not even an ethic. According to the central article of the Augsburg Confession (Article V), the Church cannot claim to be an institution directly founded by God. What *are* established in this sense (*institutum est*) are specific practices: the proclamation of the Word and the administration of the sacraments. The Church can be understood as a divine institution only as it finds itself practising the proclamation of the Word and the administration of the sacraments *in the proper way* (*recte*)— that is, in the promise of the Spirit. A pneumatological proviso of this kind is no doubt common coin for every Christian tradition in the framework of its own ecclesiology. But perhaps it would not be unduly bold at this point to take into account a particular virtue which the churches of the Reformation have to contribute here (a virtue which, needless to say, is paralleled by a whole number of equally specific vices).

Seen from this perspective, the Church itself appears as a *praxis*, shaped by the practices instituted by God to which we may give the summary description 'worship'. A theological reflection on these practices such as I should like to put forward here will of course also reduce to absurdity the attempt to raise worship, for its part, to the status of a 'foundation' for ethics. The fact that the practice is bound to repetition makes it impossible to identify a foundational claim that is somehow derived from its essence; for the knowledge of such an essence would actually make the constitutive character of the Church's worship superfluous, this constitutive character being the fact that men and women have to *attend and participate in it again and again*, so as to practise at the proper place what Barth calls 'the art of correct asking about God's will'.[1] The practical experience of worship continually impresses on the Church that it cannot simply 'possess' its own ethic, in the sense that it could also apply that ethic to an external field of action, as something it 'has' and over which it can dispose. Its ethical knowledge will always be available to it only in the mode of 'being', embodied in its own praxis. And the exemplary mode of this incorporation is simply the complex celebration of worship, which integrates the different aspects of living.

This non-foundational character of worship shows how my proposal is related to the parameters of the discussion which have become established under the labels 'communitarian' and 'liberal'; for in the case of an ethic springing from worship it is a matter of neither-nor. This ethic is not modern or liberal, for it is critically opposed to all attempts at a foundationalist claim. But for the same reason it cannot be understood as communitarian either. For the process of enquiry about what is 'behind' it in any given case threatens to end up in a 'communitarian positivism' which, for the reasons I have given, is theologically untenable. If the alternative is to make a particular community (such as the Church) the immediate and ultimate foundation for its ethics (in this case Christian ethics)—a community which could then recognize only its own self-implementation and praxis as normative—then liberal formalism would be preferable to any such communitarian positivism.

At the same time, this book has been written in the conviction that this alternative cannot be the last word. The approach

---

[1] K. Barth, *The Christian Life*, *CD* IV/4 (Lecture Fragments), 34.

I am putting forward here—ethics springing from worship—
should in fact be understood as a way out of this unsatisfactory
alternative—an ethic beyond both communitarianism and liberalism.

This will permit a new approach to another question: how ethics
can be learned. This question needs to be freed from the narrow
bounds which have come to restrict it through the widespread
orientation towards 'moral stages' such as Lawrence Kohlberg
once propagated.[2] His distinction (often uncritically adapted) between 'conventional' (heteronomous) and 'reflexive' (autonomous) morality proves inadequate in the face of the complex
relationships of an ethic 'in-formed' by worship. Ethics springing
from worship cannot simply be equated with a conventional community morality which claims the validity of a given fact, for the
formation and communication of Christian ethics in worship is
continually at stake. To listen afresh again and again is something
for which there is no substitute.

In approaching worship as the source or well-spring of Christian
ethics (using the metaphor I have consciously chosen in speaking of
ethics springing from worship), I should like first to bar the way to
some natural misunderstandings. I am well aware that these can be
anticipated only to a very limited extent, but nevertheless the
following possible misconceptions should at least be touched on
at this early point. An ethic springing from political worship has
nothing to do with either (a) an ethicization of worship or (b) the
quietization of ethics. Nor (c) has it to do with the politicization or
idealization of worship. Finally (d), what we are aiming at is neither
an ethical stance nor a meta-ethic.

(a) Ethics, even theological ethics, has often looked for its point of
departure not in worship but elsewhere—in anthropological potentialities, such as reason or an innate moral sense, or in normative
foundational norms, such as conventions, precepts, or institutions.
The reason for this may perhaps be found in a specifically theologically motivated reservation about viewing worship so directly in
the light of ethics. Isn't worship important precisely because it is
beyond ethics—an interruption of the moral continuum, where
action is suspended, where we lay our hands in our laps, or at
most fold them in prayer? Doesn't worship have to do primarily

---

[2] L. Kohlberg, *et al.*, *Moral Stages* (1983).

with what *God* does in and for human beings, who for their part
need do nothing but receive, in the hearing of the Word and the gift
of the sacraments? Wouldn't an ethicization of worship undermine
precisely this salutary passivity, if even what is intended to be a gift
to human beings is now also made their 'work'? It is far from my
intention to dispute all this, and with it the soteriological significance of worship.[3] The purpose of this study is indeed to grasp the
ethical significance of that very fact. Where does ethics begin? With
what we do? With our own judgements? Or by acquiescing in what
God does, and God's judgement?

(b) At the same time, this acceptance is for its part certainly not
quietism. It is a highly active affair, in which men and women are
fully involved. The first task of ethical reflection, and its function,
must, for good reasons, be to ask what the conditions look like in
which human beings are in-formed in the ethical sense: how their
lives are brought into a particular form by what happens to them.
For Christians, the experience of worship is seminal. It is here that
they experience the presence of the acting and judging God in a
formative way; and here, at the same time, a reflective ethics will
emerge among them—social behaviour guided by 'the law of the
Spirit' (Rom. 8: 2), a form of living which takes in all the different
sectors of existence. Accordingly, the purpose of our present study
is to describe worship as being in the fullest sense *a form of life*.

Here three levels can be distinguished, roughly speaking. First, the
ethical significance of worship is already given with the mere fact
that it takes place. Here men and women repeatedly disengage from
the comings and goings of the world, with its inextricably tangled
web of the moral and the immoral, so as to enter into God's rest;
and this witnesses to the fact that the world may revolve on its axis,
but its life does not depend on its own frenetic activity. The future
of the world cannot be secured by morality, nor can immorality
destroy it. The external testimony of worship is intrinsic to its very
existence as an interruption of the course of the world, and this
testimony subjects all total claims to an ultimate criticism. That is
the one side. Beyond that, of course, we also have to grasp the
ethical significance which belongs to worship by virtue of its inward

[3] 'For no man doth serve God unless he let God be God and work His works in
him' (M. Luther, WA 7, 595, 34 f.; cf. also E. Jüngel, 'The Church as Sacrament?', in
idem, Theological Essays (1989), 189–213).

life. It is the acting and judging of God experienced in worship which guides believers to a *specific* form of life. On this second level, the decisive point is that the formative happening takes place in the context of a human *receptivity which can also be described as acting and judging*. So the acting and judging of human beings is only an outgrowth of worship, a possibility which *then* arises of responding in daily life to the acting and judging of God which has been experienced. It is *in worship itself* that the ethical in-forming of human acting and judging comes about. By *assenting* to God's judgement (*homo-logein*) and by chiming in with what God does, men and women engage in worship. In this receptivity, in the *passivity* of worship, a specific ethos emerges; and about its inherent conceptual side ethics can then reflect. This subsequent reflection embraces the question of how the formation of action and judgement in worship can be tried and tested in the conditions of everyday life. This reference to everyday life constitutes the third level of an ethic springing from worship. It does not mean, however, that ethics takes on the function of a general theoretical way of transferring from the one reality (worship) to another (everyday life). The purpose of our present study will rather be to see how the *specific* ethical spheres of experience in worship have a significance for *specific* questions and areas of our existence in the world. The theoretical feat which this requires must not be underrated; for it means something like paying out the ample cheque of talk about the ethically relevant 'experience'[4] of worship in the actual pounds and pence which it represents.

(c) We only fully grasp the ethical dimension of worship when the chiming in with God's activity is recognized not just as the ethical forming of individual believers, but also and primarily as the forming of the worshipping community. It is the act of *sharing* in the praise of God, the consensus in the confession of faith, and the entering into God's acts 'for others' which is the mark of ethics springing from worship. This judging and acting in accord with

---

[4] The concept of experience here is formative rather than reflexive. It does not stress what German calls the 'making' of experience (*Erfahrung machen*). Here the passive element is in the foreground. Experience is not the reflecting mirror always already existent at the back of the consciousness. It is, rather, a term for what the world does with us. In its quality and capacity for expansion it is dependent on the particular forms of life in which we live. Cf. here G. A. Lindbeck, *The Nature of Doctrine* (1984), 30 ff.

God and with other believers is not merely the mark of the felicitous moment when heart, lips, and hands keep time with one another. Rather, it forms a specific, social form of life, a *communio* in which believers find their basic *political existence*. That is what is meant here when we talk about 'political worship'. In the sense in which I am using the term, it does not mean a particular type of worship in the sense of an order of service for some politically relevant occasion;[5] nor does it point to the political colouring which worship can be lent by way of an appropriate liturgical form, or particular thematic emphases.

On the contrary, here the expression 'political worship' takes into account the fact that in the proper sense *every* public service of worship in which a Christian congregation engages has a specifically political character, since it is the assembly of 'Christian citizens', 'fellow-citizens with the saints' (Eph. 2: 19), in praise of the God who, in the words of the hymn, 'ruleth on high'. Christian ethics recognizes that it is political when it considers the forming of the congregation in worship as the formation of 'a public' in its own unique sense: the particular political form of life which is determined by 'the law of the Spirit' (Rom. 8: 2).

In my view, the political understanding of worship holds the key to an understanding of its meaning for Christian ethics in general. This insight must admittedly take into account a specific difficulty. The dominance of the liberal doctrine which holds that worship belongs to private life has not merely severely narrowed down the expectation of experiencing in worship the essential impress for ethics, and social ethics especially; in addition, the way in which worship itself is actually celebrated in the Christian churches has not remained untouched by this influence either. The

[5] This expression is used in a working paper prepared by the Division for Theology of the German Evangelical Church (EKD) entitled 'Der Gottesdienst in der politischen Welt—"Politischer Gottesdienst"'. The paper uses the term to describe a long-standing tradition of church services held on days of particular significance for the political community—parliamentary sessions, council meetings, coronations, remembrance days; but also during times of war. The term 'political worship' crops up in the framework of this tradition in the eighteenth century, and in the succeeding period acquires the connotation of the political functionalization of church services in the interests of particular political communities and parties. Even though the paper's main stress is on orders of service for political occasions of this kind (pp. 10 ff.), its general reflections on the nature of the Church's worship also bring out the political dimension of every 'normal' service of worship (pp. 7 f.), as distinct from these services for special occasions.

rediscovery of worship as central to the formation of ethics will therefore have to go hand in hand with the theoretical and practical rediscovery of political worship—the essential political dimension of worship which has more or less been pushed aside. This means that it will also have to take critical stock of the history of worship's depoliticization, which can be detected especially in the clerical expropriation of the congregation's own office and ministry. This dispossession of its genuine liturgical function has engendered a corresponding consumer attitude among members of the congregation, which in its own way again obscures the political dimension.

In spite of the unavoidable criticism of the *status quo* of worship, this of course does not mean appealing to a Platonic Idea of worship, over against worship 'as it really exists'.[6] The point is rather first to awaken a new attention to the political dimension, which is embedded in the quite normal give and take of activity in congregational worship. This attention should be encouraged and should be accompanied by the diachronic and synchronic awareness of what the celebration of worship can mean in the context of liturgical history, and in the world-wide fellowship of the Church. If we look back, we can see that the particular denominational traditions of worship have a rich latent treasure of 'dangerous remembrances' for the present practice of worship, just as nowadays the encounter with other churches and their particular forms of worship is also an invitation to the renewal of our own praxis.

So even if we have to admit that an ethic springing from worship can always be only as good as the celebration of worship itself, this dependence must not be viewed as a conceptual weakness. It may perhaps be that the liturgico-ethical integrity of worship can initially be perceived only cloudily, from individual aspects of some actual 'worship practice' at a particular time and place; but even so, the remembrance of that integrity may, conversely, bring the practice of worship to a new awareness of its political dimension, and thus to practical steps of liturgical reform. Viewed from the perspective of theoretical ethics too, this mutual dependence is not a conceptual blemish. It is the necessary counterpart to the non-

---

[6] This is a play on the phrase *real existierender Sozialismus* ('socialism as it really exists'), which was applied in the West to political systems in the Eastern bloc before 1989, where practice crassly diverged from socialist theory [Trans.].

foundational character of an ethic springing from worship which we
have touched on. To try to escape it through the affirmation of an
ideal political worship would be as inadmissible as a flight into the
empiricist denial of the political character of worship 'as it really
exists'—a denial which would entirely fail to reckon with the *renewal* of awareness of the existing connection.

To assert that the key to a grasp of the significance of worship for
ethics can be found in its political character may give rise to a number
of misunderstandings, and a few preliminary observations about the
terms used may therefore prove useful. In the celebration of worship
the congregation is transposed into a particular social order. This is
represented in a definitive way in the shared hearing and proclamation of the Word, in the act of baptism, and also at the Lord's Table.
As the body of the risen Lord, the congregation is the form in which
the eschatological *polis* (Rev. 21: 9 ff.) is present in the world. In this
city, life is not subject to a self-regulating 'process' in which there is
a free play of forces; on the contrary, life in it is 'ruled'. Christ is the
head of the Church, and the life of the communities of his people
follows the law of his Spirit. In this respect it is inescapably political—aligned towards the recognition of the good that comes from
God, towards the common exploration of the good in the world,
and towards the trying and testing of that good in shared action.

Accordingly we are understanding politics here in a wider sense
than the one that has become usual today. My use of the term does
not so much take its bearings from the modern model, where
politics are understood in the light of the political will of the
sovereign subject, and are primarily considered as policies for the
implementation of particular interests (Machiavelli) or as a striving
for shares in power (Max Weber). What we shall understand by
politics in our present study is closer to the classical concept[7]
formulated by Aristotle and interpreted in our own time by Hannah
Arendt especially. Here politics is understood more comprehensively as whatever touches the affairs of citizens (*ta politika*). Politics
is civil life in the *polis*. For Aristotle, this embraces, on the one hand,
concern about objective formative orders (constitutions), but on

---

[7] For this distinction cf. D. Sternberger, *Drei Wurzeln der Politik* (1978). To the
classical and modern perspectives Sternberger adds yet a third: 'totalitarian politics',
in which the subjective politics of sectional interests which we find in modern times
are coupled with the objectifying solemnity appropriate for implementing secularized eschatological utopias.

the other, he also sees politics as political action: as action (*praxis*) as distinct from productive activity (*poiesis*), as political life (*bios politikos*) as distinct from theoretical life (*bios theoretikos*), and as the science of that activity ('politics', *he politike*)—the skill (*arete*) of political action, statesmanship, and political ethics.[8]

Hannah Arendt's interpretations of the classical Greek concept of politics have emphasized an aspect which is particularly important in our present context. She reminds us that political activity as joint action is always dependent on what she calls an *initium*, an initiating action. What one person does makes a beginning; others then join in this activity. In the process of free shared activity, power is formed. It is dispersed when people lose themselves in activity, and loss of power in its turn brings into the arena power's profoundly unpolitical surrogate: violence.[9]

This concept of politics may prove useful for our perception of the political dimension of worship. According to this interpretation, worship would be political inasmuch as God's activity provides the *initium*, an activity to which people assent in baptism, in praise, in prayer, in the hearing of the Word, in the confession of faith, and in the Lord's Supper. And, as it proceeds, the service of worship—in analogy to the classical interpretation, even if a limited analogy—is also a *co-activity* shared by God and human beings. God's activity is not exhausted when God has initiated something—in God's institution of the different elements of worship. This preceding activity (which is God's activity alone) goes hand in hand with the assent of believers: 'in, with and under' the activity of human beings, God goes on acting. Accordingly, this human activity is not free in the sense of a decision, of being able to act in one way or another. It is free in that it accepts the liberating activity of God as its rule.

This is what I mean when in this study I talk about the intrinsically regulated character of worship. The political life of believers, like life in the *polis*, is dependent on good laws and their observance. It follows 'the law of the Spirit of life in Christ'. In this light we can also understand what the power of the Church consists of. It cannot simply be presupposed as a *de facto* authority, something that can be exercised—towards believers as well; that would be a bureaucratic misunderstanding of the Church. On the contrary, in the Church, power in the political sense we have described (in which it is

---

[8] C. Meier, 'Politik', *HWPh* 7, 1038 ff.
[9] H. Arendt, *The Human Condition* (1958; 2nd edn. 1998), 175 ff.

differentiated from violence) is always first formed—and formed in worship—in the assembly of all believers, as the work of the Holy Spirit, who ensures the harmony between God's activity and the activity of human beings. Accordingly, in the framework of this study we shall not, as is often the case, take an individualistic view of *sanctification*, the traditional theme of Christian ethics. We shall see sanctification as *the empowerment for political life*.

Empowerment for political life as citizens of the church *polis* comes about through the regulated character of worship. It proves itself in the continual to and fro between experiences in political worship, and politics in state and society. In this way, political ethics arising from worship promises to lead beyond the conceptional alternative indicated by slogans about the doctrine of the two kingdoms and the kingship of Christ (an alternative which is in any case inadmissibly simplistic). Here we are not threatened with a flat and colourless autonomy in the secular spheres of economics and politics, since for them too the experience of worship is determinative; nor do we have to maintain a Christocratic linearity between what Barth talks about as 'the Christian and the civil community'; for the decisive thing is the *complex experience* of worship, which cannot be drawn out into a string of analogies.

If the *experience* of political life in the Church *polis* constitutes the ethically relevant dimension, then there is no 'content' which could be directly reflected into secular politics, or transformed into those politics, through the application of a moral theory. There is only the complex and pluriform political life which among Christian citizens spills over, so to speak, into the secular *polis*. In order to be able to describe more precisely how the experience of political worship proves its efficacy in the world, I borrow the concept of a 'grammar', which makes transferences within the complex of linguistic rules comprehensible. According to this concept, I must have internalized the rules in order to be able to say something new. Even what is new—unheard of—must not be understood as simply bursting apart the rules. It is rather an expansion of the rules to take in new cases. 'The law of the Spirit' describes the political life of Christians as a grammatical complex of this kind: as a *law* of the Spirit it aims at the regulated character of the Christian form of life—and as the law of *the Spirit* it ensures that the Spirit is not confined within a rule, but expands the rule, in the course of its application, to take in new cases.

If I try to explore how far we can get with the theoretical formation of theological ethics if that ethics takes its bearings from
political worship, this certainly does not mean conceiving of the
political category as a universal paradigm. It remains a qualifier. In
this respect the political ethics intended differs from the tradition of
political theology,[10] which aims at the politicization of the whole of
life. As I see it, 'political worship' is not bound to claim that there is
nothing beyond the political sphere. The political element cannot
be brought in everywhere, but must be looked for in its good and
rightful place. Precisely as political worship—as the original location of politics, where the activity of the Creator itself gives the
initium or first impulse—worship accordingly stands for *the salutary
limitation of the political category*, since every experience of what is
political must be tested against the experience of worship. But even
within worship itself the political element has a limited scope. It is
true that the heavenly Jerusalem is imagined as a *polis*, but that city
no longer needs to be ruled, since its citizens have the law 'written
in their hearts'. Here an eschatological differentiation is called for.
If we are talking about Christian citizens living together in God's
polis (*ta politika*), we cannot get beyond politics. But politics as (the
art of regulating) the way Christians live together (*he politike*) is not
an indefinite and unending task. It does not belong to the eternity
of that citizenship.[11] Consequently, for our present study on the
relation between worship and ethics the claim of the political para-

[10] In this tradition the political element is dominant, and theology has to be
understood as qualifier. Thus political theology has consistently been used to legitimate political purposes. These may be directed to existing forms of power. We first
find this approach in antiquity, with the definition given by Panaitos, who saw
political theology—as distinct from mythical and 'physical' theology—as explicitly
at the service of the state religion. Later came Machiavelli's utilitarian interpretation,
and later still Carl Schmitt's monotheistic justification of 'the state of emergency'.
But political theology has also been used to legitimate the revolutionary politics
which are at the service of the era to come.

[11] It is true that the vision of 'the new city' in Revelation 21 f. speaks of 'reigning'.
But this reigning (*basileusousin*, Rev. 22: 5) is significantly enough applied to *all* the
citizens of that city, all God's servants (22: 4). This idea puts an end, practically
speaking, to the political *arete* which regulates how the one is to rule over the other.
This art will no longer be required in that city, any more than a sun will be needed to
illuminate it: 'for the Lord God will be their light, and they shall reign for ever and
ever.' In these motifs we hear the echo of that ancient prophetic vision about the
eschatological city of God which 'shall not be uprooted or overthrown any more for
ever' (Jer. 31: 40) and which will be inhabited by the people of 'the new covenant',
who will not have to teach each other, because God's law is written in their hearts
(Jer. 31: 33 f.).

digm is not all-embracing either. If I say that worship can be properly understood only as political worship, this does not prevent me from saying with equal justification that it can be understood only as doctrinal, for example, in the context of the formation of Christian teaching. What can be ruled out, however, is the supposition that worship can be properly understood as non-political, abstracted from its political character.

(d) In order to show how it is possible to think in the framework of an ethic springing from political worship, I shall take as an example the ethics of politics. It may seem the obvious choice to draw on this complex of problems in order to see how the ethic in-formed by worship can prove itself in terms of practical ethics. But we must not lose sight of the fact that the political form of worship can by no means be confined to the ethics of politics, or its relevance for that. It is not only the ethics of political life which must legitimate itself as a *political* ethic in the light of worship; the same may be said of economic ethics, the ethics of marriage, or any other practical ethics. Sights must always be set on the Christian *citizen*, not human beings or Christians as such. Political ethics have to do with these people viewed from the outset as part of the political commonwealth of the Church, not simply as related to it in a secondary sense, as if there could be one ethic for Christians as individual decision-makers, and then an additional, separate ethic for them inasmuch as they are *also* citizens of the *polis* church. Seen from the angle of political worship, Christian ethics can be neither individual ethics nor social ethics, if social ethics means expanding individual ethics to cover questions touching the community. On the contrary, it will from the very outset be 'civil' ethics—political ethics. But if this is true, it must also be possible to show *how* the experience of worship empowers Christian citizens to act politically in other public spheres in which they move—the spheres of state and society. Accordingly, it must be shown that Christians are the exemplary citizens, and in what sense this can be said. With this in mind we have to look in detail at what this specifically civil experience means.

If we keep in mind the clarifications aimed at up to now, we can then also define more clearly the level on which an ethics springing from worship belongs in the context of the present theoretical debate. For it is neither one conception among others, nor does it fulfil the criteria for a meta-ethic. Ethics springing from worship do not reflect a particular stance. To claim directly for a particular ethical conception the accepted essential character of worship for the Christian life would be not merely inapposite. The word 'worship' cannot be used as a qualifier for characterizing an ethic more precisely. Liturgy can certainly be challenged at the conceptual level as to the relationship between divine and human action which is implicit in it, and the ideas about 'the good life' which it implies. But this positive ethic which is contained in worship itself does not enter into direct rivalry with the different conceptions of theological ethics. It has no desire to make these ideas superfluous, but rather aims to act as their critical reading aid; for every Christian ethic, and every ethic which calls itself Christian, must be able to stand its ground together with the central practice of the Christian faith, its worship, and must not be conceived in a way that would run counter to the ethical thrust of that worship.

So even if worship represents one source of Christian ethics, and not the only one, and if other possible candidates for this status were to be named in addition—Scripture, natural law, and Christian experience—worship can still, even among these plural sources, be viewed as enjoying a special position; for here we already have to do with a case of the specific *interaction* of those other sources in the warp and weft out of which life is formed. That is why worship must have pride of place as a 'grammar' for Christian ethics: it is no less complex than life itself. In worship we find the core principle, 'God is to be worshipped' (*deum est venerendum*), and the right use of the biblical canon, which was established precisely for the requirements of worship; and in worship both these things—and more—come together in a comprehensive sensory, intellectual, and spiritual experience. This is worship as a form of life.

PART I

WORSHIP AS THE BEGINNING OF CHRISTIAN ETHICS

'Christian ethics begins when the people of God gather to worship.'
These words of the Armenian Orthodox theologian Vigen Guroian[1] offer a good conspectus of the investigation that is to follow.
'*Christian* ethics begins when the *people of God* gather to worship.'
Who are the agents in the ethics springing from worship? Not
individual decision-makers, deliberating about their conduct. The
agent is an identifiable social entity: the 'people of God', a community living in accord with 'the law of the Spirit of Christ'. The
particular character of their *Christian* ethic cannot be watered
down by the demand—in any case outdated nowadays—that it
should be made universally applicable. Nor can it be restricted to
the social teachings of particular Christian churches and groups.
The practice of worship, unlike such theological trade marks as
'justification' or 'natural law', belongs to the 'one holy catholic
church' as such, not to a particular confessional tradition. To
explore the ethics that spring from worship, then, requires an
ecumenical sensitivity which can match the extent of God's people
as a whole. It is a 'Church' ethic, in that it is inseparable from the
Church as the place of the Spirit, the space of worship as the
'happening' of the Spirit; but it is not a church ethics in a confessional, let alone a clerical, sense.

'Christian ethics begins when the people of God gather to *worship*.'
Not, that is, when they begin a discussion about ethics. *Ethics begins
in worship and in the moral rationality proper to it*; not, as it might be,
only later, when the 'moral implications' are worked out. It begins
in worship, at the very moment it takes place and among the people
who engage in it together. We might put it this way: in worship,
ethics and ethos are woven together, and each depends on the
regulated manner of its practice. Worship is ethos to the extent
that its outward form is regulated (in keeping with Christ's words
of institution, 'Do this as often . . . '); and worship is 'ethical' to the
extent that it is intrinsically regulated—that is, that there is a clear
rule to which the acting and judging which go on in it conform.

---

[1] V. Guroian, 'Seeing Worship as Ethics', in *idem.*, *Incarnate Love* (1987), 71.

Worship therefore includes ethics not only when the sermon has a moral theme, or if it aims at some action with a pronounced ethical purpose. It is simply that its inherent structure of acting and being acted on is formed by divine action, and its exercise of judgement by the condemning and redeeming judgement of God. This moral *grammar* of worship cannot be tied down to some particular liturgical form. It does not function like an ideogram for ethics, in which the relation of signs and their meanings could be given an ideal logical form. Just as the grammar of a language is answerable to its use in speech, so the grammar of ethics is answerable to the lived ethos, the regulated performance of worship. So it is not an ethics *of* worship; nor is it a worship ethics. Worship is simply the source from which ethics springs. So the term 'ethics' itself refers to something more than a secondary reflection of the lived ethos; it is itself a practical enterprise, an induction into the particular exercise of moral accountability. Yet it is a *critical* induction, in that it presents and reflects upon the lived ethos into which it introduces us.

'Christian ethics *begins* when the people of God gather to worship.' This is not meant restrictively, as though to make a contrast between a bare beginning and an implementation that leaves the beginning behind. What 'beginning' means here is something different. It means that the primary point of moral reference is *in time,* not outside it. Christian ethics is temporal, not a-temporal; it has a 'beginning' but is not a 'foundation'; an *initium* certainly, but not a *principium*. Its structuring and restructuring are found by experience of sense-perceptible events in time, not established by reflection as a 'basis' which could be grasped theoretically at any time whatever—some 'theory of reality', perhaps, or 'theory of praxis'. No: Christian ethics *always* has to take its start, over and over again, from the event where human beings are grasped by the self-communication of God. If ethics conforms to the specifically political mode of Christian communication appropriate to the community of obedience to the Word, it is free from general strategies of a foundational kind—certainly free from *ultimate* foundations, which are always world-renouncing and, in the end, atheistic, abstracting in thought from the world as God's creation and simply designing an ethics out of nothing, with no lived ethos.[2] It is not in business to

---

[2] According to Kant, the law of ultimate foundations is that 'reason has insight only into that which it produces after a plan of its own' (*Critique of Pure Reason,* 14).

justify moral behaviour; on the contrary, set free from self-justification, even at the level of theory, it is freed for moral accountability. Moral accounting is always concrete. It is exercised for particular states of affairs. And it is exercised within the community which is assigned the task of testing the will of God, which in worship it is given to know with assurance.

This is, in effect, an *annihilatio mundi*, an abolition of the actual world, driven by a compulsion to map the universe from a zero point, where human reason has nothing to begin with but itself.

I

Political Worship: Overcoming the Functional Approach

To look at worship as the 'beginning' of Christian ethics means taking a quite different path into the topic from that which theologians have taken in recent decades. We shall approach worship not as a problem to shed light on, but as a light to shed on our problem. So we shall not attend primarily to the *functions* that worship performs, not even its function of undergirding morality, but shall concentrate on opening it up *as a phenomenon* which has light to shed on ethics. We shall not consider it as an object of perception, in whatever way, but shall view it as itself the place where ethical perception can be acquired, as the happening which shapes practical knowledge.

As we have said, theological discussions have for some time hoped to make their critical discoveries about worship, not phenomenologically from within its own dynamic, but from various viewpoints outside it, bringing theories from sociology, behavioural science, social psychology, or other sources to bear on it.[1] Typical of this functional kind of approach is the use of a master concept,

[1] Cf., e.g., the following titles: W. Jetter, *Symbol und Ritual: anthropologische Elemente im Gottesdienst*; H.-J. Thilo, *Die therapeutische Funktion des Gottesdienstes*; M. Josuttis, *Der Weg ins Leben: eine Einführung in den Gottesdienst auf verhaltenswissenschaftlicher Grundlage*. Peter Cornehl's 'Theorie des Gottesdienstes', *ThQ* 159 (1979), shows explicitly the difference between a 'theoretical' and a 'doctrinal' approach: in the former the object is viewed 'from outside' and subjected to functional analysis, a procedure which only then allows theology to learn from the human sciences (p. 179). Inspired by Schleiermacher and taught by Durkheim, Cornehl understands liturgies and festivals as 'expressive actions in which a community gives visible form to what most deeply concerns it' (p. 180). By exploring the generally applicable characteristics of such celebrations in the light of their function for individuals and the congregation ('orientating', 'expressing', 'affirming'), he arrives at a general conception of 'cult', and then declares—hardly surprisingly—that 'Christian worship is cult. There can be no doubt that these functional criteria apply to it' (p. 185). Of course these functional criteria—among others—can be 'applied' to worship. But the distinctive character of Christian worship is thereby screened out, as is its critical purchase on functional analysis.

which promises to lend a deeper insight into the essence of worship than seemed to be attainable from the immediate phenomeno-logical (in this case theological) perspective. So, for example, we are always hearing about worship as *feast*, a category used long ago by Schleiermacher as the key concept in his account of worship,[2] but which was given new prominence in the 1960s by Harvey Cox's *Feast of Fools*, and has also been followed recently by Rainer Volp, for example, in his two-volume *Liturgics*,[3] and by Ernst Lange's influential essay, 'What Use is Worship to Us?'[4] (Lange's title is revealing, showing how the functional perspective still prevails even when the subject itself is said to be 'purposeless' in its intention!) Worship is a feast, we are told—or at least it should be. But who tells us what a proper feast is? Do we learn it from other feasts? There is a close connection between functional thinking and ideal-ist generalizations, and the connection can appear very plausible.

Small wonder, then, if liturgical revision too proceeds by this functional route, which has indeed a long tradition going right back to the theology of the eighteenth-century Enlightenment. In one of those revised liturgies which sprang up like mushrooms, aiming at a 'rational' worship, we find the Eucharist commended as 'the most salutary institution for promoting active Christianity'![5] Though this may create the impression that worship is an indis-pensable instrument for fostering general moral sensibilities, there is no hiding the basic tendency of the functional perspective to emancipate itself from the means it uses and lauds. 'May God's blessing abide with you—ay, for without my asking it abides al-ready, if by godly and virtuous life ye be worthy of it! God grant that it may be so!'[6] When other more effective means are devised for reaching the same goal, or at any rate when the goal is thought to have been attained, means that have emerged historically then become superfluous.[7] Half a century before, J. S. Semler had spelled out the logic of this with great clarity. He knew well enough how to appreciate the institutions of a purely historical 'church

---

[2] F. D. E. Schleiermacher, *Praktische Theologie*, 70 ff.
[3] R. Volp, *Liturgik: Die Kunst, Gott zu feiern*; see esp. ii. 913 ff.
[4] E. Lange, 'Was nützt uns der Gottesdienst?', in *idem*, *Predigen als Beruf* (1976).
[5] From the 1797 Schleswig–Holstein liturgy of J. G. C. Adler, 163.
[6] A benediction formula from the Enlightenment period, quoted in C. Albrecht, *Schleiermachers Liturgik* (1963), 95.
[7] 'To define a thing by its function is to make it in principle replaceable through equivalents' (Robert Spaemann, 'Überzeugungen in einer hypothetischen

Christianity', just so long as they were conceived as a preparation for that more elevated 'private religion' towards which we must strive.[8] That might in certain circumstances include meetings for mutual edification; but it would be able to dispense with anything like what we normally conceive as worship.

The attitude prevailing on a broad front today, at least, seems increasingly to follow the logic of that development in every respect. When Christians in the early centuries—and today too in some parts of the world—risked a great deal, sometimes their lives, to take part in congregational worship, it was because the participation of the whole community in worship was something precious to everyone. To use a simile, how could the show go on if all the members of the cast weren't there? In the churches of the Northern hemisphere today, on the other hand, baptized Christians tend to think that their place is in the auditorium rather than on the stage—and, even then, often enough, only as an audience at some *future* performance. Worship may still have some significance in the background, and the gratifications of worship may always be kept on hold, since we never know whether we might not, after all, feel the need for them sometime or other. 'You can be a good Christian without going to church.' This neo-Protestant slogan, often with overtones of populist belligerence about 'church-going bigots', is based theoretically on notions about the changed moral (or political) age into which Christianity has supposedly now mutated in the course of its historical development.[9] In this age, it is argued, it is a significant component of the Christian ethos of freedom to be able to make individual choices about the measure of one's loyalty to the Church (which is demonstrated mainly through one's attendance). In principle, it is held, this has nothing to do with what

Zivilisation', in O. Schatz (ed.), *Abschied von Utopia?* (1977), 315). And applied to religion: 'The inappropriateness of assigning any functional interpretation of religion comes down to this: to relativize the absolute is to abolish it' (Robert Spaemann, 'Funktionale Religionsbegründung und Religion', in his *Philosophische Essays* (1994), 218).

[8] Cf. G. Hornig, 'Die Freiheit der christlichen Privatreligion', *NZSTh* 21 (1979), 198–211.

[9] This historicist speculation, which can be traced back once again to Semler, was given systematic shape in the middle of the nineteenth century by Richard Rothe (*Theologische Ethik* III/2, §§1176 f., 1009–11; see E. Jüngel, *Anfechtung und Gewißheit des Glaubens* (1976), 50–5). It was taken up in different ways in German theology after World War II by Wolfgang Trillhaas and Trutz Rendtorff.

the person is like morally. Whether or not an individual exercises his or her sovereignty by deciding for active church member-ship is a secondary question; the moral value is seen not in the worship or the commitment involved, but simply in the sovereign disposition which decides. But what is generally not spelled out is that where participation in worship is concerned, to exercise this freedom means accepting relegation to the status of an 'audi-ence', whose presence is of minor importance for what is going on.[10]

However, the triumphant progress of functionalism attracted some opposition from theologians, especially energetic on the part of Dietrich Bonhoeffer. In his lectures on the nature of the Church, Bonhoeffer characterizes the question about function as the 'deadly' question which bars the way to community. 'To ask whether I need God is senseless. What I "need", I always need for my own ends. But here, where God is addressing us, it is inappropriate to speak in these terms. So it is equally senseless to ask whether we need the church. God has spoken. He has revealed himself to us in the church ... We have simply to recognize the fact.'[11] That the functional perspective betrays a fundamental fail-ure to comprehend the idea of community is something Bonhoeffer explained earlier, in his dissertation 'Sanctorum Communio', as being an emanation of individualism, which gives our 'actual need' of worship a psychological turn, asking 'What is the point of gathering together?' Only 'the individualist enquirer' will call in question the 'organic' need for such assembly, which lies outside the scope of any calculus of benefits. We should have just as much right to ask 'why one should love one's mother' ('Sanctorum Com-munio', pp. 227 f.). 'Preaching is a divinely ordained activity *of the church for the church.* Since I belong to the church community, I come to the assembly ... This act is not based on utilitarian considerations, or a sense of duty, but is "organic" and obvious behaviour' (p. 227). This early pattern of thought is succinctly expressed in the last phase of his work on the *Ethics,* written shortly

---

[10] The liturgy of the Enlightenment period shows how, when the corporate character of the congregation is lost sight of, the idea of an 'audience' does in fact take its place. In the language of Enlightenment liturgy, it is actually addressed as such in some 'religious discourses' (formerly preaching) at 'religious meetings' (formerly worship). Cf. Albrecht, *Schleiermachers Liturgik,* 88 f.

[11] D. Bonhoeffer, *Das Wesen der Kirche,* 55.

before his arrest, in his reflections on 'the church as an end in itself'.[12]

Political Worship: 'Political Night Prayer' and Barth's Contextual Interpretation

It is just because Christian worship is not a means to an end that it is political. Just as the state, conceived of as 'first servant', turns into what Max Weber—talking about the degenerate *polis* of the ancient world—calls a consumer proletariat, so the authentic political character of the Christian community disintegrates as soon as the community is conceived under the category of audience. The state looks to elaborated political doctrines to protect it against such abuse, successfully or otherwise; but the worshipping community is different: it has an in-built resistance to being instrumentalized through the form of its central practice. No higher end can be imputed to the worshipping community; the act of worship puts this beyond doubt, since in the act of worship the Eschaton itself breaks into time. There is nothing higher than God's dwelling with his people (Rev. 21 f.), and it cannot be cashed in for some political good like liberation or welfare. The liberation experienced in worship is already political in and of itself—the blessing of being 'members of God's household and fellow-citizens with the saints' (Eph. 2: 19).

We may certainly insist that it is not the Church *as such* that endures for ever (*ecclesia perpetuo mansura sit*[13]); it is 'the city of God'. This saying then means initially only that the Church is taken into the heavenly Jerusalem. Not in every respect, of course: much in the Church as we know it will pass away. What abides is in fact the *political* form of the Church, the Church as it opens out into the city of God. But that is the social form of the Church, the Church as it is in its true self, when it is engaged without further ambition in the praise of God, praise which will one day unite with the chorus of creation and the heavenly host in a mighty *concerto grosso* (Rev. 7: 9–12).

This is the important thing for Christian ethics, this 'presence' of the Church in political worship which anticipates the city of God.

---

[12] German 'die Selbstzwecklichkeit der Kirche'. N. Horton-Smith in his translation of Bonhoeffer's *Ethics* renders this as 'a self-contained community'. But this is not perhaps the best rendering.

[13] Augsburg Confession, Article VII.

For here we find action; here we find judgements; here we find a
presence of the political which continually breaks through the going
categories of political theory. This is true particularly of the distinction between 'what is' and 'what ought to be', a distinction where
the presence of the political is absorbed into the one (utopia) or the
other (*Realpolitik*). But worship is *place* (*topos*), a temporal-spatial
extension, the site and current form of the political. In it the
peaceful coexistence of men and women, the goal of politics, is
not impossible (or reduced to the ending of war through a stale-
mate); nor is it possible (F. Alt[14]); it is simply *there*. Not of course
'there' as a sheer fact; but there—in the language of the Epistle to
the Ephesians—as the 'bond' which has to be maintained in the
unity of the Spirit (Eph. 4: 3). This gift, therefore, is given only *in* its
political form, as both a binding claim on men and women and a
bond between them.

This binding form of acting and judging, 'the law of the Spirit of
life in Christ Jesus' (Rom. 8: 2), is what constitutes the Church as a
political community, as distinct from an amorphous social process.
It has a regulated social life, and this embodied rule is what it listens
to, what it always expressly acknowledges itself obliged to. A society
(in the systems-theory sense of the word) merely follows its own
immanent laws of development, and must behave accordingly.
But—as the Greeks knew—for a community to be free to *act*, it
must have a law; and that is how it becomes a political community.
Yet, if it is to be observed, the law requires a common agreement, an
agreement which has constantly to be sought, and may also fail to
materialize. In so far as worship is an act of assent—in the confession of faith, in praise, and in the hearing of the Word—it contains
in itself the political task of arriving at consensus as a gift. This gift
requires the highest attention to procedures, but is not itself arrived
at by procedures. It is in this sense that worship can be understood
as a basically political phenomenon.

We must again bear in mind at this point that the predominant
sense of the term 'political' in this discussion is not, as in 'political
theology', committed to a specialized use of the term, but is closer
to the Aristotelian sense. We see this worked out, to take one
example, in Hannah Arendt's distinction of the three modes of

[14] F. Alt, *Politik ist möglich* (1983).

the *vita activa*:[15] 'action', as the political form of doing, stands out from 'fabrication' and 'labour' inasmuch as it pursues no further end than joint action in the political community itself. The aim of the praxis is neither a product nor even the prolongation of life itself. The point is to seize the initiative in word and deed and to make a 'beginning' in the world. When people meet to make a concerted beginning, political power comes into being, power which violence may destroy but cannot replace. Here are the points of convergence with the phenomenon of worship which make it useful to speak of its political character. Of course, after all that has been said above, it cannot be a question of applying a political theory such as Arendt's to the practice of worship. Rather, by referring to it from time to time, we need to explore the ways in which our talk about the political is *transformed* by the experience of worship.

In German theology, the idea of political worship has hitherto been at home, largely speaking, in two different conceptual contexts: the one is associated with the name of Karl Barth, the other with the movement called 'political night prayer', which developed in Cologne. My own conception differs from both, as a brief comparison will show.

'Political night prayer' developed out of an ecumenical working party founded in 1968 in the context of the protests and action groups evoked by the Vietnam War. Its aim was to work for a 'politicisation of conscience within the setting of worship too'.[16] It began at the lay Catholic Assembly (*Kirchentag*) held that year in Essen, attracted great attention, and soon found many imitators, though also provoking a good deal of criticism. So what is political about this worship? The context, we are told, and the way the worship is related to it.[17] This means that worship is conceived as political essentially from outside, by virtue of the impact of society upon it, and its impact on society. Methodically speaking, the moment of Information incorporates the former, the moment of

---

[15] H. Arendt, *The Human Condition* (1958; 2nd edn. 1998), 175 ff.

[16] K. Schmidt, 'Das Politische Nachtgebet 1968', in *Evangelischer Gottesdienst: Quellen* (1992), 298.

[17] M. Josuttis strikingly articulates the political hermeneutic employed here: 'The fact that worship always occurs within the setting of a social system, and so has a political character, means that we must always reflect consciously on our connection with this context' ('Das Ziel des Gottesdienstes: Aktion oder Feier?', in *idem, Praxis des Evangeliums zwischen Politik und Religion* (1974), 158).

Action the latter. Meditation and Discussion, which come between Information and Action in the course of a political night prayer, function as a kind of transmission system between the social input of worship and its output, which is also socially related. What is in the foreground is the question of political effectiveness, which is to show itself in the action. 'The effectiveness of a service of worship', we are told by Fulbert Steffensky and his wife Dorothee Sölle, key figures in the movement, 'turns essentially on whether it shows up a real possibility for action.' Otherwise the information about social conditions breeds resignation.[18]

Worship, then, is designed to have an outward effect. And this functionalization of worship as a whole is matched by the inward functionalization of its component elements. Of course the question here is: how political can a 'discussion' be, how free is a 'meditation', when its outcome—in an 'action' for which the plans have already been laid—has been fixed from the outset? At a closer glance, even the formal freedom to rearrange the elements which are to lead to the action demonstrates the functional subservience of the worship. For worship is not conceived to have a form which contributes its *own* meaning, its *own* dynamic, ethical among other things. It is seen as the object of a design dictated by whatever the theme may be—all of which demonstrates the truth of what the advocates of this conception explicitly claim for it: that this 'political worship' stands in the tradition of 'political theology'.[19]

Actually, political worship was not an idea devised by the movement for 'political night prayer'. As I shall try to show, it has in fact characterized Christian assemblies from the beginning, and from the eighteenth century became the term for orders of service tied to some political event. In the twentieth century, talk of political worship was given a theological slant by Karl Barth in particular. We meet it first in his Gifford Lectures of 1937–8, *The Knowledge of*

[18] D. Sölle and F. Steffensky (eds.), *Politisches Nachtgebet in Köln*, i (1969), 9 f. For criticism, cf. R. Leuenberger, 'Politischer Gottesdienst', *ZThK* 69 (1972), 100–24.

[19] This theological movement has been influential since the 1960s. Its distinctive character has been well summed up by the Swedish theologian Arne Rasmusson, in contrast to what he calls 'theological politics'. Political theology treats the struggle for liberation as the context within which to interpret the Church's theology and praxis. Theological politics goes the other way, interpreting world politics in the context of the Church's own political existence. See Rasmusson, *The Church as Polis* (1994), 177 f. On the distinction between political theology and political ethics cf. also H. G. Ulrich, *Eschatologie und Ethik* (1988), 255 ff.

God and the Service of God according to the Teaching of the Reformation.[20] Here Barth offers an interpretation of the Scottish Confession which makes an excellent introduction to his theology. Following the arrangement he has chosen, he expounds first those articles of the Confession which invite treatment under the heading 'the knowledge of God'. Then he turns to those which allow him to lay out his understanding of 'service' or, more properly, 'worship' (*Gottesdienst*).[21] This section is divided into three subdivisions, devoted to the different modes of worship. Barth first treats the worship of the Christian life, goes on to the worship-service in the church ('worship in the narrower sense of the term'), and closes with some reflections on 'political worship'.

With this 'unusual and artificial term' (p. 218) Barth deals with the subject-matter treated by the Scottish Confession under the heading 'Of Civile Magistrate'. In his view, 'political worship' comprises a third level, distinct from the previous two forms of worship he has already discussed. It is at the same time a special perspective on Christian worship as a whole, and something besides—a 'peculiar' worship distinguished as 'political' through the specific 'space' in which it takes place: the space of the world, inasmuch as this is 'still a stranger' to the lordship of Christ. To proclaim to the world the Word that Christ is *its* lord and the lord of its political order too is what constitutes the Church's 'political worship'.

In this worship there is a provisional but real 'sanctification of the world' (p. 221), in which its outward political order can be seen as a 'shadow cast before it' by the final order of love and peace. To claim the political order of the state as 'worship' means reminding those in power of their calling (Rom. 13: 6) to be God's 'ministers' (p. 223). They are admonished to fulfil the limited task given them by God in the proper place assigned to them: to secure the political virtues of provisional peace and provisional order, and to let the Church go about its business. 'The significance of the political order as

---

[20] The title given to the English translation of Barth's *Gotteserkenntnis und Gottesdienst*. The page numbers in the text refer to this volume.

[21] Although (as the English title suggests) Barth's translators favour the translation 'service of God' for the German *Gottesdienst*, the word is generally used to mean worship, in the widest sense. The term 'political' is also avoided in the translation of the Lectures, so that the phrase 'political worship' does not occur there, although Barth's apology ('unusual and artificial') for the neologistic sound of it does! By replacing 'political' by the paraphrase 'the State's', the translators narrow down unduly what Barth meant by *politischer Gottesdienst* [Trans.].

worshipful service becomes clear where the State provides and preserves *freedom* for the Church' (p. 226; trans. amended). Whether
and to what extent the state maintains the 'worshipful' sense of the
political order will determine whether the Church's political worship takes the form of active participation by its members in political life or of criticism, which, in the last resort, may go so far as
forcible resistance. But especially because force, in Barth's view, is
something in which we are all inevitably actively or passively involved in some way or other (p. 231), for him political worship is
also a fundamentally questionable and dangerous business (p. 236).

Barth's distinction between three levels of worship may in the
end prove problematical in the sense in which Barth pursues it; but
it is helpful because it helps us to see more clearly the constellation
of ideas with which we have to deal. This becomes evident when we
ask how Barth's three different forms of worship are inwardly
related. In Barth the nature of this relation is not clear. In what
sense is the Church's service of worship the 'concrete centre' of the
church's worship as a whole (p. 190)? And what precisely is the role
here of the third level, 'political worship'? Is it simply an appendix
to the other two, a further sphere which also falls under worship?
The way in which Barth arranges and presents the different sections
suggests that he sees the link between the three levels he is dealing
with in their capacity for correspondence: what makes the human
activities he is dealing with modes of worship is their character as a
response to God's Word, which gives them their definition and
calling in each given case. By concentrating on this shared aspect
of correspondence to the Word of God, Barth lends a certain
homogeneity to the three levels, thus setting their differences in
low relief. But in my view the constructive potential of his distinction is fully realized only when we concentrate on the differences.
For then 'political worship' affords us not merely an unspecific
'third level' in addition to the other two, but the *paradigm for the
relation of the one to the other.*

From our perspective, political worship, as one of the three
strands in the relationship, has its specific task as a criterion or
test case for the relation of 'church worship or service' and 'moral
service'. So the argument to be developed in the following pages on
worship and ethics will try to offer an answer to the question: 'What
is political worship really about?' Here, however, Barth's scheme
must be set right at a decisive point, the very point which he and the

'political night prayer' movement have in common. For Barth it is political inasmuch as it relates to the political order of civil society in the state. He ignores the fact that this relation to the 'political' public realm is preceded by another public realm, constituted and celebrated in liturgy, which already belongs to 'fellow-citizens with the saints'. In this light we can resolve Barth's hesitation as to whether political worship is a specific dimension of worship or a distinct subspecies of it, and declare unequivocally (against his own inclination) for the former. At the same time, 'political worship' is not just one of a number of possible ways in which the worship of God can be considered. It is the decisive case, the one which gives the others their coherence. For if we fail to understand the assembly of believers politically, 'church service' and 'moral service' necessarily fall apart. Then they have to be stuck together again, a process which, if it can be done at all, demands a secondary theological device to hold them artificially in place—precisely such a device to marry worship to social conscience as is exemplified by the programme of 'political night prayer'. Even in Barth's own case we cannot entirely overlook the hint of such artificiality, despite the fact that the relationship is presented with more nuance.[22]

We may briefly summarize our critical review of these two advocates of political worship in the sense in which it has been used previously by saying that both deploy a *contextual* idea of the political which sells short the *structural* political dimension of worship. Against Barth, we would maintain that liturgical worship is actually *political*, not merely a 'church service'. Against the Cologne programme, we would maintain that this worship *is* already political, and stands in no need of further politicization.

---

[22] Later, however, Barth relates worship and ethics in a more organic manner. In the context of his treatment of worship in the second volume of his *Doctrine of Reconciliation* (*CD* IV/2), he finds that the conduct of Christians in everyday life is 'ordained to be a wider and transformed worship' (639). And in the posthumous fragments on the ethics of the doctrine of reconciliation he reverses the viewpoint, and says about the liberty of God's children to pray that 'the invocation of God the Father is as such a supremely social matter, publicly social, not to say political and even cosmic' (*The Christian Life*, *CD* IV/4 [Lecture Fragments], 95).

2

Worship as a Form of Life:
The Grammar of Christian Life

'Agreement in Judgements'

Political worship is a form of life—nothing more and nothing less. As a form of *life*, it embraces the life of believers as a whole, not just certain parts of it, be it the political sphere. A *form* of life is at once restricted and derestricting. It is more than a life-style which can be adopted by individual men and women. It represents the ethos of a community, and critical participation in it. On the other hand, if faced by the demand for principles of conduct that are amenable to some universally valid theory, a life-forming ethics inevitably proves resistant. It envisages a universe of moral relations, but not a universal morality. In our context the concept 'form of life' is particularly fruitful in the shape given to it by Wittgenstein's late philosophy. For in his *Philosophical Investigations* Wittgenstein shows how language *always* already develops and moves in a political context, and hence can never be understood in a purely instrumental sense. '[T]o imagine a language is to imagine a form of life.'[1] We do not grasp the nature of language when we determine its basic logical form in the ideal correlation of sign and meaning—a senseless undertaking, as (the later) Wittgenstein came to realize—but by watching to see what it is really doing.

It is therefore not surprising that Wittgenstein should see language as essentially ethically based. '[H]uman beings ... agree in the *language* they use. That is not an agreement in opinions but in form of life. If language is to be a means of communication there must be agreement not only in definitions but (queer as this may sound) in judgments' (§§241 f.).[2] Agreement in judgements springs

---

[1] L. Wittgenstein, *Philosophical Investigations* (1967), §19.

[2] Aristotle had already identified this ethical—indeed, explicitly political—connotation of language in his *Politics*. According to what he says, language is there so that we may distinguish the just from the unjust. 'For the real difference between man and other animals is that humans alone have perception of good and evil, just and

from a shared ethos, and at the same time sustains that ethos. The specific forms of the shared social context of living determine the way things are perceived and the terms deployed. Where different forms of life intersect, on the other hand, or where there is no prevailing form of life at all, equivocations lurk. We think we understand, but in fact we are at cross purposes. Moral discussion is especially prone to this failure, because of the erroneous inversion of the relationship between forms of life and the way we speak of them.[3]

Because of this, where worship is concerned, two linked facts stand out as especially pregnant. On the one hand, 'agreement in judgements' as the political (life-forming) condition for an ethic and moral discussion is implicit in worship, because this consists essentially in the agreement which worshippers arrive at together: agreement with the judgement of God on sinners, who, though deserving of death, are pardoned. On the other hand, worship appears as a form of life by existing in that anti-functional way which we designated as especially political. In this respect 'form of life' can be understood as an emancipating concept. It resists the master concepts which force the phenomenon described into a functional perspective. Worship as a form of life then simply means that it cannot be understood by way of general concepts such as ritual, feast, game, therapy, and so forth; on the contrary, these terms can be understood and communicated only in the light of worship. Whatever 'feast' may mean for Christians only properly emerges in worship, and will have to be brought into line with other ideas from that point. Of course, if we set an emancipation concept over against master concepts, this also means that 'form of life' cannot itself be turned into a master concept, in place of rival concepts. In this sense worship is not an element in the Christian form of life ('Does a Christian have to go to church?'): it *is* the Christian form of life. Worship as a form of life sees worship itself as the regulative factor wherein we recognize the discipline which proves a life to be

unjust, etc. *Yet it is sharing of a common view in these matters that makes a household and a state 'house and state'* (1253a14–19 [trans. slightly altered]; my italics).

[3] Thus, in a frequently employed logic, for example, a term such as 'love' or 'faithfulness' can be passed off as a 'value', the presence or absence of which is supposed to show the ethical quality of certain relationships. What is overlooked here, of course, is the fact that it is just the concrete form of life (marriage, concubinage, etc.) which decides what the term is actually expressing.

Christian. It is this socially regulative character which is aptly described as 'being ruled by the Spirit' (Gal. 5: 16, 18).

The Regulated Character of Worship as Interaction with the Canon

As the immediate context in Paul shows, in spite of elemental metaphors like wind, breath, and fire, the Spirit of God should not be understood as vitality, as a spontaneous expression of life, as opposed to form, or as a code word for charismatic, as opposed to institutional, as the Spiritualists in the Reformation period assumed, and later Troeltsch, Sohm, and Emil Brunner too. It must be seen as a formative personal subject. The Spirit 'rules', and its fruit (Gal. 5: 22 f.) can be described just as clearly as 'the works of the flesh' (Gal. 5: 19 ff.). Here the social colouring which permeates all the different facets of the fruit of the Spirit is as striking as the anti-social, imperial character[4] of the works of the flesh. The two lists are not to be understood as congruent: they characterize the two contrary ways of being ruled—by God's Spirit or by the 'spirit of the flesh'. The fact that the fruit of the Spirit is mentioned in the singular and is yet described in an inward plurality indicates that each of the behavioural patterns touched on is a complete work of the Spirit: an efficacy into which the Spirit enters wholly, though not exclusively. When Paul says: 'If we live in the Spirit, let us also walk in the Spirit' (Gal. 5: 25), he is not viewing the Spirit as the definition of a sphere wherein the spirit is divided from the flesh, or the sacred from the profane. To walk in the Spirit means rather that God's Spirit determines the specific form a life takes, and constitutes its intrinsically regulated character.

Now, the rule of the Spirit is bound up with particular outward means of grace. In opposing the Enthusiasts, Luther insisted on the link between the Spirit and God's external Word, and in our present context this finds its specific form in the relationship between worship and canon. Eilert Herms has pointed to this in his 'Reflections on the Nature of Worship'.[5] He starts from the postulate that 'the essence of worship cannot be grasped by way of the concept of

---

[4] M. Welker (*God the Spirit* (1994), 306) stresses the expansive character of the spirit of the Western world. Welker sees the collective incarnation of this spirit in the key concept 'enterprise'. This embodies an activity of self-preservation which ruthlessly pursues its own expansion.

[5] E. Herms, 'Überlegungen zum Wesen des Gottesdienstes', *KuD* 40 (1994), 219–47. The page numbers in the text refer to this essay.

structure, but only through the concept of rule' (p. 222). Accordingly, worship is essentially 'the regular entry of believers into the original situation of faith'. Worship now finds the criterion for this 'regularity' not in the ordained ministry but in the canon (p. 225). It is here that it has 'the centre of its identity' (p. 232), like the whole Christian life. The canon decides the constituents of every possible order of worship, the identity of which (and historically evidenced structural similarity) emerges from the fact that every Christian service of worship follows the same rule (pp. 237 f.). The communal structure which grows out of this must accordingly not be confused with the rule that confers the identity.

Herms's ideas can now be deepened and linked up with what I have said above about 'form of life'. And we can then go on to say that the canon is to worship as a grammar is to a form of life. In both cases the *telos* of the first is at home in the second. Strictly speaking, grammar exists only in and for forms of life. But at the same time the grammar ensures not only that the life has form, but that the form has life. That is to say, just because of its regulating character, it also makes something new possible, by making the new recognizable in a given context of linguistic communication—born out of the continuity which it both transcends and extends in substantially expanded form. The same can be said about the canon. On the one hand, as canon it is formed in worship and formed for use in worship. It depicts the content and compass of the Holy Scriptures used in worship. But at the same time worship is regulated by the canon: what is to be celebrated in worship is given us in the canon. Here the fixity of the canon is the very aspect which makes the voyage of exploration possible, in the specific 'how' of the celebration of worship in time—makes it possible too in the specifically political sense. For the spiritual authenticity of worship—the regularity of a liturgical 'how' in accord with the canonical 'what'— cannot be ensured in any other way than through the test of a shared, critical process The continuity of the rule is not functionally secured by functionaries. The ordained ministers can at most represent the authenticity of the worship; they cannot guarantee it.

So in thinking about the fundamental question of this study—to what extent worship can be seen as regulative for Christian ethics— we may first of all say the following, from the angle of the canon. Worship is not in itself and *directly* the rule for the community's moral life; it governs the moral life as *the first instance,* so to speak, of the rule's application. If the social life of believers is to find its form in relation to this rule, it does so first of all in worship. For it is there that the primary modes of the common life can be found—as fellowship at the Lord's Table, in shared listening and speaking in assent to the Word; it is also the place where the canonical texts find their direct expression, and it is these which mediate the rule to us. So in what sense is worship itself regulative? Here the answer has to be: simply as the rule's first application—its first, continually necessary first application—its 'beginning'. The gathered congregation is the paradigmatic application of the rule, because of the promise made to it that it will be ruled by the same Spirit who has brought both the canonical writings and the canon itself into being.

Every attempt to find a foundation for ethics is exposed to the critical question whether another, deeper level cannot be brought to light—a foundation beneath the foundation on which we have set our sights. It would then seem that if we pursue this question far enough, we should finally hit bedrock in worship, in which Christian ethics can be placed on an unshakeably firm foundation. Or we could be misled by our perception that the centre of worship is the canon into maintaining a still more foundational foundation for ethics in the sense of a phenomenological reduction. Either attempt would come down to the demand for a 'worship' or 'biblical' ethics. But a political conception of worship dispenses in principle with the quest for a foundation. It is rather that the question about the properly founded form of ethos and ethics (if it is theologically soundly based) begins again and again with the canonical service of worship, or (which is the same thing) the canon used in worship. *Ethics has its foundation neither in worship nor in the canon, but it begins in the relation between canon and worship perceived in the interaction of the two: in political worship.* Consequently an ethics springing from worship will be equally critical of both the Protestant temptation to bridge this interaction by an ethical 'scriptural principle' and the Catholic temptation to short-circuit it in a clerical model where the foundation is a 'sacramental' church ethic.

The Need for Transformation

Now it must also be said that the idea of a form of life which develops and is passed on in a linguistic community is in danger of trivializing and domesticating the drama of what happens in worship. After all, it is a matter of *trans*formation here, not merely formation.[6] It is true that in talking about a form of life as a traditional phenomenon there is always an implicit link between ethos and pathos. Yet we must remember that worship is not a linear, harmonious socialization process, in which the ethical shaping of believers follows like words written one after another on a blank page. Ethical learning always proceeds in the form of a struggle between the 'old' and the 'new' man. As Paul says in his famous paraclesis at the beginning of Romans 12, it is a matter of the new *morphe* of the Christian life, as a change from the old. Consequently Paul mentions the positive task of metamorphosis in the same breath as the negative one—not to be conformed to the pattern of this world (Rom. 12: 2). Although 'the form of this world' is destined to pass away (1 Cor. 7: 31), he evidently, for all that, assigns it to the effective formative powers which put an almost irresistible spell on human beings. Even Christians are not always free of their influence; they need the reminder (the 'consoling admonition': *paraklesis*) of their freedom in Christ. These 'proofs of God's mercy' (*oiktirmoi*, Rom. 12: 1), which Paul has talked about in the previous chapters, must be continually kept before eyes and ears. So the transformation required is expected and promoted not by an iron will but emphatically through the 'renewal of your mind', the *nous* as the organ of perception in the widest sense—practical judgement.

Now for our context it is significant that the biblical word *anakainosis* is employed both in connection with baptism (Titus 3: 5) and with reference to the daily renewal by, or out of, the Spirit which Luther identified as *reditus ad baptismum*—a return to baptism (2 Cor. 4: 16). Baptism and the remembrance of baptism come into question in a special way as the context of this renewal of judgement. So if it is possible to talk at all about 'worship in the everyday life of the world', then, especially if we remember Romans 12: 1 f., 'ethical worship' cannot be played off against liturgical worship, since the *logike latreia* is characterized by the link with *anakainosis* in a clear reference to baptism.

If we have in view this close (and typically Pauline) interweaving of worship and ethical elements—an interweaving which is also manifested in the way in which the two alternate as the chapter

---

[6] On the transforming role of the Church's practices, cf. L. G. Jones, *Transformed Judgment* (1990), esp. 73 ff.

goes on (Rom. 12: 3–8)—we may sum up by saying that the renewal of discernment which is rooted in baptism and the remembrance of baptism both sets off the transformation which constitutes the Christian life and keeps it going: the transformation from the abstractions of the powers of the world to life in the form of worship—life in the Spirit, in the 'logic' of worship.[7]

The capacity for judgement renewed through the Spirit is demonstrated especially in the capacity to distinguish properly, without divorcing them, God's acts from human acts, and God's judgement from human judgements. The 'proving' or testing which is the aim of that *logike latreia* according to Paul is not an abstract, universally applicable 'art of distinction'; it identifies, through the Spirit, what is 'good, well-pleasing and perfect'. Since the renewal of the capacity for judgement is rooted in the service of baptism, this suggests that the guardianship of this capacity must also be seen as being closely linked with the congregation gathered for worship. Then the intended identification will not be illuminative, through direct inspiration, or analytical, through the application of a theory, but indirect: through the experience of what is good, well-pleasing, and perfect, as this is promised and present in worship. Here we find the operations which run ahead, before eyes and ears take in hearts and senses, which are first of all said to be *agathos, euarestos, teleios*. But this also means, conversely, that the capacity for judgement pales as this very experience recedes. What is thought to be good is then once again defined abstractly, in the light of the master concepts which the world offers in its own capacity for judgement. True, this is not something we simply have to dismiss, but its fruits are not just *worth* testing (Phil. 1: 9 f.; 1 Thess. 5: 21), they also *have to be* tested. So devoted service on behalf of the world includes the criticism that tests the world. It must be said, however, that the condition for this criticism and the enduring capacity for criticism of 'the form of this world' is that the critics themselves undergo the transformation in which 'the old man' dies.

---

[7] The tradition of Israel's ecstatic, Spirit-imbued prophets already makes it clear that God's Spirit is experienced as transformation. Thus Samuel proclaims to Saul after his anointing: 'Then the spirit of the LORD will come mightily upon you, and you shall prophesy with them and be turned into another man' (1 Sam. 10: 6). The transforming efficacy of the Spirit can also appear in the political structure, as the story about the call of the seventy Spirit-filled elders to be leaders of the people shows (Num. 11: 14 ff.). Cf. Welker, *God the Spirit*, 75 ff.

In what we said above about form of life, we looked at the ethos of worship and the ethics formed in worship in the context of the development of human language. But we must say more precisely here that worship as a form of life makes the Christian life more like learning a foreign language than understanding one's own. 'I hear a language which I did not know before' (Ps. 81: 5b). Of course, this does not do away with the importance of the idea of a form of life, which provides an orientation. Even a foreign language can only be properly learned in its own country, where terms and phrases are understood in the context of the form of life which sustains them. That this learning inevitably goes together with the (partial) un-learning of one's own mother tongue is confirmed by the experience of people who live abroad, whose thinking, dreams, and feelings increasingly move in the new language, opening up experiences which are so intrinsic to that language that they can hardly be expressed in the mother tongue, or only with difficulty and clumsily. There is no translation from one form of life to another. But forms of life can be shared, and their experiences communicated. Consequently, the ethos shared in worship and the ethics belonging to it should not be understood as a translation into a new conceptuality of experiences in the linguistic area previously inhabited (the form of life of 'the old man').[8]

For Luther, this connection between 'the new creature' and 'the new language' was of central hermeneutical importance for his whole theology: 'post Christum natum, crucifixum et resurrectum'—after Christ born, crucified and raised—nothing remains as it was. This must be true of language first of all. The Christian ought to be a new creature, since in all things he speaks and thinks other than the world judges ('Christianus debet esse nova creatura ..., qui aliter loquatur, cogitet de allen stücken, quam die welt von judicirt', WA 36, 255, 7–9). This new language is not a matter of new terms. It is a different, 'parabolic' use of the terms, which thereby acquire a new meaning (it is impossible to avoid comparing

---

[8] It is along these lines that we might also formulate some reservations about George Lindbeck's deservedly celebrated book *The Nature of Doctrine* (1984). Lindbeck's attempt to understand the Church's doctrine as the grammar of faith could equally well be fruitfully applied to Christian ethics. But Lindbeck's general approach by way of the analogy of learning a language (a mother tongue, mainly) means that the transformation aspect can hardly be included. On the problem of the translatability of moral worlds, cf. A. MacIntyre, *Three Rival Versions of Moral Enquiry* (1990), 112 ff.

Wittgenstein here). 'Nam mutatis rebus etiam verba mutantur in alium sensum et fit plane nova Grammatica'—'For as things change, words change also and acquire a different meaning and a new grammar is formed' (WA 42, 195, 20 f.). The subject of this new grammar is not the person who employs it—for a grammar is never in fact at one's disposal at all—but God's Spirit, who guides human beings in their new use of language: 'Spiritus Sanctus habet suam grammaticam'—'The Holy Spirit has his own grammar' (WA 39 II, 104, 24).[9]

In the framework of reflections about transformation in worship, we might take this a step further and even say that the new language of believers is not simply the outcome of their transformation, not a function of the 'new creature', but its material cause: the 'material' in which this transformation process fundamentally takes place. The new *morphe* is manifested first of all in the new use of language, and is itself—we might even say—itself essentially a 'new grammar'. Here we remain dependent on worship as the language school of faith, where we are introduced to the new use of terms and concepts, the moral ones included. Here the renewed capacity for judgement comes into its own as theological language criticism, a criticism which cannot be separated from the strangeness experienced in the new language.[10]

---

[9] Luther illustrates this in a sermon on 1 Corinthians 15. Picking up the 'seed' metaphor used there, he says that the dead should not be understood as 'ein stinckend, verfaulet ass oder todten bein' ('a stinking, putrifying carrion or dead bones'), but as 'eitel körnlin, die da bald sollen daher wachsen, unsterblich un unverweslich, viel schöner denn die grüne saat auff dem felde, wenn es somer wird' 'pure seeds, which are soon to grow up immortal and imperishable, far fairer than the green seedlings in the fields in summer' (WA 644, 21–5). 'Das ist nova sprach de resurrectione mortuorum' ('That is the new language of the resurrection of the dead') (WA 36, 647, 2 f.) as we encounter it in the proclamation. Cf. A. Beutel, *In dem Anfang war das Wort* (1991).

[10] Cf. also P. Wadell, 'What Do All Those Masses Do for Us?', in K. Hughes and M. R. Francis (eds.), *Living No Longer for Ourselves* (1991), 153–69.

3

Absorptions

Political worship can be relativized in two main ways, which can be distinguished from one another. Each of them in its own way undertakes to do away with worship as a form of life. The marginalization of worship as a *form* of life is associated with the name of Hegel, the loss of worship as a form of *life* with the name of Kant. We must look at these forms of absorption[1] first. We shall then consider theorems and ideas about theological ethics which follow from these relativizations in their own particular spheres. Here I shall be criticizing both a sacramental ethic, in the sense of a universal hermeneutical extension, and a eucharistic ethic, in the sense of a motivation ethic. My criticism will be targeted at the tyranny of ethics as well as at a Church ethics in the form either of a community ethic or a clerical one. First, however, we shall turn to the two philosophers who fathered the relativizations which constitute the two main ways of doing away with worship as a form of life. The way represented by Hegel elevates worship, or one aspect of it (sacrament, Word, liberation, etc.) to a principle, or generalizes it to a structure, thus dissolving its particular external form and, as we shall see, paving the way for a secondary instrumentalization. Kant, on the other hand, takes another path, pursuing a primary instrumentalization. He reduces the relevance of worship for life to one particular aspect—the moral one—and approaches this from the angle of an external criterion: practical reason.

Hegel's Absorption of Religion into a Concept, and the Problem of Sacramental Ethics

The point of departure which already emerges from Hegel's early theological writings characterizes his perspective in general. He

---

[1] *Aufhebungen*: in the Hegelian sense, the word *aufheben* can mean either to destroy or to preserve through absorption into something else, often something higher. It is sometimes translated by 'sublate' [Trans.].

proceeds from the experience of a fundamental bifurcation or dichotomy of life, whose totality he wants to win (or win back) through a comprehensive movement of reflection.[2] This restitution of the totality of life characterizes Hegel theologically: for him, it means the reconciliation of faith and reason, law and love, subjectivity and objectivity. Inasmuch as philosophy purports to fulfil this task once and for all, it is itself nothing other than worship. In philosophy Hegel seeks to 'justify' religion[3]—in its highest form the Christian religion—by simultaneously postulating that the 'positivity' of faith can be surmounted through 'the idea of the general'. For him, the essential epistemological aid here is the distinction between the content of religion and its form. 'In faith the true *content* is certainly already found, but it still lacks the *form* of thinking' (346 n.).[4]

Over against the capacity for 'speculative consciousness' to complete religion's unique 'movement *in the Spirit*' (p. 153), the cult merely has the task of *representing* this movement *externally*. The marginalization of the event of worship as a gathering of believers becomes clearly evident, for example, when Hegel discusses the subject of confession and repentance. Here there is no mention of the event which can be experienced in the service of worship—the spoken confession of sin and the uttered promise of forgiveness. Instead, 'confession' becomes the disposal of evil in thought 'through contrition'.

---

[2] For the young Hegel see K. Löwith's interpretation in *From Hegel to Nietzsche* (1965), 327 ff., to which I am indebted in the following passage. It is illuminating to see how from his Frankfurt period onwards Hegel assumed that the bifurcation was 'fated' to precede all attempts at thought, and especially also in the relationship between worship and life. Thus he closes his observations on 'the Spirit of Christianity' by saying of the Christian Church: 'It is its fate that church and state, worship and life, piety and virtue, spiritual and worldly action *can never* dissolve into one' ('The Spirit of Christianity', 301; my italics). We might then almost go so far as to ask whether the origin of Hegel's dialectic—where this very capacity for fusion is claimed—cannot be found in the *a priori* denial of the possibility of a political worship.

[3] Hegel, *Lectures on the Philosophy of Religion*, vol. ii: *Determinate Religion*, part III, 346 n. The page numbers in the text refer to this volume.

[4] The background here is Hegel's view of the three modes of reception: immediately, in feeling, through the senses; in the idea (or reflection) in which feeling is already conceptualized; and in pure, conceptual thinking. Only 'the flight into the concept' can help us out of the particular limitations of the two preliminary forms and their harsh opposition in the clarification.

Hegel's procedure becomes completely evident when he turns to 'the main sacrament', the Christian celebration of the Lord's Supper. Here he can hardly deny the sensory character of 'tasting and seeing'. At the same time, this counts only as the starting-point, which must very soon be left behind, as Hegel says, believing that the Lutheran view of the Eucharist is 'the most thoughtful' of the different confessional ways of thinking the dissolution of the antithesis between finite and infinite.[5] At this point our interest need not be directed so much to the fact that Hegel (quite evidently in complete misunderstanding of the real confessional differences) wrongly appeals to the Lutheran tradition for his own version of the *annihilatio* of the material elements. It is more important for an understanding of the connection between worship and ethics to note how the Hegelian 'concept' assigns Christian worship to the category of a 'higher' form of appropriation. Brought under the logic of 'concept' (which is basically a logic of appropriation), the receptive character of the Eucharist is simply, and without more ado, turned upside down.

In contrast, the pervasive bodiliness of the worship event—and especially in the perspective of Lutheran theology[6]—insists on the indivisibility of form and content. It is impossible to surrender or to get beyond the bodily and sensory celebration of the Lord's Supper. Where that is transcended, the content of the celebration is inevitably simultaneously diffused. The presence of Christ among his people cannot be reduced to a concept. The exemplary importance of Hegel's philosophy of religion is then to be seen in the very fact that he has put forward *in principle* (for 'the' concept as such) what will always apply in the present too to every 'simple' concept under which worship is conceived.

From this perspective it then becomes clear why an ethic springing from worship cannot be conceived as a 'sacramental ethic'.[7] To make generic talk about sacraments the starting-point for ethics

[5] 'The advance is that the individual worshipper takes up this consumption inwardly, and the sensible is first spiritualized in the subject... Here there is no transubstantiation, or at at any rate only one by which externality is annulled' (*Philosophy of Religion*, p. 339).
[6] See here O. Bayer, *Leibliches Wort* (1992), 57 ff., with detailed evidence.
[7] Cf. T. F. Sedgwick, *Sacramental Ethics* (1987). Oliver C. Quick treats the connection between worship and morals explicitly under the premiss 'A Lesson from Hegel', and proceeds from the following (frequently made) assumption: 'And the representation of the common in the holy is, we believe, the first principle of sacramental theory' (*The Christian Sacraments* (1952), 244).

already presupposes an abstraction which makes it difficult to
perceive the significance for ethics of the individual worship practices gathered together under this term—a significance which is
inherent in their *individually* characteristic movements, or in their
complex field of mutual reference. Instead of that, a *tertium compar-
ationis* is invoked, and the attributes of the individual practices
which make them a sacrament are then stylized into an ethical
principle. It may then be perhaps the 'union' or 'unification' of
the divine and the human, God and the world, which in supreme
generality is understood to be 'the sacramental principle'. This not
infrequently takes place in the framework of a universalist incarnation theology which—with the help of an incarnation Christology
derestricted in a problematical way through its pneumatological
poverty—is talked about as 'sacrament' by the world at large. In
the twentieth century particularly, this pattern of thought continually proved its attractiveness, right across the various confessional
barriers.[8]

The tradition of political theology especially has drawn on this
model. Leonardo Boff, for example, in his little book *Sacraments of
Life—Life of the Sacraments*, uses the following argument.[9] In good
Hegelian fashion he takes as his starting-point the postulate that 'A
sacrament is a way of thinking'. The second thesis follows: 'As a
specific way of thinking, sacramental thinking is universal. In other
words, all things, not just some things, can be transformed into
sacraments.' From this point it is only a short step to the identifying
link between the political struggle for liberation and the sacramental character of history. In this way a sacrament becomes the means
for drawing political forms of action into the legitimacy of the
Church's activity rather than the transformation of political life,
as is the case in political worship.

*Worship in the Kingdom of Ends: Kant's Moralization and the Problem
of 'Eucharistic Ethics'*

The other way of doing away with political worship as a form of
life is Kant's. This takes the reverse direction. It does not extrapo-
late worship to a concept or to the 'sacramental universe', but
incorporates it into a universe set up somewhere else—in Kant's

[8] For William Temple's idea of 'the sacramental universe' cf. section 5.1.
[9] Cf. the summary of his theses, 89 ff.

case, the universe of reason. In Kant's 'moral kingdom of ends', worship and its object can also come into question only as a means. Theoretical reason gets along quite well by itself. It is only practical reason which cannot avoid making use of religion.[10] Kant's moral or ethical theology constitutes an instrument which is necessary if we are to think the simultaneity of happiness and (moral) worth, by assuming the existence of a higher, moral, supremely holy and omnipotent being, who is the guarantor of this simultaneity. 'Morality leads ineluctably to religion.'[11] Thus Kant becomes the theorist of the functionalization of faith in the service of the all-embracing claim of reasonable morality. Because only the human being counts as 'an end *an sich*', for him everything must be utilized. Practical reason only 'needs' God (the German verb *brauchen* has the double sense of 'to need' and 'to use'); it does not worship him.

For Kant, prayer 'as an *inner formal* service of God . . . is superstitious illusion'. Whereas 'nothing is accomplished by it', and it discharges none of the moral duties 'to which, as commanded of God, we are obligated', 'pure' prayer would be 'the pure spirit of prayer', the disposition in which all actions are performed *as if* they were performed in the service of God. Prayer as an act of worship, in contrast, if it does not immediately give way to the superior self-reflection of the moral individual, can always have a merely functional character—'[it can] at best possess only the value of a means whereby that disposition within us may be repeatedly quickened' (p. 182). This 'invisible' worship as a matter of the appropriate disposition is certainly also represented by 'the sensuous'. But Kant thinks that this celebratory means of expression is potentially dangerous, because the representation may be equated with the thing itself, and 'through an illusion that steals over us', it is easily held to be *'the worship of God* itself, and is, indeed, commonly thus spoken of' (p. 180; trans. altered).

Thus Kant arrives at a critical evaluation of the four useful sensory (or 'sensuous') instruments which also externally represent the worship or service offered by the proper disposition: prayer,

---

[10] 'The actuality of a supreme morally legislative Author is, therefore, sufficiently proved simply *for the practical employment* of our reason, without determining anything theoretically in respect of its existence' (I. Kant, *Critique of Judgement*, 125).

[11] I. Kant, *Religion within the Limits of Reason Alone*, preface to the 1st edn., 5. The page numbers in the text refer to this volume.

church-going, baptism, and communion. Here the political dimension is always in view. For example, Kant notes that church-going is a sensuous representation[12] 'of the community of believers, not only a means to be valued by each *individual* for his own *edification* but also a duty directly obligating them as a *group*, as citizens of a divine state which is to appear here on earth' (pp. 186 f.). Communion in particular seems to him to be effective in this respect, being the 'oft-repeated ceremony of a *renewal, continuation and propagation of this churchly community* under laws of *equality*'. For it 'contains within itself something great, expanding the narrow, selfish, and unsociable cast of mind among men, especially in matters of religion, toward the idea of a cosmopolitan *moral community*; and it is a good means of enlivening a community to the moral disposition of brotherly love which it represents'. But in order to obviate any 'clerical' misunderstanding (Kant's word *pfäffisch* has a strongly derogatory flavour), he half makes a reservation: 'But to assert that God has attached special favors to the celebration of this solemnity... is a religious illusion' (p. 188). 'Means of grace' are for him nothing more than all too transparent attempts on the part of the human being to escape the moral imperative by '[busying himself] with *piety* (a passive respect for the law of God) rather than with *virtue* (the application of one's own powers in discharging the duty which one respects)... To this end man busies himself with every conceivable formality, designed to indicate how greatly he *respects* the divine commands, in order that it may not be necessary for him to *obey them*' (p. 189).

Of course we can see where Kant misrepresents the phenomenon of worship. But what should primarily concern us here is the connection which Kant's acute analysis brings out. For what he sees with complete clarity is that where worship is a means, it cannot and may not be a 'means of grace'. For the logic of the

---

[12] Since both Kant and—as we have seen—Hegel use the term 'representation' (*Darstellung*) to describe the nature of worship, and in view of the representative role that Kant and Hegel have for the dissolution of worship as a form of life, this may make one sceptical about Schleiermacher's attempt to see the particular character of worship in talk about 'representative action'. Even in this version, 'representation' remains a reflexive term which aims at a more primal Something which is re-presented in worship; worship is not seen as itself a primal efficacy of the Spirit. Thus Schleiermacher sees 'the purpose of religious observance' as being 'the representing communication of the strongly excited religious consciousness' (*Praktische Theologie*, 75).

means–end category destroys grace—just as, conversely, grace forbids the conception of all goods as means to ends. This connection must be taken to heart especially by any theology that attempts to see worship as a function of an ethic *corresponding* to grace. But that is precisely the fundamental idea behind the conception of Christianity as an ethical *motive*. This conception follows Kant in assuming that morality has to be universally valid, and must be understood as existing of itself, in splendid isolation. It also follows Kant in requiring for the actual implementation of the moral imperative yet another authority, an 'idea' which is capable of actually giving life to the disposition. What in Kant is reduced to the mere assumption of a transcendent author of the moral law, is here once again extended theologically to cover particular foundational doctrines held by the Christian Church. The recourse to salvation history, for example, or to what is received in the service of worship, then becomes the driving force, or motor, of the moral life. This specific motivation can thus appear to determine the particular character[13] of Christian ethics. As I shall hope to show in what follows from its most powerful version—supposing the best of all possible motives, i.e. gratitude—the conception of the Christian motive as the vassal of the Kantian 'kingdom of ends' cannot avoid continuing this sworn enmity to the means of grace.

If what is Christian about an ethic is seen essentially as its motivation, then, if we are thinking of its inward agreement with the content of faith, this ethic would seem to have no better form than that of gratitude. For in gratitude the problem of the relation between receiving and independent action is solved in such a way that the thankfulness I feel is, for its part, merely something for which thanks are due. Consequently, it appears as the inner impression (which becomes the outward expression in the act of giving thanks), where in the autonomous action the element of receptivity is still preserved. So does this not mean that at least with gratitude we do in fact have a form of ethical motivation which can be said to be 'a child of grace'? Is the Eucharist itself not the

---

[13] The question about the distinctiveness of Christian ethics is never able to draw level with its location within a *form of life*. To ask this question already suggests that the question whether there is a Christian form of life has, *a priori*, received a negative reply.

best proof of this?[14] But here much too rapid a leap is made with
gratitude from the Eucharist to a eucharistic ethic. For after all,
eucharistia means initially the particular act of thanksgiving (at
home and) in the event of worship.[15] Of course thanksgiving
plays an important part in the life of believers, outside the liturgical
framework too: about that there can be no question; but this does
not mean that we can deduce an 'ethic of gratitude' from this fact.
On the contrary, gratitude as motive would come into action precisely *between* the grace received and the rendering thanks for it, and
would distance these two elements from one another.[16] It does not
befit thanks to be dragged into the formation of an ethical theory—
even as its determining feature.

EXCURSUS

Consequently the Heidelberg Catechism has contributed to the formation
of a problematical tradition by answering the question about moral duties
('For what cause are we to do good works?' (Question 86)) by saying: 'For
thankfulness for so great benefits.' Of course we have to appreciate that
rejection of any thinking in terms of merit in connection with 'good works'
is the primary motive. Yet the notion that Christian ethics are based on
gratitude brings into play a turn of phrase which—involuntarily—prepares
for what was later to emerge in Kant's radical ethics of disposition in its
pure form: the functionalization of the event of worship into a psychological disposition for action—'the good will'. 1 Timothy 4 ff. makes it clear
that when the Bible talks about thanks it is following a different rule.
Talking about created things, this text insists that what is to be called
good is that which is received *with* thanksgiving (*meta eucharistias*), not
that which is performed *out of* thankfulness. The goodness of the action is
not the outcome of the thankfulness; it rather goes hand in hand with the

---

[14] The Methodist ecumenist Geoffrey Wainwright already argues along these
lines: 'Grace and gratitude are linguistically related, as were *charis* and *eucharist* in
Greek. In worship we receive the self-giving love of God, and the test of our
thankfulness is whether we reproduce that pattern of self-giving in our daily relationships with other people' (*Doxology* (1980), 422).

[15] The character of the word *eucharistia* as a *nomen actionis* is preserved, from the
term for the Jewish table benediction, by way of its extension to every devout act of
thanksgiving (especially in liturgical worship), right down to its special form as a
technical term for the celebration of the Lord's Supper. Cf. H. Patsch, 'εὐχαριστία',
EWNT ii. 221–2.

[16] William H. Willimon is still more abstract in his description of the 'ethic of
gratitude'. Here thankfulness is no longer even invoked as the *immediate* reason
(motivation) for moral action. Now 'Gratitude *engenders* a reason for being moral'
(*The Service of God* (1983), 194 f.; my italics).

thanks. 'Eucharist' remains directly active thanksgiving and cannot be turned into a disposition of thankfulness.[17]

Thankfulness moralizes the thanks, which for their part are already an ethical—indeed, a political—phenomenon, an action that mirrors the social relation to the one we express our thanks to. Consequently, the thankfulness changes if it is turned from something which is not directed towards some particular effect into a motive for action. It is reflected, as it were, out of the immediacy of the relationship to the one thanked. The *specific* grace which is mediated to believers in worship is not some good thing or other, for which they have to give thanks; it is the life with God, and of this all the individual good things (forgiveness, consolation, and so forth) are merely different facets. Here the idea of motivation evaporates. Worship is the way in which God's children, led by the Spirit, address their heavenly Abba (Gal. 4); and for that, thankfulness is a completely inappropriate description. Children express their thanks spontaneously. Gratitude, on the other hand, betrays a slave-like turn of mind. It belongs to slave morality, to the behaviour of people who have to practise gratitude in the presence, graciously conferred, of the patriarch, *because they do not have free access to him* (Rom. 8: 14–17). But the Eucharist celebrates God's presence, and does not express thankfulness arising, as it might be, from the sense of being unworthy of that presence. That awareness has its place in the confession of sin, and is overridden in the fulfilled promise of forgiveness.

It is only when the Eucharist leaves this 'bad conscience' behind that its thanksgiving can become the beginning of political ethics. Otherwise it would not reflect a free relationship, in spite of a deliberate and conscious surmounting of the 'do as you would be done by' attitude. God as the one who gives in freedom would after all be misrepresented through the expectation of thankfulness projected on to him. He would then come close to the picture of parents who 'have done everything for their children', and ruin

---

[17] The Apology of the Augsburg Confession takes account of the dynamic character of thanksgiving when it says that good works should be performed 'propter mandatum Dei, item ad exercendam fidem, item propter confessionem et *gratiarum actionem*' ('because God has commanded them and in order to exercise our faith, to give testimony and *to render thanks*'); the German version of the Apology has 'als Danksagung' ('as thanksgiving') (Article IV).

their relationship to them precisely by articulating their awareness of the fact—whether their expectation of a corresponding thankfulness is actually expressed or not. Yet, if not thankfulness, why should love itself not be the supreme 'motive' for Christian ethics? But here everyday language knows better. What love does was extolled by Paul in his hymn (1 Cor. 13). But what men and women are apt to profess they have done 'out of love' not infrequently justifies some act (it may be unfaithfulness to husband or wife, the euthanasia of a disabled child, and so forth) which is in crass contradiction to what Paul extols in his hymn. So we see that to pierce through the motivation ethic at what is supposedly its strongest point shows the elemental irreconcilability of Christian ethics with the Kantian logic of means and ends. In constructing a relationship which is in fact present as a gift, it denies the love of God as this is experienced in worship.

Ethics as the Residual Theological Task

In motivation ethics, theology, it seems to me, has arrived at the end of the long road it has pursued in Kant's discipleship. In the history of theological ethics as a discipline, theology has to a great extent followed the path which Kant pioneered theoretically. Here the content of the Christian tradition was reduced from what was formerly its decisive authority for faith and life, down to the Kantian point, the mere premiss (in its psychological colouring as motivation) for thinking the idea of God as the author of the moral code. Where theology was not prepared to accept Hegel's attempt at total mediation (an attempt already threatened with demolition in the dispute among his pupils), it could relate to Kant's moral reduction of faith with what seemed to be greater security, since here faith, even if it could be accepted only as the requirement for morality, could nevertheless be assumed to be irrelinquishable. Through the concentration on ethics as the residual theological task, the relevance of the undertaking 'theology' seemed to be permanently secured. But to the degree to which theology acquiesced in the place assigned to it by Kant, as part of the project of the moral education of the human race, it was forced to pay the price of separating the *lex bene vivendi* from its traditional link with the *lex orandi–lex credenti*. And this meant doing away with the political form of Christian ethics—its constitutive relation to a particular social entity 'ruled' by doctrine and liturgy. Instead, ethics—now conceived in universal terms—had to serve the throng of moral individuals on their way to self-determined conduct. It could now come into question only as a function of *private* morality.

This fundamental divergence from the political ethic of the Christian tradition inevitably meant that the material presuppositions of ethics—now established as a discipline—had to be abstracted more and more from the elements of the Christian faith in doctrine and liturgy which tradition had passed down. Whereas the earlier attempts had still been directed only towards making plausible the substantial identity of biblical ethics and the ethics of reason, a differentiation soon came to be made between such elements of tradition as could be allowed to count as 'reasonable' and other morally irrelevant elements which were merely Hebraic.[18] From that point it was only a short step to the specifically modern prejudice which claims that only the reason which is philosophically neutral, purged of all bonds with tradition, would prove effective in furthering the (moral) prosperity of human beings.[19]

What was left for theological ethics here except to withdraw to what was supposedly the final refuge left to it: the motivation for a morality of this kind? It is true that here too it can see itself merely as one of many alternatives on offer. But in this sphere it can now reproduce unmolested everything which it was forced to renounce for ethics as a whole. In its function as motivation, theological ethics is permitted to be as specifically Christian as it likes, and to show as much specific character as it cares to do. To bring about *this* motivation and display its own unmistakable colouring, all the elements of tradition can now be restored to favour. Even though they can make no further claim to truth, and can no longer plead any obligatory character, they nevertheless make available a varied armoury of stimuli for the moral life, which can be drawn upon on *à la carte*.

In this way, where theological ethics conceives itself to be unpolitical, detached from the social norm of doctrine and liturgy, it actually presents itself as highly suited to every kind of political

---

[18] This distinction is made by W. Robertson Smith, e.g., editor and one of the authors of the 9th edn. of the *Encyclopaedia Britannica*. Cf. A. MacIntyre, *Three Rival Versions of Moral Inquiry* (1990), 179.

[19] On this 'Enlightened Morality as the Superstition of Modernity', see MacIntyre, *Three Rival Versions*, 170 ff.

functionalization. In its essentially individualistic guise, it serves as a supply depot for privatized morality in liberal capitalist societies. Eberhard Jüngel is no doubt right when he sees the particular Protestant misunderstanding of worship as being precisely this moral instrumentalization, in the wake of Kant. Latent in this misunderstanding is the danger of a 'submission of worship to the tyranny of ethics' or to the tyranny of political goals and values (and) of a righteousness of works which makes 'the moral content of the whole effective life an *opus operandum*'.[20] The context makes clear to what extent the utilization of worship as a 'resource' for the moralization of the world ultimately regresses to the same righteousness of works whose clericalist form in the medieval sacrifice of the mass (as a human work performed *ex operato*) once raised the protest of the Reformers. Even if, by and large, the history of ethics in modern times undoubtedly endorses Jüngel's judgement—'moralizing sermons' are an essentially Protestant invention—we must not, for all that, overlook the fact that, as time has gone by, an ecumenism with a Kantian colouring has developed which blurs the lines dividing the different confessions in this respect.

The specifically Catholic form of the moralization of worship comes out, for example, in the following declaration made by Camillo Torres, the martyr of liberation theology: 'I have stopped offering mass to live out the love for my neighbour in the temporal, economic, and social orders. When my neighbour no longer has anything against me, and when the revolution has been completed, then I will offer mass again.'[21] Here the indissoluble connection between Eucharist and political righteousness and justice is seen in its most stringent form. And yet the co-ordinates have been shifted. Who is the giver of the eucharistic feast? Who is 'offering' something here? Is it not Christ himself? How far does the priest's identification with Christ actually extend? For even according to Catholic interpretation, this identification is found in his *celebrating*

---

[20] E. Jüngel, 'Der evangelisch verstandene Gottesdienst', in *idem, Wertlose Wahrheit* (1990), 306. Jüngel's quotations are taken from Schleiermacher's *Christliche Sittenlehre* and from Julius Smend. In his liturgical study, *Der evangelische Gottesdienst* (1904), Smend had raised an early objection to this moralization under the significant heading 'The independent importance of public worship' (*Die selbständige Bedeutung des öffentlichen Gottesdienstes*).

[21] Camillo Torres, *Priest and Revolutionary* (1968), 72.

the mass.[22] In asking whether the mass should be celebrated or not, the priest steps outside this identification. He is exceeding his competence. Here too it becomes clear that to moralize worship means simultaneously putting it to use, as a 'means'.

Now we may of course ask whether Torres cannot appeal for his standpoint to a particular aspect of Roman Catholic tradition, in which the ethical life of believers—like the sermon too—certainly counts initially as a preparation for the sacramental reception of grace. According to Vatican II's Constitution on the Sacred Liturgy, 'Before men can come to the liturgy they must be called to faith and to conversion' (1. 9). This can be understood as an inverted form of the idea of worship as a motivating factor which we see in Protestantism. In this case the motive operates prospectively (producing *antecedent* good works), whereas in the Protestant form it operates consequentially (producing *subsequent* good works). But this difference amounts to no more than a didactic nuance within the same motivation logic. Torres, however, seems to be remembering only the first part of the following statement made by the conciliar Fathers: 'Nevertheless the liturgy is the summit toward which the activity of the Church is directed.' He seems to ignore the second part: 'it is also the fount from which all power flows' (1. 10). It is only when the two parts are taken together (and perhaps—better—in the reverse order) that they form the closed cohesion which cannot be instrumentalized. But each part, taken on its own and detached from this cohesion, fits seamlessly into a motivation ethic, whether its provenance be Catholic or Protestant.

Koinonia *as Context—the Problem of a 'Church Ethic'*

What Torres says implies at the same time a further type of ethical theory, closely bound up with the motivation ethic, and we may now look at the relationship of this theory to the ethics springing from worship.

Torres evidently understands the Eucharist contextually. The just or unjust society is the context determining worship, and becomes the answer to the question about its legitimacy. Now, what we have already said has made it clear that worship resists any such contextual determination imposed on it from outside. It is

---

[22] Second Vatican Council, The Constitution on the Sacred Liturgy, Article 7.

not the condition of society which determines the worship; it is the community of believers which, following Christ's institution ('Do this ... '), desires the Eucharist. So would the *Church* not then have to be interpreted as the 'context' for worship, and would an ethic resulting from that not have to be seen as 'Church ethics'?

This road (the road of a contextual Church ethics) has in fact been pursued. Paul Lehmann's *Ethics in a Christian Context* (1963) sees itself explicitly as a *koinonia* ethic. It does not start from abstract moral principles or imperatives, but, as an 'indicative ethic', wants to begin with the specific congregation, as the manifest and irreplaceable context of Christian ethics (p. 14). Lehmann expressly wishes this to be understood not as the application of a general concept of 'contextuality' but in the light of the calling bestowed upon Christians. For this touches them as members of the Church and not in any other way. The decisive question we have to put to Lehmann's concept is therefore: *in what way* is the Church the given context? Lehmann answers this initially in a manner closely related to what I have said above, by talking about the political character of the *communio sanctorum*, the communion of saints: he understands *koinonia* as the Jewish-Christian equivalent of the Aristotelian *polis* idea, representing the ideal type of human sociality (p. 85). If we then go on to ask a second time in what way the Church is the given context, we are offered a historical or aetiological answer: it is the context provided by 'the politics of God', from Israel, by way of the community of the disciples, down to the church. It is true that as 'the penultimate chapter' this 'narrative' involves the thematization of the eucharistic community as a 'laboratory of maturity' (p. 101); but we are still left with the impression that the Church is essentially an entity which is available in its historical actuality as the context for Christian ethics.

This is obviously different from the ethics springing from worship which we have in view here. In the perspective of political worship, 'the politics of God' are not (as in Lehmann's view) unspecifically identified in history wherever people act in the interests of humanization, as the quintessence of political action (p. 85);[23] they are to be found at the point where God's activity can be expected as certainly promised and unambiguous. What is experienced there,

---

[23] Cf. also Lehmann's contribution to political ethics and the theology of revolution, *The Transfiguration of Politics* (1975).

in worship, then contains the rule identifying God's activity in history. In the Augsburg Confession, it is precisely the article on the Church (*De Ecclesia:* CA VII) which reminds us that we cannot speak directly about the Church at all. Here the Church is defined not merely in terms of community as *congregatio sanctorum,* the communion of saints. It is given a still closer definition in the light of the acts of worship which constitute it: 'in the pure teaching of the gospel and the proper administration of the sacraments' ('*in qua evangelium pure docetur et recte administrantur sacramenta*'). This definition has to be understood predicatively, not attributively. What makes the Church the communion of saints is simply and solely the communication of the gospel in Word and sacrament.[24] Consequently, the Augsburg Confession explicitly points out that this definition is not just necessary; it is also sufficient (*satis est*), and by no means constitutes a minimal definition of what the Church is. If it were to be pinned down further by way of particular supplementary data or conditions (organizational profile or anything else), it would be robbed precisely of its *political* form. A political ethics springing from worship certainly also reflects its ties with the Church as a social entity; but it cannot for all that ignore the danger of a 'contextual' misunderstanding, which can crystallize in a Church ethics.

If the Church in its actual historical existence as community is made the criterion for ethics, Christian ethics too are threatened by the biased judgements, misrepresentations, and rigidities—familiar to us from history—which a community ethics can take on, to the point of displaying Fascist-like tendencies. Lehmann in my view avoids this danger, even if instinctively rather than explicitly. Yet the limitation of his conception is evident, and particularly at its very centre. He certainly stresses the importance of *koinonia* for Christian ethics, and insists on a socio-ethical interpretation of the Church, over against an individualistic one: however, the *contextual* logic, which depends on the assumption that the Church is a 'given' entity, ultimately means losing sight of the political importance of *koinonia*. The fundamental question of the *koinonia* ethic which Lehmann formulates brings this out; for it is defined as 'the

---

[24] The New Testament term for 'church', *ekklesia*, was originally used in secular Greek to mean 'assembly', and hence is already related semantically to the worshipping *sunagein*; this fact points in the same direction. Cf. P. Brunner, *Die Lehre vom Gottesdienst* (1954; 1993), 106 (see Eng. trans., *Worship in the Name of Jesus* (1968)).

disciplined reflection upon the question and its answer: what am I, as a believer in Jesus Christ and as a member of his church, to do?' (p. 45). So the community ethic also remains ultimately centred on the individual. In fact, this is inevitable if, and as long as, *koinonia* is understood as *context*—as the context of the individual, who is faced with the ethical question of what he or she as individual has to do. The level of the individual decision-maker is merely socially embedded.

If, in the framework of a contextual Church ethics, we are to avoid the secondary individualistic conclusion to which Lehman falls victim, we are left with the variant of a clerical ethic. Here the Church is seen as the context determining the ethic, in the sense of the norms it lays down. The authority with which the Church speaks on ethical issues is conceived as a formal component of the Church in its 'given' nature as official authority. This first suggests the Catholic view of the interpretative monopoly of the magisterium in moral questions too.[25] And certain characteristics of a clerical ethic are in fact gathered together here, as we can read, for example, in Pope John Paul II's moral encyclical *Veritatis Splendor*.[26] On the one hand, talking about the ecclesiological basis of the Church's moral teaching, the encyclical maintains that the tradition carries forward authentic interpretation, 'whereby—as the Second Vatican Council teaches—"the Church, in her teaching, life and worship perpetuates and hands on to every generation all that she is and all that she believes"' (§27, p. 43). But this sequence of ideas—teaching, life, worship—is by no means homogeneous. For referring to the task laid upon the present to proclaim 'the truth regarding moral action', the encyclical, following the conciliar Fathers, states (ibid.) that authentic interpretation is in the sole hands of the church's magisterium, which draws on the liturgy, and so forth, as *resources* for formulating this truth.

It is clear that in this way the liturgy is understood essentially in the sense of its stock of tradition, fixed *verbatim*; it is not viewed as a confronting event of the gospel. For that would then have to be the supreme interpretative authority. In place of the (Protestant) understanding of the critical authority of the communicated gospel,

---

[25] First Vatican Council, *Pastor aeternus*, 1870, DS 3074 ('doctrina de fide vel moribus').

[26] Published in English by the Catholic Truth Society, 1993.

towards the Church in its present existence too, the Roman doc-trine places the image of the completed harmony of the interpret-ative process *within* the Church. Here the sources of tradition accord without tension with the individual binding pronounce-ments of the magisterium—'guaranteed' by the Spirit, which acts in tradition and magisterium in the same way (§§4 and 24).

It would be simplistic, however, to make the type of a clerical ethic one and the same as the conception of Roman Catholic moral teaching. For there is also a specifically Protestant variant of the clericalization of ethics. This comes to the fore especially when people are burdened by Church signatories with public appeals about their conduct, without there being any simultaneous call to political worship. Then, too, utterances on the part of the Church are in danger of being understood clericalistically *ex sese, non autem ex consensu ecclesiae*—on their own account and without the concur-ring experience of worship; on their own account, and not fed by the authority of the Word, which, after all, has its focus of action in the congregation, as the social form which it confers. Unless the Church in its own internal public character develops the political form of life which it calls for in society as a whole, its claim will be felt to be a heteronymous imposition.

But if, then, the Church cannot present itself directly as the determining context for Christian ethics (either as a community ethics or a clerical ethics), but remains for its own part determined by its worship and the communication of the gospel, do we not have to see worship itself as *the* context *per se* for Christian ethics? The dependence of the Church on worship is certainly too radical for it to be subsumed under the concept of contextuality. The worship-ping assembly of believers does not simply constitute the frame within which the movement of ethical thinking develops; the prac-tices of worship cannot be understood as an external complex of conditions wherein ethics can find support. Contextual ethics is simply the sociologically 'enlightened' variant of foundationalism. But, as we have seen, the celebration of worship is not suited to provide the 'reason' for something else. It does not represent the context; in a certain sense it is the text, or—to be more precise—the regulatory script of ethics: its grammar.

4
Worship and Ethics:
Their Traditional Correlation

We have now addressed a series of possible misunderstandings of what is meant by an ethics springing from political worship. We have seen which of the reasons advanced for ethics are not applicable. The incompatibility of the types of worship ethics we have looked at with what we mean here was due in each case to a lack of understanding of the political character of worship or, in other words, to the inability to grasp worship in its fullest form as a *form of life*. This objection was made to one variant of contextual ethics: a 'Church ethics' based on stipulations laid down by an ecclesial community, or derived from a clerical interpretative monopoly. The same objection was made to the kind of social ethics which, while seeing the individual ethical subject in the context of his or her sociality, does not from the outset view the Christian in his or her political involvement.

Every kind of moralization (and politicization) of worship proved in general to be subject to this deficiency. It is especially evident when the moralization takes the form of a 'eucharistic ethic' which makes gratitude the motivation. Also called in question was a sacramental ethics which generalizes the practice of worship, and makes it the principle for explaining or improving the world; and the same objection could be made to other concepts in which the bodily or sensory performance of worship is conceptualized into abstract ethical norms, values, and the like. As we have said, all these objections were made in the name of 'political worship'. We have also already explained that political worship must not be taken to mean any special variants among the possible perspectives of worship or the forms given to it. What is meant here is rather the character of Christian worship as a whole. If the assembly of believers is to worship in the proper sense, it is necessarily political. And if the Church wishes to be political in the proper sense, it must celebrate worship. It is this coherence, centred on the political aspect, which we shall trace in the following sections, drawing on the essential arguments for it which Christian tradition suggests. We shall first look at Luther's theology, with a view to seeing what it has to say about the correlation between worship and political ethics.

Luther: Worship as Fulfilment of Commandments and the Inescapability of Political Ethics

Since the second half of the twentieth century onwards, it has emerged more and more clearly in Luther studies that Gogarten missed the mark when he maintained that the unique character of Luther's ethics was its separation of the moral from the sacramental.[1] In a countermove, it has even seemed to others appropriate actually to talk about Luther's 'eucharistic ethics'.[2] However, initially there would probably rather be agreement if we were to describe Luther's ethics as a 'commandment ethics',[3] going on to enquire about the significance of worship from that point.

First let us see how for Luther the teaching about 'estates', or social spheres, was bound up with the interpretation of the Decalogue. What began with his sermons on the Ten Commandments in 1516/17 was developed in his first exposition of the penitential psalms in 1517, reached full form in the 'Sermon on Good Works' of 1520, and was summed up in his 'Confession' of 1528: 'For such three institutions or orders are encompassed in God's Word and commandment, but that which is encompassed within God's Word and commandment must be a holy thing, for God's Word is holy, and hallows all that is about it and in it' (WA 26, 505, 7–10). The fact that the estates 'are encompassed in God's ... commandment' means that in his commandments God points to the place where good works are to be performed and can be performed. Good works do not have to be looked for in a special, self-chosen 'spiritual order'; they are not 'outside the gates'; they are within them, within the economic and political life of Christians.

The good works pleasing to God, then, are to be hidden in everyday life, in what is a matter of course, 'in the estate ... which

[1] F. Gogarten, *Die Verkündigung Jesu Christi* (1949), 287 f. For an account of the research see V. Vajta, *Die Theologie des Gottesdienstes bei Luther* (1952), 312.
[2] M. Rathey, 'Eucharistische Ethik in Luthers Abendmahlssermon von 1519', *Luther*, 2 (1992), 66–73.
[3] Cf. O. Bayer, ' "Ich bin der Herr, dein Gott ...." Das erste Gebot in seiner Bedeutung für ... Ethik', in *idem, Freiheit als Antwort* (1995), 83–93 (see also the forthcoming Eng. trans. *Responsive Freedom*).

God hath instituted, and since God's Word and good pleasure is contained in them, *all the works*, being and suffering of such estates become holy, divine and precious' (WA 10/2, 297, 17–19). In view of the medieval esteem for the evangelical counsels, this was of course a provocative novelty. But the commandments do not merely point to the place of good works in the estates; they also make them 'assured'. It is in this connection that Luther talks about life in the estates, or stations in society—life lived according to the commandments—as worship. Where the good works have their proper place in the estates and in faith, they are assuredly pleasing to God. There they *are* worship. In his brief writing of 1522, 'The Distinction between True and False Worship', Luther sums this up succinctly: 'Now worship is never constituted other than in his commandments.' A life in obedience to God's commandments is for him 'the true worship for all estates, for all men'. At this period, it would seem, Luther confronts the sheer objectivity of the performance of the Roman mass with a definitely *ethicizing* concept of worship: 'There is no greater worship than the Christian love which aids the needy and ministers to them' (WA 12, 13, 26 f.).

However, this emphasis increasingly changes in the wake of the dispute with the left wing of the Reformation, whose iconoclastic stress on 'inwardness' brought Luther back to a sense of the importance of worship in its external form. Now the exposition of the Third Commandment in the catechisms lays down the principle that the regular, externally celebrated worship of the congregation *is* the fulfilment of God's commandment (*BSLK* 508, 12 ff.; 580, 10–586, 22). 'I tell you this now, to admonish us that we should gladly listen to God's Word and go to hear it preached, not alone because that is a strict commandment of God but because it bears the highest promise, that it is well-pleasing to God and is the highest, dearest service we can do him' (WA 36, 354, 26–9). So whereas Luther initially interpreted the Third Commandment in the light of the First—faith and love as the true, daily holy day—he more and more came to realize that the First Commandment must also be interpreted in the light of the Third. For the Word which effects faith is not grasped through a free movement of the spirit, but in the Spirit's bond with the performance of worship in which the Word is mediated. Although at that particular time these two polemical turns of phrase had become necessary, the mature Luther was able to formulate the two in the light of the context which first made them possible at all. 'It is doubtless true that the foremost and highest worship is to preach and listen to God's Word, to administer and receive the sacraments, and so forth, these being the works of the First Commandment among the ten. But yet the works of the other commandments do also all of them serve God: namely to honour father and mother, to live patiently, chastely and virtuously. For whoever lives thus serves and worships God thereby' (WA 45, 682, 22–7).

We see that for Luther commandment ethics and worship ethics are actually intertwined. His commandment ethics is an ethics anchored in worship, not a pure commandment ethics. It is only in modern purism that we find for the first time a pure commandment ethics, in the notion that there can be such things as moral principles, norms, and values which exist independently, simply on their own, as postulates of 'pure reason'. Thus the problem of modern norm ethics is not simply that it is a *secularized* commandment ethics; what is questionable is not merely the abstraction through which the enjoining power is moved from a personal God to the rule of a law of reason or—later—mere convention. The questionable thing is already the detachment from the liturgical, life-forming context in which commandment ethics in its Jewish and Christian sense was, and is, embedded, and which even a secularized commandment ethics is not able to dispense with. Consequently, talk about norms remains blind to its own conditioning matrix. For what makes norms be norms is never simply 'pure reason', 'mere convention', or the like, but has its seat in the depths of the self-reflection of a society and its own images of itself. Norms are the moral side of the idols a society worships, just as commandments illuminate in the light of love the face of God turned towards the worshipping congregation.

Now the liturgical context of commandment ethics in Luther, as we have shown it, is furnished with an explicit *political* emphasis, which may well come as a surprise to many. The inescapability of political worship probably offers the often unrecognized hermeneutical key to Luther's teaching about the 'three estates'. Luther assumes that Church, politics, and economic life were called into being by God together with human beings.[4] So they

---

[4] For the following passage cf. O. Bayer, 'Theologie und Gottesdienst', in F-O. Scharbau (ed.), *Erneuerung des Gottesdienstes* (1990), 19–35.

are not emergency measures;[5] they are in fact orders, or dispensations, of creation—unless we prefer to avoid the term in
view of its problematical historical reception, in the sense of a
primal legitimation of the *status quo* of existing orders, or dispensations. What is actually meant, however, is something very different. It should by no means be understood as a statement of
legitimation, but rather as a challenge to political thinking and
acting. It presents worship (and therefore the Church), politics,
and economic affairs as fundamental forms of life which must
not be decried or played off against each other, but which also
have their share in the commendation 'and behold, it was very
good'.

How does Luther present the connection between these forms of
life? These 'estates', instituted with the creation of human beings,
certainly count as equal in value. But for all that, the Church has to
some extent a special role in relation to the other two institutions.
As Luther says in his interpretation of Genesis 2: 16 f., God's first
word to human beings ('You shall eat . . . you shall not eat . . . '), it is
the first of the institutions to be created: 'Haec ist institutio Ecclesiae, antequam esset Oeconomia et Politia.' The church is 'the
fundamental estate' inasmuch as human beings are fundamentally
the beings to whom God speaks, created and called to respond to
him.

This general church 'outside the doors' (*sine muris*) as an order,
or dispensation, of creation embraces all human beings. 'It exists in
Word and faith—in the fact that God calls the human being to life,
in this manner "preaches" to him, "lays his word before him" and
hence "desires only this, that he praises God and renders him

---

[5] This idea, used e.g. in H. Thielicke's 'Ethics', starts from a one-sided interpretation of Rom. 13 and of Luther's writing 'On Civil Authority', where politics is
identified almost entirely with its protective function (*Polizey*). In contrast, Ulrich
Wilckens especially has pointed out that the other side of Rom. 13 (according to
which those who do good have no need to fear the sword) implies a positive political
ethics. The punitive function of civil authority presupposes that its primary task is to
make 'the good life' possible. Cf. U. Wilckens, 'Römer 13, 1–7', in *idem, Rechtfertigung als Freiheit* (1974), 203–43. It must be said, however, that in talking about *politia*
Luther himself did not always express himself unambiguously. On the one hand, he
can explain it in a pre-lapsarian sense as being a created dispensation ('Ergo cum
conditae sint Politiae et Oeconomiae, cum leges et artes divina ordinatione cum
homine concreatae sint' (WA 40 III, 222, 35 f.)). But in other places he can refer to it
in a post-lapsarian sense as an emergency measure (WA 42, 79, 3–9).

thanks, so as to rejoice in the Lord".'[6] A factual priority corresponds to this priority in time: politics and economics are always already related to worship, just as the position or office of the father of a household and the office of the prince hinge on the office or ministry of preaching.[7] But for our present context this has an important consequence, since if the two secular estates detach themselves from their relationship to worship, they themselves inevitably assume a cultic character, and mutate into idolatry. They then cannot avoid giving themselves absolute status, and become totalitarian: 'total politics' and 'the cult of Mammon'.[8] When human beings emancipate themselves from their general duty in worship to praise God as the foundation of the knowledge of 'good and evil' (which means allowing themselves to be told by God what good and evil are, without wanting to know this simply by themselves), all their forms of life collapse into the *status corruptus*. To understand *ekklesia* and *politia*, church and politics, as dispensations of creation therefore means that worship and politics are inescapable—and are inescapably bound up with one another.

Since all the estates are involved in the Fall, we must not expect the restitution of creation—the new creation—to pass these estates by, but to pass through them. The restitution will go hand in hand with the salutary renewal of those forms of life. But this renewal, for its part, takes place in the sequence and relatedness which is factually necessary, since it was part of creation from the beginning. And this means nothing other than that the Church as the worshipping community represents 'the first fruit of the new creation' in the sequence of institutional forms of life. We may therefore expect the restitution and resocialization of politics and economic life to take place by way of the renewal of the Church as the primal order of creation. But this happens where human beings are liberated from concentration on themselves and from the idolization of what is politically or economically good, and are freed for the praise of God, the Creator, Redeemer, and Perfecter. Inasmuch as ethics consists of delineating what life in those

---

[6] Bayer, 'Theologie und Gottesdienst', 20. The Luther quotations are taken from the 'Lectures on Genesis', WA 42, 79, 3; 79, 4; 80, 2; 81, 3 f.

[7] WA 11, 415, 26 f.: 'Thus it is the highest of all offices, on which all others depend and follow. And again, where there is no preaching office, no other can follow.' Cf. V. Vajta, *Theologie des Gottesdienstes bei Luther* (1952), 203 and *passim*.

[8] Cf. Harvey Cox, 'Die Inkarnation des Mammon', *LM* 1 (1993), 4–7.

fundamental forms of life can look like, its pre-eminent task must accordingly be seen as working out as clearly as possible the mode of this relationship; it must show *how* the celebration of God's 'politics' and 'economics' advances those social forms of life. If they are understood in the light of worship, this means at the same time that politics and economics cannot simply count as being a preserve of *the law,* as an unduly abridged reference to Luther's doctrine of the two kingdoms supposes. If the political use of the law (*usus politicus*) were to be understood as marking a particular preserve not touched by the gospel, it would not be compatible with 'political worship'.

The point of the teaching about created estates is in fact precisely that they bring into view the *connection* between the different forms of life, a connection which in the doctrine of the two kingdoms threatens to disappear in the distinction between the two. Luther saw this with increasing clarity in the course of his development of the doctrine of the estates, or rather, his reshaping of the traditional teaching. Initially, when he first took up this doctrinal construct, in the baptismal sermon of 1519, he still followed the traditional logic of a separation between the two spheres. He could therefore write: 'God hath ordered different estates, in which we must learn to do and to suffer; for the one it is the estate of marriage, for another the spiritual estate, and for a third the estate of government' (WA 2, 734, 24–6). Later, it is precisely the correction to what had hitherto been the centre of this doctrine which is emphasized in Luther's doctrine of estates: 'Faith and the state of being a Christian is so free a thing that it is bound to no estate, but is above all estates, in all estates, and through all estates' (WA 12, 126, 16–19).

The Reformation fusion of the previously accepted fundamental difference between the spiritual and the worldly estates (politics and economic life) in the single 'estate' of Christian life now, in its turn, occasions a new perception of the way the estates belong together. For they now no longer denote mutually exclusive forms of life. They are the different fields in which faith and love must prove themselves. Now everyone belongs to every worldly estate because everyone belongs to the spiritual one. No one can escape the *politia,* no one may despise the *oeconomia.* The Christian citizen is a citizen of the Church, a citizen of his household and a citizen of his city all in one; and this being so, every Christian inescapably lives politically. There can be no private existence for Christians.

Luther finds this endorsed in the whole of Holy Scripture too, since it shows that there is nothing holy which does not find a place in politics or economics ('quod nullus sanctus unquam extiterit, qui non versatus fuerit vel in Politia, vel Oeconomia', WA 40 III, 207, 30). In the doctrine of estates modified in this way, Luther introduces a strong counter-emphasis to the doctrine of the two kingdoms, and one which we cannot ignore with impunity[9]—or, to be more exact, he introduces a framework in which the doctrine is supposed to be protected against misunderstanding; for whereas the doctrine of the two kingdoms lives from distinctions, and particularly from the distinction between law and gospel, in the doctrine of the estates Luther brings out the connections.

If we follow the general trend of Luther's teaching here, we can see that the ethics springing from worship which he is putting forward has to be understood as a political ethics. As such, it describes the *form* of Christian ethics, not a special sphere of application or validity. This ethics is political in so far as it does not treat individual themes along the lines of applied ethics, but sees the task of ethics as a whole as a political one.[10] In line with this approach, in the further course of our study we shall have to examine especially the different facets of the public and political character of worship as a happening of the Spirit. The biblical tradition makes it clear that God's Spirit does not act merely in the private sphere; it is directed in every case towards public life, towards its formation and regeneration. Its ecstatic effect must not be understood solely in its psychological repercussions on the individual; it is always at the same time a political phenomenon. Already in the Old Testament, the fact that those imbued with the Spirit were 'beside themselves' meant that they were forced to become public figures—not infrequently against their will—and built up a specific public around themselves. Judges and prophets are no longer 'their own man'—or

[9] O. Bayer points out that the doctrine of the three estates has been absorbed into Luther's important summary and testamentary testimonies, but not the doctrine of the two kingdoms; see his 'Natur und Institution', in *idem, Freiheit als Antwort* (1995), 120 f. (see also the forthcoming Eng. trans. *Responsive Freedom*). On the relation in Luther between the doctrine of the three estates and the two governments, see also U. Duchrow, *Christenheit und Weltverantwortung* (1970), 495–512.

[10] Aristotle viewed politics as the most important of all studies. In his vocabulary (which is not always uniform) it comprises ethics, economics, and politics in the narrower sense of the study of statecraft. Cf. C. Meier, 'Politik I: Antike', *HWPh* 7, 1043 f.

woman—but are claimed by the Spirit for a public task.[11] It is in this tradition that we have to see the public character of the Church constituted by the Spirit of Pentecost. This character was generated by the efficacy of the preaching of the crucified and risen Lord, and it is in this that the Church has its continued existence.

Worship as Waiting on the Spirit: The Pneumatological Correlation

It must already have become clear where the dogmatic point of intervention in an ethics springing from worship is situated: in the ecclesiologically unfolded doctrine of God's Spirit. Here worship stands for the mutual interpretative cohesion of ecclesiology and pneumatology. Once it has been detached from Church and the Spirit, the service of worship is bound to become the individualistically functional 'work' of human beings; and in the same way, though conversely, observance of the practice of worship preserves pneumatology from a spiritualistic misunderstanding, and ecclesiology from an idealistic one. 'Worship' means at once the activity of the Spirit in the Church and the Church in the efficacy of God's Spirit. In order to guard against the assertion of the ubiquitous presence of God's Spirit, Luther insisted on the Spirit's bond with 'the external Word', the bodily and sensory practices of worship. This can be seen as the 'identification rule' of Reformation theology according to Luther's thinking, since it firmly establishes where and how we encounter God's Spirit[12]—in accordance with 'the ministry of the Spirit', which is to give assurance to men and women.

The cloudiness in which theology can land itself without an awareness of this bond is manifested, for example, in Michael Welker's concept of the Spirit.[13] Because his concept seems not to be conscious of any medium to which the Spirit has bound itself (it is not just in the index that 'worship' is missing), it ultimately surrenders itself—in spite of all its criticism of the Hegelian understanding of the Spirit—to the notion of a sheer self-relatedness of the Spirit. It is true that Welker rightly stresses that the activity of the Spirit must not be looked for either in abstract ubiquity or in

---

[11] An illuminating exposition of the action of the Spirit 'in the public transformation of powerholders and of political power structures' may be found in M. Welker, *God the Spirit* (1994), 74 ff.

[12] G. Sauter, 'Die Kirche in der Krisis des Geistes', in *Kirche—Ort des Geistes* (1976), 80.

[13] See Welker, *God the Spirit*. The page numbers in the text refer to this volume.

obscure mysticism (p. 334), but is clearly and unequivocally identifiable: in line with the whole of biblical tradition, he sees the identifying marks of the Spirit in the creation of righteousness, peace, and the knowledge of God (p. 319). At the same time, he does not fail to acknowledge the ambivalence of these things: 'Not *every* human *experience* of *liberation and freedom* is necessarily an experience of God's Spirit' (p. 336). But if, for all that—as Welker himself stresses—the activity of the Spirit has to be identified in sensory realms of life (that is to say, as experience, and not merely as a theoretical distinction, perhaps between a Hegelian self-communication and a self-giving in the light of Christ (pp. 338 f.)), his pneumatology still remains astonishingly silent at this essential point. The identifying rules for the activity of the Spirit in the world cannot be determined by way of hermeneutical operations on texts, but must be learnt in worship, at the place where the activity of the Spirit is promised and can be experienced—and experienced, as Luther says, with all assurance:

'But the Holy Spirit is such a teacher who is sure, makes sure, and does not let us waver here and there' (WA 23, 245, 30 f.).[14] Luther starts from the assumption that it is the function of the Spirit to lead us away from the diffuse experience of God to the *Deus revelatus*—to the 'sure and certain God', to the God who does not show himself in naked 'being as such' but communicates himself in worship in 'revelatory signs'. Bread and wine, the spoken Word, and the preaching ministry correspond to the incarnation, Christ's assumption of humanity. These are sure—indeed, certain—revelatory signs, without which God will not give his Spirit (*Smalcald Articles*, III, 8).

The double negation in this formulation already points to the fact that in speaking of the Spirit's efficacy here Luther by no means has in mind a sacramental objectivism. The 'sanctities' of worship remain the 'works' *of the Spirit*. When Luther talks about the assurance of those elements of worship, he is precisely concerned to stress the sole waiting upon the Spirit.[15]

---

[14] R. Prenter's book *Spiritus Creator* (1954) offers the most comprehensive interpretation of Luther's testimony to the Spirit.

[15] Accordingly, Prenter sums up: 'On the contrary, we have seen that the more *firmly* Luther adheres to the steadfastness of the revelatory sign, the more *firmly* he restricts all possible ways to God to one way only: the waiting upon *the Spirit*...For

The assurance of the efficacy of the Spirit which is concentrated on the bodily-sensory service of worship therefore serves on the one hand to avert the capricious assertion of the workings of the Spirit in the world (identifying rule). But it also serves to ward off a capricious affirmation of the Spirit *within* the event of worship. Here Luther was thinking both of the Enthusiasts, with their assertion of the direct workings of the Spirit in the heart (and in the corresponding form of worship, which Luther censured in the *Invocavit* sermons), as well as the practices of 'the Papist' mass, whose *ex opere operato,* with its performance objectivism, he viewed as on a par with the subjectivism of the Enthusiasts: for him, both alike meant an instrumentalization of the Spirit by the religious subject. Over against such attempts to put the Spirit at the disposal of human beings, instead of allowing human beings to be ruled by the Spirit, Luther stressed that the Spirit is sovereign. The Spirit is not a servant; it is 'the Lord Spirit' (2 Cor. 3: 17).

The same can be said about the Spirit's relationship to the Word. It is not confined within the Word. Its tie to the Word remains a sovereign, self-imposed tie—that is to say, it must not be understood as a unique act, as if the Spirit were to surrender its sovereignty to the communicating Word. The Spirit allows the gospel to be received as the Word which gives assurance, *ubi et quando vult,* where and when it wishes. The Spirit remains sovereign towards the Word to which it binds itself by deciding *the way in which* the Word makes its impact, as law or gospel.[16] So, according to Luther, the relationship between Spirit and Word (the outward means of grace) is of such a kind that the Spirit is above the Word; yet at the same time the Word precedes the Spirit in time, in respect of its actual efficacy in worship. This spiritual order—'that God gives no one his Spirit or grace except through or with the external Word which goes before' (*Smalcald Articles* III, 8)—is the actual *condition* of the Spirit's freedom, inasmuch as it means that all human possibilities are concentrated in the waiting on the Spirit.

the revelatory sign is not some random efficacious means of grace. It is the place where God himself is present *in hidden form* and can therefore be grasped only by the faith which the Spirit gives freely and in sovereign manner' (p. 288).

[16] 'There is no one on earth who can distinguish gospel and law and knoweth how properly to do so—the Holy Spirit alone hath this skill' (*Tischreden* (Table Talk) no. 1234, WA TR II, 3, 20–3).

This tense relationship between freedom and bond can be broken off on either side: the freedom of the Spirit is forfeited on the one hand if its efficacy is imprisoned in the Word, as for example in the framework of an 'orthodox' Lutheran doctrine of the attributes of the Word, its verbal inspiration, and its efficacies (Prenter, pp. 288 f.); but, on the other hand, the free efficacy of the Spirit in its bond with the outward means of grace can also be imprisoned (as it is in the Hegelian tradition) in a doctrine of the Spirit in which the Spirit of God and the human spirit are thought together, so that the Spirit is conceived of in a single dimension.[17] Where the Spirit is thought of as the means and object of the coming to consciousness of the devout self-awareness, it is impossible to preserve the tension which was essential for Luther's testimony to the Spirit. Whether the Spirit be imprisoned in a doctrine of the Word or in a doctrine of the Spirit, in both cases there is a failure to realize that the working of the Spirit is *primal* action, an action which cannot be traced back to any other. Once we pursue this intention of Luther's, and consider the justification for an ethics springing from worship, one thing becomes clear: it is this reflection on the *primal* activity of the Spirit in the free bond with the elements of worship which compels us to view worship in the heuristic way undertaken here as the *beginning* of ethics, not in the sense of their *foundation*.

If our approach is to view worship itself heuristically, and not in the light of its function for a particular context of one kind or another, this approach demands a specifically phenomenological way of proceeding. This does not have its sights set on a systematic concept of worship, to which individual worship practices would have to be subordinated.[18] Instead, it perceives them in their individual character and multifarious relationships. A phenomenological approach probably best corresponds to the way the New Testament talks about worship. For it is clear that there a wealth of

[17] J. Fischer offers an example in his *Leben aus dem Geist* (1994).

[18] This would be the leading principle of an expressivistic understanding of worship, such as Schleiermacher paradigmatically developed. According to this, there can be 'no true perception of the relationship of the different parts' as long as 'the common idea which underlies the whole practice of worship' has not been brought out. Schleiermacher sums up this 'common idea' under the 'general theory of representation'—the foundational aesthetic principle of the external expression of an inward condition, in this case the 'state of religious feeling' (*Praktische Theologie*, 67).

different descriptions coexist, and that these are not subordinated to any overriding concept.[19]

Now in pursuing a phenomenological procedure of this kind, it might seem appropriate to follow it up by tracing the course of the service of worship. That would undoubtedly be a possible method. It would bring out the fact that worship itself draws up the ethical agenda, so to speak, and is not used just to provide an answer to questions addressed to it from outside. However, examples show that this approach typically ends up by assigning particular ethical problem areas (Stanley Hauerwas) or confessional traditions (Hans-Martin Barth) to the separate elements of worship. In a similar way, a 'dogmatic ethics' such as Karl Barth's assigns the ethical problem sectors to the thematic discussion of the dogmatic *loci*.[20] Even if the writers concerned stress that the allocations are merely exemplary, the outcome tends to be a shortening of the perspective. For example, marriage cannot be adequately comprehended under the aspect of creation (as in Karl Barth), but only by taking in the dimension of the second and third Articles of the Creed; and similarly, it is inadequately apprehended ethically if it is allocated to baptism (as in Hauerwas). Conversely, the ethical significance of baptism can no more be restricted to 'marriage, sex and the family' than the ethical significance of the Lord's Supper can be restricted to 'economics, justice, war and peace'. Hauerwas of course knows this, just as Barth was aware of the difficulty; but that does not do away with the problem involved in such a procedure.

[19] Instead of taking over the general terms commonly used in the cultic sector in the wider sense (such as *latreuein* or *threskei*—even *leitourgia* gains general acceptance only later on), the first congregations preferred to describe the novel experience of their coming together for worship in terms tied directly to the phenomenon: for the Lord's Supper, 'the breaking of bread' (Acts 2: 42, 46; 20: 7; 1 Cor. 10: 16), 'eating' (1 Cor. 11: 33), giving thanks (Ign. *Eph.* 13. 1); and especially the semantically related terms 'to be gathered together' (*sunagesthai*, Matt. 18: 20; 1 Cor. 5: 4; in substantive form *sunaxis*) or 'to come together' (*sunerchesthai*, 1 Cor. 11: 18, 20; 14: 23).

[20] For Hauerwas, cf. his lecture plan, printed with comments in 'The Liturgical Shape of Christian Life', in his book *In Good Company* (1995). H.-M. Barth, 'Die ekklesiologische Dimension der Ethik', *KuD* 43 (1988), 42–59, understands Catholic moral theology as primarily 'baptismal', Protestant ethics as an 'ethics of the Word', and Orthodox ethics as 'eucharistic'. For Karl Barth, cf. the concrete examples given in the various 'ethical' passages in *CD*.

If our examination were to follow the course of the service of worship, it could show itself to be an 'ethics of worship'. But that is not what is intended here (and seems to me as inadvisable as a 'theology of worship', which all too easily becomes a substitute for the worship dimension of theology as a whole). Ethics *springing from* worship, unlike an ethics of worship, can be guided frankly by the questions brought to it as time goes on, the questions brought to it by life itself *in the light of political worship*. So in fact it is not worship which itself sets up the agenda for ethical enquiry; it is life, in its multifarious complexes of questions and problems. And that is pre-eminently unavoidable when we talk about *political* worship. For political worship simply means that when people celebrate worship, they are always already moving within the warp and weft of the political fabric. To see worship non-functionally by no means re-quires a blank sheet, which first has to rid itself of every question, in order then to pose these questions anew. Conversely, for us to bring our questions with us into worship does not in itself automatically mean that worship is being instrumentalized. The fact that in the light of worship our questions also make themselves felt in all their questionableness, and thereby change, is part of this perspective. In the light of this prospect, in the main section which follows (Part II) we shall be asking what a worship heuristics can bring to bear on the elemental questions of political theory which are summed up under the catchwords *polis* and *oikos, vita activa* and *vita contem-plativa*, society and state, public life and a common formulation of objectives.

Which Worship? Particularity and Completeness in the Ecumenical Perspective

First, however, we must look at an objection which does indeed raise a real difficulty. What worship are we really talking about? Is everything we have said about the ethical power of worship really met by a reality which we could appropriately describe in this way? Or is it in fact a prescriptive programme for an ethics, norms merely clothed in the description of some imaginary worship? Moreover, why should we try to meet the present (and increasing) need for ethics by associating it with, of all things, an offer which is quite evidently less and less in demand? And is not this offer little in demand today for the very reason that it proves so ineffective? We certainly have no dearth of sociologically supported theses about the creeping marginalization of worship—at least as far as the once-Christian consumer societies of the Northern hemisphere are concerned.

Now the question about the relevance of an ethics springing from worship cannot simply be settled by answering the question of whether or not we are right to talk about the crisis of worship today. The fact that in our own country many people do not celebrate worship, or no longer do so, does not in itself necessarily mean that worship would therefore have no importance for these people. For worship is always also celebrated on behalf of the people who are not present—or are no longer present—or are not yet present—and for their sake. This has belonged from the very beginning to the way in which the congregation gathered together in the Lord's name sees itself and its function. The fact *that* worship is celebrated keeps open for the absent the place reserved for them, so to speak. The prophetic function of 'throwing oneself into the breach', and the act of priestly representation, were always fundamentals of worship, and this means that its relevance can never in any case be subsumed in the categories of a statistically calculated success story.

To say this is not to deny that the celebration of worship can be, and not infrequently is, a pretty dreary affair. And if we are not to fall into the trap of adopting the Platonic pattern of a visible and an invisible church, we have of course to remember the significance of this practice, which corresponds to its promise and its charge. It was not man-made, and therefore cannot be destroyed by human beings, at least not completely. This reminder is therefore the very opposite of an invitation to evade the pressure of these challenges by escaping into the distinction between 'worship as it really exists' and 'worship as it was, or is, really meant to be'. On the contrary, everything we have said up to now about the decisive importance of worship for the Christian life and Christian ethics, and everything which we shall still have to say about it in the further course of our study, applies to ordinary worship as it is actually celebrated—the worship celebrated Sunday by Sunday in Christian congregations all over the world. If it does not apply to that, it is simply a waste of breath.

To talk theologically about worship means in fact refusing to adopt the misleading alternative of an 'empirical' or an 'idealist' approach. What we have to say about political worship should certainly not be understood as another exercise in the genre of the ideal commonwealth. 'We are not dreaming of a Platonic republic', as the Apology for the Augsburg Confession remarks.[21] It is not a formal model to be set over against the untidy reality of politics. If ethics springing from worship were to be tied down in this way to an *a priori* 'ought', as opposed to an 'is', worship would be turned on its head. It would become a project for the world. But ethics springing from worship means no more and no less than the celebration of worship according to the rule, and does not aim at a new programme *for* worship. The first thing to insist on here is not to undervalue what happens through the *regular* celebration of worship. It is hardly surprising that the actual effectiveness of this is understated in studies conducted on the basis of questionnaires, since it is generally more a matter of our acquiring ethical sensibilities in the course of things than of decisive moments at which we translate something we have heard into ethical decision, though only the latter kind of impression reaches the surface of our consciousness. The regularity of the life of worship holds open a specific time and a specific space for the moral formation of believers. It does not depend on any ideal form which worship must first conform to in order to have an effect.

When we talk here quite uninhibitedly about the 'completeness' of every service of worship, however modest and deficient it may be, this initially means simply focusing our perception of it on God's promise. To look at the act of worship in the light of its riches, not its defects, is in line with the precedence of hearing over doing which is incorporated in worship's own structure of action. But the decisive reason for using the word 'completeness' is that there is no greater completeness on earth than the fullness of the Christ present among the 'two or three' gathered publicly in his name.[22] That being so, we are inescapably bound to assume that in every service of worship, however small and obscure the congregation, the *whole* Church is represented in its catholic completeness. Now, this Church is certainly a visible reality in every congregation gathered for worship, a reality which can be perceived in bodily and sensory terms; yet it cannot be directly grasped simply

[21] In the Article on the Church: 'Neque vero somniamus nos Platonicam civitatem.'

[22] This was already stressed by Ignatius of Antioch, Smyrn. 8: 2.

in this visible appearance itself. It was to avert an objectivism of this kind that Luther framed his formula about the 'hiddenness' of the Church ('Abscondita est Ecclesia, latent sancti'—'hidden is the Church, invisible the saints', WA 18, 652, 23). This is not simply an empirical description; it invites faith in the Church as confessed in the Creed. This kind of hiddenness is not, of course, the fearful hiddenness of the *deus absconditus*, the God who hides his face. It is itself a salutary mode of the Spirit's *presence*. It is a hiddenness 'open for faith',[23] and aims at the growth of assurance in the human being—an assurance which stands in exact antithesis to the human longing for self-assurance, with its thirst for objectification.

At the same time, however, it seems to me that the hiddenness of the Church has to be given a different additional emphasis from the one Luther gives it. The Church as the *una sancta catholica et apostolica*, the 'one holy, catholic and apostolic Church' acknowledged in the Creed, is hidden even in its confessional divisions. It is these divisions which constitute the ambivalence of its hiddenness, and suggest a serious question: in view of the mutual exclusion from the Lord's Table practised by some denominations, is it possible to talk about the completeness of their worship at all? Is this very exclusiveness and supposed self-sufficiency not a sign of deficiency rather than plenitude, making these denominations incomplete and fractured? But here we have to differentiate further. Since the *una sancta*, which embraces more than any single congregation and particular church, is acknowledged in every service of worship (so that its own incompletion is explicitly formulated, as it were), the ecumenical coherence which conditions the completeness of worship is not lost sight of—even if it is obscured by the partial refusal of eucharistic fellowship. Since worship as an eschatological enterprise always draws on the completion towards which it moves—the shared participation in the eternal praise of God—the confessional divisions are certainly a very serious deficiency; but they are not an *absolute* negation of the completeness of the worship celebrated in the churches belonging to the different confessions.

But this makes one thing all the more clear: it is only in ecumenical breadth, height, and depth that the completeness of heavenly

---

[23] H. J. Iwand, *Erläuterungen zur deutschen Ausgabe von 'de servo arbitrio'* (1954), 294.

worship is made present under the conditions of this aeon at all. No church and no service of worship can arrive at this ultimate completeness at any time. But to accept this truth for oneself is therefore in itself an act of faith in the 'visibly hidden' *una sancta*. It is only the synchronic and diachronic perception of the communion of saints in its full extent which keeps us from a myopic empirical perception of worship, which either idealizes it in a sectarian and Enthusiastic way, or confronts its drab appearance with an accusatory 'ought'. In this perspective, we have no need to screen out existing deficits. They are certainly experienced, although in the perspective of another reality of worship, an ecumenically plural one—not in the perspective of a non-reality, in the sense of an ideal condition, either imagined or affirmed. Seen rightly, it is precisely the ecumenical horizon of the service of worship in its completeness which makes it possible for us to perceive our own deficits, because in this context there is no need for us either to accept them resignedly or to compensate for them through some projection or other. The *ecclesia semper reformanda*, the church which is always in need of reform, undoubtedly has its centre in worship. And this means that the synchronic and diachronic perception of the communion of saints too will always take the form of a reformed worship in the individual churches and congregations. Here, of course, what is intended is not a programme for a synthesis, a mutual adaptation at the cost of what is special to each, but rather a continual process in which we learn from one another, in one-to-one encounters.

EXCURSUS

One example is the mutual learning process which we have seen happening between the Roman Catholic Church and the Protestant churches with regard to the importance of the frequent celebration of the Lord's Supper on the one hand, and, on the other, the importance of the (vernacular) proclamation of the Word. Because this involves the attempt to understand the other, with a view to a reform of one's own practice (and is also a path leading to a common practice), it also brings with it a recognition of the *political* character of worship. For that always includes a continual impulse towards reform. This certainly also affects the structure of worship—the order of service, for example—but it primarily affects the way in which worship is celebrated. *How* does the congregation pray, *how* is the sermon preached, *how* is the Lord's Supper celebrated, *how* is the life of the congregation reflected in the notices, announcements, or 'intimations', etc.? The problem—at least for the church in Germany—is bound up with the fact that as a rule a great deal of time, effort, and imagination is devoted to the 'programme' for a second and third service, targeted at particular groups. Here the participation of lay men and women in preparing and conducting the service has become a matter of course, largely speaking. But in the regular Sunday service, which is the spiritual centre of the congregation, the procedure approximates to economic rather than to political life. Here the dominant logic seems to be that of a professional offer on the one side and a consumer response on the other.

Worship is politically celebrated, however, only when the congregation assumes its own office or function in that worship—if it is *able* to assume it, and does not remain stripped liturgically of its competence; and if it *wants* to assume it, and does not remain stuck fast in the consumer attitude to which it has become accustomed. Worship is political when the intercessions bring before God the needs of this particular congregation, its individual members and the congregation as a whole, and learn from this immediacy to pray in equally specific terms for village, town, country, and the world. Worship is political when a congregation is actively involved in responsibility for the proclamation, and when imagination is invested in the question of how this can be brought out appropriately in the church service. (It is then, and not as the outcome of theological educational programmes, that theology would also come to be seen as something the congregation needs, and its very own affair; so that the cleft between religious object language and metalanguage would cease to be so wretchedly wide.) Worship is political when the pool of the charismata existing in every congregation is brought out in the notices or announcements, so that these gifts are made mutually available and can be drawn on by others too. Worship is political when the 'peace' before communion is not merely practised as a non-committal sign of general solidarity, but is also taken seriously as an act of reconciliation between people 'who have something against each other'.

What may perhaps have become plain from these fragmentary suggestions is that much depends on the willingness of individual congregations to learn ecumenically. Political worship cannot be guaranteed or organized on any national or regional level; it cannot be enforced or directed centrally. As long as congregations are islands in their celebration of worship, bound together at most through their use of the same liturgy or order of service, political worship is improbable. It is true that, on the one hand, political worship can only come about in the celebration of a *particular* congregation, when its members meet and live together under the guidance of the Spirit. Yet the political form is always threatened by a self-contained focus on one particular community, and remains dependent on ecumenical experience with other congregations and churches.

Worship and Ethics in the New Testament: 'Serving Tables' for the World

The close connection between worship and ethics has been received wisdom in the Christian Church from the very beginning, not least because of Israel's own tradition (cf. Part II 1. 2.1). This was more or less implicitly accepted and practised as a matter of course, rather than made a specific subject for reflection. In the New Testament, the worship of the congregation counts as the *telos* of the Christian ethos, its innermost well-spring and its goal. The indicative–imperative structure which Rudolf Bultmann stressed as being the centre of Pauline ethics is rooted in the understanding of baptism.[24] Paul speaks of dying to sin (Rom. 6: 2) or being freed from sin (6: 6, 12), of 'putting on Christ' (Gal. 3: 27; Rom. 13: 4), and 'crucifying the flesh' using both the indicative and the imperative. Although the Christian ethos springs from celebrations of worship—the ethically central notion of the congregation as an organism of active members springs from the Lord's Supper *paranesis*, 1 Corinthians 10: 14 ff.[25]—it is also directed towards these celebrations.

Accordingly, the praise of God appears as the goal of good works in a double sense. On the one hand, Paul's admonition to live for mutual edification leads on to the purposeful: 'so that together you may with one voice glorify the God and Father of our Lord Jesus Christ' (Rom. 15: 2–6). On the other hand, the Sermon on the Mount describes the *telos* of good works hidden from the doers themselves as also being praise of God—praise uttered by the people who see the works: 'Let your light so shine before men that they may see your good works and give glory to your Father who is in heaven' (Matt. 5: 16; picked up in 1 Pet. 2: 12). Taken as a

---

[24] R. Bultmann, 'Das Problem der Ethik bei Paulus', *ZNW* 23 (1924), 123–40.
[25] W. Schrage calls this the 'sacramental' foundation for ethics: see his *Ethik des Neuen Testaments* (1989), 178 ff. H. von Soden, 'Sakrament und Ethik bei Paulus', in *idem, Urchristentum und Geschichte* (1951), already argued in the same direction.

whole, the connection pointed to here is succinctly expressed in
Ephesians 2: 10: if we are created 'for good works which God
prepared for us beforehand, so that we should walk in them', it is
in worship that the hearing and looking, the 'tasting and seeing', of
those works of God takes place, the works which the Christian
ethos explores practically, and Christian ethics explores intellec-
tually from within.

Apart from these explicit connecting lines, a series of other
observations testify to the way in which worship and ethos were
intertwined as a matter of course. This is already evidenced by a
striking and unique terminological feature. Whereas for liturgical
acts, 'secular' terms such as *leitourgia* were used, or purely phenomenological ones ('coming together', 'breaking bread', etc.), particularly *cultic* terms were used for the worldly activity of believers. It
was not only Paul's activity as an evangelist that could be called an
'offering' (Rom. 15: 16). The same word could be used for every
good deed, a gift of money, or the whole commitment of a life lived
as 'reasonable service' (Rom. 12: 1 f., AV). Accordingly, functions
and ministries rooted in worship are also presented as liturgically
and socially intertwined. This may be said especially of the
deacons, as servers at table and carers for the poor.[26]

EXCURSUS

In the Hellenistic environment of the earliest congregations, *diakonia* was a
purely secular term, and meant the acts of service performed in connection
with a banquet. These included inviting the guests, greeting them, washing
their feet, and showing them to their places, as well as the preparation and
serving of the dishes.[27] Since Jesus himself used this slave service to
characterize his ministry (Luke 22: 27, a logion which is translated into
narrative in the Johannine foot-washing scene, John 13: 1–20), and since it
appropriately represented the significance of his table fellowship with his
disciples, and its resumption in the eucharistic celebration of the post-
Easter community, *diakonia* could become the quintessence of the Christian ministry. Paul could therefore call everyone who worked to build up
the congregation a 'deacon' (1 Cor. 3: 5), and could see his own apostolate
too as falling under this overriding term (2 Cor. 6: 4).

[26] On the following excursus cf. J. Roloff, 'Zur diakonischen Dimension ... von
Gottesdienst und Herrenmahl', in *idem, Exegetische Verantwortung in der Kirche*
(1990), 201–18.
[27] Ibid. 205.

On the other hand, in Philippians 1: 1, and later in the pastoral epistles (1 Tim. 3: 8, 12), the diaconate could also appear as a special ministry, different from the others, and could be used to describe the special function of 'serving tables' in the context of celebrations of the Lord's Supper, which were presided over by the *episkopos*, acting as paterfamilias. Here, from the very beginning, the social, charitable character of these table fellowships was of the essence, as we are reminded by the summary in Acts 2: 42–7, where the breaking of bread and *koinonia* are mentioned directly side by side. Since the first Jerusalem congregation consisted for the most part of Galileans who had moved with their families to Jerusalem, where they had little or no economic base, this connection was of urgent importance, although that does not, of course, 'explain' it.

The material adjustment between the well-off and the less well-off was, at all events, an essential criterion for the *koinonia* (Acts 2: 44 f.), and it was already implemented in a basic way in the framework of the Lord's Supper itself. On the one hand, this was a proper meal designed to fill the stomach, a meal to which everyone contributed something, according to how much he or she possessed. On the other hand, what was left over was then distributed to the poor.[28] So it is significant that the first conflict we learn about in the early Church arose from insufficient regard for the diaconal element (provision for the Hellenistic widows). 'The first inner crisis of the church was accordingly the result of a failure in the diaconal components of Christian worship.'[29]

What the book of Acts stylizes into an 'installation account' of the diaconate as a separate ministry (Acts 6: 1–7) reflects the failure at an important point of the diaconal congregational element, which had its central place in the Lord's Supper; but nevertheless it insists on the inward connection, under the diaconal aspect, of ministries which were now drifting apart: the ministry of the Word—the ministry of 'serving tables'. Although since that time *diakonia* has become a word for Christian charity and commitment to the needy in general, its original roots in worship should not be forgotten. On the other hand, the extension of the liturgical 'serving tables' to characterize the whole of Christian life is in line with the way Jesus's

---

[28] The custom of distributing to the needy gifts of food brought to the eucharistic feast endured long after the Lord's Supper had been separated from a meal for satisfying hunger. This is shown, e.g., by the provisions in the Scottish Episcopal Prayer Book of 1637, cited in G. Wainwright, *Doxology* (1980), n. 1034.
[29] Roloff, 'Zur diakonischen Dimension', 211.

meals with the disciples and the poor in Palestine before Easter were extended to the meal Christ shares with the Church drawn from all nations, to the end of time and the world.

If we survey the interrelation between worship and *diakonia* in its whole New Testament context, we can see that it is impossible to play off worship and active life against each other. An abstract liturgism would miss the mark as completely as the ethicism of a pure 'everyday worship in the everyday world'. The awareness of this integral character of Christian worship—its social spirituality or its spiritual sociality—flickers up even in the popular prejudice against 'bigoted church-goers', where the imputation is centred with complete accuracy on what worship is really about: the unity of faith and life, liturgy and ethics.[30]

Lex orandi—lex credendi—lex bene operandi

The will to grasp this complex more precisely is behind the attempts made in recent years to expand the interpretation of the patristic Church's formula: *lex orandi—lex credendi* (the law of prayer corresponds to the law of belief). This formula—so the argument runs— ought to be supplemented by a third term: *lex bene operandi* (the law of good works); this would accord with the New Testament maxim about 'faith working through love' (Gal. 5: 6).[31] However, the traditional formulation of the lay brother Prosper of Aquitaine (made round about 435–42) goes beyond the mere assertion that the two dimensions belong together, and says something about the actual way in which these elements cohere. Consequently, in considering our own question it is worth casting a closer glance at the formula and the discussion it has evoked.

The declaration originally had a limited connotation. Prosper, a literary disciple of Augustine's, wishing to avert semi-Pelagianism, argued as follows: the apostle's commandment to 'make intercession for all men' (1 Tim. 2: 1–4) implies the duty *to believe too* that faith in its full scope, from the inception of the good will until its

---

[30] For the prejudice according to which 'institutionalized religion' is bigotry, cf. R. N. Bellah *et al.*, *Habits of the Heart* (1985; rev. edn. 1996), 78 f.

[31] Cf. T. Berger, *Lex orandi—lex credendi—lex agendi*, *Archiv für Liturgiewissenschaften*, 27 (1985), 430 ff. The three-term expansion of the traditional formula is referred to in the subtitle of G. Wainwright's systematic theology, *Doxology*, esp. 218–83. Cf. also D. B. Forrester, 'Lex orandi—Lex Credendi', in D. B. Forrester (ed.), *Theology and Practice* (1990), 71–80.

perseverance unto the end is a work of God's grace. The unqualified need for intercession (for all human beings) proves the unqualified need for grace; the church's practical intercessory practice therefore endorses the Augustinian doctrine in this respect. Prosper then generalizes that connection into the principle that the law of prayer defines the law of belief (*ut legem credendi lex statuat supplicandi*).[32]

The most interesting interpretation of this formula, and the one that sheds most light on our own question, is offered by Aidan Kavanagh in his brilliant study *On Liturgical Theology* (1984). Over against the usual shortened form given to the formula (*lex orandi—lex credendi*), Kavanagh insists on the predicate 'grounds' (*statuat*). For this preserves both the 'communitarian' content of the statement and its unequivocal thrust.

In the first place, Kavanagh maintains that the personal subject of the two activities, prayer and belief, is one and indivisible. The people who observe the law of the church's practice are no other than those who are concerned with the law of its doctrine. Thus the formula remains critical of the divergence of liturgy (in which the people are involved) from doctrinal theology, as the discipline of a special guild of theologians.[33] Even though Kavanagh does not mean to deny theology's right to existence as a separate academic discipline, he does differentiate it as *theologia secunda* (theology of the liturgy) from *theologia prima* (liturgical theology), where Prosper's formula, with the interplay of the two 'laws', has its true place. As Kavanagh puts it, *theologia prima is* 'proletarian'. It is not a clerical or academic, elitist phenomenon; nor is it an individual achievement: it is 'communitarian', a joint enterprise, and it is 'quotidian', not projected from time to time, but springing from the regular performance of liturgical acts.[34]

The last definition is particularly important for Kavanagh, because it points to the fact that in this primary sense theology can be related neither to an isolated liturgical act, nor to the liturgy *per se*. Rather, it identifies the activity of critical reflection on the 'change' wrought in the worshipping community as it goes from one liturgical act, one service of worship, to the next, and of the 'adjustment' of each new act of worship to that change.[35] In this sense theology

---

[32] *Indiculus de gratia Dei* 8 (DS 246).
[33] A. Kavanagh, *On Liturgical Theology* (1984), 91.
[34] Ibid. 89.
[35] Ibid. 73 f.

must be viewed as the dynamic interconnecting of liturgy, intrinsic to every individual act of worship, yet not understandable in the light of that act alone. Theology is not primarily something contained within each liturgical act, whether as an element of it or as its doctrinal substance. More important than that, and making that possible, it is the intellectual stock-taking of the change which each encounter of the community with God brings with it.

Without the fundamental distinction between these two levels of theology and the location of its primary form as 'intermediary' in the liturgy—in the regularity of worship—Prosper's formula, and with it the whole connection between liturgy, doctrine, and the active life, can only be viewed in the sense of a disastrous 'who controls whom?' But it is just this which, as time has gone on, has come to be the determining question; under its domination the subject and the object of the formula have shifted, and the result is what Geoffrey Wainwright treats and advocates under the catchword 'doctrinal control of liturgy'.[36] It is by no means fortuitous that this transformation should be reflected in the changed meaning of the word *orthodoxia*. Originally and literally, *orthodoxia* means true worship in all its fullness, and comprises the three 'laws' of prayer, belief, and life; but it came to be more and more reduced to what would have to be more accurately rendered as *orthopistis*, correct belief, or *orthodidaskalia*, correct doctrine.

Kavanagh calls the English Act of Uniformity of 1549 a milestone in this long development, which from the sixteenth century onward was especially intensified by the ecclesiastical controversies. The Act assigns control over orthodoxy—quite explicitly in the sense of correct doctrinal tenets—to a centralized authority, with exclusive power to establish an absolute, unified standard for liturgical texts and celebrations by way of parliamentary statutes. This unified standard was the Book of Common Prayer. To the degree to which 'orthodoxy' became something to be established and secured by 'secondary' theology, the service of worship turned from being the location of true orthodoxy—that is, primary theology (which is what it had been up to then)—into being a mere *locus theologicus* in Wainwright's sense of the term[37]—that is, a *locus* which an

---

[36] Wainwright, *Doxology*, 252 ff.
[37] G. Wainwright, 'Der Gottesdienst als "Locus Theologicus" oder: Der Gottesdienst als Quelle und Thema der Theologie', *KuD* 82 (1982), 248–57.

independent secondary theology makes use of, whether it is required for the correction which secondary theology makes to particular theological developments or whether secondary theology makes corrections to primary theology in accordance with particular theological developments. In the framework of this monistic concept of theology which Wainwright espouses, the disastrous control syndrome in the description of theology's task cannot at all events be escaped.

It is true that Wainwright himself makes a similar-sounding distinction between 'first- and second-order language'. According to this, worship would be the immediate place of 'religious language'; but for him, theological language is a language belonging to the second order. 'It is the language of reflexion upon the primary experience. The language of worship mediates the substance on which theologians reflect.'[38] But with this common modern pattern of experience and reflection, object language and metalanguage, the phenomenon 'worship' cannot be grasped at all. On the contrary, a pattern of this kind bursts apart the intertwining connection in worship of the two (or three) *leges*, which can be understood only in the framework of a distinction *within the theological activity* such as Kavanagh, for example, has undertaken.

But if, entirely contrary to the intention of the patristic formula, the task of theology (a theology not inwardly differentiated) is so stepped up that it is assigned an 'architectonic' or 'critical' function towards liturgy (theology, in its *primary* mode being demoted to 'religious language'), then the doxological character which Wainwright bestows on it, in the sense of its controlling influence on liturgy,[39] seems all the more problematical. Even the supposed evidence from the Fathers with which Wainwright supports his view, drawing on the tradition of the Eastern Church (according to which the true theologian is 'the person who prays'), can only be misunderstood in the framework of an undifferentiated concept of theology. As Kavanagh rightly comments, the point of the traditional dictum is not to ascribe a doxological quality to the work of a devout (second-order) theologian; its purpose is to lend a theological quality to the (first-order) activity of believers in their celebration of worship.[40]

[38] Wainwright, *Doxology*, 21.
[39] Ibid.
[40] Kavanagh, *Liturgical Theology*, 124.

It is instructive to see how an interpretation of theology such as the one we find in Wainwright affects the definition of the relationship between worship and ethics. Here Wainwright talks about the need for a 'two-way movement', a movement which, starting from the liturgy, asks about consequences for life, and, conversely, starting from life, enquires about liturgy.[41] So liturgy and life come into question as two relational entities, which have to be mediated to each other in theological thinking. Whether the outcome of this theological mediation is understood 'architectonically', or rather in the sense of an intellectual reconstruction of a natural oscillation between the two spheres, may be left in doubt. The essential point, at least, for this achieved mediation too, is that it establishes or reveals the relationship of two entities which are viewed primarily as separate spheres.[42] It is hardly by chance that here Wainwright brings into play the distinction between 'the sacred and the secular or profane', where 'an absolute [sic!] separation' cannot be made. So he attacks one-sidedness in the relationships of these spheres ('sacralization' or 'secularism'), knowing 'that sacred and secular can be falsely related'.[43]

To think in different spheres like this permits only mutual relationships which are conceived of in the typical pattern of the 'effect' of the one on the other, and back again. This two-way movement is pursued by Wainwright in the modern triad of 'liberty, equality and fraternity'. According to this, for example, the proper practice of liturgy would promote the political freedom which in its turn would contribute to the free practice of liturgy.[44] What cannot emerge in the logic of this relationship, however, is the very characteristic which is decisive for political worship: that the liturgy itself is understood politically—as praxis which encapsulates a *particular* freedom, which does not merely promote civil liberty but challenges it too—that is to say, calls its premises into question. Instead of that, in Wainwright political liberty emerges only as an 'effect', as something on which liturgy either works, or which works back on the Church, in the sense of its own conditions for political freedom. But this can only be said in the perspective of a 'second-

---

[41] Wainwright, *Doxology*, 408, 410.
[42] Raimundo Panikkar's liberation theology proceeds analogously: see his *Worship and Secular Man* (1973), sec. 3.1: 'Worship towards and versus Life.'
[43] Wainwright, *Doxology*, 406 f.
[44] Ibid. 418.

ary' theology, which no longer reflects on the perceptions of primary theology, but objectifies them into 'religious language', which is now only in a position to provide the 'substance' for theological reflection. Unlike primary theology, which itself constitutes the heart of Prosper of Aquitaine's formula, a secondary theology such as this looks in separation at the 'laws' addressed, so as to be able to relate them to each other, again in a secondary way.[45] But here what was previously wrenched apart is not put together again at all. As we have seen, the relationship between worship and ethics *as the outcome of a mediation* cannot avoid being something different from what it is said to be in Prosper's (expanded) formula.

Over against this, we should accept the valuable sense of the traditional formula, expanded by its third term, taking it up in such a way that our attention is focused on the way in which ethics is formed *in* worship, and—conversely—on the identification of the liturgical or cultic dimension which every ethics necessarily involves. 'We imitate the one we revere,' as Augustine, Prosper's authority, knew. What has been said may have helped to explain further why I prefer to talk about the liturgical and secular *dimension* of worship, rather than about a liturgical and secular worship. Talk about 'political worship' or about 'worship as a form of life' also sees itself as a critical movement directed against a two-way movement, and tries to think in a 'secondary' theological way about the rule of primary theology: *lex supplicandi statuat legem credendi et vivendi*.

---

[45] It may perhaps be asked here in passing whether 'secondary' theology does not frequently acquire its material simply by ignoring basic perceptions of primary theology.

PART II

WORSHIP AS THE CRITICAL POWER OF CHRISTIAN ETHICS

Christian Citizens in a Torn and Divided World

A. WORSHIP AS THE PRAXIS OF RECONCILIATION

The next two main parts, II and III, are devoted to political ethics in the broader sense of the world. Here we shall attempt to show how the awareness of political life changes through the experience of worship. But awareness here is not confined to a mere passive cognizance. It also means an appropriation of what is perceived. It includes both the development of a particular view of political existence and the given political reality, and participation in this reality in the sense of 'political life'. In the first part of this section, emphasis is on the *critical* development of the power exercised by the worshipping community on the ideas about political life which it encounters, and on existing political circumstances. Here I should like to show how, in the light of political worship, the classic tensions in political life between the public (*polis*) and the private (*oikos*), freedom and necessity, the contemplative and the active life (*vita contemplativa* and *vita activa*) can no longer be understood as the *essential antinomies* out of which political theories have emerged. And since I propose to show how in worship these antinomies can be experienced as surmounted (through the reconciliation of people who actually embody them in their social classes or ways of life), this first part (A) may be paraphrased by the catchword 'Reconciliation'. The experience of reconciliation as the new form of political life in the *polis* of the Church ruled by the Spirit challenges the alleged ontological need to think about political life in terms of the antinomies we have named, and to find a balance between the demands of the ideal and the real. In this first section, this thesis is largely developed in discussion with the classic political theories, so that in the following section (B) we can relate it to the conditions for political identity in modern and postmodern society.

5
The Political Dimension of the Church—Modern and Postmodern

First, however, we shall approach the questions we have raised by asking how the political dimension of the Church can be properly understood at all. For this purpose, I should like to analyse two fundamentally different concepts, both of which we find in the Anglican tradition. The first of them shows how the significance of the Church for the secular political commonwealth can only make itself felt in its full scope if the Church itself is viewed as a political commonwealth on its own account; while the second example shows how the political form of the Church's existence is related to definitions of the nature of political life and of the Church itself. The first concept was William Temple's, and is a representative modern approach. John Milbank's—the second we shall be looking at—tries to take into account the conditions of postmodern discursivity.

5.1 THE MARGINALIZATION OF THE CHURCH AS SOCIAL FORM

The Priority of Principles

In William Temple we meet a kind of thinking about social ethics which is still widespread, and puts its mark especially on official Church statements about social and political questions. In the tradition of British Hegelianism and the 'incarnationalism' prevailing at the end of the nineteenth century and the beginning of the twentieth, Temple developed the ethical side of the then prominent notion of the sacramental universe. Temple's ethical ideas are most easily accessible in his *Christianity and Social Order* (1942), a little book which achieved best-seller status.[1] Here he showed how the Church can and should exert an influence on political and social life. The book's argument runs as follows.

---

[1] For Temple's theology in general, cf. M. A. Ramsey, *From Gore to Temple* (1960), and for his social ethics, A. M. Suggate, *William Temple and Christian Social Ethics Today* (1987).

Contrary to the widespread assumption that the Church has its own (religious) enclave in society, and therefore ought to keep out of the others, Temple defends the Church's right to intervene in public affairs. History shows that the Church has in fact always intervened in this way (pp. 46–57). But just *how* should the Church intervene? Temple says: in three ways. It must certainly intervene politically *in individual cases* now and then; but the fundamental level of its contribution is the educative influence it can exert on society, by making 'good Christian men and women', who do their Christian duty as members of their families, and as citizens (pp. 40 ff.). With this aim, and in addition, the Church must contribute to the fundamental orientation of society by making available to it 'a scale of values for the political field . . . some ordered system of principles which represents the real "good" ' (p. 42). In short, says Temple, 'The main task of the Church must be to inculcate Christian principles and the power of the Christian spirit' (p. 45).

In his book Temple presents just such a series of Christian social principles in the systematic form of 'primary' and 'derivative' principles. Primary principles are directly deduced from the fundamental doctrines of the Church, and are more or less general in kind. Temple mentions two: God and his loving and salvific purpose, and the dignity as God's image of human beings, who must therefore not be made the economic or political means to an end (pp. 58 ff.). As derivative principles (which are deduced from these and are very much more concrete), Temple names freedom, social fellowship, and service. Freedom is defined as a person's freedom for self-determination. But since it is thought of as the freedom of the person who always already exists in social relationships and is actually constituted by them, not as the freedom of an abstract individual, the second principle, 'social fellowship', is brought into play as freedom's balancing counterweight (pp. 69 ff.). The tension between these two principles gives birth to the third: 'The combination of Freedom and Fellowship as principles of social life issues in the obligation of Service' (p. 73). This principle—the obligation of service—applies both to individuals and their work for the well-being of the whole, and to social groups and associations; but it applies pre-eminently, of course, to the Church itself.

What is really decisive here, however, is not so much the choice and formulation of the principles which Temple undertakes in his book as the way he defines the task of the Church in the light of these principles. Put briefly, the Church has to 'announce' the principles, and this completes its task *as Church*. After that, it is for *individual believers* in their own particular walks of life to see to it that these principles are put into practice in society.[2]

The notion that the Church's political function is to act as the 'provider' of social and moral principles is an essentially modern one. It presupposes a unified, harmonious reason which will prevail both in the Church's presentation of the principles and in the acceptance of these principles by society. And a unified rationality is in fact quite explicitly the premiss of Temple's concept. Accordingly, 'the priority of principles' is tied up with the need for 'some general system of thought or map of the intellectual world by which we may be helped to judge which of several principles should prevail' (p. 78). This in its turn sheds light on the important role which Temple allocates to experts in formulating social and ethical maxims and putting them into effect. Experts prove themselves, as it were, by their ability to survey the whole map of which he speaks. Just as the Oldham Groups consisted of experts and responsible people from different spheres of society (generally chaired by theologians),[3] so the Church itself is seen as being an expert for social principles.

The background of the pre-eminence Temple gives to principles and experts is his Platonically moulded philosophical standpoint, according to which the nature and goal of the world process are to be found in the control of spirit over matter. And the linear character of the world process is, in its turn, based on the incarnation. There transcendence entered into immanence and, in a reverse

[2] 'The Church must announce Christian principles and point out where the existing social order at any time is in conflict with them. It must then pass on to Christian citizens, acting in their civic capacity, the task of re-shaping the existing order in closer conformity to the principles. For at this point technical knowledge may be required and judgements of practical expediency are always required' (*Christianity and Social Order*, 58). Just how influential this concept still is even today in Anglican ethics can be seen especially in official Church reports on 'the state of the nation'. For example, in 1987 the Church of England's Board for Social Responsibility brought out a study entitled *Changing Britain*, which tried to solve the pressing problem of 'social diversity and moral unity' (the study's subtitle) through recourse to 'basic principles' (p. 67). Temple's combination of liberal and personalistic thinking is not hard to detect in the argumentation.

[3] On the theology of 'the middle axiom' popularized by J. H. Oldham and W. A. Visser t'Hooft, and its close connection with Temple's concept, cf. D. B. Forrester's critical evaluation in his *Beliefs, Values and Policies* (1989), 17–35.

movement, thrusts forward the Spirit-guided process which was already fulfilled in the incarnate Christ, the process in the course of which immanence is brought back into transcendence. Since then, the form of this reality can only be properly understood as sacramental. Thus 'the sacramental principle of the universe', or 'the sacramental view of the universe', becomes the central category for an apprehension of the whole of reality, including ethics. And this category in its turn rests on a generalization of worship such as we analysed in Hegel and his theological disciples. The connection described here can be seen particularly clearly in Temple's most philosophically orientated work, *Nature, Man and God.*[4]

In this book, the incarnation, as the culminating point of history, is fitted into the framework of a philosophy of spirit, where the spirit drives forward the cosmic process in which God's 'own nature of perfect spirit' is fulfilled (p. 492). Temple's pneumatology is shot through with the idea of self-realization, whose inner necessity is development. God's self-realization in the spirit is for Temple clearly visible in the evolutionary development of the world's reality in its various stages. This (age-old) idea of the progression of being (inorganic matter—organic matter—the human mind—the divine spirit (p. 492)) presents a more subtle form of the definition of the relation between matter and spirit which Temple calls sacramental. In the movement from the lower to the next higher stage, which for its part is dependent on the stage below, matter is not degraded in a Manichaean sense. It remains 'goodly creation'—in its necessity *as material for the evolutionary process*. 'Matter exists in full reality but at a secondary level. It is created by spirit—the Divine Spirit—to be the vehicle of spirit and the sphere of spirit's self-realisation in and through the activity of controlling it' (p. 493). Thus the development of 'the sacramental universe' appears to be a matter of the actualization of mind over matter, as the elevation of the spirit, 'not by ignoring matter but by controlling it' (p. 477). Since in the human being this controlling function of the spirit is exercised through the reflection of the intellect, the consequence for Temple is inescapable: 'Here the logical, if not also the temporal, order is thought first and thought last with physical movement as its mode not only of expression but of self-actualisation' (p. 495).

---

[4] The Gifford Lectures, 1932–3 and 1933–4. The page numbers in the text refer to this work.

At this point it seems important to observe the logical connection of Temple's thinking about ethical principles with this 'metaphysics of mind'. For the same linkage recurs in my own argument—though in reverse. It is evidently substantially unavoidable. So I shall hope, on the one hand, to show with the help of the later Wittgenstein (Chapter 9 below) how the metaphysical divorce which Temple presents between the bodily and the spiritual, feeling and thinking, saying and meaning, represents the basic form of that 'hermeneutics of suspicion' in which political ethics suffocates. On the other hand, the same connection has to be developed in a positive sense; for the authentic perception of the political dimension of the Church presupposes a 'Hebraic', anti-metaphysical view of the human being, where physical utterances or manifestations do not function as the *expression* or—the other side of the same coin—as the *concealment* of an already existent 'spiritual' reality of ideas and concepts, but themselves contain the meaning itself in the very mode of its utterance. The subordination of matter to the spirit that controls it finds its correspondence in the will or need to find the true reality of social life in an aseitic sacramentality, as the fundamental epistemological principle *per se*, instead of in the sensory and particular practice of worship. Thus Temple unreservedly understands sacramentality as 'conception' as 'clue to our metaphysical problem'. As the intellectual solution to the classic problems of metaphysics ('the relation of the eternal to history, of spirit to matter' (p. 482)), sacramentality is not merely the essential means of grasping and solving those problems with the greatest possible universality—'a clue to the general interpretation of the universe'—but is in itself a generalization. Consequently Temple does not proceed from the special sacramental act of the congregation; his point of departure is the assumed fact that sacramental rites are 'a common feature of human religion' in general, the Christian sacrament being for him to some degree the highest peak in this homogeneous range (p. 483). God's general revelation through the world process precedes the possibility of his special revelation, which Temple in no way denies. The sacramental principle of the world merely *makes its appearance*, we might say, in the specific sacrament.

How, then, does Temple pin down more precisely the place and function of the celebration of the sacrament within the framework of the sacramental constitution of reality as a whole? True, sacramentality as universal principle exists, as we have seen, prior to the special sacramental practice of the worshipping community, and independent of it. But according to Temple, this is the apprehension of an 'adequately sensitive mind' which can grasp the interpenetration of all life through the divine Spirit. Since this sensibility is generally lacking, however, it would seem 'that all must deepen their insight by periods of adoring contemplation, which alternate with periods of activity inspired and guided by what is then apprehended' (pp. 493 f.). Here the difference from the approach taken in our present study emerges quite explicitly: for Temple, worship has to do with *the deepening of an insight* (which can be acquired elsewhere too). It is not the place of *perception* and transformation. Whereas I see worship as a primal institution, in Temple it appears to be an emergency measure, established at a secondary stage.

The Separation between Knowing and Doing: Political Idealism

A critical evaluation of Temple's concept from the perspective of its political dimension, however, would now, above all, have to begin at the point where the alleged universality of his 'explanatory principle'—the sacramental view of the universe—presupposes a decidedly *strategic* standpoint. This permits the principles he brings to bear to be maintained with such certainty that they seem to be as such unassailable, much as a general surveys the map of a whole terrain, where the positions of the various units, etc., are all marked. In Temple's blueprint the strategic potentiality of the Church as expert body suggests that the insufficiencies always lie on the side of their implementation by individual Christians. The principles themselves appear to be sacrosanct. In their claim to timelessness, they resemble Plato's eternal Ideas.[5] But mustn't the perception of principles as unassailable entities of this kind then also correlate with the thrust to *implement* them accordingly in the reality of social life? And doesn't their implementation signify in a positively paradigmatic way the good end which is supposed to justify the means? Thinking in terms of ethical principles does in fact mean that the end-means category strikes root in political life.

---

[5] These are existent *before* the act of their translation into material reality—for example, as 'model' in the craftsman's head—and remain identical with themselves, as model for further realizations, even after a successful or unsuccessful fabrication process. Plato lays great stress on this point. Cf. here H. Arendt, *The Human Condition* (1958; 2nd edn. 1998), 141 f. The page numbers in the following Excursus refer to this work.

As Hannah Arendt shows in *The Human Condition*, in her analysis of Plato's political idealism (to which Temple continually appeals), this category is inescapable once the doctrine of Ideas, which stems from the experience of fabrication, is implanted in political life.

EXCURSUS

In a fascinating chapter on 'The Traditional Substitution of Making for Acting' Arendt traces this line of thought in Plato's thinking. She starts from the fact that fabrication (*poeisis*) as a form of activity which is distinguished from purposeless action, in that it is conceived as a means to an end other than itself (that is, the product), always inevitably includes an element of violence. Thus, in order to realize the Idea (the 'model' of a chair, for example), the craftsman, whom Plato chooses, by no means fortuitously, to exemplify his teaching about Ideas, is forced to do violence to the material (in this case the wood). 'This element of violation and violence is present in all fabrication, and *homo faber*, the creator of human artifice, has always been a destroyer of nature' (p. 139). Whereas action, as the political form of free co-operative activity, is pierced through by temporality, must continually begin anew, and leaves behind it unforeseeable consequences in every case, fabrication is associated with the durability of the product, in which the material world to some degree receives a share in the eternity of the Ideas.

Arendt believes that the reason why Plato applies the doctrine of Ideas to political life, thereby putting fabrication in the place of action, is the desire to bring into the sphere of human affairs the 'solidity' and order which belong to fabrication (p. 225 f.). His proposal that the state be given a philosopher-king can be seen as the attempt to replace the unsurveyable co-activity of the many by an activity for which all that is required is a single individual who 'would remain the complete master of what he had begun, not needing the help of others to carry it through' (p. 222). 'In the *Republic*, the philosopher-king applies the ideas as the craftsman applies his rules and standards; he "makes" his City as the sculptor makes a statue; and in the final Platonic work these same ideas have even become laws which need only be executed' (p. 227).

We may compare Arendt's analysis here with what Temple says: 'it is in the sacramental view of the universe . . . that there is given hope of making human both politics and economics and of *making effectual* both faith and love' (my italics); and further, as he looks at what a person with social ideas of this kind can actually bring about: 'He can work upon his environment to ensure that it shall in future afford illustrations of those combinations of elements which hitherto have existed only in his thought. He can compare the good offered by circumstance with a good apprehended only in idea, and can deliberately forgo the former in hope of thereby making actual the latter.'[6]

The other characteristic of political Idealism which Arendt stresses can also easily be recognized in Temple's ethic of principles, where the task of Christianity is presented as divided into two: the Church as body has to enunciate the principles; individual believers have to implement these principles in society. We find the basic type of this political 'division of labour' in Plato's *Politicus* too. There the two stages of shared political action, *archein* and *prattein*, the inception and the application, are reinterpreted as two independent types of human activity, which are, in addition, distributed between different determining subjects. Now the one who 'begins' becomes the ruler over those who only implement what the other gives them to do. The division of function into ruler and ruled goes hand in hand with the separation between knowing and doing which, as Arendt elaborates, still forms the root of all theories of rule even today.[7] In Temple, the concept of the Church's role stands in a similarly dualistic tendency between experts on the one side and the executive roles on the other. This reflects the divorce which separates the philosopher-king from other people; he differs from them precisely because of his insight into the eternal Ideas, an insight which for him makes the good so certain that he can and may enforce it on others, even, if necessary, by using the method of deception. This form of 'political' influence on the public—the introduction of guiding principles—is of course in itself unpolitical. The model from which it takes its bearings is rather the *oikos*, the household as it was viewed in the ancient world, where it was enough if the paterfamilias knew how things stood, and out of this knowledge passed on directives to the members of his family and the slaves or servants. Here knowledge is indeed power, and power is no longer that which is formed by co-operative action. The result is the identification between knowledge and rule on the one hand, and between action and the mere implementation of directives on the other.

---

[6] W. Temple, *Nature, Man and God* (1934, repr. 1979), 486, 487.
[7] 'Plato was the first to introduce the division between those who know and do not act and those who act and do not know' (Arendt, *Human Condition*, 223).

Even a democratically cushioned version of social principles cannot escape this fundamental logic. Here too we have to say that ultimately the idea of principles and application acts as a brake on the formation of a political ethics, which itself would have to be nourished by a specifically political praxis. But this praxis is bypassed in the false ecclesiastical logic which divides the Church as a body of experts from the individuals who are the executive. As a political commonwealth, the Church does not appear in Temple at all. It is political only *in reference to* political life. But the derivation of social ethical principles is a solitary affair, fundamentally so (just as the Platonic 'theorist' must first emerge from the cave of human affairs and the life of the community in order to contemplate the eternal Ideas). Such a derivation can, basically speaking, be undertaken by an individual too, provided that he has enough insight into the fundamentals and mechanisms of social life, even though it is normally undertaken by ecclesiastical boards, commissions, and working parties, and is then mediated to the public. The really political thing, the collaboration of the many, comes into play in Temple only at the application stage, with the implementation of the principles in a local situation.

Here, however, we are faced with a decisive question: *how* should individual church members then provide for the implementation for which they are always dependent on other people too? If they are to act politically—and that means not simply forcing something through—Christians must not just be equipped with the right principles; they must above all be made *capable of political action*. But this capability is not already inherent in the principles themselves; for, as we have seen, the logic of the principles tends to encourage enforcement. So the capability must be acquired elsewhere. And for this the Church must imperatively be seen as a sociality which is in itself already political, where it is possible to learn what political life among men and women looks like—that is to say, regulated life lived in consensus, which renounces the use of violence. But if the Church as *polis* itself provides the essential experiences for the political actions of Christians in society and state (though not directly as a model to be copied), then the logic of thinking in terms of principles is turned upside-down. Whereas here things depend primarily on men and women, who contribute their experiences in the *polis* of the Church to the secular commonwealth, in thinking in terms of principles it is precisely the personal factor which is eliminated from the concept of rule.[8]

More important still: behind the hegemony of principles it is not only the person of the ruler that disappears; it is the public in general.[9] In a similar way, in a Christian 'principles' ethic the Church as a political sociality also disappears from view. This ethic does not start off from the plurality of members who act together; it is essentially speaking monistically structured, following a unified rationality, the unambiguousness of the principles, and the solitariness of its experts. This monism is undoubtedly at heart violent, just as violence is inherent in the metaphysical motif of the control of matter by spirit, a motif which for Plato guarantees the continuity of the moral life. The one who rules himself is fit to rule others. The man who has himself under command, the man whose emotions are ruled by reason, is qualified to determine political life. In the individual, the mind should rule over the body, and the higher regions of the soul over the lower ones; and the political order in the state should follow the same pattern. The logic of political Idealism which we see here (and its offshoot, ethics taking its bearings from 'principles') differs essentially from an ethics which takes its bearings from the political life of the Church in the following way: whereas here, in the political life of the Church, a social plurality is the starting-point, there political life is viewed on the pattern of the individual and the constitution of his soul, and is structured accordingly; whereas here the determining experience for political life springs from association with others, there it derives from association with oneself.[10]

---

[8] This consequence of political Idealism is already prefigured in Plato: 'The greatest advantage of this transformation and application of the doctrine of ideas to the political realm lay in the elimination of the personal element in the Platonic notion of ideal rulership' (ibid. 226–7). What is seen in the *Republic* as the direct claim to rule of philosophers could in the *Laws* be transformed into an impersonal claim to rule on the part of Reason. The principles don't care who maintains them.

[9] 'In the realm of action, this isolated mastership can be achieved only if the others are no longer needed to join the enterprise but are used to execute orders' (ibid. 222).

[10] Cf. ibid. 239 f. It should be said that towards the end of his life, Temple evidently sensed this ecclesiological deficit in his social doctrine. In an autobiographically coloured essay he pleaded for a new alertness to 'the theological status of the church'. He now formulated the insight that 'the individual Christian is helpless except as a member of the Body, the Church. So the Church, alike as ground and object of faith, and as the agent of the Kingdom endowed even now with its powers, has a new prominence in the minds of thoughtful Christians. We did not fail a quarter

Where the Church's character as a political entity is *under*estimated, its political task 'outwards' can easily come to be *over*estimated, if it is viewed as the guardian of the Christian character of society. So political thinking remains caught up in the alternative, which has often enough been explored but is nevertheless unsatisfactory: the alternative between the vision of a 'Christian' society determined by the Church and a secular society with Christian legitimation.

The Church as Hermeneutics of the Gospel

The central significance for political ethics of the Church as a social and political entity in its own right was not adequately perceived in the tradition of the great Anglican social reformers such as Charles Gore and William Temple, in spite of their sacramental view of the universe (or rather, just because of it). But on the Anglo-Catholic wing of the Church of England this significance was recognized, and by Eric Mascall particularly. In a criticism written at the beginning of the 1950s, Mascall took up a clear stance over against a universal sacramental hermeneutics and the falsely deduced affirmation of the social implication of the sacraments which went with it: 'The sacraments have social implications, the Church has social implications, only because the Church itself is a divine and supernatural society... The Church has many functions *in* society, but it can never become a mere function *of* society, for it *is* a society—the Society of God, the life of the Holy Trinity communicated to men.'[11]

But for the Church to live and embody the 'principles' which it passes on to the public life of society is not simply a matter of the Church's credibility or its principles. The relation to other forms of public life becomes *substantially* different once the Church learns to see itself as 'a public', and proves itself to be so. The way it lives also determines what it says and the way it says it. But if, on the other hand, a relation between the public and the Church is *constructed*, a bridge of this kind actually bypasses the real point about the proper influence of the Church on public life. The Church in its

of a century ago to insist on the necessity and claim of the Church. But this was secondary and derivative, now it is primary and basic' (W. Temple, 'Theology To-Day', in *idem, Thoughts in War-Time* (1940), 103 f.).

[11] E. L. Mascall, *Corpus Christi* (1953), 45 f.

own political existence always *already has* a public influence—since it is a letter from Christ, read by everyone (2 Cor. 3: 3 f.)—before it concerns itself about the influence of its public statements; and a failure to see this generates the clericalism which we have already analysed (Chapter 3). Then official Church statements tend to provide answers to questions nobody is asking. But this awkward phenomenon, whenever it crops up, should be seen not so much as a sign of the decadence of a society without any interest in the gospel and a godly life, as a question put to the ethos of a Church which is incapable through the way it lives of *awakening* the questions it would like to answer. (Perhaps this incapacity also explains the widespread tendency to see the Church's 'real' task as being to provide answers to the questions which people are 'really' asking.) Even if the perspective developed in our present study does not exclude public statements made by the churches, but in principle covers them too, we should not lose sight of the premiss: that the Church does not just have the task of interpreting the gospel *for* society, but also, and primarily, of acting as a 'hermeneutics of the Gospel'.[12]

This gradation in priorities can be given a particular stress with the help of Bonhoeffer's formula about the Church's 'qualified silence'.[13] As long as the Church is not capable of qualified silence, it is not qualified to speak in public either. But what we have already said must have made clear what this qualified silence consists in—a point Bonhoeffer leaves open. For it consists in nothing other than the qualified *life* of the Church, the political existence of the Christian community as the sociality ruled by the Spirit, the 'politics of God'. It is only a life which is articulate even in silence which will put the Church in a position for qualified speaking. If the political life of the Church is itself articulate, its attitude to its own statements can be a relaxed one. It will have no need to stimulate an echo artificially. On the contrary, the marginal glosses with which the Church perpetually accompanies public life might well make us ask whether in turning outwards in this way the Church is perhaps trying to escape its inward political unimportance. But it is with the qualified silence Bonhoeffer talked about that the Church's public task really begins. It *begins* there, not just when the Church raises its

[12] L. Newbigin, *The Gospel in a Pluralist Society* (1989), 227.
[13] D. Bonhoeffer, *Sanctorum Communio*, 251.

voice: 'It is better to be silent and to be, than to speak and not to be' (Ign. Eph. 15. 1).

The test of this view is political worship, as Bonhoeffer also shows here with his formula about the 'objective' Spirit which builds structure in the practice of the cult. If there is a failure to recognize this, all that remains is the obvious (but for all that falsely deduced) alternative between Church and sect in the form Ernst Troeltsch gave to it—a distinction which permits only an élitist group with 'a Christian order based on love', cut off from the world and without influence on public life (the sect type), or a mass institution which acquires its influence on the shape of society at the expense of an inevitable accommodation to it, and does not get beyond a compromising ethos (the church type).[14]

A Christian social ethics such as we met in William Temple, based on the communication of principles, cannot escape this impasse, and will always remain a conformist phenomenon. The very notion that society can be moulded through principles of this kind also involves a conformity *to* modern society through the adoption of the aspects which are constitutive for 'principle' ethics: the belief that general rationality will prevail of itself, coupled with the notion that this rationality can be made universally accessible through the generalization of Christian truth (a truth which finds expression in worship). But the universal claim of Christian worship, to which all human beings are called, is wider than the claim to universal plausibility made by a Christian imperative. As an eschatological enterprise, worship reaches out in principle beyond every measure of understanding and the practical implementation of what has been understood. Accordingly, it refuses to abide by the separation between knowing and doing which so largely determines political theory and practice. It does not proclaim the universal plausibility of its ethical directives as the premiss of its public relevance and the subsequent translation of these directives into practice, which is the logical consequence. Worship's universal

---

[14] E. Troeltsch, *The Social Teaching of the Christian Churches* (1931, 1981). Our analysis is confirmed when we note how in Troeltsch this distinction is explicitly based on the negation of political worship. Thus he assumes that the gospel was originally 'free personal piety... without any tendency towards the organization of a cult' (p. 993). It is true that he sees 'the worship of Christ' as 'the centre of the Christian organization', but 'this again developed out of the fact that the new spiritual community felt the necessity of meeting together' (p. 994).

claim depends precisely on its particularity, its special, unmistakable and irreplaceable experience. It is this which makes it the touchstone for every ethical concept and practice. This particular character of ethics springing from worship, which is critical of the modern viewpoint represented by William Temple, may now draw our glance expectantly to the second example—a concept which thinks theologically about the conditions of postmodern discursivity.

5.2 THE CHURCH AS EMBODIED ONTOLOGY OF PEACE—A POST-POLITICAL THEOLOGY?: JOHN MILBANK

On its appearance in 1990 John Milbank's *Theology and Social Theory* attracted considerable attention.[15] If we compare his concept with Temple's, we can see that he has taken two essential steps forward which are of relevance to our own discussion. Milbank radically adopts the postmodern discursive paradigm, which leaves behind the assumption of a unified rationality, and for the question about the determination of social life as a whole, assigns to the Church an outstanding conceptional significance as a form of life of its own. However, a positive evaluation of these new directions still permits a question: how far is the ontological colouring of Milbank's ecclesiology inclined to obscure the possibilities of a political ethics?

The Ontological Priority of Violence

In an extensive analytical section, Milbank tries to narrate the rise of modern social theories in a way which will bring out the scarlet thread running through them all: the assumption that violence is an ontological necessity. Violence is perceived as a primal datum, as it were; as a given fact, it is the unavoidable social way of dealing with the elemental experience of difference. Consequently 'politics', in the sense of a purposeful shaping of social life out of conditions that have to be surmounted, always represents an inherently violent phenomenon. 'Antique thought and politics', he writes, 'assumes some naturally given element of chaotic conflict which must be tamed by the stability and self-identity of reason. Modern thought

---

[15] For the reception cf. *New Blackfriars*, 73 (1992) and *Modern Theology*, 8 (1992), numbers which were devoted to discussions of Milbank's book. The page numbers in the following passage refer to this work.

and politics (most clearly articulated by Nietzsche) assumes that there is *only* this chaos, which cannot be tamed by an opposing transcendent principle, but can be immanently controlled by subjecting it to rules and giving irresistible power to those rules in the form of market economies and sovereign politics' (p. 5). Under the heading 'Theology and Liberalism', Milbank traces the 'invention' of the secular as a particular space which is spanned, filled, and maintained by the simultaneously established and independent disciplines of 'political science' and 'political economy'. He shows that the establishment of these 'autonomous' sciences—from now on freed from the alien rule of religion—is concerned with its own, sectional spheres of life; but that, in turn, rests on decidedly theological modifications of traditional Christian doctrine.

Milbank pursues the trail of the ontological qualification of violence further through the development of modern social theories, from political economy to the establishment of sociology. In comprehensive analyses of the concepts of Hegel and Marx,[16] he shows that their particular forms of dialectical thinking are forced to pay tribute to violence as a necessary transition. Beyond the constitutional place given to violence in the key explanatory attempts of French and German sociology, Milbank points to the fact that the claim of this discipline to be a 'master discourse' forcibly inverts the originally prevailing relationship to religion and theology. The earlier attempts to understand 'the social' as an entity in its own right proceeded from the assumption that it possessed a God-given quality. Sociology was therefore theologically based; that is, it was explicitly conceived in the framework of theological definitions. But the positivist assumption advanced by Auguste Comte that 'the social' was an original phenomenon, not derived from anything else, meant that now everything, religion included, could be completely explained by the 'laws of social life', which would soon be discovered. 'Here lies the further paradox; sociology is only able to explain, or even illuminate religion, to the extent that it conceals its own theological borrowings and its own quasi-religious status' (p. 52).

Even if Milbank's genealogical procedure is indebted to French deconstructivism, he by no means shares its perspectivistic attitude to truth. In his view, the scarlet thread exposed in modern social discourse suggests, rather, the unavoidable presence of a unified

---

[16] J. Milbank, *Theology and Social Theory* (1990), 147–205.

organizing logic, within which the story is told. Here Milbank pleads for a self-confident challenge to sociological logic on the part of theology, and an abandonment of the false modesty with which theology itself increasingly promised itself enlightenment from sociology about the reality of social life, the religious sphere, and itself, thereby becoming incapable of subjecting the theological presuppositions of the secular discipline to the appropriate criticism.

The postmodern ascription of all the allegedly 'discovered' or 'objective' concepts of social, economic, and political life to the 'will to power' is taken up by Milbank, but is then turned against the genealogical-nihilist narrative community itself. Is the discovery of the myths of modernity as deriving from the Nietzsche paradigm not itself a myth?

Does the Church Embody an 'Ontology of Harmonious Peace'?

Milbank counters this with a specifically Christian social theory, in which difference appears not as a reason for violence, but as a harmonious coexistence of what differs. He defines peace as 'the *sociality* of harmonious difference' (p. 5). In order to put forward a counter-story which is at least no less plausible than the violence story of the social theories of antiquity and modern times, Milbank sets out three levels on which the various counter-modes have to be demonstrable. The priority of violence must be confuted on the historical level, on the ethical level, and on the ontological level. In this way Milbank aims at the conception of a counter-*history*, in which the interruption of history in the Christ event is claimed as the criterion of history as a whole, a counter-*ethics* in which virtue is understood no longer heroically but as *agape*, and finally a counter-*ontology*. For the latter he draws as model on Augustine's concept of the two *civitates*. In Augustine, Milbank particularly works out the complex in which he shows that the claim of the *pax romana* is unfounded, because the 'peace' was itself violent. It rested on the violent subjugation of peoples, and could be maintained only by means of a continual violent intervention. No community can claim true peaceful coexistence unless the chain of violence is broken by the practice of forgiveness (p. 406). But this is the mark of the Church on the way to 'the other city', a city without walls, which is not an 'asylum' in which the pacified, subjugated peoples rejoice over the 'protection' of those who have subjugated them; it is a citizenship in which 'the ontological priority of peace over conflict' is lived (p. 390).

EXCURSUS

Milbank shows how Augustine conceptualizes the distinctive perception of difference in the Church: the experiences of difference between individual soul and community, *oikos* and *polis*, as well as between *polis* and world, are examples; but they are now understood musically, so to speak, not antagonistically. In an interpretation of Augustine's *De musica*, Milbank works out an understanding of difference according to which harmony appears as the *telos* of differentiation, while still being dependent on the difference (pp. 404 f.). Thus he stresses that Augustine's social theory may be described in summary form as a microcosmic-macrocosmic relationship of correspondence between smaller social entities (individual soul and body, family) and larger ones (congregation, *civitas Dei*), as well as a non-subordinate relationship between the part and the whole, in which the whole is present in every part (pp. 409 ff.). It is true that in the pagan world of antiquity harmony was held to be the ideal designation of social relationships; but, Augustine argues, this was only possible by way of the principle of control, in which higher powers rule over the lower ones—the soul over the body, for example—and allot them their proper place in the ordering framework. 'Harmonious orders' of this kind must be constructed by means of violence, since they lack the third level, where the nature of order itself finds its own ordering. It is only belief in the Creator which is able to perceive the differences in the true harmony. For belief understands both, soul and body, as equally primal good things of creation, where difference does not have to be understood in terms of hierarchy, and where social order does not have to be seen in terms of subordination.

Of course the decisive question is now: *in what way* is this differentiating harmony present in the Church? How can the social reality of the Church be adequately described in terms of the Augustinian concept of a harmonious peace? Here Milbank, it seems to me, points in precisely the right direction: 'In such a position, no claim is made to "represent" an objective social reality; instead the social knowledge advocated is but the continuation of ecclesial practice, the imagination in action of a peaceful, reconciled social order, beyond even the violence of legality' (p. 6). At this point, however, we have to enquire more closely. For the fundamental difficulty which Milbank's concept has to combat is the very question of how the conceptual significance of the Church as a social entity *sui generis* with a corresponding claim to 'reality', can be understood for political theory and ethics, and can yet avoid falling victim to an ecclesiological foundationalism ('objective reality').

The following critical comments should be understood as an attempt to take up the valuable thrust of Milbank's thought in the direction he himself points, and to take it a stage further. Here it must be clear that the question about the (ontological) quality of the Church in its significance for a Christian social theory can only be grasped with the required depth and precision if cloudy talk about 'ecclesial practices' is given more distinct form by referring it to the key practice of worship. The following observation may serve as a starting-point. Milbank subtracts the question of the Church's *relationship* as *polis* to the existing political community almost entirely from the question about possible *behaviour* towards that community. 'The Church, to be the Church, must seek to extend the sphere of socially aesthetic harmony—"within" the state where this is possible; but of a state committed by its very nature only to the formal goals of *dominium*, little is to be hoped. A measure of resignation to the necessity of this *dominium* can also not be avoided' (p. 422).

However, Milbank finds in the Church as a historical entity above all the 'failure to be the Church'—the *de facto* decline of the Church into a 'hellish anti-church' which has largely adopted the world's violent form of reaction. It would seem that only an ontological leap can rescue it from this impasse. Milbank puts forward what he calls counter-modes; but among these, 'counter-history' (pp. 382–98) and 'counter-ethics' (pp. 398–422) resemble, rather, separate islands adrift on an open sea, which are no more able to offer a firm stance than the postmodern discursive paradigm. Only 'counter-ontology' (pp. 422–32) seems to provide firm ground from which the offensive can be launched. For it was also a particular ontology which Milbank detected on the side of the various social theories, as their fixed point in the flux of various phenotypes. In a similar way he conceives the ontological dimension of the Church as representing what lies behind its 'counter-history' (in the sense of his accepted narrative perspective) and its counter-ethics, as its 'ought', so to speak, or its potential, which it in fact generally fails to implement.

As we saw above, Milbank succeeds in a remarkable way in exposing the violence ontology of secular social theories. But the assumption that this ontology can be promisingly countered only by another ontology, is by no means self-evident. The assumption would seem much rather to be strategically prompted, pursuing a pattern of argument bearing the hallmarks of orientation towards a goal. Thus, in connection with the introduction of an alternative Christian 'myth', Milbank talks explicitly about a necessary 'strategy' (p. 279), which promises to solve the problems that have been recognized from Attic philosophy onwards, but have been insufficiently treated—for example, the relationship between the individual and society (p. 330). Accordingly, Milbank does not merely trace back the distinct practice of the Christian Church as 'harmonic peace' to its dogmatic foundation (the relations of the divine Trinity *ad intram*); he conceptualizes this still further in the direction of a general 'construction' of the infinite 'not as chaos, but as harmonic peace' (pp. 5, 427 ff.). 'In the speculation, social ontology . . . is grounded in a general ontology (concerning the ratio of finite and infinite) and a "counter-ontology" is articulated' (p. 423).

Since in the eleven critical chapters which act as a prelude to his own concept, Milbank makes use of the methods of postmodern deconstruction, his counter-concept is also drawn into the problem of every genealogical proceeding which deconstructs the new in what is already known. Doesn't the demand for a counter-ontology also bring the new 'ethics' and the new 'history' back to the sphere of the one common problem—the appropriate definition of the nature of difference? Shouldn't the successful exposition of the secret ontology of violence (which underlies genealogical thinking not merely in substance but structurally and methodically too) have made Milbank more cautious about ontological thinking—at least in its 'strong' version? As it is, he arrives at a remarkable disjunction: on the one hand, we are presented with a great self-confidence on the part of the Church, its 'gigantic claim' to be the critique of all human community (p. 388) and the end of all philosophy and politics (p. 430); and on the other hand, we are faced with the seemingly inescapable resignation with which the book closes, as Milbank contemplates the tragic 'fate of the counter-kingdom' (p. 432)—in view of the historical failure of the Church to live out this ontology.

Yet is the Church to be properly understood at all as an embodiment of 'harmonic peace'? This seems questionable, both on the fundamental ecclesiological level, and for the question of how Church and peace, Church and conflict, belong together. For the affirmation of 'harmonic peace' as the concern of a 'being' tends to iron out the question about the political form. Viewed in this light, it would bring Milbank's study involuntarily close to doctrines such as the tenet held in the post-war socialist societies of Eastern Europe about the 'objective' concern of the working classes, as opposed to which no competing individual or group interests 'can' exist. (Because there can be no conflicts about the nature and goal of a socialist society, the question about the political form becomes superfluous—and conflicts which do actually arise will be suppressed through the intervention of a quasi-political power machinery.)

We must at least ask about the significance of the fact that for the Church peace apparently cannot offer the ontological quality which violence can provide for the secular state. In biblical tradition, the Church appears rather as the battleground where forces clash: the force of peace and the force of violence (Eph. 6: 10 f.; Heb. 12: 4). Peace is not just a given fact, in the sense of a primary datum. It is tied to the practice of worship, in which the Church experiences peace by claiming victory over the forces of violence through the form its life takes. With this, one form of life initially confronts another—the form of life springing from worship, which proclaims the disempowerment of violence, and the form of life which, following the appearance of things, believes that violence is inescapable, and practises it accordingly. Milbank shows convincingly that in spite of some common 'material', Church and secular life do ultimately tell different meta-narratives, which cannot be harmonized. But what he does not sufficiently take into account is the fact that this irreconcilability is manifested not merely on the level of *content*, where contrary concepts of difference, social identity, virtue, and so forth are developed; it is just as fundamentally evident in the *form* taken by the two. Whereas the proclamation of violence legitimates itself ontologically—that is, *re*insures itself by forming a theory about the given 'essential presuppositions' of social life, the proclamation of God's peace is bound to *promise*. Where peace is grasped as promise—in the development of a political form of life which reflects life in the future city of God—an ontological argument is neither possible nor necessary. The category of promise is alien to ontological thinking, and the converse is equally true. 'It has not yet appeared what we shall *be*' (1 John 3: 2), but as those who 'are called God's children and are so now' (ibid.), we live from that which we receive.

Worship as an Act of Expression?

The authority to criticize political ontologies of every kind cannot therefore be ascribed to the Church directly, as the exemplary social entity which embodies the harmony of opposites; it belongs to the Church indirectly, as the congregation gathered together for worship, which in this practice receives that which actually makes it the Church. The practice of worship is the only form of activity—or form of life—which truly is that which is all too easily hypostasized as 'the truth of the Church': it is instituted by God himself. The Church is the divine institution whose character can be made the standard for all human community only as the community at worship, not *per se*. To put it in the language of apostolic tradition, what is established by God is not an essence of peace identical with the Church but 'the ministry of reconciliation' (2 Cor. 5: 18 ff.); not the *essence* of peace but the *ministry* of reconciliation; not the essence of *peace*, but the ministry of *reconciliation*. The Church is not a divine institution *per se*, but only in reference to its ministry to teach the gospel and administer the sacraments.[17] So if the Church is to be the Church, become the Church, and remain the Church, it is fundamentally dependent on this happening in worship. If it wanted to emancipate itself from this permanent dependence— even by assuring itself of its own ontology—it would degenerate, and become no longer divinely established, but a human establishment, an institution in the bureaucratic sense of the world. Moreover, the very recourse to a definition of its own being, in a search for legitimation, would deprive it of its critical force.

This variant has developed its own problematical ecumenical form. Whether the act of worship is viewed in the (neo-)Protestant sense along the lines of Schleiermacher's hermeneutics, as the expression (or 'representation', as he puts it) of the religious state of feeling of gathered believers,[18] or (as in the Catholic form) conforms to the notion of worship as 'the self-implementation of

---

[17] Augsburg Confession V: 'Institutum est ministerium docendi evangelii et porrigendi sacramenta' ['The ministry is instituted for the teaching of the gospel and the administration of the sacraments'].

[18] Schleiermacher, *Praktische Theologie*, 75. In his *Christliche Sittenlehre* Schleiermacher describes 'representative action' (*darstellendes Handeln*) explicitly in terms of expressivistic logic, saying that 'representative action is nothing other than the assumption of outward form by what is inward, the expression of feeling in organic acts' (ii. 156).

the Church',[19] the difference merely illustrates the varying confessional dead ends in which the same wrong ecclesiological turning
can end up.

EXCURSUS

The two concepts are conditioned and connected historically in a way
which explains their present interplay. The Roman Catholic assertion
that the Church in its existing institutional form *per se* offers a criterion of
truth was bound not only to lead to a denunciation of the Reformation as
heretical but, equally inevitably, to provoke a violent clash between the
newly emerging confessional churches. The religious wars of the sixteenth
and seventeenth centuries, in their turn, were an essential presupposition
for the modern privatization of religious life in the Western world, since
'religion' as constitutive factor in *public* life seemed to have disqualified
itself. Seen from this angle, the privatization of religion is by no means an
invention of the Enlightenment, which had merely to conceptualize what
had previously been 'achieved' by the Church itself, through its failure to
keep the controversy on the right level, by word but not by force (*sine vi sed
verbo*, Augsburg Confession, Article XXVIII) and within its own boundaries. In view of the supposedly irreversible fate of religion in the modern
world as a privatized body, the further turn to an expressivistic understanding of religious life seemed unavoidable, if the churches were not to lose
their social relevance completely. To the extent to which both confessional
parties at that time, by entering into violent conflict, acted in conformity
with a 'Catholic' concept of the Church, as an institutional criterion of
truth, both found themselves later in a position which predisposed acceptance of the 'Protestant' understanding of the Church along the lines of an
expressivistic hermeneutics.

Milbank's ecclesiology represents a particular 'Catholic' type of the
problem involved, inasmuch as for him, as we have seen, the
Church's practice appears as the expression of a harmoniously
differing ecclesial character. Accordingly he can understand the
conceptualization of Christian practice in the sense of a particular
social theory (pp. 380 ff.). But would it not be more appropriate to
understand worship quite explicitly as the elemental formation of
social life, *instead* of a social theory, since, as pneumatological
happening, it negates all systematizable knowledge about the way
'the nature of the Church' can be realized? If theology were really to
see itself as a *description* of the rules of this praxis, as Milbank

[19] K. Rahner, *Grundkurs des Glaubens* (1976), 403 f.

himself occasionally puts it (see, e.g., p. 380), it would have to absorb its own specifically critical form into itself. But then—to use Milbank's own vocabulary—Christian social theory too would be 'not exactly theory', and the counter-ontology 'not exactly ontology'.

We have seen how the Church is to be understood, rather, as primary place of the conflict between the forces of violence and the power of peace—as a community which lives by *celebrating* the victory of God's peace. The victory of the power of peace is then not the same as the replacement of a false ontology by a true one. On the contrary, precisely by renouncing quite practically the assertion that its own form of life has an ontological quality, the Church is in a position to undermine the ontological claim of others too. It undermines the claim of social history narratives about the ontological quality of violence, by paving the way for recognition of that to which it itself testifies, that in the new aeon the rule of violence is *always already* a thing of the past, and therefore has no true being. Since the rule of violence has no future, it is not a 'must' in the present either; it is not natural—at least it is not in accordance with creation—nor is it timeless.

The End of Politics or a Struggle about Politics?

In her essay *On Violence*, Hannah Arendt has shown by differentiating between power and violence how the semantics of power (which Milbank marks down pejoratively) can be given a deeper and more positive meaning. 'Power and violence are opposites; where the one rules absolutely, the other is absent. Violence appears where power is in jeopardy.'[20] On the other hand, Milbank's deconstructivism fits precisely into Arendt's analysis, since it is able to show how the secular conception of sociality as power play invades the vacuum generated by the failure of the Church to live in accordance with its real nature. Where the invoked power of social peace is paralysed, violence pushes its way in. But, on the other hand, power can also weaken violence; and Milbank fails to ask how, if power can also, conversely, rebut violence, this fact can become a *political* hope, mediated through the Church.

Here we are forced to remember that it was actually the Church in the form of its martyrs, who refused to submit to the power of

[20] Hannah Arendt, *On Violence* (1970), 56.

those who were stronger, which gave what was perhaps the most forceful political thrust towards the dissolution of the Roman Empire, as people withdrew from the political worship of the Empire. The effect of the Christian martyrs must, of course, not be interpreted to mean that the principle of non-violence proved superior to Roman violence. Their impact was not based on any ontological ascendancy of non-violence over violence. It was due to the fact that the refusal to go along with the worship of the gods of war, who represented the imperial claim to rule, pointed to the question about the authorization or *empowerment* for such action. If Christians found this empowerment in their worship, that worship did not merely reflect the impossibility of joining in the worship of Roman tyranny; it also showed the possibility of seeing this risky refusal through. Even today, the decisive constructive question of political ethics is the question about the formation of power.

If political ethics is to be replaced neither by a political theology (J. B. Metz, J. Moltmann, D. Sölle) nor by an anti-political theology (Milbank), it should be borne in mind that the Church has its own 'politics' (and economics), its specific way of dealing with the differences in social life. This praxis, which follows 'the law of the Spirit', obtains *within* the Church. At the same time, since it conforms to God's will for the shared life of men and women, the praxis must be defined as the true form of political life in general: political worship. For the Church, this claim is as inescapable as the built-in consequences of confrontation with the everyday world of political power play. This means that it enters into a struggle which is certainly not directly political (since it does not follow the prevailing political rules) but is primarily a struggle *about* politics, a struggle for the true form of political existence. The prevailing paradigm of political power play cannot be denied ontological status by way of a simple affirmation; the Church has to bring its own form of political praxis into the game, by playing along, but with other rules. The rules of a game cannot be changed from outside, but only within the community of the players, and only if the revision opens up new dimensions of the game for those playing it. With this hope, the Church is permitted to intervene, and must ultimately intervene, if it doesn't want to undermine its own acknowledgement of Christ as Lord of the world. Consequently, it cannot leave the political sphere to its own devices and to the secular heresy of its alleged autonomy. It is only in the context of an active but distinctive participation in political life that—picking up a distinction made by Jürgen Habermas[21]—we can talk about the 'saving criticism' which the Church would have to contribute, instead of a criticism that merely makes people aware of something, which is all that would be achieved by confrontation with a better 'ontology'.

It cannot be denied, however, that the Church itself too, outwardly and in its internal relationships, was and is continually entangled in the politics of violence. But the essential point is still that this fact should not be interpreted simply and solely in negative terms, as a failure. From the angle of political ethics, the fact that because of the tension of the aeons the Church still has to fight against the tendency to violence in itself too, can come to be seen as hopeful. For it is precisely this tension which can open up the experience of the way violence must be, and can be, unlearnt. In the hopeful alternative of the Christian form of political praxis, accordingly, it is not just a question of a *rethinking*; what is required is a *relearning*, in the widest sense. If the Church in its ethos were simply to embody an alternative ontology, and were not at the same time to reflect upon and throw open the path along which the politics of violence can be forgotten, it would be no more than a moral élite—a mere antitype, which would simply magnify the hopelessness of the entanglement of political existence in violence.

In the course of this chapter we have seen from two examples how the political dimension of the Church can be underdefined in two different ways. In William Temple we could trace how the *direct* political claim of the Church (as expert for social principles) can obstruct recognition of its political 'nature'. And from John Milbank's concept, the converse became clear: we saw how the claim that the Church is political in 'nature', in the sense of an ontological definition, screens out the question about political ethics. We saw, further, that the political reference of the Church can only be properly perceived, and is not abridged either through a direct relationship to politics outwards (Temple) or through a direct relation inwards (Milbank), if worship is seen as its organizing centre. For here the question about 'nature' or 'essence' does not reach out towards a metaphysical reality behind the Church or above it,

[21] J. Habermas, 'Bewußtmachende oder rettende Kritik: die Aktualität Walter Benjamins', in S. Unsell (ed.), *Zur Aktualität Walter Benjamins* (1972), 173–223.

which its praxis would first have to embody, but is dependent on the bodily presence of Christ, always already present in the sociality of the Church, which arrives at its true status and mandate in worship. The rejection of violence is essential to the Church only in so far as its members learn—and are called to learn—to renounce it. And they learn this at the place where they respect (and heed) the freedom of the Spirit; where they do not procure for themselves the assurance necessary for a peaceful praxis—even if by way of onto-logical speculations about the nature of the Church—but if they receive and claim this assurance *together with* the works of the Spirit in worship.

6
The Surmounting of Political Antinomies in Worship

In this section we shall look at the political dimension of worship against the background of some key problems in political theory. I shall try to show how the reconciliation experienced in worship by men and women who were hitherto pinned down to their separate worlds also means overcoming the contradictory definition of the relationships of those worlds and forms of life. Since women and men, poor and rich, barbarian and Greeks, Gentiles and Jews, bond and free, are all called to God's one same citizenship, *oikos* and *polis*, freedom and necessity, can no longer be seen as dividing antitheses—as total worlds which can be inhabited only exclusively and in exclusion of others.

In turning to the difference between the ethics of Christian citizenship and the political theory of the ancient world, I am able to draw not only on Milbank's analyses, but also on the work of two women to whom political theory is considerably indebted: Hannah Arendt and Jean Bethke Elshtain. Each of these three writers has a different emphasis and a different evaluation of the significance of Christianity for politics, and these tensions can be fruitfully accommodated in our own study. Nevertheless, the three share one essential concern: that the dignity of the different spheres of social existence should be respected in their difference, and that they should not be held cheap in the interests of a single, total perspective. Their analyses continually revolve round the attempts made from Greek antiquity right down to the present day to drive out the differing forms of human activity through the hegemony of only one of them (Arendt); to disparage the sphere of the necessary and those who represent it, in favour of the superiority of political life (Bethke Elshtain); or, it may be, to bring all life's different spheres under the domination of a single destructive paradigm (Milbank). Taking up these analyses critically, I should like to maintain that the worship practice of the Christian Church illuminates the fundamental alternative, the 'saving criticism' of that totalizing drift which imposes itself on us in history as if it were inescapable. This has to be demonstrated both by looking back to the turn which, from its beginnings, Christianity gave the history of political thought and action, and by looking forward to the possibilities of political existence in the postmodern age. Before we can discuss the 'reconciliation in worship' of the different and allegedly antinomic spheres of life and activity, we must look at the entanglement which has accompanied political theory from its beginnings in the ancient world. This can be more precisely described as the structural connection between political totality and political exclusiveness.

6.1 THE SURMOUNTING OF POLITICAL TOTALITY AND EXCLUSIVENESS

Citizens and 'Idiots'

A renaissance of classical (and especially Aristotelian) thinking goes hand in hand with the debate about liberalism and communitarianism, and this, not least, may be a reason for pointing to the parasitic character of the classical political model and its significance for political theory. In *The Human Condition*,[1] Hannah Arendt describes how what was fundamental for the Greek political model was not merely the distinction between the private and public spheres, but their strict severance. The person who is restricted to his own sphere (*idion*) remains as *idiotes* in a private ('deprived') existence: he is deprived of the public life which is essential if he is to be a truly human being (p. 38). For to become a human being in the full sense, a 'second birth' as a political animal is required, in which a person is seen and heard and can distinguish himself from others, instead of being merely different (pp. 176 ff.). It is here that the person's identity is first formed, as he raises himself above the transience of existence by means of 'the immortal deed'. At this point the need to think of political existence in its totalizing claim is evident: 'Without this transcendence into a potential earthly immortality, no politics, strictly speaking, no common world and no public realm is possible' (p. 55). Consequently 'a well-founded body politic should be immortal' (p. 314 n. 77), in order to prepare 'the permanent space of action' for the deeds of political beings (p. 198).

---

[1] See H. Arendt, *The Human Condition*. (1958; 2nd edn. 1998). The page numbers in the text refer to this book.

Political life is parasitic, however, since it cannot be thought and maintained without a dark sphere out of which, now and then, an emergence into the bright light of public life can occur. There are only free citizens when there are *idiotai* too. Thus access to political life is restricted to a relatively small minority of free, prosperous citizens. There is no room at this inn of freedom for women, slaves, and barbarians, or for artists, the poor, the ugly, and the deformed. This exclusive character of political life (the *bios politikos*) goes hand in hand with an explicit disparagement of domestic life, the life of the *oikos*. Political exclusiveness and the assertion of the inferiority of life's other sphere legitimate one another mutually. So historically, it would seem to be by no means fortuitous 'that the foundation of the *polis* was preceded by the destruction of all organized units resting on kinship' (p. 24). The disparagement of the *oikos* was justified particularly by this link with the realm of the bodily and the necessary, as we can see from the later description of the lower classes as the 'proletariat'—those who are concerned only with the fundamental necessity of life, the sheer survival of the human race (p. 72). The Greek cult of 'the body beautiful' is no contradiction here, since it paid homage above all to the body as it was purified from everything 'necessary'—work, sexuality, and the rearing of children: this was the body leisured, sexually sublimated, and homo-erotically male.

Taking the example of Plato's thinking about the ideal state, Jean Bethke Elshtain shows from a feminist standpoint the enduring potency of the complex of political exclusiveness and totality (which cannot simply be identified with totalitarian forms of government), which remained effective even when there was a degree of participation.[2] It is true that at times of political decadence (the democracy of his time) Plato recommends withdrawal to private life; but even this withdrawal remains exclusively and functionally related to political life: not as *oikos* but as *symposion*, where, in homo-erotic relationships between teachers and pupils, men engage in the preparation of a 'real' *polis*, which promises to fulfil the true goal of their lives: politics and war (pp. 23 ff.). In an illuminating interpretation of the *Republic*, Bethke Elshtain shows in her book how the totalization of political existence in Plato can be interpreted as resistance against the forces of the bodily and the feminine, so that a public life shaped only by men can be

[2] See J. Bethke Elshtain, *Public Man, Private Woman* (1981; 2nd edn. 1993).

maintained. 'The question to be put, then, is not just what politics is for but what politics has served to defend against. That question is best explored through the prism of the public and the private' (p. 16).

EXCURSUS

Bethke Elshtain does not illustrate the connection between these things by pointing to the old familiar aspect of Greek misogyny, which Plato shares. She focuses precisely on what is thought to be Plato's strongest point—the passages where he proclaims the equality and participation of women in the Guardian class. It is true that Plato envisages the admittance of specially endowed women to be trained for the office of Guardian. But at what cost? The participation in political public life reserved for 'persons of gold' (according to the allegory of metals) can be had by these women only at the cost of renouncing their natural relationships to their children and husbands—relationships which are now to be reduced to the necessary acts of conception and birth. Otherwise they are allowed neither permanent lovers nor any further contact with their own children, who are passed over immediately they are born to central nurseries and wet nurses.

Here the political problem goes beyond what is ultimately still a functional use of the Guardian women for the reproduction of the ruling caste (pp. 31 f., 34 f.); for what this means is the complete absorption of private and natural life into the political sphere: away with marriage, family, the upbringing of children; all these natural ties potentially endanger the undivided devotion to the state. Here we see how the connection between the totalizing of political existence and the absorption of natural life retains its violent and exclusive character even with an extended participatory base. The mythical idea of 'autochthony' supports this structure, because it is supposed to make the Guardians believe that they have not been conceived naturally, but spring from the sacred *polis*—earth itself—just as then, in the Golden Age in general, birth will be possible without mothers.[3]

In this way women are given a share in a crack male unit in the interests of a political world organized through and through by violence. It is in any case only a minority of women who can enjoy political privileges. The admission of 'political' women means at the same time their separation from other women, the non-political women of inferior rank. The paradigm of power relations is now implanted in the world of women too, which thus becomes the mirror of the male world.[4] This dualistic metaphysics

---

[3] Plato, *Republic*, 414d and e.

[4] Bethke Elshtain recognizes the same problem in such concepts in the feminist movement, which propagate an autonomous ideal of social life, without family, and

still governs Plato's late work *The Laws*, as the matrix of a totalitarian political concept. There the reason given for the admission of women to the public life of the *polis* is precisely their 'natural' weakness, which binds them to lower social constellations;[5] the aim being to free them from this anarchical power of natural life—though within the bounds of what is possible for women, bounds which are of course narrower than those for men.

These ideas were retained in Aristotle's realism too, in spite of the well-known differences between his reasoning and Plato's thinking about the ideal state. Although in his *Ethics* he praises moderation and the golden mean, he emerges as a political thinker who provides the rationale for this quite extreme political praxis of his time, which was imperialist, misogynist, and based on slavery.[6] Women were now to be excluded without exception from the 'good life' of the *polis*, as well as from the contemplative life, the *bios theoretikos*—an exclusion which Aristotle justifies by their biological and naturally given inferiority. The notion that human life begins as a homunculus, implanted by the male seed in the vessel of the female body, provides him with the biological illustration of the epistemological analogy according to which the relationship between men and women has to be seen as the relationship between form and matter—an idea which was later taken up again by Hegel.[7] In Aristotle too, fear of the binding forces of the feminine and natural shows through when he demands that a man cut himself off, externally and internally both, from the *oikos* and its sphere of influence. Here too, then, the self-sufficiency of political

hope that the abolition, largely speaking, of the private sphere will bring about a beneficial political change (see *Public Man, Private Woman*, 325 f.). To this Bethke Elshtain objects that the equality of women ought not to be directed against the family, but should be accepted in families as well as in public life. So there must be a struggle in the political discussion for the recognition of the sphere which is in the best sense socially and socializationally necessary. But in the politicization of the *oikos* the feminist movement is in danger of 'losing its soul', if this politicization takes place at the expense of children and mothers (pp. 333, 337). Where the dignity of the woman is supposed to appear only in the paradigm of 'political women', women in home and families experience an additional degradation.

[5] Ibid. 35 f.

[6] For Aristotle's treatment of the slavery question in his *Politics*, see 1253b24–1255b15; 1325a25 f.; for the Greek claim to rule over all others in the case of the formation of a unified state—a claim which he justifies on the grounds of climate—see 1327b29–33; for the rule of the patriarch over wife, children, and servants, 1259b36–1260b19.

[7] Bethke Elshtain, *Public Man, Private Woman*, 44, 175.

life is justified by the 'natural' character of the *polis*: the man has no true need which could be satisfied only in the *oikos*, and not equally well—or better—in the *polis*. The highest good is to be found in the *polis*, whereas the benefits of the *oikos* are inferior in kind.[8]

Here Aristotle directly deduces the 'naturally given necessity' of relationships of dominance and submission from their existence as an empirical fact, postulating a 'community of interests' between those who are destined by nature to rule and those who can be recognized by their very nature as destined to be ruled.[9] The difficulties raised by this train of thought in its consequences for the fate of most people in the ancient world is obvious. But the problem is already implicit in the concept of 'the good life' which is the postulate, since this appears to be possible at all only by way of hegemony over others. According to Aristotle in his *Politics*, it is only the man who can surpass and subjugate others who is good: 'Actions cannot be good and excellent unless the one who acts himself enjoys a measure of superiority over others as great as the superiority of a husband over his wife, a father over his children, or the master over his slaves.'[10]

Political Exclusiveness: The Necessity of Violence

How does all this tie in with the celebrated 'discourse' ideal picked out today, often in considerable isolation, from the political legacy of antiquity? It is true that the rhetorical form of non-violent persuasion was stressed as being the fundamental form of political action, so that the rhetorician could soon be equated with the politician. In this respect the *polis* saw itself in express antithesis to the patterns of reaction which could be encountered in the home and in barbarian empires, where patriarchs and despots ruled purely through their arbitrary power. Of course there was speech here too, but it was *aneu logou*—speech without further meaning.[11] Where the necessities of life ruled, things could not be regulated through the noble form of verbal dispute, but had simply to be decreed. Here the ruling principle was: necessity justifies violence.[12] The political form of the free interchange of free citizens could, in the awareness of its infinite superiority, cut itself off from this sphere of 'the pre-political'. However, the relationship between necessity and power of

---

[8] Bethke Elshtain, *Public Man, Private Woman*, 51. [9] Ibid. 44.
[10] Aristotle, *Politics*, 1325b3–5. [11] Arendt, *Human Condition*, 27.
[12] Ibid. 33.

course worked two ways. The connection between the two did not only affect the sphere of the necessary; it applied to the emancipation from the necessary too. The violence-free sphere of political existence was itself a violent construction, which resembled a heavily armed fortress for protection against the onslaught of the 'prepolitical'. (So the fact that the term *polis* originally meant fortified military camps may well seem more than fortuitous.) The much-vaunted equality of citizens was similar. It did not merely 'exist' as distinct from unequal forms of life; it was actually *based on the concept* of the inequality between *oikos* and *polis*. So the *existence* of a majority of unequal people was not simply the political precondition for the *polis*. In the concept of the *polis* these people were actually *destined* to lead an existence of this kind, as 'useless idiots'. The ancient world solved the problem of necessity and violence through the violent assertion of a space free of necessity.

This means that we cannot reject out of hand the question whether the ancient world's concept of joint action on behalf of the good life of the *polis* should not very largely be understood instrumentally—for the benefit of the self-fulfilment of a political class. Doesn't its structurally conditioned exclusiveness expose the whole concept of 'the good' as being, after all, interest politics? What we can learn from the ancient world's conjunction of political exclusiveness and totality in its bearing on the development even of modern societies with a wider participation base is this: participation, as the right to share in the political process, *taken by itself* will merely slow down or disguise the selection process in the political conflict of interests which is the ancient world's legacy of exclusiveness. Political exclusiveness cannot be ended as long as the total claim of political existence is maintained. It is only if political existence is limited that the participation can become real, for it is only when politics are not everything that everyone can take part. And participation requires limitation. In contrast, we have seen that the classical world's way of limiting political existence as a territory already clearly staked out at its frontiers—a territory which simultaneously restricts the sphere of the unpolitical (the *oikos*)—actually maintains the total political claim. So what we would have to set our sights on would be another way of limiting political existence, one which does not act parasitically on life's other spheres.

In addition, the attempt to preserve a pure political and ethical culture by excluding other spheres of life does not disqualify only the people who are excluded. This proceeding in its turn also reacts on the community of freemen. What determines the exclusion determines the life of those included too: the struggle for good places. So although Aristotle certainly presents the model of 'the magnanimous man' who gives rather than receives, this preference for liberality is itself seen in the framework of contest, and is therefore directed against the 'womanish' element of receptivity. Moreover, the magnanimous man—guided by moral wisdom (*phronesis*)—knows very well how to distinguish between the more and the less useful recipients of his beneficent deeds.[13]

The political hermeneutics of the classical world, whether it now meant life in the *polis* or in the philosopher state, did not take its paradigm from social life itself; its lodestone was the life of the self-controlled individual. In the inner life of human beings, the reasonable parts of the soul are supposed to arrive at the highest possible degree of control over the passions; and in the same way, the patterns of relationship in public life are determined by the model of the most highly individuated magnanimous man, who does not 'suffer' his relationships but controls them.[14] So, in the political concept of the ancient world, the fear of binding ties and dependencies, whether familial or other in kind, leads to an early form of what Charles Taylor (following Isaiah Berlin) calls negative freedom—a freedom which returns in the guise of modernity. Since the Aristotelian ethic is differentiated not only from contemplative life but also from the 'pre-ethical' realm of fabricating action, *poiesis*, John Milbank may not be entirely wrong in seeing the idea of *phronesis* as a precursor of the cold theoretical gaze of the modern world and its concept of an autonomous technology.[15] And the modern divorce between religion and morality, expressed not least in the establishment of ethics as a separate discipline, can accordingly also be seen as a new, modern edition of the Aristotelian separation of the *vita contemplativa* from the *vita activa*.

It must be said, however, particularly in view of the new criticism of Aristotle presented here, that some objections to the practical relations of life in the *polis* could very well be put forward in the name of the Aristotelian political concept of participation itself.

---

[13] J. Milbank, *Theology and Social Theory* (1990), 352.
[14] Ibid. 370.
[15] Ibid. 354.

The point of such a criticism of Aristotle by Aristotle would then be to establish that an honourable place must be assigned to political existence, because it is from this that change proceeds—beyond the limits of what Aristotle himself thought conceivable. An honourable place of this kind for political existence is, however, threatened precisely if that place is granted absolute status; for political existence can win recognition only if, fundamentally speaking, the participation of *everyone* is in view.

What these reflections drawn from the example of the ancient world may have shown is this: at the very point where ethics is concentrated on some imaginary political space, the possibility of a political ethics is suspended. In this model, political ethics cannot prosper, any more than it can thrive in modern forms of limitation, where ethics are confined to private life, or—the postmodern form—are segregated into stereotyped patterns of life which cannot be mediated to each other.

How Worship Challenges the 'Political Sphere'

In this sense the political dimension of worship (to which we now turn once more) can be seen as the practical challenge to separate spheres of this kind:[16] the worshipping congregation can neither confine itself to the sphere of private religion, nor can it recognize the autonomy of political existence. It can neither abstain from the *via activa* in favour of the contemplative life, nor will it politicize the latter. What has to be brought out is, rather, how the *reconciliation* between these forms of action and the spheres of life which belong to them comes to be experienced in worship. This reconciliation is not something we can achieve for ourselves, either by fabricating the appropriate conditions, or theoretically through the constructions of political theory. The reconciliation of forms of action and spheres of life which are experienced as antinomies cannot be achieved theoretically, because it cannot be separated from the reconciliation of the people who represent them. Women and

---

[16] Bonhoeffer's criticism of 'thinking in terms of two spheres' (*Ethics*, 168 ff.) is well known. It is directed against the self-styled autonomy with which individual spheres cut themselves off from each other, and struggle for supremacy. But Bonhoeffer's criticism is confined to the separation between the religious and the secular sphere. Beyond that, as it seems to me, it is the antagonistic separation in the secular fields themselves (*oeconomia* and *politia*) which must be particularly included in criticism of a 'thinking in terms of different spheres'.

men, parents and children, the free and the unfree, citizens and non-citizens, can all live from the reconciliation which they experience in worship. Consequently the life steadfastly lived in worship *is itself* the reconciliation of the *vita activa* and the *vita contemplativa*, private and public life, freedom and necessity.

The celebration of worship, however, always also acts critically and therapeutically on developments in the Church itself which legitimate thinking and living in separate spaces or spheres by making a total theological claim for any one of them. This may be said of theologies of the politicization of life which, in right-wing or left-wing Hegelian variants, propagate the total claim of political life, which may either mean a re-formation of the Christian redemption hope into concepts of political liberation,[17] or the assertion (inspired by Richard Rothe's vision of the absorption of the Church into the State) of a 'political' or 'ethical' age which Christianity has allegedly now entered. Whether theology now claims for itself the sphere of political existence, or legitimates theologically the political claim to autonomy, makes little difference, structurally speaking.

It is true that it is hardly possible to overlook the fact that worship itself can also be drawn into this way of thinking, and can lose its cutting edge if, following the Aristotelian separation between the *vita activa* and the *vita contemplativa*, it is wholly annexed to the latter. But worship in its traditional ritual form, more than the thinking itself, proves resistant to attempts to make it conform to a particular paradigm. What is sometimes deplored as worship's slowness to move, and as a drag on the Church's political activity, can in this sense be seen as politically highly important, since a certain inertia on the part of liturgy, over against the dynamic of theological concepts—even the concept of political liturgy—also helps to preserve the political dimension of worship. The resistant power of worship is admittedly not unlimited; nor can it be postulated directly of every individual service of worship. There are undoubtedly worship formularies which do indeed fail to reflect anything except 'concepts' of this kind, and the fashion for talking

---

[17] Gustavo Gutiérrez, for example, starts from the 'universality of the political sphere' to which a comprehensive politicization of society would correspond, a politicization which theology would also have to make the starting-point and the goal of its enterprise, in the sense of reflection on the (political) experience of liberation. See his *Theology of Liberation* (1973), 47.

about worship as a 'creative enterprise'[18] mirrors this problem. And yet history shows—and not least in the form of movements for liturgical reform—how, at all events in respect of the height, breadth, and depth of the *una sancta*, more worship is always present, in the strong and resistant sense, than concepts of politicization or depoliticization are able to destroy.[19] There is always at least sufficient worship present for something about it to be open for renewal. That is surely the heart of the promise that the Church 'will be and remain for ever' (*ecclesia perpetuo mansura*, Augsburg Confession, Article VII), a promise which can all too easily be cited as an encouragement to the self-complacency of a particular denomination concerned to assure itself of its continued existence.

Worship again and again interrupts the course of the world.[20] Through worship the Christian community testifies that the world is not on its own. And this also means that it is not kept alive by politics, as the business of politics, which knows no sabbath, would have us believe. That is why the celebration of worship is not directed simply against this or that totalitarian regime; it is directed against the totalization of political existence in general. It does not just interrupt labour and 'fabrication'; it also suspends political action in the world. In this way it affords a salutary limitation of

---

[18] It must of course not be forgotten that the *praxis* of worship always includes an element of *poiesis*. But the relative position of the two must not be reversed. If the *praxis* itself becomes a function of the *poiesis* ('worship as a creative enterprise'), and the liturgical, formal element does not, conversely, position the practical and political one, worship loses its focusing place.

[19] The ecumenical dimension of the Church's capacity for reform in the light of worship must also be stressed, because it can very well get lost on the level of individual congregations, churches, or groups of churches. The Dutch Reformed Church in South Africa (NGK) is a recent example, since its worship praxis of interpreting Scripture was entangled with the ethical praxis of apartheid, in a vicious circle. Through the refusal to live out the truth experienced in worship (which was originally racially mixed), the worship itself came in time to be deformed, and Scripture as it was expounded there was misused to legitimate the existing apartheid. Once this church had silenced the prophetic voices in its own ranks (by making the members concerned leave the church), conversion (which began in 1994) was possible only through attempts at reform made from outside, through the reaction of churches in the ecumenical community, which for the reasons given above had severed relations with the NGK. For the connection between ethical obedience and the ability to hear God's Word, see S. E. Fowl and L. G. Jones, *Reading in Communion* (1991), 84 ff., with a more detailed analysis of events connected with the NGK.

[20] Schleiermacher already stressed the 'interruption' character of worship as the essential mark of the cult as 'feast' (*Praktische Theologie*, 70). Cf. here also E. Jüngel, 'Der evangelisch verstandene Gottesdienst', in *idem, Wertlose Wahrheit* (1990), 283–310.

soteriologically charged expectations addressed to politics. These expectations have continually changed their form: the ancient world's investment of the whole life on behalf of the *polis* was later succeeded by the consumer-bourgeois vision of an omnipotent political welfare machinery; and this in its turn found its reverse side in the bored disenchantment with politics which no longer expects anything, and which in resignation over 'politics as they really exist' actually assents to the total political claim. Thus the self-contained business of politics may be nourished by the self-contradictory attitude of 'private citizens', so that the link forged in the ancient world between the exclusiveness and the totality of political existence is once more endorsed. For the more a claim is made to private life as a closed space, shut off from the rest, the easier it becomes to see political life as a sphere of its own too. Today, this inner pressure to reproduce the ancient world's dilemma is of course lapped round by the semblance of voluntary choice with which people affirm their private sphere, and by so doing reverse the thrust of political exclusiveness. In contrast, when in worship political existence is freed from total claims of this kind,[21] its liberation makes a political ethics possible.

The De-totalization of Political Existence: Israel and the Early Church

This de-totalization of political existence is already part of Israel's tradition, irrespective of the new dimension which it took on in the worship of the early Church. Israel's acknowledgement of creation in the Priestly Writing (Genesis 1) can be viewed as being a stylized challenge to Babylon's political myth, in which divine descent and authority were claimed for the ruler. The de-totalizing trend runs like a scarlet thread through the biblical narratives: the period of the Judges (who were only appointed *ad hoc* and for a limited period)— the disputed establishment of the monarchy (1 Sam. 8)—and then the Deuteronomistic criticism of every single king, each of whom was judged according to his awareness of his dependence on Israel's God. Accordingly, even where it was ultimately affirmed and accepted, the monarchy in Israel took its legitimation to a strikingly

---

[21] Thus Hannah Arendt is in some degree right in terming freedom *from* politics as perhaps the most important part of our Christian heritage: see *On Revolution* (1963); cf. also her 'Religion and Politics', *Confluence*, 2 (Sept. 1953). However, Arendt is not able to see this emancipatory aspect in connection with the politically formative one which we have before us in worship. Cf. here section 6.5 below.

small degree from the kingship of God. It is only seldom that any connection is made between YHWH's heavenly throne and the earthly throne of the king. 'YHWH is king' was not so much understood in the light of experiences of the monarchy; it was rather the reverse: the monarchy was seen in the light of the king-ship of YHWH. It is largely on the basis of their relationship to YHWH that Saul and David allow themselves to be understood and judged as kings in Israel's sense.

The era of the prophets provides a particularly enduring contri-bution by widening the focus on the rulers in two different direc-tions. On the one hand, even foreign potentates such as the Persian Cyrus, the ruler of the mighty empire to which Israel was subjected, can be apostrophized as instruments in YHWH's hand—as 'whistled up' (like Assyria and Egypt earlier, Isa. 7), so that Israel may be judged and restored (Isa. 45: 1–5). As long as Israel pins its hopes on political measures and alliances, instead of 'waiting on YHWH', this judgement will be inescapable (Isa. 7: 30). On the other hand, the prophets' social criticism is turned towards internal conditions, and associates the question about the oppression of the poor with the other question about proper worship. However, this criticism does not simply aim to bring about the just social condi-tions which would have to accompany the YHWH cult if it were not to be 'vain', and merely correctly practised in the ritual sense. This is not criticism of an ethics which clashes with the proper worship of God. On the contrary, for prophets like Amos, Israel's worship stinks to high heaven because *the practice of worship itself* is inescap-ably impaired by the faulty social behaviour of the worshippers. It turns into idolatry because the unjust conditions prevailing in Israel mean that the deity worshipped can no longer be identified with 'the God of widows and orphans' (Amos 5: 21–7).

Israel's most important contribution to the de-totalization of political life, however, can probably be found in the tradition about the prohibition of images (Exod. 20: 4). This does not just mean refraining from moulding God into an image—and an image was an excellent way of representing the historical power of worldly rulers, who used to carry representations of the gods with them as a banner, demonstrating this power. What was also of special importance for political ethics was a further aspect of the prohib-ition, which forbade the making of idolatrous images of 'what is on earth'. The prohibition which forbade the people to degrade God to an idol, an image made 'in the likeness of male or female' (Deut. 4: 16), had a reverse side: no human being was to be elevated through stylization into an idol of this kind. Consequently, the prohibition also includes precisely total political claims which are put forward in the name of a particular vision of 'the true nature' of human beings, in the name of 'humanity', or in the name of nature itself (or its preservation).

But political ethics springing from worship cannot be developed merely by negating total claims. The interruption of action on the stage of public and political life in itself means more than merely a negative political dimension of worship, since the form of this interruption is itself political: the shared action that enters assentingly[22] into the great acts of God. The power of the Church is to be found in this assent.[23] The demythologizing of political life could not remain without consequences in history for the relationship of Christendom to the representatives of political power as well. These could no longer be revered as quasi-divine figures, and it is characteristic of the epochal change that only a few centuries later a Roman emperor could be called to do penance like any normal believer for 'crimes committed'—it was actually said—'in the name of the state',[24] and that he obeyed the command. The public power

[22] On the 'assent' to the acts of other people as the formation of power, and as the original form of political praxis, cf. Arendt, *Human Condition*, 199 ff. Although Arendt does not explicitly use the term, it does, I believe, bring together the two essential elements she develops: the beginning and the assenting association in action.

[23] In 'Der Beitrag der Kirchen zur politischen Kultur' (1994), Hartmut Löwe, the Bonn representative of the Evangelical Churches in Germany (EKD), tells the following anecdote. He describes the service held immediately before the election of the new Federal President on Whit Monday 1994, and goes on: 'It did not influence the result of the vote, and no recommendation was given either directly or indirectly. No one would have followed such a recommendation anyway. But the tension in the party meetings before the service and afterwards, the calculations and counting, the bringing into line . . . was interrupted by the service. The politically powerful, the candidates, the voters all entered another world, the world of the wisdom of the Bible, the pentecostal prayer for the Holy Spirit ("Kindle a light in our understanding . . . "), glorious church music. For a whole hour—perhaps for some people who were still restless and absent in thought it was only a few minutes—about a thousand people, half of them voters, stood before God. Politics was no longer the be all and end all. The pushing and bustle was interrupted in a salutary way. "We beseech you that the election of the new Federal President may take place in dignity and may serve to bring our people together—Lord have mercy upon us!" '

[24] In the year 390 Ambrose, bishop of Milan, refused communion to Emperor Theodosius until he had performed public penance for a cruel punitive expedition

that had hitherto been uncontested had now to answer to another throne, whose presence in the world is represented by a community in which the least member is to enjoy the greatest honour.

Nietzsche propounded the theory that the Christian 'reversal of values' was the avenging revolt of the slave caste; but Jean Bethke Elshtain rightly points out that this theory fails to take account of the moral change that took place here. 'Authentic moral change incorporates and transforms the old.'[25] Anyone who merely fits an event like this into the familiar pattern of the power play between secular and ecclesiastical power has failed to recognize its novel element. It was not a bishop in the power of his office, or simply the charismatic figure of an Ambrose of Milan, that was able to constrain an emperor. The emperor did penance before the God to whom all Christians bow the knee. This was not an act of political subservience; it was a penitential worship ritual. It was doubtless difficult for the Constantinian link between Church and political world which was then developing to retain this fundamental detotalization of the political sphere, and not to slide into a power game between Church and State, or a mutual relationship where the one legitimates the other. Nevertheless, this new relationship proved itself to be more or less continuously existent, in worship especially. Even in the 'Caesaro-Papist' East, in worship the emperor had no higher rank than that of a subdeacon. A completely new feature, in addition, was the potential duty of Christians to resist public authority, a duty which was also bound to be awakened by worship. Christians had to refuse their assent to the Roman state cult, because it was incompatible with the political dimension of their own worship. That would have been inconceivable for the political theory of the ancient world. Plato, for example, paints the picture of his teacher Socrates as a citizen who celebrates even his own execution as proof of his political loyalty. Instead of fleeing, he deliberately accepts the cup of hemlock as a faithful citizen of the state—and accepts it from the hand of the corrupt representative of state power.

Over against this was a fresh concept which was of decisive importance for the new definition of the exercise of the ruler's power in Christendom: the practical exercise of the *potentia* which

---

against the people of Thessalonica. Cf. the account in P. Brown, *Power and Persuasion in Late Antiquity* (1992), 110–13.

[25] Bethke Elshtain, *Public Man, Private Woman*, 59.

a person possesses in the private or public sphere has now to be related in each case to the *potestas* of God—the unlimited power to rule which is his alone. In classical theory, *potentia* means the power of absolute disposal enjoyed by the free citizen over his household. But in its Christian application it not only designates the power exercised in the social sphere (power which was fundamentally restricted). It also determines the form that power assumes through this answerability to God's *potestas*, and the way in which is exercised. This implementation came increasingly to be understood in the light of the 'synkatabasis' ideal, the gracious inclination of the powerful to the needy. So in Shenoute's sermons, for example, the mighty are exhorted to lower themselves as Christ also lowered himself: '[The powerful] also should learn to bend as Christ had bent: they also must forgive the insubordination of their inferiors and must show mercy to the poor, to petitioners, and to their own servants.'[26]

An essential element in the revolution which Christianity introduced into the political world of late antiquity was its fundamentally different attitude to the body. The totalization of political life in the ancient world had expressed itself particularly as a total claim to the body of the human being. 'The classical, pre-Christian view, then, is that the city-state should have *complete control of human bodies* for the purpose of labor, procreation and war.'[27] This purely functional view and treatment of bodily life underlies the categorial supremacy of the political over the private sphere, and simultaneously intensifies its effect. Against this background, the view of the human body as 'the temple of the Holy Spirit' (1 Cor. 6: 19) was bound to act politically like gunpowder. What Paul brings to bear over against the idea of 'self-possession' is no less valid where the possessions of others and the claim to their use is concerned. This freedom could be a life-saver in the quite literal sense—for example, in the case of raped women, who according to the Roman view were encouraged to commit suicide, an obligation from which Augustine in Book I of his *City of God* explicitly freed them. It could also certainly lead to the final extreme, for when the claim of the state to the body of Christians collided with the claim of the spirit of Christ, the political claim could be enforced only by

[26] Brown, *Power and Persuasion*, 156.
[27] J. Bethke Elshtain, 'Christianity and Patriarchy', *Modern Theology*, 9 (1993), 110.

violence—through the killing of the body. In this way the true character of this totalitarian claim became, on the one hand, radically evident: it was a claim 'to the death'. But, on the other hand, in the ultimate sense the claim finally lost its force. For the power of the Spirit is still efficacious even in the dead, in the resurrection of those killed, and—*sanguis semen ecclesiae*—in the building up of the Body of Christ, as a community of bodies set free.

6.2 'FELLOW CITIZENS WITH THE SAINTS AND MEMBERS OF THE HOUSEHOLD OF GOD': THE RECONCILIATION OF *POLIS* AND *OIKOS*

Now as its roots in worship show, the de-totalization of political violence in Christianity is not the result of a simple process of relativization. It comes about through confrontation with another absolute priority: discipleship of Jesus Christ for the sake of the kingdom of God. Here the important point is to see how the call to discipleship relativizes the obligations of the life previously lived in the *oikos* (that is to say, relates them to the kingdom), but without disparaging these spheres of life in principle. We can see this peculiar dialectic in Jesus's own proclamation. On the one hand, the proclamation of the kingdom of God makes all existing ties provisional (Luke 14: 25; Mark 12: 25); on the other hand, the Proclaimer of this kingdom is concerned for the success of a marriage feast; the one who himself lives as a celibate takes the marriage feast as a favourite image for God's coming kingdom (Matt. 22: 1–14), and speaks in defence of marriage with a radical emphasis previously unknown (Mark 1: 11 f.). Even if the new community of the disciples as 'the family of God' (Mark 3: 34 f.) could sometimes be set over against natural family obligations (Luke 9: 59–62), from the very beginning the Christian Church avoided presenting itself as a kind of super-family. Tension between the claims of family and gospel could not be ruled out; but for all that, it may be said that in the apostolic tradition as a whole, natural ties are not something to be fearfully avoided or disparaged for the sake of ties with the new community. They are fully acknowledged and are to be cherished.[28] As we shall see in the following sections, one reason why

---

[28] It must of course be said that individual texts have different emphases in this respect. As opposite poles we might name Q and the pastoral epistles. Q is ascetic in tendency, whereas the epistles have a more domestic orientation.

the Church was able to avoid the danger of presenting itself as a new super-family was precisely because its new community could in any case not be fully comprehended in the image of 'the family of God'.

The Political Self-Understanding of the First Congregations

In his sociological study of the first urban Christians,[29] Wayne A. Meeks explores the extent to which the early Church took over the different contemporary views of social life with which it was faced, or modified them. He compares characteristics of the Pauline congregations with characteristics of the Graeco-Roman household, the voluntary associations, the Jewish synagogue, and the philosophical schools, and comes to the following conclusion: 'The fact is that none of the four models we have now surveyed captures the whole of the Pauline *ekklesia*, although all offer significant analogies' (p. 84).

EXCURSUS

Meeks's study makes available to us valuable insights at particular points which can continually throw light on the following discussion. But in the context of the question we have been looking at, we can also see its limitations. Why does Meeks confine his comparative study to these four models, leaving out the concept of public life in the political sense? Are we supposed to assume that this played no part in the way the first congregations saw themselves? This omission also leads to a methodological narrowing down, a narrowness which is in any case latent in the sociological perspective. Where the Church is viewed in the light of other, already existing social models, the perspective is foreshortened, and its particular character does not sufficiently come into view. Meeks is unable to show *how* the way the congregations saw themselves was related to the analogies to—and differences from—the social patterns of the surrounding world which he has previously investigated. Yet it is precisely this question that would show which prevailing *theological* norms led to one or the other modification. Not only that: the question would also bring to light the theological *claim* made by the fundamentally new order of social life, a claim which comes out clearly in the New Testament testimonies themselves. Of course, this would not merely necessitate a comparison between individual social models and the model of the *ekklesia*; it would above all require a discussion of the complex relationship between public and private life, for this characterizes the relationship to the Church in a much deeper

[29] Wayne A. Meeks, *The First Urban Christians* (1983).

way than any individual aspects can do. But then it would be difficult to ignore the political character of the Church to the degree to which Meeks does.

It is true that if we compare it with the Greek 'invention' of the opposition between private and public life, the appearance of public life had changed considerably by New Testament times. As the opportunities for political participation became to a great extent marginalized, the sense of citizenship in the Roman Empire mutated into an unspecific cosmopolitanism. The possible ways of defining political status in the towns had become much more differentiated in the mixed Roman–Hellenist societies of the Mediterranean area. Thus there were not only full Roman citizens side by side with the indigenous population; there were resident aliens too. These—the Jewish community, for example—often constituted something like a state within a state,[30] a *politeuma* of its own. For some social classes—the *liberati*, or freedmen, for example—opportunities for advancement were available in certain spheres, and some upper-class women broke through the now more permeable confines of the household. Yet the classic antagonisms between the public and the private sphere, free life and life bounded by necessity, remained determinative, and had even to some extent worsened. Thus the parasitic and arrogant relationship between urban landowners and the towns, on the one hand, and the increasingly enslaved tenant farmers in the country, on the other, had hardened into permanent hostility between the two worlds.[31]

Meeks's theory about the social classes to which members of the Pauline congregations belonged confirms this impression. According to the classic view (Celsus, Nietzsche, Deissmann), the first Christian congregations were a catchment area for the socially downgraded. Contrary theories maintained that in a hierarchical society the triumphal progress of Christianity could only have moved from above to below. Meeks takes a different view. He contends that in the apostolic period, what evidently characterized at least those Christians who are named in the epistles because of the role they played was not so much their adherence to a particular class as their *status inconsistency*. For example, talking about the 'strong' members of the congregation in Corinth, he assumes:

[30] Ibid. 25.   [31] Ibid. 14.

'These may enjoy a high rank in some dimensions, such as wealth, identification with the Latin element in the colony, support by dependents and clients, . . . but they may be ranked lower in others, such as origin, occupation or sex' (p. 70). The relevant New Testament passages give us a picture of congregational leaders who in their own person, as it were, embody the antagonism between private and public life, and suffer under it: in private categories they are privileged, being affluent and the heads of households; but as freed men, independent women, and so forth, they are still downgraded as far as public recognition or their actual origins are concerned.

Meeks stresses the attractiveness of the congregations for people suffering under status inconsistency of this kind; and in this respect his thesis is in line sociologically with that of the proponents of the classic position we have mentioned; for they too tried to find definite evidence for the upward mobility of Christians in a class society. But to explain the background in this way tends to screen out what these congregations (apart from the consistency management of individual members) may have meant for the antagonistic forces, and hence the prevailing antinomies, in society itself. The apostolic texts testify to an experience which is nothing less than the actual reconciliation of these antinomies. When the Epistle to the Ephesians talks about the wall of hostility between Jews and Gentiles which has now been broken down, this means that the Church reconciled with God in a new body through the cross (2: 16) is nothing less than *the new humanity* (4: 13) in which the eternal mystery of Christ has now become manifest (3: 3 ff.). What Paul's pupil describes here as the universal significance of the 'slain enmity' between Jews and Gentiles is by Paul himself applied to the paradigmatic series of antagonisms in their consequences for social and political life.

The contrasting pairs Jew–Greek, man–woman, freeman–slave, listed in Galatians 3: 26 ff. represented—and represent still—fundamental differences, ethnic and religious, sexual and economic. All these differences were experienced as antagonistically and hierarchically structured conditions, and the last two also stood for the division between the private and the public sphere, and the political dilemma that went hand in hand with it. It must already be noted at this point that the unity brought about through what Christ did and suffered—a unity conferred in baptism—does

not depend on the abolition of the antitheses as such. The problem
is not solved by doing away with it. Slaves are initially left in their
economic sphere;[32] believers continue to see themselves as Gentile
Christians or Jewish Christians; and women and men do not stop
being women and men. (Paul even insists on the head covering
which traditionally differentiates the sexes.) This shows that the
intention was not to abolish these antinomies in general. They are
to be set aside in a quite precise sense: the political one. As we saw
in the previous chapter, the functionalization of the difference is
spelled out in the hierarchical structuring of social conditions which
constituted a fundamental political phenomenon in a society of
totality and exclusiveness. In this respect, and in this respect only,
'there is no difference'. But the personal experiences of unity in
Christ which Jews and Gentiles, men and women, freemen and
slaves, can enjoy in the *polis* of the Church could not then, certainly,
leave unchanged what being Jew or Gentile, man or woman, slave
or freeman, meant in general. Through their experience of a new
citizenship, Christians came to be aware of a new form of politics.

Ekklesia *as* Polis*: The New Language*

This experience was to find expression in a new language, as is always
the case with a new form of life.[33] This language is not of course
simply invented. It develops out of the linguistic world which is
already inhabited. The New Testament took up the vocabulary of
citizenship side by side with the vocabulary of family which was
customarily used in religious communities, and the conceptual
importance for political ethics of this adoption has not hitherto
been sufficiently appreciated Here Meeks is in good company,

[32] Slavery was a constitutive factor in the economy of the ancient world, where the
slave market to some extent fulfilled the same function as the labour market today,
serving to expand the working capacity of an economic unit (at that time the *oikos*)
beyond its own resources. Seen in this light, the—uncontested—economic function
of the master–slave relationship counted as secondary in the early Church compared
with the political status of slaves as full citizens of the Church's *polis*, and as brothers
of their masters. This priority showed itself, for example, in the case of marriage,
where the Church stood up for the slave's right 'to marry in the Lord'—if need be,
against the master's will. At a later period the head of a Christian household was also
obliged to consent if a slave decided for the monastic life. Cf. here O. O'Donovan,
The Desire of the Nations (1996), 264 ff.
[33] Cf. Luther: 'All words are made new when they are transferred from their place
into a different one' (*Omnia vocabula fiunt nova, quando e suo foro in alienum transferuntur* (WA 39 I, 231, 1–3)).

inasmuch as he is unable fully to appraise the details he himself presents—for example, when he points out that *ekklesia*, the term which the early community used for itself, already had a political background. In Greek it was most often used as a term for the voting assembly of free citizens of the *polis*. This was still the case even under the Empire, although by then this assembly was already marginalized.[34] We have to take this background into account, at least in the Gentile and Hellenistically influenced Pauline congregations.

It is true that the Christian use of the term (in its early form as *ekklesia tou theou*, 'the assembly of God') was probably mainly prompted by the term *qᵉhal el*. This was used in apocalyptic Judaism for 'God's End-time gathering', so it fitted in well with the way Christians saw themselves—as the community of the End-time.[35] But it is nevertheless striking that what was chosen as central self-designation should not have been a term drawn from life in the contemporary synagogue—or indeed from the life of the Hellenistic associations.[36] The preferred term had a distinctly political colouring. The secular Hellenistic background of the popular assembly shines through the biblical usage, especially where *ekklesia* is used to describe the specific act of the local community in gathering together. Here the political connection of worship is as clear as the fact that the constitution of the Church's *polis* was based on worship. 'In its meetings for worship, it displays its character.'[37] *Ekklesia* was a wide term which could cover both the individual house-congregation and the church of a town or province, which was made up of house-congregations, and it could reach out as far

[34] Meeks, *First Urban Christians*, 79, 108.

[35] J. Roloff, 'ἐκκλησία', *EWNT* i. 1000. The article indeed points out that the etymological derivation of *ek-kalein*, 'to call out', is hardly taken up in the biblical tradition, but in the light of this derivation too a connection can be seen which comes out in the theological motif of the 'gathering' of the End-time people of God. The gathering of the Church from all nations goes together with the 'calling out' from houses and families, and from economic, political, and national contexts. Thus the reconciliation of forms of life begins when their representatives are called out of their exclusive adherence to these forms of life (a household, a political community, a nation).

[36] This is all the more striking since the organization of the early Christian congregations as house-churches is closely parallel to the life of the synagogue. Many synagogue communities—supposedly 480 in Jerusalem in New Testament times—also met in large private houses. See J. Roloff, *Die Kirche im Neuen Testament* (1993), 72.

[37] Ibid. 85, 98.

as 'the church of the nations'. This comprehensive use shows that its political dimension was seen to be distinct from the usual concepts. The *ekklesia* is not tied to any particular external political concept. What turns the different social groupings into the *ekklesia* is rather the inner form of their existence in each case—the same form of life. It is this, and not the way in which the *ekklesia* differs from particular political concepts of sociality, or the need to draw a line between itself and other representatives of the same concept (a particular house as distinct from other houses, a city as distinct from other cities, a people among other peoples), which constitutes its political existence.

We can see the same thing from the way the term *polis* was explicitly taken over to describe the life of the *ekklesia*. Here too a Jewish term was probably initially taken over from the Septuagint; but with reference to *the* city, Jerusalem, what had been a somewhat unspecific designation had taken on a specific theological colouring, with an eschatological slant. But at the same time, in the political understanding of the *ekklesia*, this eschatological colouring had its presentative aspect. It is true that in the Epistle to the Hebrews hope for the future city, the city 'with a firm foundation', goes together with the awareness that here we have 'no abiding city' (Heb. 13: 14); but for all that, the same epistle can describe the nomadic existence of the wandering people of God in politically presentative terms as 'having come to the city of the living God' (12: 22). And although in the book of Revelation the eschatological expectation of the holy city (*hagia polis*, Rev. 21: 2) is contrasted with the present experience of what the city is, in the form of Babylon–Rome, its citizenship is none the less seen as recruited *in the present* from the throng of the men and women who 'resist'.

EXCURSUS

In an interpretation of the final vision of the heavenly Jerusalem in the book of Revelation,[38] Dieter Georgi has worked out how the term *polis* which the book adopts is linked with specific details which allow us to say 'that the book of Revelation offers political theology' (p. 352). In his view, the description of the heavenly *polis* presents the vision of the ideal

---

[38] D. Georgi, 'Die Visionen vom himmlischen Jerusalem in Apk 21 and 22', in *Kirche: Festschrift für G. Bornkamm* (1980). The page numbers in the text refer to this essay.

Hellenistic city (p. 368). Georgi works out the way in which Revelation modifies Ezekiel's prophetic vision of the heavenly Jerusalem (Ezek. 40–7). Whereas in his description of the coming city, Ezekiel concentrates almost entirely on the Temple, the Temple is missing altogether in the Johannine vision of the new city (Rev. 21: 22). 'In Ezekiel the Temple is the seat of the divine *kabod* (43: 2); in John that seat is the city itself (21: 11)' (p. 362).

The gates of the heavenly city are always open (Rev. 21: 25). They no longer stand for the need for security and separation among people and political communities, but allow the gaze to travel inwards, to civil life within the walls. 'Whereas in the oriental and Greek city the sanctuary or sanctuaries were in the centre of the city, and the city was orientated towards them, the hellenistic city... is defined by its population, and is characterized by its streets and squares as a place where the people gather together to communicate with each other. The new Jerusalem is an open, democratic city of this kind' (p. 368).

The use of the terms *politeuma* and *politeuomai* in the New Testament writings fits in with this finding; but at the same time it raises another question. A survey of the usage[39] shows that the explicitly political meaning of *politeuomai*, 'to be a citizen', is to be preferred in all the instances discussed to the unspecific meaning 'to live or conduct oneself', which was also common. The question which then arises is of fundamental importance. On the one hand Paul can talk about 'our *politeuma* being in heaven' (Phil. 3: 20), but on the other hand he admonishes the same congregation to 'be citizens' (*politeuesthe*) in their present lives 'worthy of the gospel' (Phil. 1: 27). The problem touched on here is the difficulty of a many-stranded citizenship, in heaven, in the Church, and in the secular community. And we can focus on it more clearly if we note how in their differentiating use of words the New Testament traditions have taken up constructively their own contemporary political experience in the Roman Empire. Even before New Testament times, the absolute division between *polites* and *idiotes* in the *polis* of Greek antiquity had broken down through the emergence of an intermediate level. Between full Roman citizens, the indigenous population, and the downgraded, there were now what were known as *paroikoi*, a group of foreigners (themselves differentiated into different groups) who were permanently resident in the cities of the Empire. These

---

[39] U. Hutter, 'πολίτευμα; πολιτεύομαι', *EWNT* iii. 310–12.

were not integrated into the framework of civic rights, like the Jews, for example, with their independent *politeumata*; yet their opportunities for participating in public life had grown in the course of time.

This difference between full citizens and 'strangers', those without full civil rights, is taken up by the authors of the New Testament epistles as a way of describing the existence of believers. On the one hand this distinction is used in the Letter to the Ephesians to describe the change in status which members of the congregation have experienced in the *polis* of the Church. As Gentiles they had formerly been 'strangers' or 'aliens', and although always included in the divine plan in which everyone was to be drawn in, they had nevertheless been practically speaking excluded from the *politeia* of the people of the covenant (Eph. 2: 12). But now they have been 'brought near' through Christ, and have been made fellow citizens with the saints (Eph. 2: 19).[40]

This distinction is used a second time, however, to describe the relation between the *polis* of the Church and the public life of the state.

Citizens and Resident Aliens

Here the existence of the Christian community is now defined precisely in the sense of the worldly political status which has been left behind in favour of the political status enjoyed in the Church. Now Christians will let themselves be addressed as *paroikoi* (strangers), *parepidenoi* (sojourners), and *xenoi* (foreigners), people who are aliens in the earthly *polis*, not full citizens, newcomers not native inhabitants, foreigners not 'nationals'.[41] Although these terms become noticeably more frequent in writings

---

[40] See H. Schlier, 'Die Kirche nach dem Brief an die Epheser', in *idem, Die Zeit der Kirche* (1972), 176. With 'the God-fearing' and the proselytes, the Jewish religion too accepted varying shades of adherence to the people of God.

[41] I Pet. 1: 1, 2: 11; Heb. 11: 13, and elsewhere. Cf. here in general R. Feldmeier, *Die Christen als Fremde* (1992). The Christians evidently saw themselves as a separate civil community within local life in the civil polity of the empire, even if they were not recognized as such by the state. This is emphatically documented in a testimony dating from the second century, the Epistle to Diognetus: 'Yet while living in Greek and barbarian cities . . . and following the local customs both in clothing and food and in the rest of life, they shew forth the wonderful and confessedly strange character of the constitution of their own citizenship. They dwell in their own fatherlands, but as if sojourners in them; they share all things as citizens, and suffer all things as strangers' (5.4 f.; trans. Kirsopp Lake).

belonging to the period when the state authorities became increasingly hostile, this self-interpretation was nevertheless still part of the apostolic inheritance, and there was no way of getting around it. It is formulated, for example, in the salutation of 1 Clement. 'The church of God, which is a stranger in Rome, to the congregation which is a stranger in Corinth.' Life as a Christian continued to be determined by this dialectic. However the worldly political status of a believer was defined, in the Church he was raised to full citizenship; whatever the definition of a believer's political status in the world, as a full citizen of the Church's *polis*, he can be no more than a *paroikos* in the secular community.

This dialectic permits neither the simple contrasting of the two statuses, nor simply the notion of 'the citizen of two worlds' who has to behave according to his status in the place where he happens to be. (This was a traditional though questionable interpretation of the doctrine of the two kingdoms.) The point here is rather what has always been presupposed by both ancient and medieval thinkers, and in modern thinking too: the assumption that the relative position of different statuses in a person's life must always involve a particular trend. The one status is always partly determined by the other, and this is bound to make itself felt at latest where the two conflict. For citizens of the Church in the first century, this conflict still had deadly consequences, as the Roman authorities were obliged to require Christians too to put their secular political status first. But because Christians saw themselves primarily as citizens of the Church, this 'status inconsistency' led in many cases to suffering. They thereby testified to the fact that, since in the *ekklesia* there are only full citizens, in the world these people can only be 'strangers'. To put it in pneumatological terms: God's Spirit, which rules the *ekklesia*, relativizes the ties with all the different political, economic, and ethnic systems which are determined by another spirit, the spirit of self-preservation.

Nevertheless, there were undoubtedly examples showing that the upward mobility of *paroikoi* was possible, even their rising to political careers; and these instances also show that this Christian definition of existence, where it touched on the contemporary model, could not be understood as negative *in principle*, in the sense that it could be understood to mean exclusion from the political life of society as a whole. For as *paroikoi*, Christians did not live as emigrants from society, either in the abstract or in fact. They lived *in*

society as 'resident aliens'.[42] So in 1 Peter the congregation's interpretation of itself as 'strangers and guests' is directly related to the
way its members behaved (and had to behave) as citizens of the
state (1 Pet. 2: 11, 13 ff.). Initially, political abstinence on the part of
Christians with regard to the sharing of political power apparently
seemed appropriate on both sides—that is, by both State and
Church—and was unavoidable, in view of the religious grounding
of political life in the Empire;[43] but the image of the *paroikos*
nevertheless implies that political participation was a possibility in
principle.

In actual fact, however, participation presupposed that politics
would renounce its totalizing character, and that its concept of citizenship would move away from the claim that this status has to
dominate all others. But from this perspective it now becomes evident that, through its very resistance, Christianity contributed decisively to the demolition of any such claim, so that it itself, as it were,
made it possible for Christians to share in public life and political
power. This line of development is admittedly difficult to fit into the
scheme of Church history as a falling away, a history which shows
how the pristine ideal of the early Church, with its apolitical character, foundered in the age of the 'Constantinian temptation', when the
Church was no longer able to resist the seduction of power.[44] Instead
of applying any such template, we should note that the possibility of
explicit political participation in power is already implied in the
narrative perspective of that history, which has to do with the
reconciliation of the antinomies on which every form of political
totality depends. In what way is this reconciliation present in the
language of the New Testament? We have already seen how both
the basic linguistic worlds are taken up—the world of the *oikos* and
the world of the *polis*. The community of Jesus Christ sees itself
both as 'the family of God' and as 'citizens of heaven'.

---

[42] Cf. the best seller by S. Hauerwas and W. H. Willimon, *Resident Aliens* (1989);
also W. Stringfellow, *An Ethic for Christians and Other Aliens in a Strange Land* (1978).

[43] Tertullian, e.g., could still say: 'For us nothing is more alien than public life'
(*Nobis nulla magis res aliena quam publica* (*Apologeticum*, 38)).

[44] This is not to dispute the fact that this temptation existed. But it did not arise
for the first time in the Constantinian era. It was already present once the Gallienus
Edict of 260 increasingly opened up opportunities for Christians to participate in
public communal life. Particularly in this intermediate period, when civil life was still
pagan through and through, Christian soldiers, members of the municipal authorities, or state officials in the performance of their civic duties always had to tread a
tightrope if they wanted to avoid apostasy—or martyrdom.

But another observation is important too. For it is not only that these two ideas are taken up to describe the life of the Church, somewhat naively, in spite of their tension. We also find texts which explicitly and unequivocally express the reconciliation in the Church's new form of life of forms of living that had hitherto been antagonistic. It is not surprising that the most concentrated evidence for this should be found in the Epistle to the Ephesians, which thinks about the meaning of the Church particularly profoundly. Here the writer points to the politically exciting consequence of the fact that through Christ both Jews and Gentiles have access to the Father in the one Spirit. 'So you are now no longer strangers without citizens' rights. You are *fellow citizens* with the saints and members of the *household* of God' (*sympolitai ton hagion kai oikeioi tou theou*, Eph. 2: 19). It must be said, however, that explicit formulations of this kind are somewhat rare, which rather suggests that the congregations originally took a naïve view in this respect. The sparseness of the references indicates that the congregations did not at first develop a concept of the bond between *oikos* and *polis*. Instead, the texts testify to a growing awareness which had grown up gradually with the experience of the new life in the Body of Christ: the awareness that here a form of life has come into being which cannot be fitted into the traditional antinomies.

Such a growing theological sense of this new, special modality also emerges in another writing, which is marked by special interest in the programmatic character of the Church's life: Luke's Acts of the Apostles already etches these intertwining forms of life into his account of the growth of the Pauline congregations. According to Luke's narrative, Paul tried to find connecting links for his mission both in the *public* life of the forum or synagogue and in the houses of *private* patrons or professional colleagues, such as Prisca and Aquilla. This accepted intertwining of public and private worlds, even in the founding period of the congregations, reflects the ecclesiological definition of the community of believers which Luke sees to be of the essence. In order to understand the extent of what was new for the life of the Church as it is described in the summary accounts in Acts, it may be helpful to remind ourselves of the antagonism existing in the life of the *polis* as the ancient world saw it. As Hannah Arendt comments, this meant 'that man received "besides his private life a sort of second life, his *bios politikos*. Now every citizen belongs to two orders of existence; and there is a sharp distinction in his life between what is his own (*idion*) and what is communal (*koinon*)." '[45] It was precisely these two Greek key-words, showing the contrast between two orders of being, which—surely hardly by chance—we find related to each other in Luke in a completely different way: 'The company of those who believed were of one heart and soul, and no one said that any of the things which he possessed was his own (*idion*), but they had everything in common (*koina*)' (Acts 4: 32). Is Luke not also pointing here to the departure from the hitherto obtaining 'ontology' of political life, where the sense of these counter-orders of being— the private and the public, the domestic and the political—were viewed as antagonistic?

It is true that in discussing the summary account in Acts scholars also talk about a romanticization of the real circumstances (or at least of the extent to which these circumstances actually existed); but the fact remains that this truly revolutionary 'grammar' of political life was not something that was simply affirmed; it went hand in hand with the establishment of a form of social life in which this reconciliation was really lived. So when in the second century the pagan apologist Celsus described the Christian congregations as attracting only the simple-minded, the disreputable, slaves, women, and little children, he may not have captured the actual sociological structure of the congregation, but he undoubtedly hit the nail on the head politically. A religious group which saw itself as a political community in its own right, and at the same time turned the existing foundations of political existence upside-down by pronouncing representatives of the *oikos*, the useless 'idiots', to be full citizens of their 'commonwealth',[46] was bound, as Celsus real-ized, to be either deranged (in both senses) or dangerous. As Augustine was to find at the end of the Roman Empire, both verdicts were to prove well founded: because through Christianity the ancient ontology of political existence was so fundamentally deranged, the Empire, touched at its vital spot, was unable to survive.

---

[45] Arendt, *Human Condition*, 24, quoting Werner Jaeger's *Paideia* (1945), iii. 111.
[46] The striking inclusiveness of the Christian congregations, in the sense of 'the universal way'—the *via universalis*—could be seen especially in the regard they paid to the poor. Whereas in the late period of the Roman Empire, this increasing group was excluded from the traditional proofs of beneficence offered by the notables—it was citizens' rights which opened the way to these donations, not need—the welfare

Worship as the Public Life of the Congregation

The Church's new form of life was rooted in the practice of worship, and it is there that it is manifested in a primary way. It will hardly be by chance that the context of most of the texts cited above points to the connection between the two: form of life and worship. Thus in his famous words in Galatians 3: 26 ff. about the differences which have been abolished, Paul talks about those who have been *baptized* into the one body, and in Luke's description of the community of property practised in the early congregation, he explicitly associates this in the preceding section with devotion to the apostles' teaching, fellowship (in worship), the breaking of bread, and prayer (Acts 2: 42, 44). In worship, the congregation experiences the reconciliation of antitheses which had hitherto been deemed irreconcilable. The new relation between private and public life was the structural mark of Christian worship, and can be traced back to its beginnings. Even if the tradition that crystallized in the first centuries seems to have been still very open, and to have taken many forms, and even though the documentary evidence as a whole is too fragmentary for us to draw a complete picture of the worship life of early Christianity and the early Church, certain elements can still be clearly identified.

We are indebted to Dom Gregory Dix in his epochal work on liturgical history[47] for tracing the development of eucharistic worship in a meticulous study of the sources. His thesis, that Christian worship had a double origin, is still generally accepted today, even if the emphasis would sometimes differ. According to Dix, worship was fed by two different sources, and their confluence in Christian

---

of the poor belonged to the subjective viewpoint of the Christian congregations from the beginning. And this was not just a matter of a gracious condescension. *Pauperes*, the poor, was a word which Christians applied to themselves early on. It shows that the congregations felt that in some sense they belonged to that 'other city' which could describe the quarters of the poor. As John Chrysostom stressed, this universality was based on the fact that beggars and the wealthy stepped into the baptistry together, and were all fed by the gifts of the altar (*Homiliae in I Cor.* 10, 1; PG 51, 247 AB). In accordance with this viewpoint, the poor were not left alone in the semi-obscurity of charitable care, but played a particular public and (ecclesiastically) political role. For together with other groups marginalized by Rome's civil law, the unmarried monks and virgins, they escorted the bishop as mounted entourage on his public appearances, and as his special clientele played an important part in the choice of a new bishop, as the designated 'friend of the poor'. Cf. Brown, *Power and Persuasion*, 77 f.

[47] G. Dix, *The Shape of the Liturgy* (1945).

liturgy already points to its double (public and private) character. The one source was the public worship of the Jewish synagogue, the other the meeting in private houses to celebrate the Lord's Supper.[48] In the first centuries these two forms of liturgical celebration—the *synaxis* (an assembly whose order comprises reading, sermon and prayer, following the model of the synagogue) and the Eucharist—exist independently of each other but also in combination (the *synaxis* preceding the Eucharist), and from the fourth century onwards the two are regularly linked together in a single service of worship.

Dix then draws the following picture of the private/public character of worship as it developed, and the problems raised by his analysis will concern us here. After Jewish Christians had been excluded from the worship of the synagogue (an exclusion which took place at widely different periods in different regions—in the Syrian area, for example, Christians participated in Jewish worship right down to the fourth century, or formed a synagogue congregation of their own), Christian worship had become 'a highly *private* activity', and had hence reverted to its original character: 'Their specifically Christian worship is from the first a domestic and private thing' (p. 16). This only changed three centuries later, according to Dix's analysis, when in the period of tolerant or Christian rulers, with their encouragement of Christianity, it was possible to talk about a shift 'From a Private to a Public Worship' (pp. 304 ff.). Dix sees the unmistakable sign of this transformation in the place where worship was held, as this moved from the closed-off world of private houses to the largely visible publicity of the early basilicas, which from the middle of the third century accommodated the growing number of believers.

Now, this historical outline simplifies the question about the public character of worship in a way that blocks perceptions which are of essential importance for political ethics. In my view, it is not least the textual witnesses which Dix himself analyses which make it clear that to be public does not merely, as Dix's account suggests, indicate a frame of reference for early Christian worship which is determined by the external conditions in any given case. The Church's central celebration does not acquire its public character from the access it offers to a surrounding public, to which it can

---

[48] Ibid. 36.

relate or on which it can rely. On the contrary, as we shall see, it constitutes a public life of its own. If Dix's theory were correct, it would mean, strictly speaking, that the Christian congregations would have had to understand their God in analogy to the household gods of Rome; these were worshipped in private, and had a more personal relationship to the house-communities they patronized than did the gods of the civil religion, who were publicly worshipped for the benefit of the state, and whose cult put its stamp on the rhythms of life and its festivals in the state as a whole.[49]

If the Christians had viewed their worship as a private domestic cult, they could easily have enjoyed the religious tolerance bestowed by the Roman authorities in this respect, and would have been spared the experience of martyrdom. As it was, martyrdom was inevitable, since the *ekklesia* was bound from the beginning to celebrate 'political worship'. It could not worship the Lord of the cosmos as the penates were worshipped; it had to do so in a way which its pagan environment could not avoid viewing as an insult to the gods of the state, and was bound to suffer the sanctions imposed upon an 'atheism' hostile to the state. From this viewpoint, the pagan opponents of the congregations grasped the claim of Christ as 'civic God' better than many Christians and theologians in the later course of history, especially in modern times. In the worship of the God of the Christians in their services, however, forms of speech and forms of life were intertwined in the way analysed above. As civic God, he was not fobbed off with the contribution which citizens of the Empire could spare for the public deities, which was often paid merely as a matter of duty. He was also worshipped as Abba, dear Father, in accordance with the familiar and emotional language which in the pagan environment was normally reserved for the household gods. It was precisely Christ's claim to the whole of life which really disqualified him as the God of a civil religion. For all that, in the course of its historical existence Christianity repeatedly allowed itself to adopt the civil religion role; but this was possible only at the expense of the 'family' claim of Christ.

EXCURSUS

In spite of Christianity's recognition of state authority in principle (Rom. 13: 1–7; 1 Pet. 2: 13–17), the establishment of its own public life in wor-

---

[49] G. Dix, *The Shape of the Liturgy* (1945) 316.

ship—and it was only this that made Christian assemblies of such interest for the authorities—went so far in certain sectors that some functions of state sovereignty were claimed for the Church's own public life. In 1 Corinthians 6: 1–7, for instance, Paul demands that civil disputes, if they cannot be avoided, should not be settled by pagan courts but should be laid before internal congregational tribunals. Here, where the new congregational form of life is at stake, the state is to be conceded no power to judge. This admonition led to the development of an institutionalized assumption of the task of arbitration. This arbitration was entrusted to a Christian 'synhedrin' composed of presbyters and chaired by the bishop, which met regularly. In the light of the admonition in the Sermon on the Mount to be reconciled with one's adversary before offering a sacrifice (Matt. 5: 23)—an injunction already taken up in the instructions about the eucharistic celebration in the *Didache* (14. 2)— the Syrian *Didascalia of the Apostles* required these arbitration tribunals to be held at the beginning of the week, in order to allow enough time for matters to be settled before the Sunday. The part played by the kiss of peace before the Eucharist makes it clear that the service of worship was effective not only as the driving force for reconciliation, but because it itself put a seal on the reconciliation. The exchange of this sign of reconciliation between believers, which was taken over from Judaism, was sometimes accompanied by the crying out of 'formal precautions' ('Is there any one of you who has something against the other?') or admonitions ('Let none (give the kiss) hypocritically').[50]

The unavoidably public character of worship is indicated in a special way by the distinction made between different forms of assembly in the Christian congregations themselves. Dix has clearly traced the way in which this differentiation soon came to be terminologically unified. From Paul onwards, *ekklesia* means the formal assembly of the (whole) congregation, its *synaxis* or *eucharistia*. There was another kind of meeting in addition (the *syneleusis*), for the purpose of instruction, for mutual edification, or for the celebration of the *agape*, as love meal. This form of assembly, which was geared rather to private peer groups in the congregation, had a religious character, but not a liturgical one, since the public exercise of the ministry (by specifically ordained persons) was missing. These different levels were strictly differentiated, at latest from the time of Justin,[51] and in Ignatius we find urgent admonitions not to misunderstand these private meetings for edification as a

---

[50] Ibid. 106 f.
[51] Ibid. 20.

substitute for participation in public worship (Ign. Mag. 7. 1). It is public worship alone, as the central celebration of the local *ekklesia*, which makes it possible to fulfil as a Christian the duty of a 'personal' liturgy. The strong stress on the role and presence of the ordained minister in Ignatius, for example, must not be interpreted too hastily as already the inauguration of a 'hierarchical Catholic ministerial principle'. What it expresses initially is rather a sense of the *public* character of worship, where the difference from private meetings for edification is shown by the presence of the ordained office.

The fact that Dix and others[52] fail to perceive the significance of this difference in its bearing on the character of the worshipping assembly, which was public from the beginning, may be connected with the circumstance that both forms of meeting took place in private houses.[53] This could suggest that the domestic context of the meeting also determined its form. It is true that the warm family atmosphere of these meetings, which extended even to their language, would fit in with this assumption, as would the fact that the heads of households had themselves baptized 'with their whole house', which at that time could have included not only the nuclear family but other relations, slaves, and freed persons, as well as people employed on a wage basis, tenants, and business partners. At a time when it was usual for clients to share their patron's religion,[54] and when large households, at least, could also serve as base for an association or cultic group, it might therefore well seem plausible to see the early Christian house-congregation as an analogy. In addition, it must have been wealthy citizens who were able to accommodate the congregational services in their houses, and to provide food and drink for the congregation. The New Testament leaves us no doubt that patronage of this kind certainly offered an important base for the worshipping life of the first congregations. Some of these

[52] P. F. Bradshaw, 'Gottesdienst IV', *TRE* 14 (1985), 40 f., follows Dix in describing 'the development from private to public worship'. He deduces that worship was originally 'private' from the fact that its central moment was open only to Christians (arcane disipline). But here too an over-simplified concept of 'public' (where 'private' can be understood only in antithesis to the public life of the state) hinders further differentiation within this counter-existence to public life as the state knew it.

[53] See here generally H.-J. Klauck, *Hausgemeinde und Hauskirche im frühen Christentum* (1981), and, more recently, *Gemeinde zwischen Haus und Stadt* (1992).

[54] See Meeks, *First Urban Christians*, 31.

heads of households are named, finding a mention when local congregations are called 'the *ekklesia* in so-and-so's house'.[55]

In spite of this, however, there were significant differences between the congregation gathered for worship 'in so-and-so's house'
and both the customary household cults and the social model of the
household in general. The very fact that it was the *public* worship of
the local *ekklesia* which required a sufficiently large assembly room
(unlike the meeting of friends in a small group) means that we have
to be cautious about over-hasty analogies. Moreover, the congregation 'in so-and-so's house' was normally by no means identical
with the patron's house-church. On the one hand, the religious
freedom of individual members of the *oikos* to refrain from
attending the meeting of the *ekklesia* could not be denied, and on
the other hand, the number of participants in the meeting of the
ekklesia extended in principle beyond the members of the house
hosting the assembly. The dramatic situation which inevitably
arose for Jewish Christians when houses were thrown open for the
worshipping public is reflected in the events which followed the
'council of the apostles'; these circumstances had led Paul to make
sharp attacks on Peter and other Jewish Christians, after they had
first implemented the previously agreed fellowship with the Gentile
Christians through table fellowship with them, and then, under the
influence of the strict Jewish–Christian group around James, revoked it (Gal. 2: 11 ff.). The background of these events was probably the contemporary Jewish practice of encouraging non-Jews to
participate in the worship of the synagogue, and of at least tolerat-
ing their presence in the outer courts of the Temple,[56] while strictly
forbidding any association with them in private houses (Acts 10:
28). The unusually sharp tone of Paul's expostulation now becomes
doubly understandable when he publicly (*emprosthen panton*) 'with-
stood [Peter] to the face' (Gal. 2: 14), accusing him of departing
from the truth of the gospel; for what was at stake here was not just
the fellowship between Jewish and Gentile Christians in the church;
it was also the fact that went with it—that the (worship) life of the
church could not be made congruent with the *oikos* paradigm.

---

[55] Ibid. 75 f.
[56] On this complex problem, cf. S. Safrai, *Die Wallfahrt im Zeitalter des Zweiten
Tempels* (1981).

Another observation confirms this, since it signalizes a profound difference between the order of social life in the *oikos* and that in the congregation. The household (in Latin the *domus* or *familia*) was structurally defined in the first instance not through kinship but by relations of dependence and subordination towards the paterfamilias.[57] In the community of the church, relations were different. Direct dependence on the patron and absolute subordination to his natural authority in the household broke down, since now both parties, clientele and patron alike, were subject to the same Lord. When Paul sends back the runaway slave Onesimus to his master as 'brother', his starting-point in his expectation of the way Philemon will behave is that he will accept that Onesimus's new status as citizen of the church's *polis* takes precedence over the traditional disentitling definition of his status as slave and non-person. So here, contrary to traditional usage, the term 'brother' should really no longer be understood as a word taken from the language of the family. It belongs to the political vocabulary of the church,[58] and determines the 'brother's' role in the *oikos* too, giving it a new direction. Consequently Paul can also couch his recommendation in the tones of apostolic authority; for the authority enjoyed by the head of the household has now to be employed in responsibility towards another authority still: the authority of God, the congregation of his people, and its leader.

We find a particularly striking example of this remodelling in the dispute in which Paul was forced to engage in the community in Corinth, in connection with the eucharistic celebrations there (1 Cor. 11: 17 ff.). He complains that when the congregation meets, it is not the Lord's Supper (*kyriakon deipnon*) that is celebrated. On the contrary, everyone eats his own supper (*idion deipnon*), and some go hungry while others get drunk. Gerd Theissen offers an interesting analysis of the possible socio-morphological background of this conflict, believing that light can be thrown on it if we assume that there was a clash between two social classes in the

[57] Meeks, *First Urban Christians*, 30.

[58] Accordingly Paul also stresses the double character of Onesimus's newly acquired brotherhood for his master Philemon: 'both in the flesh and in the Lord' (Philem. 16). The (really unnecessary) mention of 'the flesh' is aimed at the possible misunderstanding that 'in the Lord' means that the brotherhood must be seen according to a purely religious perspective. Through his addition Paul makes it clear that the brotherhood does not exist just in God's eyes, but is a political category which defines the particular character of social relationships within the congregation.

community which was already mirrored in the domestic setting.[59] According to his view, the 'have-nots' were shamed by 'the haves', the people who 'had houses' where they could also eat. These people would eat their own lavish fare (*idion deipnon*), which they had brought with them, before the Eucharist, so that all that was left for the 'have-nots' (some of whom probably also came later, straight from work) was what was required for ritual consumption.[60]

EXCURSUS

Theissen compares the situation in the early Christian congregation meeting in the house of a wealthy host with other occasions on which a patron of this kind would give a banquet. It was then usual to invite both the freed clientele as well as various friends or business partners. However, these invitations also gave the host the opportunity to parade the social differences between the guests through the arrangement of the tables and the differing quality and quantity of the dishes served to equals and to dependents—a fact which is the subject of frequent comment in the literature of late antiquity.[61] So when a certain Gaius, for example, opened his house for the whole *ekklesia* in Corinth (Rom. 16: 23), it would not be particularly surprising if he saw himself in the role of a host in the ancient world when he organized the eucharistic service together with a preceding class-specific meal designed to satisfy the hunger of the guests.

In his essay, Theissen reminds us that 'the wealthier Christians were not simply inviting the whole congregation, but in doing so were also at the same time inviting some of their peers who belonged to it. Within the framework of social intercourse among Christians of equal standing, those ordinary standards for solicitousness and hospitality, which applied socially apart from the congregational life, could not suddenly be suspended. It was part of such expectations, for example, that there would be meat to eat (1 Cor. 10.27–28).' In addition: 'To justify the exclusion of other Christians from "their own meal", the wealthier Christians could formally appeal to the paradosis of the Lord's Supper itself, which applied only to bread and wine. Whatever went beyond that could be declared part of a "private meal".' (p. 161)

If Theissen is correct, the target of Paul's criticism would have been not only the specific bad behaviour of a greedy section of the

[59] G. Theissen, 'Social Integration and Sacramental Activity', in *idem, The Social Setting of Pauline Christianity* (1982), 148–51.
[60] Ibid. 151–6.
[61] Ibid. 156–8.

congregation but also, once again, the interpretation of the practice
of worship as an analogy to the private world in general. The heart
of his criticism would then be that the Lord's Supper is not a private
celebration. This interpretation is endorsed if we note the emphatic
language in which Paul expresses his criticism. According to this,
the 'meeting' would not be a 'Lord's Supper' because everyone
enjoys his 'own' supper (*idion deipnon*). As we have already seen,
idion is a word used to signalize the private sphere. So Paul's
challenging contrast seems quite logical: 'Do you not have houses
(*oikias*) to eat and drink in? Or do you despise the church (*tes
ekklesias*) of God?' (1 Cor. 11: 22). Here Paul makes it unmistakably
clear that the house-congregations are not to live by the laws of the
private household; for the (worship) life of the *ekklesia*, as a public
and political affair, has to be distinguished from private life. It is
surely this that is the target of the phrase about 'distinguishing the
body' (*diakrinon to soma*, v. 29; RSV: 'discerning the body'). It is
calling not for a distinction between the sacred feast and 'profane'
meat and drink, but for respect for the body in its special political
significance.[62]

The Integration of the 'Household' into the Political Order of the Church

We have seen that already in the New Testament worship did not
belong to the sphere of the private cult; nor could it be understood
structurally as belonging within the paradigm of private life. It was
indeed its public character which broke up patterns of behaviour
which had hitherto been unquestioned in the worlds of both public
and private life. In the reconciliation of the two forms of life, the
public character of worship could not mean that private life was
now to be ignored, but the new relationship had to bring out the
political dimension of private life as well, in its significance for the
public life of the church's *polis*. Where one person had something

---

[62] J. Roloff, 'Heil als Gemeinschaft', in *idem, Exegetische Verantwortung in der
Kirche* (1990), 194. The older assumption was that the criticism is aimed not so
much at a privileged social group as at the spiritualist Enthusiasts in Corinth, whom
Paul talks about in another passage. But even if this theory were to be preferred to
Theissen's thesis, the conclusion drawn above still stands. For the lofty 'spiritual'
attitude of these Spiritualists, which was 'above' the marginalia of physical existence
(a superiority which may have covered their own gluttony just as much as the hunger
of other people) is ultimately based on an individualistic, private conviction which is
interested only in private experience, the public existence of the congregation being
at most of instrumental importance.

against another, however 'private' that something might be, the public life of the congregation was affected. It was then no longer able to celebrate worship as *ekklesia*, the *whole* body of Christ.

The life of a community as a whole is inescapably marked by the conflicts provoked by the dissimilarity of its members (a fact which was conducive to the political exclusiveness which we noted in Greek political theory); and this is also true of the church. The church differs from other communities not because it experiences itself directly as an original harmony, but because it constitutes a social order in which the regulation of conflicts takes a different course, following neither the barbaric form of merely giving free rein to antagonistic forces, nor the method followed from Greek antiquity onwards, where the problem is viewed as a 'constitutional' one, so that the solution itself has to be incorporated in the community's outward structure. The church, in contrast, is called to solve afresh any conflicts which arise, instead of trying to exclude them through some formal *a priori*—perhaps through the constitutional exclusion of persons or groups which have proved to be the source of special conflict. But its special political character means that the form of life in which it exists in salvation history—that is, reconciliation—is also the *medium* through which it solves conflicts.

The much despised and abused *Haustafeln* (or rules for governing the household) are themselves an example of the way the political form of action is brought into the *oikos*. For their tenor is the demand that believers should behave in essentials no differently at home from the way they behave in public worship. The underlying trend of the *Haustafeln* is that a person should respect the other more than him or herself, and that Christians should subject themselves to one another (Eph. 5: 21). The aim is a way of life springing from recognition of the different charismata in worship, in which the least important function is the one most honoured (1 Cor. 12: 24). It is therefore not surprising that the passages which are usually set aside as *Haustafeln* in both Ephesians and Colossians follow directly on a paranesis about worship in each case. The way the two (*Haustafeln* and worship) are linked in Ephesians through the same grammatical construction (*hypotassomenoi*, Eph. 5: 21) makes it clear that the *Haustafeln* do not so much indicate a new beginning, in the sense of a thematization of private life; in the context of what we have described, they indicate the further development of the 'worship' form of activity in the life lived in the *oikos*, which is now no longer conceived in a private, self-contained sense. Seen in this light, the very existence of the *Haustafeln* provides an important indication of the political character of New Testament ethics. It is a question whether in their present form they should perhaps be understood as a conservative reaction to the unheard-of degree to which the sphere of the *oikos* had changed through its absorption into the *polis* of the church (a change shown, for example, by the fact that women had become Christians even against their husbands' will, 1 Cor. 7: 13); but quite apart from that, their existence as a separate genre shows how the sphere of the household was integrated into the politics of the *ekklesia*. Domestic life was no longer simply a pre-political and pre-ethical sphere, where relations and patterns of behaviour were largely regulated according to the traditional hierarchical functions, and were subject to the patron's power of disposal. Now the patron too is among those who are admonished, as husband, father, and head of the household.

If we look more closely, what proved to be especially significant is the fact that women, children, and slaves are now thought worth admonishing, and are told to fall in with the way of acting practised in the *polis*. The people who up to now have simply had to *behave*, are now called to *act*, and are freed for action. It is true that the same phenotypical demands can be made (for obedience, and so forth) which marked the pattern of the household in antiquity; but since they stand side by side with explicit breaches with the old pattern,[63] they indicate that there was a political awareness of this pattern. Obedience to the old authorities is now also adapted to a new 'obedience', obedience to the authority of the new Lord (Eph. 6: 1, 9) and his citizenship. This obedience can liberate for both subordination and resistance: because subordination is no longer presupposed as 'natural', it can be entered into freely; but it can also be resisted if circumstances so require. Life in the Christian household is not regulated traditionally, according to the accepted hierarchy of powers; nor does it turn this arrangement upside-down in any revolutionary sense. It does not barbarically give free reign to the given forces, but orders them in the field of force of God's

---

[63] Thus Christian slaves were supposed to be prepared to bear suffering 'for conscience's sake'. What is probably meant is preparedness to resist participation in the slave-owner's pagan house cult. Christian women are to live in such a way that they win over their husbands to their own new faith; cf. 1 Pet. 2: 19, 3: 1.

Spirit. That is the political point of the New Testament's *Hausta-feln*, in so far as they are seen in the context of political worship. Abstracted from that, they would certainly be just what they have often been thought to be: a reanimation of the ancient concept of order, with a new Christian colouring.[64]

As we have seen, from the perspective of political worship, the household seems to have been integrated into the political order of the church, inasmuch as it can claim for itself no form of action that follows its own laws. But if the *oikos* is also to be understood 'politically', does this not mean that it disappears altogether as a sphere with a dignity of its own? A politicization of this kind is clearly not the case, however. There is no talk of abolishing or disparaging this form of life anywhere in the New Testament—on the contrary. The ancient world's recognition of the household's specific form of activity (labour, meaning dealings with the neces- sities of life) went hand in hand with a belittling consignment to the pre-political sphere, whereas its *political* interpretation corresponds to the Christian form of acknowledgement of this form of life: it is worthy of action.

The profoundly thought-out formula in Ephesians 2: 19 which we have already cited illuminates this connection in its own way: 'You are therefore no longer strangers without citizens' rights; you are fellow citizens with the saints, and members of the household of God.' It is first of all clear that the assurance of citizen status for all members of the *ekklesia* now also means that the connection

---

[64] The New Testament writings which tend most strongly in this direction are undoubtedly the pastoral epistles. Their 'class' paraneses and their 'mirror for office- holders' belong to a specifically domestic congregational order. They make the *oikos* the paradigm for congregational structure and behaviour. On the other hand, the book of Revelation, which was written about the same time, concentrates on the *polis* motif. Unlike the treatment of the *oikos* motif in the Pauline tradition, the theme in the pastoral epistles is not so much aimed at the community of believers as 'family of God' as at the institutional character of a household order (*oikonomia*, 1 Tim. 1: 4) for that community. In the congregation as 'God's home economics', the office- bearer, who represents the heavenly 'house despot' (2 Tim. 2: 21), fulfils the representative role of steward (Titus 1: 7). The theological problem raised by the pastoral epistles is therefore not, as has been continually said, their tendency towards an adaptation of Christianity to civic society. The precise opposite is the case: the problem is that they do not sufficiently take the civic and political aspect into account. The difficulty is the one-sided domestic orientation, which must be judged a regression from the reconciliation between *oikos* and *polis*, and their mutual interpenetration, which we find in the picture of Christian ethics presented in the New Testament as a whole.

between *oikos* and *polis* can no longer be solely the affair of the paterfamilias, who had hitherto been the only person who had occupied both spheres. But in addition, the specific way in which the language of family and citizenship in the text is related to life with God, or with one's fellow human beings, is surely not fortuitous, but has a theological basis: it is as fellow householders with God that Christians are fellow citizens. Because in Christ all 'have access to the Father' (Eph. 2: 18), human relationships in the church can only be perceived and lived in a political sense.[65]

At this point we have to consider a possible objection: is the reconciliation of *oikos* and *polis* today still so far-reaching that we can continue to see it as fundamental for political ethics? Can the *oikos* especially still count as an exemplary form of life at all, at a time when in the urban centres single life is increasingly in vogue? Are these 'households' and the households of ancient, medieval, and pre-industrial times not worlds apart? This objection can only be partly countered by pointing out that life in families is the form of life which has determined history as a whole and still determines it at the present time, if we take the world as a whole. Moreover, from the perspective of Christian ethics we must also say that *polis* and *oikos* are fundamental forms of human living, which cannot in principle be superseded. After all, even the attempts to live without

---

[65] John Milbank, in *Theology and Social Theory*, also considers that the antinomy between *polis* and *oikos* in antiquity has been overcome, 'because every household is now a little republic...and the republic itself is a household, including women, children, slaves as well as adult males' (p. 403). However, Milbank ascribes the surmounting of this antinomy to Augustine's conception, and does not derive this idea from the description of the Christian form of life itself. So he pronounces, as a decisively new insight, that difference does not have to mean conflict but can mean peace. It is illuminating, in contrast, to see that Paul, in the very same passage where he talks about 'one body with many members' (a metaphor which could most readily be used to support the notion of 'harmonic peace'), talks about conflict and ambition among the members, and the way they play off the one against the other (1 Cor. 12). Against this, Paul does not directly put forward the inner plausibility of the idea that a body can function only if its members do not act against one another. It is not the concept of the harmonic fusing of differences which is the theological heart of his argument (though it is this idea which underlies the metaphor of the body with many members); it is the fact that the body, as the Body of Christ, comes into being out of reconciliation (through the crucified body of Christ) and exists in reconciliation, which is the new form of the congregation's life. Just because this means that we must expect the differences to be displayed between Christians in the church too (although they know better), the form of life in the church exists in the constant practice of reconciliation, which cannot be put down to the church's nature, but surely to its status in salvation history.

family ties and without political allegiance feed parasitically on these fundamental forms of life, without which they would not be possible at all. At a time when many people try to escape the antagonisms between these forms of life by simply withdrawing from both (instead of seeking their reconciliation), the Church is therefore faced with an additional task. Where fewer and fewer spheres are available where people can meet with family and political life, the Church (which must always be both a family and a political sociality) is challenged to keep these forms of life in view as open to experience.

6.3 THE PRIESTHOOD OF ALL BELIEVERS: STATUS AND MINISTRY IN WORSHIP

Leitourgia: The Irreplaceable Ministry of the Congregation

The end of political exclusiveness in the Church's *polis* did not come about by way of a concept of participation on the basis of equal rights. It ended practically, with the endowment of specific charismata which 'fellow citizens with the saints' accept as their particular office and ministry in worship. In the exercise of these ministries they cross the bounds of their private sphere (their *oikos*, to use the Greek term) and 'become visible'. By acquiring a share in the ministry of reconciliation (2 Cor. 5: 17 ff.), they are no longer *aneu logou*, wordless; what they say and do becomes important— eternally important. In the political thinking of the ancient world, the connection between a person's dignity as a citizen and the office he holds is clearly seen. Aristotle was able to define the citizen in no better way than by saying that he was a man who holds an office.[66] In this light, it is surely not fortuitous that talk about the private citizen (which is actually a contradiction in terms) arose in the pre-liberal, post-feudal phase of the early nation-states, at a time when 'private persons' as the object of the public monopoly of power, were more or less identified as being persons without any office. They were 'the public' in the modern sense of the word: onlookers,

---

[66] *Politics*, 1275b18 f. But Aristotle also numbers among the tasks of every state 'the care of worship'. In this respect too the political offices were conceived in exclusive terms: 'Neither a peasant nor a lower-class artisan may be installed as priest. For it is fitting that the gods should be honoured by citizens' (*Politics*, 1328b15; 1329a28 f.).

who can only meekly say 'yes' to the politics 'made' by a political class.[67]

The political understanding of the Church as the *communio sanctorum*, the communion of saints, is also determined by the meaning of office—a meaning which is already implicit in the self-designation itself. For *communio* is the term used for an association which is identified through a common office or duty (*con-munus*). The Greek term *leitourgia*, which is used as a technical term for the performance of Christian worship, and which has a definitely secular and civic background, points in the same direction.

The word *leitourgia* belongs to the constitutional vocabulary of the Greek city-states, and, as 'people's service', initially meant the service performed by an individual or a group on behalf of the political community. It will hardly be by chance that, in taking over the term for the practice of worship, the Church adopted the usage of the Septuagint, which preferred this term for Temple worship rather than *ourgia*, which was the word normally used for cultic observances in the private or more arcane sense associated with mystery cults, rather than with state religion. In the New Testament the use of *leitourgia* varies. It can designate the priestly ministry in the Temple, or the Pauline mission—even the collection made for the congregation in Jerusalem. But we also already find it applied to the worship of the *ekklesia* (Heb. 8: 6) and, significantly enough, it is used by Paul to mean worship in a wider and inclusive sense: '*leitourgia tes pisteos hymon*'—'the service of your faith' (Phil. 2: 17).[68]

It is in line with this that in his First Letter to the Corinthians, in the chapters about the order of worship, Paul continually urges the multiplicity of the charismata, and the need to see them as practised ministries from which no one is excluded: 'When you come together, *each one* has something: a psalm, a teaching, a tongue, an interpretation. Let all things be done for edification' (1 Cor. 14: 26). The New Testament *ekklesia* certainly had specially called office-holders too, but their ministries, even over against the congregation, are always viewed as serving the ministries of 'the multitude of believers'; they do not marginalize these ministries, let alone replace them. So the Epistle to the Ephesians sees the different

---

[67] Cf. J. Habermas, 'Öffentlichkeit', in *idem, Kultur und Kritik* (1973), 68.
[68] H. Balz, 'λειτουργία', EWNT ii. 858–61.

ministries as related to each other in such a way that the specially
called ministries serve to equip believers for the exercise of their
own particular ministries, and the purpose common to them all is
the building up of the Body of Christ (Eph. 4: 11 f.).[69] Consequently, the existence of specially called ministries in the Church
can by no means be identified *per se* with the clericalization of the
Church's ministry as a whole. It is only when the multifarious,
mutually irreplaceable, and non-interchangeable ministries are
subsumed under a few ministries, professionally exercised, that
the outcome is the inner-church form of exclusiveness which cor-
rodes the political dimension of worship.

In tracing the development of the Eucharist, Dom Gregory Dix
shows[70] that this problematical trend did not make itself felt simply
as emphasis on the episcopal office increased, or when particular
functions in the worship of the early Church came to be set apart for
the bishop, but only when the bishop's functions increased dispro-
portionately compared with those of other office-holders (including
the members of the congregation). In the pre-Nicene period, the
functions which were reserved for the bishop were initially confined
to preaching (in the framework of the *synaxis*) and the offering of
the eucharistic prayer at the Lord's Supper.[71] All other ministerial
acts were the responsibility of other office-holders, ordained or not.
The congregational liturgy had its especially prominent place in the
offertory—the bringing of gifts to the altar. Everyone brought some
bread and wine, or other fruits of the field and their labour, which
were then blessed. The degree to which this liturgical act was seen
as something for the whole congregation is brought out by a custom
in the congregation at Rome, where the 'have-nots', orphans from

---

[69] Orthodox tradition too has retained the view that ordination is not a 'status' of a
separate kind, since in this tradition baptism and confirmation are fundamentally
viewed as introduction into an *ordo* of the Church. In his pneumatologically shaped
ecclesiology, *Being as Communion* (1993), John Zizioulas points out that in the
Orthodox tradition this is precisely the purpose of the ritual union of baptism,
confirmation, and the receiving of the Eucharist: 'The theological significance of
this lies in the fact that *it reveals the nature of baptism and confirmation as being
essentially an ordination*, while it helps us understand better what *ordination itself*
means.' For the person who is baptized and confirmed becomes not merely a
Christian but also a member of the specific *ordo* in the eucharistic community
(ibid. 215 f.).

[70] Dix, *Shape of the Liturgy*.

[71] Ibid. 40.

the papal choir school, brought the water which was mingled with the wine in the chalice.[72]

The trend towards clericalization from the fourth century onwards therefore also showed itself especially in the abolition of the congregational offertory, and in the growth of the prayers surrounding the *b^erakah*, the blessing or thanksgiving, which was taken over from the Jewish domestic liturgy and was now central to the bishop's function. The prayers of intercession too, which were at first offered by the congregation itself—even if generally in silence—and were only 'gathered together' by the deacon (in the collect) were increasingly offered by the ordained office-holder. So in the Middle Ages a fatal equation could develop which has still not been surmounted in many churches, where the relation between ordained ministers and the congregation is the equivalent of the relation between active and passive. Between 'the work of the people' and a proceeding in which some 'say mass', whereas the others 'hear mass',[73] there may historically be only a few centuries; but politically the two are worlds apart. It will hardly be by chance that in the middle of the fourth century the linguistic usage changed in a way which crystallizes this trend. The office of presbyter, till then largely understood in the sense of the Jewish office of elder, becomes 'the priesthood', which is now understood clerically, no longer as the function of the whole congregation.[74]

Even though the churches of the Reformation reversed these trends, and endeavoured to revive 'the priesthood of all believers' according to 1 Peter 2: 9, the politically decisive factor in this idea was even then not always seen with sufficient clarity. Luther's differentiation between 'status' or 'position' (*Stand*) and 'office'

[72] Dix, *Shape of the Liturgy*, 104.

[73] Ibid. 12. Dix lists the shifts in vocabulary which indicate the change, and stresses how the early phrase 'doing the liturgy' was used quite indifferently of laity and clergy alike.

[74] Ibid. 34: 'Thus "priesthood", which had formerly been the function of all members of the church with the bishop as "high-priest", becomes a special attribute of the second order of the ministry.' In the wake of this trend towards depoliticization, in the sense of the loss of a political ethics grounded on worship, it is hardly surprising that in the same breath elements of the imperial court ceremonial could also be incorporated into the service of worship. Cf. Bradshaw, 'Gottesdienst IV', 41.

(*Amt*)[75] illustrates this; for the distinction could easily be taken to mean that although everyone who has been baptized enjoys the *position* of priest in general, *the actual exercise* of the priesthood is still tied to the 'office' and remains the preserve of specially called office-bearers. Even though Luther himself undoubtedly understood the priesthood of all believers quite practically, and wished to distinguish it from the 'office' only in the interests of the Church's 'order', historically speaking the influence of his distinction, in which the 'ministry' was largely reduced to the ordained preaching ministry, surely contributed to the fact that talk about the priesthood of all believers in Protestantism withered into rhetoric, which was largely speaking without consequences. In view of these developments, the primary task of political ethics for the Christian churches today must be looked for not so much in political influence in particular cases or sectors, as in regaining the position *and* function of the congregation in worship, where they can develop their political form of life in accordance with the gospel.

Ethical or Ontological Exclusiveness: Excommunication and Reconciliation as Political Discipline

The worship of Christian congregations is always exclusive too in some sense, and that should not be forgotten here. When Paul reckons with the possibility that outsiders may find their way into the assembled congregation (1 Cor. 14: 23), and for their sake wants to give preference to language they will understand, he will have meant this inclusiveness to apply to part of the liturgical assembly, the *synaxis*, but not to the Eucharist, as the intimate celebration of the congregation with its Lord. We can be sure that this indeed was highly exclusive, as Dix stresses, although, as we have seen, it cannot be understood as conforming to the pattern of private meetings. Even the prayers in the *synaxis* already marked out the intimate sphere, and before they were spoken, those who were not—or not yet—baptized were formally asked to leave[76]—whether the Eucharist was to follow or not. This arcane form of exclusiveness of

---

[75] 'For all Christians are truly of the spiritual estate and there is no difference among them save alone for the sake of the office' (*Denn alle Christen sein warhafftig geystlich stands, und ist unter yhn kein unterscheyd, denn des ampts halben allein*, WA 6, 407, 13–15).
[76] Dix, *Shape of the Liturgy*, 38, 42.

course presents no problem from a political aspect. The exclusion was limited in time, and was in intention actually bound up with the contrary objective. The catechumens who were now asked to withdraw were 'outside', on their way 'inside'. The fundamentally missionary attitude meant that this 'inside' was destined to dissolve, for as wandering people of God the congregation was on its way to acquiring an eschatological form, where there can no longer be any 'outside'—that is to say, once the *polis* 'from all nations', whose walls are always open (Rev. 21: 25), has been finally reached.

What is directly relevant from the perspective of political ethics, however, is the other kind of exclusiveness, which was practised in the early congregations: *ethical* exclusion. Following the practice of congregational discipline enjoined in the 'ecclesiastical sayings' in Matthew 18, where the extreme form was the exclusion of unrepentant members from the congregation, Paul addresses a specific case in Corinth, and thereby makes clear what this exclusiveness means: 'I wrote to you in my letter not to associate with immoral men; not at all meaning all the immoral of this world, or all the greedy, and the robbers, or the idolaters, since then you would need to emigrate from the world. What I meant was: do not associate with any one who calls himself your brother if he is guilty of immorality or greed, or is an idolater, reviler, drunkard, or robber—do not even eat with such a one' (1 Cor. 5: 9–11). Ethical exclusiveness is not to be directed against 'an outsider'. It is an internal mark of life in the congregation. As such, it does not simply forcibly exclude someone, but to some extent achieves the self-exclusion of those who have put themselves outside the church through their behaviour (Titus 3: 11); for what they do does violence to the praxis of the congregation. The two cannot go on existing together. But what is of particular political importance here is that what the excluded person has done is *not ontologized*. The excluding character of their conduct is not made a definition of their nature. It is precisely this deontologizing way of viewing the practice of exclusion which Paul formulates in the hope that the 'spirit' of the evil-doer will ultimately be saved, partly as a result of the exclusion (1 Cor. 5: 5); and it is the same hope which makes the author of the Second Epistle to the Thessalonians enjoin his readers not to view the excommunicated person as an enemy, but still as a brother (2 Thess. 3: 15). This kind of exclusiveness differs from an ontological one in two respects. First, it is aligned towards the resocialization of the evil-doer, instead of ontologizing what he or she has done, thereby eternalizing the exclusion. Second, it is directed not against particular groups and types of people, but against certain ways of behaving, which are incompatible with the church's praxis. Consequently, the exclusion is basically open to revision, and aims at conversion, repentance, and the reconciliation of the penitent. It therefore already presupposes a political ethos, and is in this way distinct from the 'political' exclusiveness which uses exclusion as a policy, or as the presupposition or instrument of policies, and by so doing actually excludes a political ethics.

However, the ethical exclusiveness of the church as a disciplinary and disciplined community (*communio disciplinans et disciplinata*) does not simply constitute a historically interesting difference from political exclusiveness in its ancient or modern forms. It is indispensable for the political identity of the church itself.[77] Exclusiveness cannot simply be dispensed with, as if it were not a matter for discussion at all. We have seen how the attempts to abolish political exclusiveness through a comprehensive claim for participation merely create more subtle channels in which exclusive political behaviour can operate. Consequently, only an ethical form of exclusiveness can show what is wrong with political exclusiveness. The penitential office of the patristic Church accordingly manifests a complex political teleology. The one form of exclusiveness is practised so that the other can be dispensed with. For this the patristic Church developed the differentiating instruments of the penitential office, which by establishing a separate temporary status, the status of penitent, avoids the politically devastating alternative of either ontological exclusiveness or a morally indifferent participationalism.

This suggests two consequences. First, where the need for ethical exclusiveness is disputed in the name of an indifferent participationalism, the door is thrown wide open for the very phenomenon which the comprehensiveness was actually supposed to prevent— political power. For as the opposite pole to ethical exclusiveness, this allows itself to be readily drawn into the vortex which ensues if there is a vacuum in this sphere. The second result is accordingly

---

[77] It was not only Calvin who numbered Church discipline among the *notae ecclesiae*, or marks of the Church. Luther did so too. In 'Von Conciliis und Kirchen' ('On Councils and Churches'), Luther numbered the public office of the keys among the seven marks of the Church (WA 50, 632, 10–20).

that where an attempt is made to introduce the 'political' concept of ontological exclusiveness into the Church, the Church is bound through the terms of its very existence to take a stand. In the period of Nazi dictatorship, too few people perceived this consequence, and that is the tragedy of German church history in modern times. For even in the Confessing Church, the conflict was largely viewed superficially, on the level of the relation between State and Church, rather than as a problem of political ethics. So what were in the foreground were the incursions of the State into the Church's right to self-determination, not the ontological exclusiveness practised and ordered by the State, the denial of people's rights as citizens because they were 'by nature' Jews, Sinti and Roma, homosexuals, or disabled. It was this that the Church should have countered early on, by way of its ethical exclusiveness: anyone who practises this ontological exclusion cannot approach the Lord's Table.

EXCURSUS

To take a contemporary example: the way the politically fundamental difference between ontological and ethical exclusiveness was discerned in the ecumenical community of the churches is shown by the exclusion from the World Council of Churches of the racially exclusive Dutch Reformed Church (NGK) in South Africa. The learning process which the ethnically divided NGK in South Africa has undergone since then on the way to reunification[78] once again makes the connection between the two forms of exclusiveness clear. It is also possible that the conversion from ontological exclusiveness can be followed through to the end only by way of ethical exclusiveness—through the excommunication or self-exclusion of 'ontological hard-liners' who in the end refuse to be converted.

The Ordination of Women

Against the background of the political importance of the inclusiveness of worship, we can also see the full significance of a question such as women's ordination. In view of the political status of the ministry, the question whether women can be excluded from the ordained ministry shows itself to be not a question about Church politics in the narrower sense (in which case it could be solved in either the one way or the other) but a question which affects the

[78] In October 1994 its synod resolved that reunification with the three non-white sister churches should be fully implemented by 1999.

political ethics of the churches as a whole. And the answer to this question says something about the state of political ethics in the Church in general. To that extent this subject can claim exemplary relevance for the complex we are discussing here. The Church already began to push women out of its official leadership in the post-apostolic period. What it lost, with the waste of women's specifically feminine charismata, has not yet even been fully described. Yet this impoverishment also meant losing part of the political empowerment which God had destined for the Church as a new form of life, a reconciled community which no longer requires any ontological exclusiveness whatever.

The failure to see this was bound to prove fatal for the political existence of the Church. For a direct path—even if a long one—leads from the patriarchalizing of the Church as the reprivatization of women to the privatization of faith and Church, a privatization which today obscures their political character. A point that is frequently overlooked is that the patriarchalization of the Church provoked, and still provokes, a reaction, and not perhaps in the form of feminism alone, but first of all in the 'feminization' of the Christian religion and the Church itself.[79] It is stripped of its publicly relevant claim, and pushed back into the private sphere, with its image as the refuge of women to which it itself has contributed. The ordination of women was introduced in a number of churches during the twentieth century; and the fact that in the eyes of many people this seems to be no more than the Church's follow-up of developments in modern Western society (if not actually a capitulation to 'the spirit of the age') makes the loss suffered in the course of this development all the more evident.

This can be said in the strongest terms. But we must also remember that the political existence and political ethics of the Church depend on a ministry which, if it is concentrated on, let alone reduced to, an ordained leadership, is contracted to its own detriment. What bearing does this have on women's ordination? The Church—and the doctrine of the Church—cannot be interpreted in the light of the clerical ministry. It begins with the ministry of the Word—the sacramental word, or the verbal sacrament—from which the Church

---

[79] A. Douglas, *The Feminization of American Culture* (1977). On early forms of the patriarchalization of Church and ministry from the second century onwards, cf. E. Schüssler Fiorenza, *In Memory of Her* (1983), 288 ff.

lives (2 Cor. 5: 17 ff.).[80] It is on the freedom of *this* ministry that the political form of the Church directly depends, not on the form and order of the clerical ministries. Nevertheless, the order of the ordained ministry in each case has its effect on the ministry of the preaching of reconciliation, which is entrusted to the Church as a whole, either strengthening or weakening it. The effect of this correspondence must now be looked at on two different levels. Here a question such as the structuring of the ordained ministry (three-fold, single, etc.) has a different political relevance from the question about its limitation to a particular race or a particular sex. The *order* of the ministry can resemble this or that existing political model, hierarchical or democratic, single-strand or multi-stranded,[81] with-out betraying the political existence of the Church; but where polit-ical exclusiveness or inclusiveness is in question, it *must* correspond to the structure of the priesthood of all believers, which is open to all races and classes, and to both sexes. And whereas an order of the ordained ministry which is more or less appropriate to this general priesthood influences the effectiveness of the Church's ministry in general on the first level, on the second level it cannot avoid affecting the political existence of the Church as a whole.

This 'inductive' importance of the ordained ministry as test and starting-point for evaluating the general priesthood in the Church can itself, however, already reflect a theologically problematical concentration, within which questions such as women's ordination

---

[80] M. Luther, 'The ministry of the Word makes the ministers, not ministers the ministry of the Word' (*Ministerium verbi facit ministros, non ministri ministerium verbi*, WA 39 II 182, 1).

[81] In spite of these concessions, we can, I think, see a certain trend in the question of how the order of the different ministries can best be in keeping with the lordship of Christ. Since in this aeon the lordship of Christ is a hidden one, we should resist the temptation to lend it a visible representation in a hierarchical leadership. The lordship of Christ in the Church is experienced through the Spirit, which for its part rules through its *multifarious* gifts. In so far as these all contribute to the *oikodome* of the Church's political household, they always already incorporate the Church's centripetal character, the lordship of Christ being the centre towards which it is drawn. The lordship of Christ itself needs no official authority to represent it. It is, so to speak, the direction or orientation of all the charismata, the centre at which they all aim, in a common movement from different directions, the centre which these charismata in their convergence *leave free*. The rule of Christ through the Spirit exists directly *in* the political life which the joint exercise of the gifts of the Spirit brings about in the congregation. These gifts find their primary place of application in worship, where they experience their order as a 'sacramental' order—not as a systematic gradation, but as a functional order.

are unfortunately discussed not just politically but ideologically as well.[82] What so easily allows this dispute to become ideological (as can be seen in the Church of England at the beginning of the 1990s) is the fact that in many churches the ministry as a whole has largely become the exclusive preserve of the clerical office. Seen as 'the Church's power centre', concentration reflects a long process of profanation, in the course of which the ministry was more and more reshaped in analogy to secular offices (the bishop as city governor, the pope as emperor, the council of elders as municipal authority, and so forth). It is understandable that, in the climate that ensued, the dispute about women's ordination should be carried on with such grim determination, on the one side as the fight to conserve a male power centre, and on the other as women's fight for an egalitarian 'admission' to this power centre. In this struggle the political importance of the fact that at no period of Church history were women excluded from the ministry, but only, at times, from one aspect of it—the *episkope*—is easily disregarded.[83] Just because of this ideologization, which is rife in both reactionary and progressive clericalism, it is essential to have an eye to developments of the ministry which set counter-emphases, and refuse to be brought completely into line. In this context, those aspects of ministry which today are so little understood and appreciated deserve particularly to be valued for their political importance.

Among the supporters of this counter-moment in the ministry are the celibates who, like the itinerant missionaries of former times, resist the absolutization of the *oikos* as a settled, familial form of life. Among these people were the mendicant friars, whose form of life challenged the total claim of economics, and Christians living in communities under obedience, who dispute the necessity of democracy as the ministerial structure which in today's view is the only one possible. Another characteristic or mark of the

---

[82] I am indebted to Oliver O'Donovan for this point, and for the following one about the 'counter-moment' of the ministry.

[83] It is along these lines, for example, that the Catholic feminist theologian Bernadette Mbuy Beya, from Zaire, has raised objections to the concentration on the clerically determined ministry in the African churches: 'The point is not to turn women into feminine clerics. Male clericalism is bad enough. The fact that in Africa's churches and congregations so many women come forward spontaneously as "spiritual leaders" is a sign of the times which the church as the community of believers must not despise, let alone overlook' ('Die Last des Schweigens abschütteln', 25; German translation in *Publik Forum*, 22 (1994)).

Christian ministry belongs here, because it offers yet another example of independence from a democratic view of ministry: that is, the ministry of children and the disabled. Here what are in the forefront are not the conditions of access and legal claims to participation with which individuals challenge the political community. Here thinking runs in the opposite direction: the Church's *polis* is not *complete* without the contribution of individual Christians with their own special charismata. This different thinking is intensified if we look at the political role which children, for example, or the mentally handicapped are conceded. Whereas even in democratic communities they have no right to political participation, in the Church's ministry they play a fundamental role. The praise of the worshipping congregation is the Church's central political practice, and this is incomplete as long as it cannot be said that 'Out of the mouths of babes and sucklings thou hast brought perfect praise' (Ps. 8: 2; Matt. 21: 16).[84]

Do the Structures of Ministry Make the Church Resemble a Family?

Just how important the unity of the Church's ministry is in the political sense also emerges from the fact that the double reference of *oikos* and *polis* (which was already constitutive for the understanding of the general ministry in the New Testament) was supposed to apply to the specially called ministers as well. This unity must not be lost by setting laity and clerics over against one another, or by contrasting private and public life. For Machiavelli, the direct contrast between public and private morality was the survival principle of power for its own sake: it was precisely because he was 'a bad man' that 'the Prince' was a good politician, and vice versa.[85] But the exact opposite is required of the Christian who

---

[84] The importance which disabled children have in this respect for Christian ethics has been recognized by Stanley Hauerwas. Thus he stresses—for example, in connection with the many attempts to take moral possession of their existence— that respect for their independence of us is based on the fact 'that we are each called to service in God's kingdom' ('Children, Suffering and the Skill to Care', in *idem, Truthfulness and Tragedy* (1977)).

[85] See J. Bethke Elshtain's interpretation, which takes special account of the gender component in this view of politics, where recognition of the category of private behaviour (which Machiavelli recognizes entirely within its own bounds) seems suicidal. So, for the role of women, which for Machiavelli must in any case be judged according to the conditions of domestic life, the principle has to be: 'Women are morally superior *because* they are publically inferior' (*Public Man, Private Woman*, 94; the page numbers in the text refer to this work).

holds an office. In the pastoral epistles, the 'code for office-holders' (see 1 Tim. 3: 1–13) shows that anyone who took over a special ministry in the Church had to prove their suitability in their private lives: 'For if a man does not know how to manage his own household, how can he care for God's church?' (v. 5).

Now, a requirement of this kind could well provoke the criticism which Jean Bethke Elshtain formulates in the epilogue to the second edition of her book *Public Man, Private Woman*, where she castigates a dangerous tendency towards the 'overfamiliarizing of politics' (p. 360), a trend which she believes has grown up in recent years:

It turns on our recognition that the rules of conduct that flow out of private relationships—loyalty, intimacy, fidelity—are not altogether transferable to public relationships where different criteria, including the capacity for provisional alliances—no permanent enemies; no permanent friends—are required. We need ever more to teach ourselves and our children what it means to be held accountable to the various rules of public life and private relationships if we are to avoid a disastrous overfamiliarizing of politics. To engage in politics is to be called out; to go beyond; to enter the unfamiliar. (p. 363)

The trend in North American society towards 'identity politics' suggests that there is, or should be, a simple identification between private and public existence—an identification which works both ways. On the one hand, the rejection of someone's politics can be turned into a rejection of the person in their identity as a whole. They are reduced to the embodiment of the politics they support (p. 357). On the other hand, age-old 'undercover politics' acquire political respectability, weak points in the private lives of individuals in public life being tracked down in order to prove the questionableness of these people's politics. In view of the transparent attempts of political opponents to undermine the political integrity of people such as John F. Kennedy or Martin Luther King by publishing details of their sex lives, Bethke Elshtain goes on: 'It should be noted that a cramped and cribbed, narrow-minded set of Christian moralisms frequently affixes itself to the terms of the Machiavellian deal: a marriage not made in heaven. Under the guise of bringing morality to politics this deal only brings moralisms to the private lives of political figures and ignores a public morality altogether' (p. 342).

But mustn't this criticism then also be levelled at the connection between the private and the ministerial ethos which is demanded in 1 Timothy in its code for the behaviour of office-holders in the Christian congregation? After all, this code also explicitly requires that the candidate for an office in the Church should 'be tested first', and that people can only exercise an office if they are found 'blameless' (1 Tim. 3: 10). Aren't the rules of conduct for private life simply extended to the political sphere here, so that, for example, the demand for faithfulness to one husband or wife (vv. 2, 12) would have to lead in the sphere of public service to a preoccupation with 'permanently monogamous alliances' (Bethke Elshtain's phrase) which would in a critical situation put loyalty to a coalition partner above political reason?

If we look at the matter more closely, however, a different picture emerges. First, it is noticeable that the behaviour demanded (to be gentle, not violent—not to be quarrelsome—not to be a lover of money—not to be puffed up with one's own conceit—not to be slanderous, but serious, reliable, and so forth) are not arbitrary forms of good behaviour in domestic life. They are forms of inter-action in the life of the community which are certainly politically relevant. Marriage and hospitality are associated most closely with the sphere of the *oikos*, but it is precisely these which are seen to have an explicitly *political* colouring in the *ekklesia*, as we have seen from the New Testament as a whole. The conduct of marriage is removed from the self-regulating mechanism of the patriarchalism of antiquity or Judaism, and is transferred to the form of life actively lived 'in Christ'; and the opening of one's own house for the worshipping congregation is no longer to be viewed as an act of private hospitality. So it may rather be said that Christian aspirants to the office of bishop or deacon must not simply prove themselves through exemplary private lives; they must show that they already lead their private lives 'politically', in the sense of the new way of acting practised in the *ekklesia*. Seen in this light, by proving themselves in the one ministry (which is shared by all Christians), they qualify themselves to take on another.

Nevertheless, it cannot be denied that the Christian moralism whose political effect Bethke Elshtain so deplores does undoubt-edly exist. The pastoral epistles particularly are certainly not com-pletely free of it, although their moralism can be seen not so much in the demand for unified Christian conduct in private life and in the ministry *per* se as in the peculiar way this demand gets limited to the clergy. Where the office-holders are alone in having to achieve a consistent standard in their family and their public life, *oikos* and *polis*, it is tantamount to giving up the attempt at a harmonized Christian morality altogether.[86] It must be judged a sign of the loss of the Church's political self-awareness if it misunderstands the ethical connection between conduct of life and the conduct of the ministry as being a professional problem; where it requires the ethical connection only or mainly in the narrow sector of the recipients of benefits where the Church is given *power* over its employees, instead of proclaiming the unity of conduct and ministry *sine vi sed verbo*—without force but by the word—for all its members as intrinsic to the exercise of their priestly ministry.

As we have seen, the Christian insistence on homogeneous standards for private life and official conduct must by no means lead to the 'familiarization' of political life. It is not a question of transferring family modes of conduct to political forms of action; the point is the ethical orientation of *persons*, whose identity is determined not by the particular context, be it private or public, but by the same law of the Spirit. Nevertheless, certain forms of action can also be identified as characterizing this ethos at the particular point where *oikos* and *polis* interact. Paul recognizes that the different charismata and the correspondingly different ministries in the congregation bring with them the danger of a struggle for position; and in the image of the body with many members he puts forward the organizing principle that the member which is seemingly least important should be given the greatest honour (1 Cor. 12: 24). This is in line with what Jesus had to say, when the disciples were wrangling about their position in the

---

[86] The struggle for the 'homologous' ethical identity of Christians (considered in more detail here in section 7.2) throughout all the different roles is reflected historically, for example, in the resistance of bishops in the closing years of the Roman Empire to the 'avarice' or unjustifiable piling up of wealth by tax officials, in the face of the growing impoverishment of the people. Contrary to such admonitions on the part of the bishops, Christian tax-collectors (who permitted themselves without restraint to appear in church splendidly dressed) were accustomed to make the significant objection that the same moral standards could not be applied to tax officials as to monks and priests. What bishops such as Ambrose or Maximus still disputed, in the name of the *single* form of Christian life, was in the course of time absorbed into the idea of the 'evangelical counsels', a special moral standard, elevated above normal Christian requirements. Cf. Brown, *Power and Persuasion*, 147 f.

heavenly 'commonwealth' (Mark 10: 35–45): 'Whoever would be great among you must be your servant.' So Jesus does not answer by saying what is so readily read into the passage—that in the sight of God all are equal. Instead of levelling talk about equality (or at least equal value), he puts forward a new definition of greatness: greatness shows itself precisely in its recognition of what is generally considered to be of small account. Jesus's antithetical saying makes it clear that this should be explicitly understood in the political sense: 'You know that those who are supposed to rule over the Gentiles lord it over them, and their great men exercise coercive authority over them. But it shall not be so among you' (vv. 42 f.).

The way Luke 'places' the scene where the disciples dispute about position, and the stresses he puts, reflect the extent to which this new definition of political behaviour was anchored for the Christian congregation in worship; for this passage (Luke 22: 24–7) follows directly on the Last Supper pericope—no doubt provoked by the question in Luke's Marcan source about the 'seating plan' at the Lord's table. Jesus's answer about the primacy of the server is here clothed in addition in the image of the liturgical office of 'server at table' (deacon): 'Which is the greater, one who sits at table, or one who serves?' The end of the pericope then makes the new definition clear by stressing the contrast to the usual power politics: 'Is it not (normally) the one who sits at table? But I am among you as one who serves.' The new order of life in the *polis* of the Church is therefore presented as the political seating plan at the Lord's table, where service is recognized in its constitutive importance for every public ministry in the Church.

Again, what we have before us here is anything but an extrapolation into political life of the domestic scene. Rather than that, one could more readily understand Jesus here along the lines of the classic Greek theory of political existence, when he distances himself from 'barbarian' power politics, in which the arbitrary power of the patriarch customary in the domestic sphere is practised as the political way of acting. But the difference from the Greek model is also patent. The Greeks elevated the struggle for position (even if that struggle was purged of its barbarian aspect, the application of sheer physical force), and made it the very life-blood of political life by defining politics as the art-form of the contest for excellence.

(We find this concept of politics as 'war by other means' returning with full force in modern economic and political theories.) But the 'politics' of Jesus expels this central notion, providing a higher standard than that of excellence. According to this new standard, the truly great person is not someone who makes other people feel small. It is the person in whose presence other people can also acquire honour and greatness. It is therefore perfectly proper when, as we have seen, the Epistle to the Ephesians makes the motif of 'being subject to one another' the connecting link between the public and the private ethos (Eph. 5: 21).

6.4 THE RECONCILIATION OF FREEDOM AND NECESSITY

The reconciliation of *oikos* and *polis*, private and public life, under the same 'law of the Spirit' (Rom. 8: 2) goes together with the reconciliation of necessity and freedom. In the light of this reconciliation, there can no longer be a public realm of freedom which depends, parasite-like, on a domestic realm of necessity, which has to do exclusively with the ignoble physical requirements of the sheer struggle for existence.

'The Two Kingdoms' of Political Life?

The political worship of the Church both requires and makes possible a totally different definition of the relationship between freedom and necessity. They are now no longer antithetical and opposed; they are complementary. Whereas the sphere of the necessary is carried into public worship in the person of its representatives (slaves, women, artisans, etc.) and their affairs, what was conceived of as political and public freedom *from* necessity is 'earthed', and must now itself deal expressly with the necessary. To associate politics with what is necessary simultaneously means de-totalizing them. Politics are now no longer there to serve the self-realization of political life; because they are dependent on the necessities of daily bodily life, they themselves become 'a mere necessity'. But what does 'mere' mean? Even though Christians have continually been tempted to view politics as a necessary evil, Christian worship, rightly understood, actually permits only a fundamentally positive attitude. As a worldly affair which is, when all is said and done, necessary, politics are not to be despised but, like private life as well, represent the necessary space in which faith proves itself, where the purpose is solicitude for human beings in their bodily, social needs, as a joint attempt to alleviate their lot.

In what follows we shall look more closely at the way this new definition is arrived at. Here Luther's 'vocational ethics' especially can strike out a fresh path—and not least through the thickets of misunderstanding which have gathered round this idea itself. First, it must be remembered how exclusively the relationship between freedom and necessity was embedded in the classic concept of politics. Where there was necessity, there could be no freedom, and freedom for its part had to acquire its form in complete emancipation from necessity. Seen in this light, the only connecting link between the two spheres was again a necessity—the necessity of violence. Whereas in the realm of what was necessary for life, violence was in any case considered to be indispensable, it was also in some sense necessary for freedom too, for the suppression of the pre-political sphere.[87]

This antithesis is still viewed in a very similar way in Marx (as in some varieties of political theology too), since for him the realm of freedom in the classless society can decidedly be expected only 'beyond the realm of necessity', since then the working class would be freed not just from the exploitation of their working power but ultimately from work itself.[88] Even though Marx's revolutionary programme was explicitly anti-political, he too recognized that the intervention of violence was necessary for the attainment of freedom, a necessity implicit in the logic of this definition of the relation between freedom and necessity, and one envisaged in classic political theory. Whereas Marx expected freedom to follow the death of both the public and the private sphere in Communist society, the societies of the West (and the post-socialist East too) seem today to aim at what is practically a reversal of the ancient

[87] Hannah Arendt points to the connection: 'What all Greek philosophers, no matter how opposed to *polis* life, took for granted is that freedom is primarily a prepolitical phenomenon, characteristic of the private household organization, and that force and violence are justified in this sphere, because they are the only means to master necessity—for instance, by ruling over slaves—and to become free. Because all human beings are subject to necessity, they are entitled to violence towards others; violence is the prepolitical act of liberating onself from the necessity of life for the freedom of world' (*Human Condition*, 31).

[88] Thus Marx says in this connection: 'Beyond [the realm of necessity] begins that development of human energy which is an end in itself, the true realm of freedom, which, however, can blossom forth only with this realm of necessity as its basis. The shortening of the working-day is its basic prerequisite' (*Capital*, iii. 799 f.).

relationship between freedom (in public political life) and necessity (in domestic life). Today freedom is increasingly sought in private life, while political life, in contrast, now appears only as a necessary evil, legitimated only by the extent to which it is able to contribute to the preservation and increase of the freedom of private individuals. The totalization of private life, however, cannot conceal its destructive potential for both spheres: on the one hand it ruins politics which, once they have thrown off all desire for co-operative endeavour, must certainly wither into the necessary evil of an instrument for the bureaucratic distribution of welfare—which indeed is what they are largely considered to be. But on the other hand it becomes evident how private life itself is eroded in the attempt to meet the claim for a complete realization of freedom.

As we can see particularly in the sphere of partnership, marriage, and the family, on which this claim is concentrated today, the concept of private freedom becomes impossible at the very point where it feverishly demands its realization. For to the same extent to which a cold, functionally and bureaucratically organized 'necessary' outside world intensifies the need for a warm, existentially experienceable private sphere of 'true freedom' and 'regeneration', it simultaneously diminishes the chance of achieving this freedom and regeneration in the private sphere.[89] On the one hand, human beings find themselves faced here with the difficulty of effectively changing their ways of reacting when they transfer from the one world to the other; the person who has to 'function' in the outside world finds it difficult simply to 'be' when he or she is at home. On the other hand, an expression such as the 'regenerative function' of private life indicates that the concept of private freedom bears a close resemblance to a new form of instrumentalizing private life; and seen in this light, it approximates more closely to the model upheld in the ancient world than it would no doubt like.

Freedom from and for the Necessary

We find the counter-vision to these unsuccessful attempts to arrive at a successful relationship between freedom and necessity in the Sermon on the Mount (Matt. 6: 25–34). Jesus too, it would seem, recognizes the violent element which is intrinsic to the sphere of the necessary, and which exerts its mastery over men and women so

---

[89] Cf. U. Beck and E. Beck-Gernsheim, *The Normal Chaos of Love* (1995).

pitilessly. For Jesus, this connection between necessity and violence is present in the anxiety which so easily enslaves people when they try to secure the necessities of life for themselves. Yet Jesus shows us a completely different solution from the one we find in the classic concept. It does not bring into play a higher power which will help us to emancipate ourselves from the tyranny of the necessary. It is not the necessary which has to be surmounted; it is worry about it. 'Do not be anxious, saying, "What shall we eat?" or "What shall we drink?" or "What shall we wear?" For the Gentiles seek all these things; and your heavenly Father knows that you need them all.' It is true that here too Jesus sets a 'political' priority: 'Seek first the kingdom of God and his righteousness.' But other than in the classic concept, the freedom in this priority does not depend on there being a sphere of necessity supporting it, out of sight and out of mind, but, 'all these things shall be yours as well'. The necessary things are to be hoped for *within the freedom of the kingdom itself*. The violent constructions of freedom depend in each case on the notion that freedom is the outcome of human efforts for liberation, when a person (or a group) rises up against the domination of the necessary and becomes his—or their—own master. But the Christian reconciliation of freedom and necessity begins with the opposite experience.

As Luther expounds in his treatise on freedom,[90] freedom cannot be acquired; it comes to us as a freedom from outside ourselves. It comes to us in the word of the divine promise, which frees us above all from the mistaken view that a person has to create his freedom for himself. So the promise 'For freedom Christ has set us free' (Gal. 5: 1) liberates us from necessity in a different sense: it liberates us from the necessity of the 'works' through which people strive to attain freedom as liberation from the necessities of life. Luther says all this in reference to 'the inner man', while in the second part of his treatise he goes on to contrast this inner man with the 'outward' one. With this distinction he provoked a whole series of interpretations which, even though they overlook the heart of the matter, have nevertheless had almost as much historical weight and influence on people's thinking as what Luther actually intended to say.

---

[90] M. Luther, *The Freedom of a Christian* (1520), *Works*, iii. 343 ff.

EXCURSUS

Herbert Marcuse's interpretation of Luther's distinction is typical of the continually recurring misunderstanding about Luther's 'apolitical ethics':

> Luther's treatise on *The Freedom of a Christian* for the first time brings together all the elements which constitute the specifically bourgeois concept of freedom . . . : the allocation of freedom to a person's 'inward sphere', 'the inner man', with a simultaneous subjection of the 'outward' human being to the system of worldly authorities; . . . separation between person and works . . . with a 'double morality'; justification of a real lack of freedom and real inequality as consequence of 'inner' freedom and equality.[91]

This judgement is uncritically reproduced by a whole series of writers of repute, John Milbank[92] and Jean Bethke Elshtain[93] among them. Bethke Elshtain heads her chapter on Luther 'Private Piety, Power Politics'. To support her judgement that Luther's 'pietistic soul' was bound to subject outside life entirely to the existing circumstances, 'for freedom belonged to the inner man', she cites as evidence the famed double definition with which Luther begins his *Freedom of a Christian*: 'A Christian is a perfectly free lord of all, subject to none. A Christian is a perfectly dutiful servant of all, subject to all.'

What all these interpretations overlook is that both perspectives, the 'inner' and the 'outer' man, are related to the person's *freedom*. And in each perspective the human being as a whole is meant: 'inwardly' in that God acts on him, 'outwardly' inasmuch as he has to do with the world and his neighbour. This makes the relation to freedom more complex. Whereas the inner man is free through the outward Word, he preserves and retains this freedom by turning to the outward world, as outward man, acting in the strength of the Word in the 'inner man'. It is true that it certainly seems as if the inner and the outer man are in a sense related in the same way as freedom and necessity. Whereas the inner man, through the Word apprehended in faith, is completely free from all compulsions, and most of all from 'works', the outer man is considered explicitly as the one who has to deal with the necessities of bodily and social life,

---

[91] H. Marcuse, 'Studien über Autorität und Familie', in *idem, Ideen zu einer kritischen Theorie der Gesellschaft* (1969), 57 f. (see ET *Towards a Critical Theory of Society* (2001). The quotation has been translated from the German text.

[92] Milbank, *Theology and Social Theory*, 17.

[93] J. Bethke Elshtain, *Public Man, Private Woman*, 80, 83.

and for whom therefore 'works' are also necessary. 'Although . . . a man is abundantly and sufficiently justified by faith inwardly, in his spirit, and so has all that he needs . . . yet he remains in this mortal life on earth. In this life he must control his own body and have dealings with men. Here the works begin' (*Freedom of a Christian*, 358). However, in acknowledgement of the creatureliness of existence, the freedom of faith (as the freedom of the inner man) can only be freedom, and remain so, if it is exercised as the freedom of love (that is, as the freedom of the outer man). To this extent, therefore, the necessary is absorbed into a Christian's freedom, not as its prerequisite—that is soteriologically impossible—but as an 'ethical' necessity which emerges from faith's overspill into love: 'We conclude, therefore, that a Christian lives not in himself, but in Christ and in his neighbour. . . . He lives in Christ through faith, in his neighbour through love' (p. 371).

The free man or woman 'dwells' *in* his or her neighbour through love, and does not merely turn to that neighbour, as it might be, out of a free decision, seeing the neighbour as the object of his good deed; and similarly, freedom is drawn into necessity in such a way that in some sense it 'indwells' it. The criterion of freedom is now no longer the degree to which the person can control the circumstances of his or her life. The measure of freedom is not even any longer what Kant, in the sense of 'communicative freedom', defined as 'the only original right belonging to every man by virtue of his humanity', that is, 'freedom (independence from being constrained by another's choice) insofar as it can coexist with the freedom of every other in accordance with a universal law'.[94] Whereas this liberal concept of freedom sees the liberty of the one as constrained by the liberty of the other, freedom in Luther's sense must not merely be compatible with the freedom of our neighbour; it must even, and particularly, be compatible with his *un*freedom, his actually infringed freedom, his practical distress and necessity. 'As our neighbour is in need and lacks that in which we abound' is the way he formulates the law of acting out that freedom.[95] The Christian never possesses his freedom in himself but always outside himself, in God or his neighbour; and consequently he does not, either, *as person* himself form the link joining the two kingdoms of

[94] Kant, *Metaphysics of Morals*, 30.
[95] M. Luther, *De libertate christiana*, WA 7, 64. Here I am following the Latin text.

freedom and necessity, in such a way that he could go backwards and forwards between them, like the free man as a patriarch at home and a citizen in the *polis*. What links freedom and necessity is not the mobility of the free Christian, but the fact that in both freedom and necessity the Christian has to do with God and his neighbour, 'in' whom his freedom is to be found. In this respect the freedom of the Christian 'citizen', if it is viewed in a foreshortened concentration on the 'Christian man' (the *Christenmensch* of Luther's title), seen as the object of medieval state tutelage, is as much misunderstood as it is if he is interpreted as 'subject', the way in which—in the wake of Hegel—subject has come to be conceived in modern times.

It is not least the history of the false interpretation of 'the freedom of a Christian' which makes it clear how difficult it is not to wrench apart this two-stranded–single-stranded freedom. It is all the more essential to see where we can already set eyes on the unity of this freedom. Luther's treatise on freedom certainly does not say explicitly that the unity has its origin in worship, but it is the premiss (as Luther expounds elsewhere) without which the connection cannot be thought. For both as the 'inner' person on whom God acts and as the 'outward' person who turns to his neighbour, the Christian is present and involved in worship—as are God and his neighbour too.

The Lord's Supper as Political Community of Goods

In answer to the question, in what way is freedom given to 'the inner man'?, Luther replied: through the Word, which communicates all good things so superabundantly. But in order that there should be no misunderstanding about the nature of this divine Word—that it should not, perhaps, be interpreted as an 'inward Word' experienced by the individual in the heart—Luther asks: 'What then is the Word which confers so great a grace, and how shall I use it? Answer: it is nothing other than preaching...' The form in which freedom is communicated is the act of proclamation of the outward Word in community and in worship. In an explicit refutation of the Enthusiastic 'metaphysical distinction' which divides inward and outward, and through which men 'propose to be fierce judges between the spirit and the letter',[96] Luther insists on the unity of the 'bodily' Word in its inward and outward efficacy; it

---

[96] WA TR 3, 671, 10–673, 31 f.; WA 50, 245, 9–11. Cf. here O. Bayer, *Theologie* (1994), 78, 84.

is this which his own distinction between the outward and the inner man serves.

For our political context, however, the place where Luther's double freedom is most emphatically rooted in worship is of course the Lord's Supper. In his 'Sermon on the Blessed Sacrament of the Holy and True Body of Christ and concerning the Brotherhoods' Luther already (1519) describes how in the Lord's Supper the 'exchange of property', or 'community of goods', which is essential to his logic of freedom, comes about; and the mode of the 'exchange' as he depicts it also manifests the political significance of this freedom. 'The meaning or work of this sacrament is the communion of all saints ... that Christ with all saints is one spiritual body, just as the people of a city are one community and one body, each citizen a member of the other and of the whole city. Thus are all saints members of Christ and the Church, which is the one spiritual, eternal city of God.'

The *polis* of the Church means a community of goods consisting of mutual rights and duties.

This fellowship consists therein that all spiritual benefits of Christ and his saints are mediated and given as his property also to the one who receives this sacrament. Conversely, all sufferings and sins are also common to all, and thus love is kindled for love ... As in a city that city's name is common to all its citizens, with its honour, liberty, commerce, usages, customs, aid, support, protection and the like, so also, conversely, are all dangers, fire, flood, enemies, death, injuries, tribute and the like.[97]

So in the Lord's Supper the political dimension of freedom becomes manifest, since there its two perspectives are kept together; for the Lord's Supper is the social realization through which Christians ever and again have conferred on them afresh the ministry conferred on them in baptism as citizens of the Church (in his treatise on freedom, Luther calls it the office of the royal priesthood, which is tantamount to the same thing). When the outward man turns to the world, what he does is rooted in the ministry of all believers, as this is constituted in worship. Here there is no difference in the form through which freedom proves itself: just as Christians, as 'inner' men and women, intercede for each other

[97] Translation follows the text in M. Luther, *Ausgewählte Schriften* (Insel edn.) ii. 54 f.

before God as priests, they do the same as 'outward' men and women in their direct dealings with their neighbour.

We have seen, then, that this freedom cannot be pinned down anthropologically, by being deployed between a person's different 'provinces'. There are probably two closely connected reasons why Luther's distinction has nevertheless continually been understood in this divisive sense. The objective reason is no doubt the failure to perceive worship as the location of freedom, where the two perspectives are found together in a way that cannot be mistaken. The history of the misunderstanding of this freedom is therefore the history of its abstraction from its well-spring in the worship praxis of the Christian congregation. It is also, at the same time, the history of the relegation of freedom to one or other of the two spheres, either 'inwardness' or 'world'—whether the relegation was in the narrower sense religious, or took a wider form in the shift into anthropology (Feuerbach) or history (Hegel). The deeper reason for this abstraction is of course that the worship form of 'outward' freedom (received in the outward Word and necessarily proved in service to one's neighbour) is in continual tension with the striving to assure oneself of freedom which has put its stamp so profoundly on history.

In this respect, the study by the Canadian moral philosopher Charles Taylor, *The Sources of the Self*[98] (which received considerable attention) also falls short. Taylor pays tribute to the Reformation contribution of 'the affirmation of ordinary life', which he sees as one of the essential 'sources of the self', a source from which 'modern identity' can learn to understand itself. He certainly distinguishes the Reformers' intention in this affirmation of ordinary life from its modern temper; but by applying the concept of secularization, he none the less feels able to trace a direct line between the two phenomena which obscures the constitutive significance of worship for the Reformers' concern. But a narrative of 'the making of modern identity' which wants to lend adequate force to the impulse given by the Reformation's affirmation of daily life must appreciate the fact that modern 'inwardness' could only have its anti-political effect because, at the centre of the Protestant concept, 'the affirmation of everyday life' underwent a decisive transformation, as worship moved away from 'political worship' and became an affair of

---

[98] See C. Taylor, *Sources of the Self* (1989), 211 ff.

inwardness. Since worship was no longer understood as the central praxis for *both* perspectives of the Christian life, but now belonged wholly to 'the inner man', freedom as Christian freedom—which Luther understood comprehensively as the necessity of life in all its domestic and public aspects—was reduced to the sphere of private piety. Either that, or freedom was cut loose altogether from what was undoubtedly too narrow a strait-jacket, and was to be assured in terms of general anthropological or historical categories.

EXCURSUS

We may note here in passing that the liturgical development of Lutheran worship from the seventeenth to the nineteenth century (but not Lutheran worship alone) reflects this misunderstanding in phenomena which are externally contrary, although they are in fact structurally closely connected; for as time went on, the political ethics of worship was either forced to submit to the primacy of state politics or was constrained into the patterns of domestic behaviour.[99] In early German Protestantism, worship reflected the religion of the ruler, and with that the public life of the state and its hierarchy. This was even reflected in the seating in churches. Since religion was a state concern, the authorities watched over church attendance.[100] This form of church life then gave way to the neo-Protestant family religion of the middle classes. The widespread privatization of worship[101] can be seen in the liturgies of the Enlightenment period, among other things in the systematic development of the cycle of rites of passage, and their interlocking with the stages of family life (baptism as the celebration of a birth, confirmation as marking arrival at maturity, etc.), an association to which the transference of these rites of passage to private houses also testifies.[102]

Later history shows how vulnerable this liberal cultural Protestantism was to the 'political liturgy' of National Socialism, since this too was based on a magnification of aspects of natural life with the help of a diffuse religiosity.[103]

---

[99] Cf. P. Cornehl, 'Gottesdienst VIII', *TRE* 14 (1985), 54–85.

[100] Ibid. 59.

[101] The box pews which came into fashion in English churches in the nineteenth century are a symbol of this development. These closed-off compartments in the nave of the church could be rented or bought by individuals, or by individual families. They were rationalized as being 'practical' (i.e., warmer); but in fact they served to separate better-off families from one another, and all of them from the poorer (perhaps infectious) members of the congregation. In this way privacy made its way into the public worship of the congregation as a privilege and sign of gentility. The result was that members of the congregation as a whole never saw each other face to face at all.

[102] P. Cornehl, 'Gottesdienst VIII', 63.

[103] Ibid. 69, 71.

Privatized religion especially is highly vulnerable to political instrumentalization. The historical conjunction of the two things, privatization and
political instrumentalization, particularly in conjunction with the terrible
balance sheet of German Protestantism during the Third Reich, shows the
degree to which specifically Christian political worship is continually exposed to the danger of heteronomy, either political or private.

Luther's Battle against the Flight from Political Life

As we have seen, however, it is by no means true that, as Bethke
Elshtain puts it, 'Unlike Augustine, Luther's city lay primarily
within his own being,' and that he therefore left politics to the
Devil, both programmatically and in fact.[104] In fact, Luther by no
means confined himself to praying for the worldly ruler, as Bethke
Elshtain maintains (p. 84). He continually admonishes the princes
in highly practical terms, reminding them of their Christian duty to
exercise their sovereignty in responsibility before God and his
Church. 'It would be rebellion should a proclaimer of the Word
fail to tell the princes and lords of their vices. These are sham and
unprofitable preachers.'[105] This understanding of Romans 13,
which sees that civil obedience must in certain circumstances take
the form of criticism, did not for Luther merely include constructive advice and demands, aimed at a wide range of practical measures, for example in the field of education; it could also cover
extremely plain condemnations of existing conditions (usury) or
contemporary policies (the treatment of serfs).

The political essential of Luther's ethics can also be grasped with
particular clarity at the point where he lodges an attack on the
refusal to enter into political existence which he believed he could
detect both in contemporary monastic life and among the Enthusiasts.[106] Luther is not prepared to accept the claim of the mendicant
friars that they were obeying to perfection Jesus's call to discipleship; for their way of life did not in fact mean that they had 'sold
everything', since they remained dependent on what others made
available to them, economically and politically. 'That is indeed a
most glorious idea, to live from the property of others, idle and
secure! And out of poverty or the "forsake all", they make just what

[104] Bethke Elshtain, *Public Man, Private Woman*, 84, 91.
[105] WA 31, I, 196, 25 f.
[106] O. Bayer, 'Nachfolge-Ethos und Haustafel-Ethos: Luthers seelsorgliche
Ethik', in *idem, Freiheit als Antwort* (1995), 147–63; see also the forthcoming ET
Responsive Freedom.

is called in common parlance "possessing"'' (WA 39 II, 40, 1–3). The Enthusiasts also thought that they had to meet God's demand by putting themselves outside the ordinances of worldly life. As the 'love communism' of the Anabaptist kingdom in Münster illustrates, Spiritualists could reject both property and monogamous marriage, and for them there was no question of assuming public office in civil society, since that was the sphere of 'the princes of this world'. The Augsburg Confession, by contrast, in its criticism of these two 'escapist' ways of life, affirms civic life in *oikos* and *polis* with all possible clarity. After listing affirmatively all the things which Christians are permitted to do 'without sin' in the fulfilment of their duties in their worldly positions or 'estates', the Article 'Of Civil Affairs' (Article XVI) goes on:

Our churches condemn the Anabaptists who forbid Christians to engage in these civil functions. They also condemn those who place the perfection of the Gospel not in the fear of God and in faith but in forsaking civil duties. The Gospel teaches an eternal righteousness of heart, but it does not destroy the state or the family. On the contrary, it especially requires their preservation as ordinances of God and the exercise of love in these ordinances.[107]

Luther sees the affirmation of worldly existence and Jesus's call to radical discipleship as belonging together, as different ways of acting in the light of the first and second Tables of the Decalogue. If we are considering the First Commandment, then we must indeed forsake everything: 'And though they take our life, goods, honour, children, wife, / Yet is their profit small; these things shall vanish all.'[108] But if a *status confessionis* in this sense has not arisen, then, in the light of the second ('economic and political') Table, we must hear Jesus's call to discipleship in the following way: 'But other than the matter of the first Table and the acknowledgement

---

[107] Translated from the Latin in *The Book of Concord*, ed. T. G. Tappert (1959); but the Latin text is perhaps even more forceful than the translation: 'Damnant Anabaptistas, qui interdicunt haec civilia officia christianis. Damnant etiam illos, qui evangelicam perfectionem non collocant in timore Dei et fide, sed in deserendis civilibus officiis, quia evangelium tradit iustitiam aeternam cordis. Interim non dissipat politiam aut oeconomiam, sed maxime postulat conservare tamquam ordinationes Dei et in talibus ordinationibus exercere caritatem' (*BSLK*, 70 f.).

[108] Verse 4 of Luther's hymn 'Ein feste Burg ist unser Gott', in the translation by Thomas Carlyle.

of God, everything is to be acquired, retained, defended and administered' (WA 39 II, 40, 23–5). Luther's achievement as an ethicist can therefore be summed up by saying that he is not prepared to admit that 'house' and 'discipleship' are the alternatives they are assumed to be both by the medieval (monastic and Enthusiastic) forms of life and by modern sociology of religion, with its schematic apparatus of 'itinerant radicals' and later 'bourgeois ethics'.[109] In fact, Luther's own radicalism basically recognizes both radical forms—the abandonment of civil forms of life, as well as involvement in them. What his radicalism does not permit, however, is a totalization of either one of the two forms, since it is able to distinguish the one which is appropriate at any given time.

The necessities of life can be dealt with in a freedom which does not depend for its security on the safeguarding of these necessities. Just because this freedom can also 'let go' (*dahinfahren*, as Luther's hymn says), it is free to use the necessary as something good—as a limited good—but without absolutizing it, either by the way it is used (consumerism) or by renouncing it entirely (asceticism).[110] In contrast, as we have seen, the escapist form of life chosen by both the monastics and the Enthusiasts could not, in spite of their own claim, count as *eschatological* existence, inasmuch as their aim was to bring eschatological existence into an institutionally secured form. Politically speaking, their conduct (which was in a sense parasitical) can be viewed as a religious variant of the Greek concept of freedom. Both there and here, freedom is an élitist phenomenon enjoyed at the expense of the unfree, an artificial free space hewn out of the realm of the necessary. A practical symbol of the theological connection between Christian freedom and 'necessary' life in the worldly positions or 'estates' is not only the introduction of the vernacular, but also and especially the catechism. Here Luther found a contemporary way of communicating the political ethics rooted in worship. The catechism—itself an exposition of the main elements of the service of worship which were regularly taken as subjects for preaching—was a bond between the main spheres of socialization: church, home, and school. 'With the catechism and its main parts as guideline, the service of worship opened up an

---

[109] Bayer, 'Nachfolge-Ethos und Haustafel-Ethos', 147 f.
[110] For more detail on this 'eschatological aesthetic in Paul and Luther', see B. Wannenwetsch, 'Die Freiheit der Ehe', *Evangelium und Ethik*, 2 (1993), 231–54.

entire world, an interpretation of the whole of life drawn from the Word of God.'[111]

Summing up, we can say that in worship the reconciliation of freedom and necessity can be experienced in a kind of dialectic: as a free undertaking in the praise of God, rather than as a means to an end. Worship is not 'necessary' in the instrumental sense, like work or—Arendt's word—manufacture; as praxis it has no *telos* separate from itself. Though looking towards the kingdom of God, it nevertheless does not screen out the realm of necessity; it incorporates the worldly sphere too, as this is characterized by its dependence on intercession in worship. As political worship, worship practises the alternative to the political thinking of the ancient world (and to modern privatization too), although it does not simply do away with it, but absorbs its elements of truth, even if in essentially modified form. Among these elements is the important insight that politics is not possible where there is only necessity and no freedom to emerge from the immediate pressure of necessary things. Politics needs to be able to sally forth into the freedom of pondering, meditating, and reflecting; it needs time and space for thinking, judging, and joint action.

Consequently, worship as *happening* is already an elemental presupposition for the (Christian) person's freedom for political life. But this departure from the realm of the necessary, in the sense of its interruption, does not mean that the necessary is disparaged. It is simply set in relation to the kingdom of God. In this way the political and the private are each given back their own dignity, which would be destroyed if either the one or the other were to be totalized. The recognition that both spheres of worldly life are God-given spaces where freedom can prove itself, rules out the subordination of one to the other. The good things of each sphere are to be recognized in their own particular character. They cannot be attained equally well in another way or in another place. The reconciliation of necessity and freedom therefore constitutes a form of life which does not dissolve the two spheres—neither dissolves the one in the other, nor dissolves both in a third form of reality. Instead, it gives to each of them its own dignity by setting them both in relation to the kingdom of God.

[111] Cornehl, 'Gottesdienst VIII', 57.

6.5 THE RECONCILIATION OF THE CONTEMPLATIVE AND THE ACTIVE LIFE

Does Christian Contemplation Mean the Debasement of Political Existence? (Hannah Arendt)

In antiquity, escape from the necessary took two forms: political life and the *bios theoretikos*; and in the present section we shall look at the relation between them. In developing the way in which these two forms of life as *vita activa* and *vita contemplativa* are connected, and are experienced in worship as reconciled, I should like to start by taking issue with a thesis of Hannah Arendt's, put forward in *The Human Condition*, where she postulates that the new definition of the two forms of life in Christianity was bound to mean the beginning of the end for political existence. It will become clear that although in respect of its theological premisses Arendt's thesis fails to grasp the objective connection between these two forms of life, the intention behind her thesis is actually very well taken care of in political worship.

As Arendt points out, the concept of the *vita activa* only developed in the Middle Ages. But as a translation of the Greeks' *bios politikos,* it already implies the essential transformation of ideas that had taken place since antiquity; and it is this transformation which is the object of Arendt's criticism. By the term *bios politikos* Aristotle meant only activity which was related to political life in the narrower sense—'action', the public practice of free communicative co-operation which is motivated by the fundamental human condition of plurality itself. Excluded from this were the activities of craftsmanship or production (*poiesis*), in which the human being deals with the factual, objective world, and labour, whose fundamental condition is the sheer necessity to stay alive, and whose purpose is the preservation of life itself. In distinction from 'action', these two activities, which simply bring about what is necessary and produce what is useful, cannot constitute a *bios*, a form of life worthy of the free man.[112]

According to Arendt, the problematical development began when, with the disappearance of the Greek city-states, action increasingly lost its genuine political character and was 'brought down' to the level of the other two types of activity; together with

[112] Arendt, *Human Condition*, 12.

these, it could then be seen consequently as that complex of related activities which is meant by the medieval term *vita activa*. The essential expression of this development, and its essential factor, is now the primacy of contemplation, to which in Hannah Arendt's view Christianity decisively contributed. It is true that the *bios theoretikos* was already distinguished in Attic philosophy from the *bios politikos*, and came more and more to the fore.[113] But what in the ancient world was generally thought of as a merely temporary retreat, and would be claimed as a privilege to be enjoyed by only a few, was now the common coin of Christianity, available to every man and every woman, and made, as it were, the commonly expected form of activity.[114] This dignification of the *vita contemplativa*, Arendt argues, meant that until the threshold of modern times, the *vita activa* in all its variations was viewed from the outset as negative. It was now primarily understood as defective, as un-quiet, *neg-otium, a-scholia,* and was in tendency disparaged. Two connected aspects of this process are now the target of Arendt's criticism. Under the supremacy of the *vita contemplativa*, the contours of the *vita activa* become blurred. 'Seen from the viewpoint of contemplation, it does not matter what disturbs the necessary quiet, as long as it is disturbed' (p. 16). This leads inescapably to an 'abasement' of political existence, which is thus positioned on the same level as 'unfree' activities—and is hence increasingly drawn into their forms of activity.

Let us pause for a moment at this point. Isn't Hannah Arendt presenting us here with a distorted notion of the contemplative life in Christianity? It is true that Arendt's description does fit some contemplative ideals, but in Christianity these were essentially élitist phenomena. They were by no means 'everybody's business' in the Christian congregation. In this sense they are in a way closer to late antiquity's idea of the *bios theoretikos* than to the character of normal worship, which Arendt's picture doesn't really cover. In spite of this obvious weakness in her grasp of the specific contribu-

---

[113] Aristotle's account of free ways of living is noticeably guided by the ideal of *theoria*, and Plato derives the philosopher-king's capacity to rule in the ideal state from this very familiarity with 'theoretical' life, in the promotion of which, conversely, the goal of political order itself is to consist. Thus, in the philosophy of late antiquity, 'political' freedom from the necessities of life was put side by side with *schole*, leisure, as freedom *from* public concerns.

[114] Arendt, *Human Condition*, 14.

tion of Christian worship, however, it would be inadvisable to dismiss her analyses too hastily or defensively. For in intention they agree largely with what we have called the critical dimension of political worship. Arendt's positive concern is nothing other than the plurality of human life itself, which has to prove itself through recognition of the different forms of life which taken together—and only then—make up human existence.[115]

With this conviction, Hannah Arendt comes surprisingly close to Luther's political ethics as we described them in the previous section. These were apparently a closed book to Arendt; her view of Luther in *The Human Condition* would seem to have been influenced by Max Weber's thesis about 'inner-worldly asceticism' (p. 251). We have seen how Luther's passionate reverence for the elaborate warp and weft of creaturely life, and his fight against the disparagement of the diverse forms of activity in public and private life, was rooted practically and conceptually in political worship—and was therefore always determined by hope. Conversely, Arendt's 'archaeology' of modern society conforms to the pattern of a history of decline. Its tendency towards resignation is understandable, since her limited perception of the contemplative life prevents her from any explicit expectation of a political worship in the Jewish or Christian sense. It would therefore be more possible to postulate that the development Arendt describes was bound to take place not *because of* the spiritual influence of Christianity, but at the very point where the specifically Christian character of political worship was obscured—even if this obscurity may indeed have been the mark of certain contemplative Christian modalities.

The Worldliness of Worship: Communal, Verbal, Sensory

The archaeological approach we have touched on constitutes the methodological relationship between Arendt's work and the work of John Milbank and Jean Bethke Elshtain, the other two writers to whom I have frequently referred in this part of our study. Where they differ is in their evaluation of the contribution made by Christianity. All three pay tribute to the antithetical position which Christianity came to assume towards antiquity, and would assent to Bethke Elshtain's judgement when she describes Christianity in

---

[115] Thus in her discussion of the *vita activa* Arendt starts from the premiss 'that the concern underlying all its activities is not the same as and is neither superior nor inferior to the central concern of the *vita contemplativa*' (*Human Condition*, 17).

the political sense as 'Aristotle on his Head'.[116] But when they come to modern times, their opinions diverge. Whereas Milbank and to some extent Bethke Elshtain see antiquity and modernity as both together standing over against Christianity, Arendt puts Christianity and modernity together, over against antiquity. Here Arendt's analysis in *The Human Condition* reads like an inversion of Milbank's theory, according to which the development of modern social theories should be understood as springing from a disregard or reversal of the genuinely new Christian approach. For Arendt, it is precisely Christianity's new approach (even though she views it differently) which marks the beginning of that decline of political theory and life which modernity has almost brought to completion.

In this analysis her conception of the *vita contemplativa* in Christianity plays the decisive part. For Arendt, as *The Human Condition* makes clear, the heart of this *vita contemplativa* and its essential tenet is 'the immortality of individual human life' (p. 314). Because the Christian enjoys this immortality in contemplation, and elevates contemplation so that it becomes the central activity of the Christian life, Christianity sets the seal on 'the abasement of the *vita activa*' (p. 16). For the vision of eternal life leads inescapably to a till then unknown dignification of temporal life, as the beginning of the eternal in the Here and Now.

Arendt explains why in her view this assertion of 'life as the ultimate point of reference' in Christianity (p. 313) 'could not but be disastrous for the esteem and the dignity of politics. Political activity, which up to then had derived its greatest inspiration from the aspiration toward worldly immortality, now sank to the low level of an activity subject to necessity, destined to remedy the consequences of human sinfulness on one hand and to cater to the legitimate wants and interests of earthly life on the other... It is precisely individual life which now came to occupy the position once held by the "life" of the body politic' (p. 314). Whereas the Greek *polis*, like the Roman *res publica*, was thought of as the primary guarantee against the transience of life, the 'Christian immortality that is bestowed upon the person' inevitably—or so Arendt concludes—undermined the efforts which had led to the invention of political life and remained necessary for its continuance. 'Without this transcendence into a potential earthly immor-

---

[116] Bethke Elshtain, *Public Man, Private Woman*, 56.

tality, no politics, strictly speaking, no common good and no public realm, is possible' (p. 55). With the coming of Christianity, this fundamental heroic political virtue was found not merely to be unnecessary; even when it still strove to make itself felt, it was denounced as 'vanity'. For in a world which is in any case doomed to destruction, the person who strives to bring about something permanent in that world must inevitably himself fall prey to futility. 'Worldlessness as a political phenomenon is possible only on the assumption that the world will not last' (p. 55).

Theologically, this raises a number of questions. We might ask, for one thing, whether Arendt's talk about the 'immortality' or 'deathlessness of the person' does not rest on a misunderstanding of Christian eschatology. We could at least show how in her definition of the relationship between eschatology and ethics Arendt falls victim to the old liberal error whose fundamental assumption was the eschatologically motivated and fundamental 'worldlessness' of the Christian ethos; thus the Pauline *hos me* ('as if') of I Corinthians 7, which actually means a form of having and using the world, was inevitably misinterpreted. But what is incontrovertible is the fact, stressed by Arendt, that the Christian view of the world was bound to lead to a disparagement of political existence—if this was understood in a totalizing sense. But it must already have become clear that this reduction was certainly not meant pejoratively, but was rather intended to be understood as an 'earthing' of political life. Here, however, we are concerned with the central reason Arendt gives for her judgement of the political significance of Christianity. She presents Christianity as an early 'philosophy of life', which begot the vitalist impulse which smothered politics—an impulse which, detached from its dogmatic foundations, is still influential today. In a comment which does not appear in the English edition, she goes on (the addition is in square brackets): ['Nowhere does the true spirit of Christianity, at least of primitive Christianity, show itself more strikingly than in the unquestioned postulate that life is the highest of all goods.'] 'The fundamental belief [of a Christian society] in the sacredness of life . . . has even remained completely unshaken by secularization and the general decline of the Christian faith' (p. 314).

We may remind ourselves that Arendt derived this view from her interpretation of Christian contemplation. And it is from this same standpoint that she can be confuted. We saw that it was Christian worship particularly which enhanced the status of life in all its everyday aspects. Manufacture and work are now also recognized as activities which accord with creation and which, together with their representatives, have their place in worship. Does this mean a glorification of 'life as the highest good'? When Jesus talks about gaining and losing life, the connection between the two things seems, at all events, to be considerably more complex: 'He who finds his life will lose it, and he who loses his life for my sake will find it' (Matt. 10: 39). There is hardly another saying which we find so frequently, in analogous form, in the gospels (Matt. 16: 25; Mark 8: 35; Luke 9: 24; 17: 33; John 12: 25). And the tenor of the saying is that it is not life itself which is to be regarded as the highest good; it is life *in Christ*—of which Paul can say that it is ours 'whether we live or whether we die' (Rom. 14: 8).

Finally, the lives of the early Christian martyrs, and their importance for the Church, provide little evidence for Christianity as an early 'philosophy of life'. As we have seen, the refusal of the martyrs to sacrifice to the political deities of the pagan world of antiquity (a refusal grounded in worship) was itself political in character.[117] This fact is all the more striking when we see it in the light of its difference from the Stoic marginalization of the vital instincts. Whereas the Stoic is prepared to renounce quite light-heartedly the aspects of life which appeal to the emotions because he considers them to be ultimately valueless, like bodily life as a whole, for Christians the reverse is the case. The loss of life is the loss of a great good, although it can be viewed as a 'gain' for the sake of Christ, who is life itself (Phil. 1: 21). Arendt's alternative, to elevate to the status of highest good either political life or life as such, ultimately comes down to the mere possibility of reversing the Greek totalization of political life, a reversal which Christianity allegedly introduced into political history. This would simply be to reproduce Nietzsche's well-known thesis, the genealogical logic of which rests on the basic scheme of just such a reversal, and absorbs the percep-

---

[117] The real problem about the early Christian understanding of martyrdom, on the other hand, arises at the very point where it has (sometimes) been interpreted along the lines of Greek political thinking, where death appears to be the instrument for immortalizing the memory of the young hero. But from the standpoint of faith, it is actually unpolitical if death is striven after for its own sake, or because of its immortalizing consequences, instead of being suffered as an unavoidable consequence of the political worship of the Church.

tion of a new quality into the concept of the eternal return of the same thing. The agreement with Nietzsche at this point is all the more striking since his talk about Christianity as 'a religion for slaves' fits in excellently with what Arendt says about the early 'philosophy of life'; for to reverence life itself as the supreme good, which Arendt believes is the Christian view, among the Greeks counted as proof that the person holding such a view was a slave by nature.

The understanding of new phenomena can go astray if they are pressed into familiar structures, even if particular points of difference are correctly observed; and this is what we can continually see happening in Arendt's analysis. She undoubtedly perceives that contemplation in Christianity is determined by a new 'content', the vision of life itself. But by seeing the activity itself as worldless, according to the pattern of the Greek *bios theoretikos*, she is ultimately bound to misunderstand both what Christian contemplation as worship means and what its 'content' is. This also conditions the other conceptual error which Arendt makes. According to what she says, the higher status given to the contemplative life in Christianity was a 'debasement of the *vita activa*', which was to be of decisive importance for the fate of political existence in modern society. Here too the essential connection is obscured, hidden in the shadow of a reduced alternative. For the political importance of Christian contemplation cannot be seen in its contrast to the *vita activa*—anything but.

It is not the degree to which the contemplative life contrasts with the active life and is given paramount status which is decisive for an understanding of political existence; the real question is how contemplation itself is perceived—the quality that is ascribed to it. Important is not so much how a worldless activity is weighted over against a worldly one; the question is whether the 'worldless' activity really is as worldless as Arendt presupposes.[118] But if

---

[118] Arendt's own study of Augustine particularly might have enlightened her at this point. For what he says in the *City of God*, talking about the question of the two elementary forms of life in the ancient world, suggests that believers can be at home in both theoretical and political life. This indifference towards the question of preference of course springs from the specifically Christian insight that these forms of life are in any case intertwined in the *City of God*. 'We should not give ourselves up to leisure so entirely that in our withdrawal we take no account of the needs of our neighbour, nor should we absorb ourselves so entirely in the public service that we find the contemplation of divine things unnecessary' (book XIX. 19).

contemplation in the sense of the Christian faith and its worship is recognized as being itself a worldly affair, then it is at most in its distorted forms that it can be pressed into service as a proof for Arendt's archaeology—which then admittedly, as far as these distorted forms are concerned, becomes all the more apt, and can be ignored by theology only to its own disadvantage. Since Arendt's perception of Christian worship was determined by an insufficient differentiation between this worship and the ancient world's ideal of contemplation, we must now remind ourselves of the structural differences between the two activities. We may provisionally sum up the matter by saying that in the ancient world's conception the contemplative life appears as an a-social, wordless and bodiless experience, in which, even though it has a reference to political life, the possibility of a political ethics is in tendency excluded. Unlike the immortality which is bound up with political deeds, the experience of 'the eternal' has no reference to any activity whatsoever.

EXCURSUS

Being for Plato 'unutterable' (*arretos*) and for Aristotle, 'wordless' (*aneu logou*) (*Human Condition*) (p. 20), contemplation as an inactive condition is hostile even to thinking, which is dependent on words. As Plato's cave parable in the *Republic* makes plain, it can be had 'only outside the plurality of men . . . in perfect "singularity"'' (ibid.). In the cave, a man must first free himself from the fetters which chain him to other men, in order to be able to leave the cave of solidarity with others for the solitary contemplation of the eternal Ideas. It is true that he returns to the world of human beings, but that is not itself the goal of the *theoria*. On the contrary, the dazzling power of the Ideas only forces him back to social life because that power cannot be endured for long. Yet even in this 'involuntary' committal to social life,[119] contemplation retains in Plato its de-socializing character. The 'theorist' who has been furnished with superior knowledge through the contemplation of the Ideas returns as someone who knows himself to be set apart from others, in the sense of a hegemony: the philosopher is destined to rule. The fact that Plato explicitly envisages the 'necessity' that the ruling theorist will in certain cases also implement this knowledge by lying to the public, reveals how the concept of *theoria* can itself imply a rejection of the claim of political ethics.

Whereas in Aristotle the strict distinction between the *vita contemplativa* and the *vita activa* (the dianoetic and the practical virtues) ultimately makes ethics too the field of application for *techne* (which must draw

[119] *Politics*, book VII, 561c.

phronesis also into its instrumental vortex), political ethics in Plato falls victim precisely to the linearly constructed connection between the contemplative and the active life, even though the two are differentiated. Aristotle puts *phronesis* and *techne* on one and the same level, as practical virtues, seeing them both (in distinction from the theoretical virtues) as related to the *contingent*, which can be either so or so, and is therefore subject to human activity. But in Plato the connection between theory and its practical application is embodied by the immortal soul; and the order of the soul (in the sense of the rule of reason over the emotional and desirous parts) also reflects the order which *necessarily* obtains in the state. So whether theory and practice are thought of as fundamentally different, as in Aristotle, or are thrown together, as in Plato, makes very little difference where the possibility of a political ethics is concerned. Whereas for Aristotle ethics is confined entirely to the practical political sector, and is completely separate from theory as the form of life which deals with the immutable, for Plato, justice, as the most political of all virtues, does not depend on the existence of a real political community at all. True justice can in any case be found only in the Idea of justice, which is espied in contemplation.[120]

Christian worship, on the other hand, can be understood neither in the sense of a primary separation between the contemplative and the active life, nor in the sense of their secondary alliance. It is rather characterized by the interlacing of the two forms of life. To divide the two would make worship as the service of God into the service of human beings. Then God would be made the object of theory, and out of the 'contemplation' of worship a power, endowment, obligation, motivation, or whatever would be engendered through which this theory could be translated into action. Hannah Arendt is certainly not the only one who has run aground on this old-new misunderstanding about the character of the Christian worship of God. We could list many a development in Christianity itself, past and present, whose liturgical and ethical conception is marked by this misunderstanding. But for all that, even in these developments, the awareness that the two forms of life are intertwined has not as a general rule been entirely lost. Monasticism, for example, has by no means always meant the refusal to participate in active life which Luther criticized so sharply in the mendicant orders, but has itself sought to dovetail the two forms of life.

It is true that the Benedictine formula *ora et labora* could, for example, easily be understood in the additive sense of a parallelism;

---

[120] See here in general the discussion in Milbank, *Theology and Social Theory*, 370.

but the very reason given by the Augustinian Rule for physical labour (*Epistolae* 21) is that it enables the monasteries to practise neighbourly love, and that unlike overly absorbing activities like buying and selling, physical labour could actually promote contemplation.[121] Even mysticism does not lose the awareness of this interweaving of the two forms of life. Meister Eckhart's famous sermon on Luke 10: 38–42 interprets the relation between the *vita contemplativa* and the *vita activa* (symbolized by the sisters Mary and Martha) in an integrative sense. Thus Mary must ultimately 'absorb' Martha into herself, in order not merely to have chosen 'the better part' but so as to make the very question of precedence obsolete.[122] The crux of such movements was certainly not infrequently an awareness that an integration of this kind *has to be accomplished*, rather than a perception of it as being already *given* in the character of worship itself. But it was this, as we have seen, which was Luther's essential rediscovery, and one which constitutes the heart of the Reformers' 'vocational ethic'.

Unlike the ancient world's concept of contemplation, the worship of the Christian Church appears as a social, sensory, and active happening which does not undermine the possibility of a political ethics but already practises it in a particular form. Here contemplation as 'it looks upon the works of God' is not a solitary affair; it is primarily a corporate act. The shared act of worship provides the matrix for private spirituality, not vice versa: the first rule in the language of prayer is not 'my God' but 'our Father'. Strictly speaking, there is for Christians no such thing as a purely private devotional practice, since every invocation of God is always already encompassed by the communion of saints, and remains related to that.[123]

The difference between Christian contemplation and the contemplative model of antiquity is shown most clearly, however, where the Christian service of worship is a service of the divine and human *word*. It is not bound to be *aneu logou*—wordless—because all dependence on language would be disparaging. Instead, it actually consists of speaking and listening. This makes it an inescapably social event, and inescapably sensory. Its 'object' is

---

[121] E. Delaruelle, 'Le Travail dans les règles monastiques occidentales du 4ᵉ au 9ᵉ siècle', *Journal de Psychologie Normale et Pathologique* 41/1 (1948).

[122] Meister Eckhart, *Deutsche Predigten und Traktate* (1995), 280–9.

[123] Cf. here B. Wannenwetsch, *Innen und Außen?* (2004).

itself *logos*, the Word which communicates itself (John 1: 1 ff.); it is not a wordless Idea of the good, as Plato would have it. Nor is God as the 'object' of contemplation what Aristotle would like him to be: the one who, himself unmoved, enjoys and thinks himself. Whereas Aristotle (here following Plato) felt that every thought of God's directed towards something outside himself would be a weakness of the Unmoved Mover, Luther viewed this Aristotelian God as in fact a 'most pitiable Essence' (*ens miserrimum*): 'The Supreme Being sees (only) himself. If he were to see anything outside himself, he would see the wretchedness of the world. At this point Aristotle tacitly negates God.'[124] Whereas the self-related character of contemplation in antiquity already thinks its object as existing in pure self-relatedness, in Christian faith and worship God is viewed not *meta*physically but physically. The 'object' of contemplation in worship and theology is not God in the monistic sense, but is named by Luther in the following definition: 'The subject of theology is the human being, guilty and lost, and God, justifying and saving' (*Subiectum Theologiae homo reus et perditus et deus iustificans vel salvator*, WA 40 II, 328, 1 f.).

Now this does not, as it were, make 'community between God and the human being' the theme; the theme is the interaction between the two: not life 'in communion with God' but 'life with God'.[125] Oswald Bayer puts his finger on the essential point when he interprets the *et* ('and') conjoining the two halves of Luther's formula about theology not in the sense of a general state of affairs in which the relation of the two sides is mediated, but actively, as 'a heated exchange of words'.[126] For Christian contemplation, it is not a matter of an intelligible divine object which the observing human subject through its self-elevation beholds. Instead, human beings in worship experience themselves as drawn into the dramatic happening in which God communicates himself bodily, in word and sacrament, and in which human beings respond: listening, tasting, and seeing. That is why Luther, contrary to the understanding of his own time and our own, understood even private

---

[124] WA TR 1, 57, 44 f. and WA TR 1, 73, 32. The translation follows the German translation by O. Bayer, *Theologie* (1994), 54.

[125] *Freiheit im Leben mit Gott* is the title of H. G. Ulrich's volume on freedom in the tradition of Christian ethics. On the objective of the above distinction between life in fellowship with God and life with God, see the editor's introduction: 'Die "Freiheit der Kinder Gottes" ', 15 f.

[126] Bayer, *Theologie*, 41.

meditation not as a matter of religious inwardness, but explicitly in the light of the Word which comes to meet us from outside, as something to be carried on and practised outwardly, something to be recited and repeated out loud.[127] Speaking and hearing opens the door to the world, or even constitutes 'a world' as our sphere of communication. How could Christian worship as an event of the Word ever be 'worldless' or produce 'worldlessness', as Hannah Arendt assumes is the case in Christianity? Where men and women testify to the *Logos* as the mediator of creation, without whom 'not anything was made that was made' (John 1: 3), worship as the event of that 'exchange of words' becomes itself the birthplace of the 'world' which presides between human beings.

But it is just this 'gathering' world which—according to *The Human Condition*—Arendt sees disappearing in Christianity. The public and political space of an assembling world is in her opinion replaced by 'the unpolitical, non-public character of the Christian community', whose political principle, 'charity and nothing else', as it were takes the place of the world (pp. 53 f.). In its very turning to the world, Arendt descries the supreme Christian denial of the world. In Jesus's admonition to give alms in secret, and not to let the left hand know what the right hand is doing (Matt. 6: 1–4), she sees the 'curious negative quality of goodness, the lack of outward phenomenal manifestation' (p. 74). The 'worldlessness inherent in good works' (p. 76) and their lack of substance means that active goodness represents 'renunciation' as a form of life, a forsaking which can flee only to the fellowship of God as the sole possible witness. This goodness seems to Arendt to be not merely severed from any reference to the world, but to make active negation of the world a positive principle. 'Fleeing the world and hiding from its inhabitants, it negates the space the world offers to men, and most of all that public part of it where everything and everybody are seen and heard by others' (p. 77). This reproach cannot be lightly rejected. For if Arendt's assessment of the hiddenness of good works were correct, the unavoidable consequence would indeed be that the Christian ethos has to be considered as private *in*

---

[127] In his new definition of *meditatio*, compared with *oratio mentalis* ('mental prayer'), which had increasingly come to be conceded a higher status in the course of the Middle Ages, Luther picked up the patristic Church's practice of praying and reading the Scriptures aloud—though 'the heart' was of course involved. Cf. M. Nicol, *Meditation bei Luther* (1984), 73–83.

principle—as an ethos which could certainly develop a kind of social ethics (because of its relation to common obligations), but not a political ethics. For a political ethics depends on a public life in which ethics itself is made a theme—and this means that the deeds must 'appear', just as Arendt demands. But what she overlooks in her appeal to the Sermon on the Mount is the other saying about the 'hiddenness' of works: 'You are the light of the world. A city set on a hill cannot be hid . . . Let your light so shine before men, that they may see your good works and give glory to your Father who is in heaven' (Matt. 5: 14–16).

The supposed contradiction between this and the saying which Arendt quotes is resolved if we note the different perspectives which are presupposed in the two sayings. The good works are to be hidden *from the person who performs them*. It is his left hand which ought not to know what his right hand does. So in the saying about giving alms it is ultimately the complacent glance at oneself which is also to be excluded. The public character of the good work would increase this self-regard, because of the approving looks of other people. But with his saying about the city set on a hill Jesus makes it clear that this does not mean that the public character of the works is to be excluded altogether. For it is only when the works are openly seen that it becomes evident that the *telos* of the works is not the moral perfecting of the doer. The Christian teleology of public manifestation is thus utterly anti-Greek. Here public manifestation does not provide the lasting condition in which the acts arrive at the goal of immortality through enduring public remembrance of them. Instead, the manifestation imparts a *telos* of good works, which goes beyond that: the praise of God. It is not the deeds that endure but God's praise for the deeds. The public character of the works is thus carried over into the public character of the praise of God. This 'enhypostasis' of good works in the praise of God then also sets free that uninhibitedness with which these works can also be made public in worship itself.

In this way, as we know, the mention by name of particular Christians and their lives in the worship of the patristic Church was the origin of what was later formalized and institutionalized as canonization. The publicizing of the acts of those witnesses to the faith took place primarily for the praise of God, but in a secondary sense it was also supposed to provide an ethical model for other believers. The almost entire loss of this uninhibited mention of good works and the doers of them, especially in the Protestant churches, raises the question whether this loss is not based on one more serious still? We have to ask whether there is in general a failure to see that the teleology of works as a whole is to be found in worship, instead of being transferred into a teleology of 'liberation', the 'integrity of creation', 'Christian self-perfection', or more besides. It is all too easy to make the mistake of thinking that, theologically, the question about the teleology of good works can be settled through the *via negativa*, so to speak. Provided that it is soteriologically established that the works are not put to use in the interests of 'a righteousness of works', it would seem as if the further definition of their *telos* could be left without more ado to the free play of ideological thinking.

The Intertwining of the vita activa and the vita contemplativa

In our discussion of Hannah Arendt's theses we have seen where their limitation is to be found. By understanding contemplation in Christianity on the pattern of contemplation as it was viewed in the ancient world, Arendt fails to perceive the special character of Christian worship, which consists of the reconciliation of the contemplative and the active life. The pattern of theory and praxis acts as a system of co-ordinates into which the meaning of Christianity is to be inscribed. Luther, on the other hand, insisted that Christian faith is not subject to this scheme, but bursts it apart from within: 'Lest we be led astray either by the active life with its works or by the contemplative life with its speculations' (*ne vita activa cum suis operibus et vita contemplativa cum suis speculationibus nos seducant*, WA 5, 85, 2 f.). No more than theology can the Christian life be subsumed under either one of the two categories. Instead Luther brings in a third category which he calls 'passive life' (*vita passiva*).[128] This 'vita sui generis', as Bayer calls it, now provides the point of reference for the two traditional forms of life. These are drawn into the *vita passiva*, as it were. They are not of course thereby annihilated, but are transformed in such a way that they no longer relate exclusively to each other. This new form of life has its home in worship, and it is characterized by a receptivity which is in the highest degree active.

---

[128] For this phrase see, e.g., WA 5, 165, 35 f.; 166, 11. Cf. Bayer, *Theologie*, 42–9, and Christian Link, 'Vita passiva: Rechtfertigung als Lebensvorgang', *EvTh* 44 (1984), 315–51.

Because the Word communicates itself as 'bodily Word', to 'suffer' what God does is not a pure, stolid passivity, but is sensorily open. The passive life consists of listening, not closing one's ears; of tasting and seeing, not despising what is offered. But because this sensory activity is always one which is awakened by the creative power of the Word itself, it is as pointless here to divide activity and passivity as it is to divide theory from practice. Consequently it is a highly significant 'inconsistency' when instead of always using the word *passiva* in talking about faith and theology, Luther can just as freely use the word *practica*. [129]

It is only this intertwining of the contemplative and the active life which guards Christian talk about the 'work' of the liturgy (*leit-ourgia*) against the misunderstanding that something could be put into operation in liturgy from the human side—even if it were the work of God. Here Luther perceived that in the light of the *vita passiva*, the dispute about the relative importance of the active and the contemplative life (which Hannah Arendt later made the principle of her interpretation) is like the shadow-boxing of two opponents who are really playing into each other's hands.

Luther saw quite clearly that people for whom the gospel is theory, a 'human figment and idea', are bound to demand that it must now be put into practice. The pattern of theory and practice leads them astray, so that they say: 'Faith is not enough, we must now perform works'. In other words, sanctification must be added to justification, in a second act, as the human response to God's word. Luther saw that in the very same degree to which the word that initiates faith pales into theory and idea, the demand that idea be realized in practice is inevitable. The theorization of faith is matched by a moralization, ethicization of life . . . If faith is neither a theory nor the praxis of self-realization, but passive righteousness—God's work in us, which we experience sufferingly and thus die to justifying thinking as well as to justifying action—then faith is by no means thoughtless, any more than it is inactive. On the contrary: through faith, thinking as well as action becomes new. [130]

As we saw from the example of William Temple (section 5.1), the connection between the theorization of faith and its moralization

---

[129] Cf. the instances cited by Bayer, *Theologie*, 43 f.
[130] Ibid. 48 f.

cannot be ascertained in a merely historical sense, as the swing of a pendulum, the one being the result of the other; it characterizes the logical connection in idealistic thinking, where what is first perceived or theoretically 'enacted' is then 'realized' or 'put into practice'. In this framework it is immaterial where the role of faith is positioned—whether faith is ascribed predominantly to the aspect of cognition, as in Temple, or to 'realization' (via 'motivation') as in ethical rationalism, or whether it is located between the two as their 'connecting belt' (via 'interpretation') as in some conceptions of liberation theology.

Admittedly, if worship is ignored, as the place or—better still— the praxis where the reconciliation of the contemplative and the active life is experienced, Luther's formula about the 'passive life' too can only be misunderstood. It then degenerates into the legitimating of the quietism which is generally thought to be more characteristic of Lutheranism's political ethics than is Luther's formula. A point we can do no more than touch on here is that insight into the danger of the theoreticization and moralization of faith does not necessarily mean that these things are surmounted, as they come to be in the experience of worship. This insight can also present itself as an attempt to reach out beyond this experience. That is always the case if the Christian interlacing of the different forms of life is not left in the place where it is engendered—the practice of worship—but is supposed to be transferred in a post-Christian sense into definitions which are anthropologically, historically, philosophically, or theologically 'more fundamental'.

EXCURSUS

Schleiermacher, for example, was well aware that faith is exhausted neither by its cognitive dimension nor by its ethical one—that, as he says in his second Speech, it is neither metaphysics nor morality.[131] Like Luther, he counters these reductions through a third dimension which is supposed to describe faith in its all-embracing characteristic: 'feeling'. This is by no means a simplistic sentimentality, and thus a new reduction. For that, Schleiermacher's concept of feeling is much too comprehensive, at least as he develops it in the years following the publication of his Speeches (which are not very precise in this respect). Moreover, it is especially the receptive element in feeling as 'the feeling of absolute dependence' which is

---

[131] F. Schleiermacher, *On Religion: Speeches to its Cultured Despisers*, 18 ff.

taken into consideration. But nevertheless, Schleiermacher's third quality comes down to something different from what Luther meant by his *vita passiva*. Whereas Luther's passive life is born in worship (not as a 'given', but in its actual practice), in Schleiermacher we see the reverse. The repeated celebration of worship is born from the feeling of absolute dependence. This feeling itself cannot, certainly, be thought without a preceding relation to worship, but the relation nevertheless remains an ideal one: only as a 'given' does worship precede the feeling or the perception; as actual practice it is conceived of *a posteriori*: as an act of expression.

Seen in this way, the 'feeling of absolute dependence' tends in fact to absolve us from the radical dependence of worship. As dependence *per se*, it embraces the dissociation from practical dependence on the practice of worship. As a result, the affirmation of faith as a fundamental state of mind takes the place of the communication of word and sacrament, which according to the Augsburg Confession (Article V) are instituted 'in order that we may obtain this faith' (*ut hanc fidem consequamur*). But if, to some extent as a precautionary measure, this affirmation—like every other affirmation of what is supposed to be 'given' with faith as a state of mind—sets itself above the criticism which it would be bound to experience in worship, faith loses its critical potential. As a result, instead of addressing these affirmations critically, it ultimately becomes itself the object against which the criticism of religion is directed. To anchor the essence of Christianity in the self-consciousness of the devout may evade the criticism which Marx levelled at the (Hegelian) theorization of faith, and Nietzsche at its (Kantian) moralization. But this of course merely brings Freud on the scene, the third of the three 'masters of suspicion', whose psychological criticism of religion determines popular awareness today to a very much greater degree than either Marx or Nietzsche was ever able to do. For the Freudian criticism of religion has only to apply the principle of romantic hermeneutics to the concept of faith itself, tracing back the encountering word to the motivation of the author. In this sense Schleiermacher did theology no service, especially where political worship is concerned. Since worship too is now understood as an act of expression on the part of pious interpreters, designed for the mutual enhancement of their awareness of God, what was really meant to be the sharpest critic of the hermeneutics of suspicion is now turned into its most complaisant pupil.

In sensory worship—so far our reflections have brought us—the 'bodily Word' communicates itself, and resists every form of 'absorption'—either into concept or act, or into a hermeneutical, Christological, or ecclesiological principle. There 'thinking in different spaces' is destined to be overcome; there we can expect the reconciliation of theory and practice, the *vita contemplativa* and the *vita activa,* which engenders a truly political ethics.

B. WORSHIP IDENTITY IN (POST)MODERN SOCIETY

7

The Total Claim of Society

Augustine saw redemption from sin as liberation from the domination of political, economic, and psychological compulsions.[1] This redemption took political form in a community, 'the city of God' (*civitas Dei*), in which the tyranny of political, economic, or psychological forces (in the sense of their total respective claims to human life) is overcome. As we saw in the previous chapters, the power to break these total claims can be found in the political worship of the Church, which reconciles representatives of these antithetical forms of life. But today the liberation from total claims needs thinking about in another respect as well: the claim made by 'society'. For today society is putting forward a universal claim to integration which seems to be even greater than the total claims of political or private life. These became separate from one another in that each staked out its separate terrain, so that they were in a sense aware that their own field was limited by the other; but the claim of society is so unrestricted precisely because it maintains that it includes both spheres—and not merely the private and the political spheres themselves, but also the way the two are related to each other. In this light, the view which Friedrich Gogarten voices in his *Political Ethics* must almost be turned upside-down; for he described men and women as 'in thrall' to the state, but 'free' and 'autonomous' in respect of society.[2] On the one hand, there has come to be a widespread attitude towards the state which is critical to the point of complete disenchantment—an attitude which overlooks the fact that there are public obligations which do not mean freedom *from* politics, but set politics themselves free. On the other, and not least because of the triumphal march of the mass media, an

---

[1] For more detail see J. Milbank, *Theology and Social Theory* (1990), 391 f.

[2] F. Gogarten, *Politische Ethik* (1932), 149 f.

impersonal dictatorship of 'the crowd'[3] has come to the fore, where
the pressure towards conformity makes any talk about society as the
space of human freedom increasingly obsolete. In this part of our
study I shall therefore consider the critical relationship between the
worshipping community and the claims of society.

7.1 SOCIETY AS 'SUPER-SYSTEM' AND THE CHALLENGE OF POLITICAL WORSHIP

Today more than ever, society's claim is presented in the form of a
comprehensive pressure towards socialization—as the attempt to
'socialize' individuals, to make them 'fit' the pattern of society; and
this means that our discussion will have to grapple particularly with
the question about identity and the way identity is formed. Consequently in the first part, after an introductory analysis (7.1) of the
relevant social theories of Hannah Arendt and Niklas Luhmann, we
shall try—in dialogue with postmodern concepts of identity worked
out by Richard Rorty and Wolfgang Welsch—to elicit how in the
experience of the communion of worship a political identity for
Christian citizens can be developed which is socially hard to do-
mesticate (7.2). We shall first turn to the different ways in which the
claim of society is described today.

Society as the 'Going Public' of the Household

Hannah Arendt's trenchant analysis in *The Human Condition* of
'The Rise of the Social' (pp. 38 ff.) makes the connection between
society and the household clear. In her view, modern society should
be understood as essentially the 'going public' of the household
(p. 38), and it is on the pattern of the household that the public
realm is then treated—that is, administered. Arendt identifies the
birthday of society as the moment when private property ceased to
be a private affair and became a matter of public concern and public
negotiation. When wealth became 'capital', it broke out of the
privacy which bound it to the household, simply as something to
be used, and it was in the interests of its accumulation that the
society of private owners grew up (pp. 68 ff.). With this, the view of
political life changed. It was now understood essentially as a function of (economic) interests. Society and interest politics were born

---

[3] D. Riesman, *The Lonely Crowd* (1954).

in the same hour. What private owners now primarily expected of their rulers was protection of their private property; and at the same instant political life ceased to be viewed as the affair of citizens who *emerge* from private life; it increasingly also came to conform to the paradigm of the person of private means who pursues his own vital interests in public life as well.

The rise of the national economy as a colossal family business bureaucratically administered is matched on the political side by the professional politician, who in a society of job-holders also does his 'work' as a way of earning his bread. 'Society is the form [of co-existence] in which the fact of mutual dependence for the sake of life and nothing else assumed public significance and where the activities connected with sheer survival are [not only] permitted to appear in public [but are allowed to determine the face of the public domain].'[4] Thus *action* is actually excluded, being replaced by the *behaviour* which society expects of its members, making them 'socially acceptable' through the rules it lays down. Spontaneous action and outstanding achievements are sacrificed to social norms. Since social behaviour can now also be viewed as a 'political' form of reaction, it takes the place of politics in their original sense.

In this post-political refusal to engage in political life, modern society resembles the *oikos* of antiquity. It is true that the earlier principle of despotic rule is actually reversed, since in modern society nobody at all is supposed to rule. 'But this nobody, the assumed one interest of society as a whole in economics as well as the assumed one opinion of polite society in the salon, does not cease to rule for having lost its personality' (p. 40). Bureaucracy as form of government presents Arendt with the most cogent proof of this thesis. In a bureaucracy, 'the realm of the social' in the form of mass society has reached the stage at which all its members are equally embraced and controlled: '[Mass society shows the victory of society in general; it is the stage where there simply cease to be groups outside society at all.] Society equalizes under all circumstances' (p. 41).

In theology, however, the dispute with society in its specifically modern, functionally differentiated sense still leads a somewhat

---

[4] H. Arendt, *The Human Condition*, 46 (1958; 2nd edn. 1998). Here and in following quotations the passages in square brackets do not appear in the English edition and have been translated from the German (1967) text.

shadowy existence. The challenge it presents to theology has
certainly been repeatedly descried by individuals,[5] but it has hardly
been taken on board to its full extent. Perhaps what was first
needed was a way of pursuing the discussion about the complex
of 'the functional society' theoretically, over against a fully expli-
cated theory of society as 'social system', further refined by a
description of the function of religion, church, and theology. This
may be found today in the work of Niklas Luhmann especially.
That discussion cannot and need not be pursued in detail here. But
I should like to put forward some starting-points for the discussion
with systems theory from the aspect of political worship.

Unlike the ancient world's thinking about the ideal state, and
unlike a religiously motivated social doctrine, system theory purports to be programmatically abstemious; its explanations permit
merely functional judgements about the 'capacity' of a system,
which the application of the theory can therefore improve merely
on the level of the 'organizational system-formations' within the
social system.[6] The functional differentiations themselves, however, must be understood in a strictly system-immanent sense,
and by no means as the object of planning guided by theory. It is
true that the movement of modern societies can undoubtedly be
accurately described by terms such as 'differentiation'; but the
evolutionary perspective that is kept in view leads to a far-reaching
reduction. For this perspective makes it impossible to perceive
suffering in and from the movement itself, which, after all, as
'system' has basically already solved the problems for all time,
and is open at most for other, perhaps faster, but functionally
equivalent solutions. This perspective restricts the critical tools
available to the duality 'functional–dysfunctional'.

Over against a reduction of complexity like this, which promises
to overcome the suffering caused by systematization through still
further systematization, theology should insist that an elementary
distinction is indispensable: the distinction between the people who
make up a society and the way the society is constituted. For the
formative forces can only be pin-pointed if in the concept of the

---

[5] An exception here is Heinz-Dietrich Wendland, who in the 1950s made an
attempt in the name of a 'theological social doctrine', which has never found much
of an echo. Cf. e.g., 'Das System der funktionalen Gesellschaft und die Theologie',
in *idem, Botschaft an die soziale Welt* (1959).
[6] N. Luhmann, *The Differentiation of Society* (1982).

social system they are not fused with the people involved. Theology is accordingly especially challenged where, in the idea of the *autopoiesis* (self-creation) of a system, no agents can be detected any more in a 'process' which then purports to be 'self-controlled' and 'unguided'. Instead, theology will be concerned to identify the forces which are in fact in control.

The specific contribution which theology makes to 'society' can of course probably be best described in regard to the Church as political community as the *disempowerment* of anonymous forces—a disempowerment based on the lordship of Christ. Contrary to Luhmann's evolutionism, this aims at the need for a *guided* movement of society. Inasmuch as people are always determined by forces which they themselves are not able to control, a community is always under rule. In 'the state', this necessity emerges from the obscure mists of anonymity. Consequently, the state must not be turned into a mere function of society. Rather, it has to be acknowledged as the authority which guides society by way of law and politics, which for their part would be hopelessly underdefined if they were to be described as 'part-systems'. In the state, the controlling forces are positively identifiable, negotiable—in a word, political. Theological ethics discerns the state as a necessary (and therefore serviceable) counterpart to society, and views politics and law as forms of action which determine the path society takes, and not vice versa; and in the same way it will also remain critical of the systems-theoretical positioning of 'religion'. It will hardly be by chance that it is precisely in his talk about 'the function of religion'[7] that Luhmann thrusts forward to formulations which reveal both the theological quality of his theory and, at the same time, the quasi-religious claim of 'society'. It is of essential importance for Luhmann that religion too is not in a position to substantiate an 'extra-social being'. On the contrary, for religion, determination through the concept of society is unavoidable. In this context he formulates society's quasi-religious claim by saying: 'In each case, the social system which governs the relations of human beings to the world *ultimately and comprehensively* acts as society. Society is *the social condition which constitutes sensory being-in-the-world*. To the degree to which the nature of this constitution

---

[7] N. Luhmann, *Die Funktion der Religion*, 3rd edn. (1992). The page number in the text refers to this work.

system is understood in terms of systems-theory, society is understood as well' (p. 75, my italics).

Here one must welcome the clarity with which Luhmann spells out the quasi-religious claim, which is often described in much more diffuse form in other comments about 'society'. But at the same time, Luhmann thus remains bogged down in the same *theological* misunderstanding which he believes he has avoided in the total claim of society. He merely reassigns religion's own precinct by shifting it from outside society to within it. In seeing religion as a special system for the inner mastery of social affairs (meaning, contingency), Luhmann ultimately remains the confederate of a particular complex of theological tradition, in the liberal amalgam of pietism, Enlightenment, and romanticism.

It should be remembered, however, that Luhmann is able to draw on a development in the Church itself when he advises the Christian religion to use its own differentiation into the sub-systems church, *diakonia*, and theology as a way of increasing its functionality (and ultimately its transformation into civil religion). For example, he points to the different roles assigned to clergy and laity which have developed historically, where this process could be detected or extrapolated.[8] It is certainly true that the clerical form of role differentiation in the congregation pushed forward the disintegration of Christian citizenship as a form of life, and in this way prepared the shift from person to role which systems theory conceptualizes. As Luhmann points out, evolutionarily advanced societies are characterized by the increasingly hard and fast division between person and role. They underpin 'their structure and the dependability of their expectation of behaviour through roles rather than through persons'.[9] In the wake of systems theory, it is impossible to avoid an identity model such as is taken up in the postmodern presentation of the self (which we shall look at later). If the nature of human beings is identified as societal, individual forms of life pale into mere roles in society's libretto. The identity of the role-players then consists of the shared relationship to society of their different roles. Like an invisible hand, the relationship to society

[8] N. Luhmann, *Die Funktion der Religion*, 3rd edn. (1992). 103.
[9] N. Luhmann, 'Moderne Systemtheorien als Form gesamtgesellschaftlicher Analyse', in J. Habermas and N. Luhmann, *Theorie der Gesellschaft oder Sozialtechnologie* (1976), 23.

integrates the different role expectations, which would otherwise be bound to lead to unendurable tensions in the life of the individual, who has increasing difficulty in bringing them into accord.

In this perspective, society with its integrating power undoubtedly takes the place of evolution, inasmuch as the fate of the individual is seen completely from the angle of the whole and its continued existence. The multifarious subjects disappear in the one social system, whose 'environment' they constitute. From this evolutionary viewpoint, the predicament of part-systems which can less and less be mediated to each other is alleged to be a virtue. As the differentiation of the individual subsections of society increases, these acquire, each for itself, an increasing measure of competence and efficiency—a functionality which, according to Luhmann, is bound in its turn to contribute to the good of the whole. But in his view this functionality increases precisely because the individual sub-systems confine themselves to their own individual dynamic, and cut themselves off from each other in a way which counters defensively the claim of individual systems to any overall efficacy, or the right to set an agenda. But if the social system 'society' is supposed to be best served as a whole when the individual systems immunize themselves against one another, it is obvious that in the systems-theoretical view of society, politics are reduced precisely to the administrative affair which Hannah Arendt talked about.[10] It would therefore seem no more than consistent for politics itself to be understood as just such a sub-system, which shares with all the others the trend towards self-preservation and self-expansion. For where the autonomous laws of the systems are themselves made the principle by which society functions, politics is left with nothing but the tedious task of somehow balancing out the various different interests—in the sense of the self-control of administrative power. According to Luhmann, the specific political medium of communication is in fact power, just as wealth is the communication medium of the economy, truth that of science, love that of the family, and faith that of religion. The search for shared convictions and a

---

[10] The summing up of society in terms of systems theory in fact offers the precise pendant to Arendt's analysis of 'the household going public'. It is not by chance that Luhmann presses into service for the system the same logic which we first met with in the rise of an economic theory, or economic theology: the belief propagated by Adam Smith that individual egoism (whether the egoism of private persons or that of self-sustaining systems) is ultimately bound to be for the good of the whole (the 'economy' or 'society'). Systems-theoretical thinking is at heart capitalist.

shared activity which would go beyond the balancing of sub-systems is already a dead letter, conceptually. All that is left is a *realpolitik* which, it must be said, is more at home in Arendt's grey bureaucratic business suit than in Machiavelli's princely apparel.

Social Criticism: Political, not in the Name of 'Community'

A political ethics springing from worship, in contrast, will not be able to avoid a critical position towards society. But before making any attempt to change society directly, by changing the emphases in the systems complex, its concern must be to call in question quite practically the whole concept of society as the dominating social model. Over against the de-subjectivization of morality and polit-ics, political worship keeps a firm hold on the 'ethical subject', even though this subject is not autonomous. Here, as we have seen, action in all the spheres of life follows the law of the spirit of Christ, not the supposedly autonomous laws of society's part-systems. Where Christians do not cede the formation of their identity to some anonymous social complex, but preserve a 'homologous'[11] identity throughout the different social roles, the question about the conditions in which this identity can be learnt becomes acute. This means that we shall have to go on to clarify how far these roles can be learnt in worship in a way which begets a hope for political action and not just social behaviour. As such, this learning process cannot fall back on the dominance of a particular role paradigm to which

---

[11] I am using the expression 'homologous' because I do not want to use the word 'homogeneous' in connection with Christian identity, and yet want to indicate the unity of the biographical and ethical interpretation of the Christian 'story'. The unifying demand for homogeneity would not do justice to the variety of the charis-mata. But above all it would contradict the political character of Christian identity (see my essay 'Members of One Another: *Charis*, Ministry and Representation: A Politico-Ecclesial Reading of Romans 12', in Craig Bartholomew *et al.* (eds.), *A Royal Priesthood: The Use of the Bible Ethically and Politically* (2002)). In contrast, however, the identity of the Christian citizen can be described as homologous in so far as it remains constitutively related to the specific praxis of the shared assent (*homo-logein*) to what God does, and to the praise and confession of faith of the congregation. It exists neither in an outward unity, either already demanded or given; nor can its homologous character be understood merely in the sense of an inward coherence ('authenticity'). The consonance between the praxis of living and the '*Leit*story' is invested in the Christian Church with a specific outward applica-tion. In the 'outward' sense too, it is always a matter of a homologous identity: the consonance in the individual praxis of living with other people and with their praxis of living (which may very well be different). The 'play' that is in question can only be jointly interpreted.

behaviour in all the other spheres must conform. Instead, attention
has to be focused on the way in which interplay in the act of worship
actually permits the freedom to perform different social roles, and
develops the capacity for so doing, in such a way that it is still always
possible to see what 'play' is being performed. The life of believers
can quite properly be understood as 'performing the scriptures',[12]
and the unity of the ethical subject can be comprehended in this
general interpretative task (in the performative sense, not the hermeneutical one); and this fact again illustrates particularly the
contraposition to 'society'. For in defining ethical subjecthood
enhypostatically, as it were, Church and society arrive at agreement
in a way which also makes their rivalry plain: is ethical identity to be
found in the functional relation to society, or in the general relationship to the Christian 'story' through which Christian identity is
interpreted?

As 'society', the self-definition of human sociality has conceptually and pragmatically challenged Christian thought and action to a
greater degree than perhaps any other historical forms of totalization, political or private. For inasmuch as it fought against the
Christian life, even 'total' politics still thereby acknowledged that
form of life as its opposite number. In the form of modern society,
however, the totalization of social life has taken over everything;
here everything has its place—except for political worship. The
homologous ethical identity of political worship is something fundamentally different from the functional integration of different
social roles in a 'context of meaning' which is conceded to the
Church and its expressions of life. Even if this were to be defined
religiously or in Christian terms, it would still only integrate the role
expectations of society, and therefore cement its autonomous laws
and its differences. But politics are not merely to be understood as a
'balance of power'; they depend on the free formation of conviction
in the community. There is therefore an eminently political aspect
to the resistance which has to be practised in worship to the implied
presupposition that the different systems in society cannot in
any case avail themselves of consensus processes.[13] In the rediscovery of political existence, hopes can be pinned on people who
preserve and prove their ethical identity in a plurality of allegedly

[12] N. Lash, 'Performing the Scriptures', in *idem, Theology on the Way to Emmaus* (1986).
[13] See here the first section of Chapter 10.

incompatible roles. They keep alive a healthy mistrust of the suspicion—elevated to a sociological truth—that life must first be torn apart ('differentiated') before it can be raised to a higher unity. In this light, what we already diagnosed about the relation between the *vita contemplativa* and the *vita activa* (section 6.5) emerges once more. Hannah Arendt's thesis about the Christian origin of 'society' is at the very least a dangerous simplification.

Arendt traces society as the public form of *oikos*, or the home, to the Christian social concept of the Body of Christ as *familia Dei*, the family of God. In her view, this initiated a tendency in the course of which further concepts of social life were then also apprehended in the paradigm of the family, from the medieval order of the estates down to nationalism (the nation as family). Accordingly the rise of modern society is merely the secular end of this development, which, regardless of its dogmatic emancipation from its Christian roots, still preserves their fundamentally anti-political character.[14]

As we saw in the earlier section on the reconciliation of *oikos* and *polis*, the *familia Dei*, structured through worship, itself already constitutes a political community which can by no means be subsumed under categories of domestic behaviour. But Arendt's genealogy, in which society is the offspring of Christianity, is dangerous, because it turns what is potentially the strongest counter-force to the totalizing concept of society into its opposite. In this way she involuntarily strengthens society's claim fundamentally to anticipate every criticism through the universal standard of its tolerance.[15] Because 'society' presents itself as the critique of traditional total claims of social forms of life, which it integrates by levelling them down to the rank of part-systems, it is able to understand any critique only from within. Every criticism brought against it then becomes the medium for the 'development' of society, which cannot permit anything outside itself.

[14] Arendt, *Human Condition*, 53 f.: 'The unpolitical, non-public character of the Christian community was early defined in the demand that it should form a *corpus*, a "body", whose members were to be related to each other like brothers of the same family. The structure of communal life was modeled on the relationship between the members of a family because they were known to be non-political and even anti-political.'

[15] Cf. here my article 'Die Grenzen liberaler Toleranz', *LM*, 11 (1993), 31–2.

In spite of the reservations about Arendt's genealogy, her contribution here must not go unrecognized. The strength of her concept of society becomes clear when we see it over against the one which Ferdinand Tönnies developed two generations earlier, and which even today still exerts a far-reaching influence on theology, by way of Max Weber's reception. Unlike Tönnies's famous contradistinction between 'community and society',[16] Arendt shows precisely how the two hang together. She sees society not as an antithesis to community, but as an extrapolation of the family pattern in public life. In so doing, she does justice to the *de facto* claim of modern society—which is precisely its ability to mediate all the different forms of life to each other, or to exist as being itself their mediation. It is only this background which makes fully clear what the claim of the Church's political worship really aims at. For it cannot be related and restricted solely to the sphere of 'community' (although this has also continually put itself forward as an element in the Church's self-perception), but claims to be itself the integration, the *reconciliation* of different forms of life. In that perspective this can no longer be a matter of strengthening an element of community *within* society. It is rather that thought and action are challenged to grasp the mutual relationship of the different forms of life not socially but politically.

This task is much more radical than that which could be expected of a 'communitarist' criticism of society in the name of community. For it would mean showing how the different forms of life can be perceived each in its own dignity without their becoming autonomous; how these forms of life can be so related to each other that their specific characteristics are not absorbed into the hegemony of any one of their paradigms of behaviour, but find their common dimension in a law of action which transcends these behaviour paradigms. And it would mean showing how this third, common dimension must not purchase the shared relationship of the different forms of life at the expense of the subjecthood of its representatives, but that the relation can exist precisely in the preserving and proving of a homologous ethical identity. We have to talk about this identity not merely because of the simple fact that

---

[16] F. Tönnies, *Gesellschaft und Gemeinschaft* (1887). Tönnies describes the forming of a community in the characteristic style of domestic vocabulary as resting on emotional and traditional ties, whereas the formation of a society is determined by rational and utilitarian processes and relationships based on interest.

it is the same person who acts in the different roles. We rather have to ask about this identity in the sense of the consistent interpretation of a central story, a '*Leit*story' so to speak, *in* these different roles. That brings us to the following correlation: in listening to the Christian '*Leit*story' of Jesus Christ, in practising their own roles in worship, Christians learn to live their lives in harmony as creaturely beings and as neighbours in such a way that the interpreted 'text' of the *story*, the play itself, remains recognizable right across the different role expectations.

In the following section we shall consider how this 'homologous' identity, which is open for consensus, can be defined in the context of the dispute with postmodern concepts of identity.

7.2   MORAL VOCABULARY OR ETHICAL GRAMMAR?

The difference between the 'neighbourliness' we have touched on and the liberal model of 'solidarity' is on the same level as the distinction between a homologous ethical identity and the postmodern ideal type of the 'liberal ironist' whom the American neopragmatist Richard Rorty has characterized in his programmatic book *Contingency, Irony and Solidarity* (1989). A discussion of Rorty's argument is important here not only because Rorty lodges a more bitter offensive than almost anyone else against the search for a unified form of life and moral discourse, against the reconciliation of public and private life. It is also especially necessary because in Rorty we see the extreme case of a kind of argumentation which makes the total claim of (liberal) society the starting-point and ruling criterion of an ethics.[17] Rorty fits the character of that society as we have outlined it in so undisguised a way that a closer look at what he says promises to be worthwhile. This examination will also show, for one thing, that Rorty is subject to a delusion, and for another, that it is not possible for him within the limits he himself lays down to perceive the fact. It is only a theological

---

[17] 'We cannot assume that liberals ought to be able to rise above the contingencies of history and see the kind of individual freedom which the modern liberal state offers its citizens as just one more value. Nor can we assume that the rational thing to do is to place such freedom alongside other candidates (e.g., the sense of national purpose which the Nazis briefly offered the Germans, or the sense of conformity to the will of God which inspired the Wars of Religion') (R. Rorty, *Contingency, Irony and Solidarity* (1989), 50; the page numbers in the text refer to this book).

interpretation which shows the potential for self-deception in Rorty's arguments.

'Solidarity and Self-Creation': The Irony of Postmodern Society (Richard Rorty)

The ideal type of person in Rorty's universal liberal utopia of a society dominated by a 'post-metaphysical' culture is 'the liberal ironist'. His essential mark is awareness of 'the contingency of his or her most central beliefs and desires' (p. xv). To bring home in radical form the historical fortuitousness of all concerns, of human language, human consciousness, and human society, goes hand in hand with the rejection of all 'metaphysical' attempts to gather political and individual life into a single, all-embracing movement. For every attempt of this kind would inevitably mean relating to some authority outside the various inhabited linguistic worlds from which an 'inner nature' for the world or the human being would be postulated, a nature which we should have to express or describe 'adequately', and would have to accord with morally. Rorty considers any such metaphysical recourse to be both historically superseded and politically inexpedient. Instead of prolonging any further the series of attempts to fuse the private and the public, and to unify the different moral vocabularies either reductively or expansively, Rorty pleads that their difference should be respected, and 'that we should then use them for different purposes' (p. xiv). In this way the two exemplary different 'vocabularies', the vocabulary of individualism and the vocabulary of solidarity (as well as their respective philosophical exponents), would no longer have to be played off against each other in the dispute about liberalism and communitarianism. Instead, Rorty proposes '[treating] the demands of self-creation and of human solidarity as equally valid, yet forever incommensurable' (p. xv). The irony which is the appropriate attitude then no longer needs to choose between antithetical moral languages and their philosophies; it merely has to decide in each case when which of them can be usefully employed, and where.

In his demand that different (moral) vocabularies should be viewed as instruments, and employed as tools for the appropriate private or public purposes, Rorty appeals to the linguistic philosophies of Ludwig Wittgenstein and Donald Davidson. From Wittgenstein's logical confutation of the possibility of a linguistic theory of meaning, Rorty deduces the general assertion that human language is a fortuitous product. This, of course, is surely to turn Wittgenstein's intention upside-down. The epistemological progression in Wittgenstein's late philosophy compared with his attempts in the *Tractatus* is guided by the insight that language cannot be understood in independence of social forms of life; but this means that it can only be talked about—can only be traced back to—forms of life as the 'given'. 'What has to be accepted, the given, is—so one could say—*forms of life*.'[18] According to Wittgenstein's thinking, not to try to go behind the actual spoken language particularly includes the positive assertion of its 'contingency': no recourse to a sphere beyond the forms of life, neither a realm of necessity nor a realm of fortuitousness. This renunciation is simply the other side of the renunciation of the search for a logical fundamental structure for language. For Rorty, language evidently consists simply of vocabulary and sentences: 'Since truth is a property of sentences, since sentences are dependent for their existence upon vocabularies, and since vocabularies are made by human beings, so are truths' (p. 21). What Rorty's understanding of truth leaves out is grammar. Yet it is only grammar which regulates the use of vocabulary in sentences, so that they are understood as statements, and can be tested for their 'truth-value'. Consequently the question whether languages are made by human beings cannot be answered by the assertion that vocabularies can be manufactured. It is only if grammar could also be plausibly made an artefact that Rorty could properly appeal to the perceptions of linguistic philosophy.

According to Wittgenstein, however, it is possible to see how a grammar works only as it is used; we cannot see how it is 'made'. To deduce one rule from another which regulates its use, and whose own use is in its turn regulated by yet another rule, allows no methodological limitation, in the sense that at the end we are left with some fundamental rule whose content, once we know it, would be at our disposal for the 'production' of a grammar.[19] Consequently, it is not surprising that Wittgenstein can see grammar quite directly in association with theology, when it is a matter of stating the essential which cannot be methodologically captured and secured, yet determines our actual use of language: '*Essence* is

---

[18] L. Wittgenstein, *Philosophical Investigations* (1967), II xi 226e.
[19] Ibid. §84.

expressed by grammar... Grammar tells what kind of object any-thing is. (Theology as grammar.).'[20]

Rorty's postmodern ideal type of the 'liberal ironist' is therefore unmasked as an illusion, since it suggests that moral languages can be used and changed simply by way of their vocabularies. But what he is really demanding of his liberal ironist is the use of different grammars, and that means nothing less than a change of convictions in accordance with the declared purpose in each given case. Yet with this demand he by no means cuts free from the overpowering pressure of previous unified metaphysical constructions; he all the more imposes on postmodern existence something which people are hardly able to endure. To rationalize the change of convictions as he demands by asserting their fortuitous character cannot blind one to the fact that this demand could be met only at the cost of a pathologically deformed identity.[21] The fact that the postmodern ideal 'type' can be versed in the use of different vocabularies does not mean that he really speaks the languages to which these vocabularies belong. As long as 'speaking' is not part of the form of life which belongs to every individual language, it communicates nothing; it does not really become the communicative language game, but remains on the level of vocabularies—rhetorical toys, so to speak. Just as with Wittgenstein we can understand that the meaning of a word is the way it is used in the language (§43), so the meaning of a (moral) language only becomes evident 'bio-grammatically', through its use in the given form of life. Consequently, philosophers such as MacIntyre and Taylor are right when they press for 'identity' to be seen only in narrative terms, as a history of fundamental orientations and ways of living. For the same reason I am describing ethical identity springing from worship as 'performative' and 'homologous'. To this identity there belongs a performance in which the Christian form of life in all its pluriformity is nevertheless able to be homologous, because it sees itself as the biographical interpretation of the role which is practised

[20] Ibid. §§371, 373.
[21] This is one of the motifs which Charles Taylor has brought out in his extensive aetiology of modern identity, *Sources of the Self* (1989). It is entirely in line with the 'grammatical' viewpoint demanded here when he talks about the inescapable moral frameworks without which human beings cannot properly live—that is to say, cannot live meaningful and fulfilled lives. Accordingly he shows that such fundamental guiding convictions secretly exist among the exponents of naturalistic and utilitarian models too, even though programmatically they reject anything of the kind (p. 71).

in worship and which belongs within God's one salvation history with men and women. In this perspective, the grammatical observation is unavoidable. It shows that as linguistically constituted beings we are required to seek a form of life which embraces both private and political existence.

Here, as was suggested above, Rorty's own mode of argumentation provides a demonstration. According to what he says, the language of 'self-creation', which belongs to the individual sphere, and the public language of 'justice' and solidarity should be viewed as 'equally valid yet forever incommensurable'. If we look more closely at the use which Rorty makes of the two moral languages in the course of his argument, we cannot avoid the impression that where Rorty is really at home is only in the language of self-creation.

Solidarity or Neighbourliness?: The Grammatical Simplicity of the Moral Life

This will only become really evident when Rorty's use of these moral languages is tested theologically. If we put the biblical language game of 'neighbourliness' together with Rorty's talk about 'solidarity', it becomes clear that neither of the two could serve as translation of the other into its own vocabulary. For the difference is actually grammatical: whereas 'neighbourliness' is determined by the need of the other person, Rorty understands by solidarity the *self*-determination to behave socially. The exemplary story of the Good Samaritan in Luke 10: 25 ff. counts as providing the rule for Christian neighbourliness. But whereas Jesus tells it in order to criticize and transform the question about the scope of what it enjoins ('Who then is my neighbour?'), Rorty declares that the mark of 'solidarity' is actually the fortuitous and arbitrary limitation of its sphere of action. Even its expansion, however desirable, would then be no more than the expression of a contingent development to 'more' solidarity. Yet Rorty is well aware of the grammatical difference from Christian love of one's neighbour, and explicitly distances himself from it, recognizing that his position is 'incompatible' with any such attitude (pp. 191 f.). What he of course fails to see is that this incompatibility does away with the other incompatibility he maintains. For in the light of this fundamental difference, it becomes clear that the allegedly incommensurable moral languages of 'self-creation' and 'solidarity' are opposed to each other only on the vocabulary level. Grammatically, they belong to the same linguistic family of *autopoiesis*, to which the language of systems theory also belongs. Rorty sees solidarity too as an artefact, as 'the fortunate happenstance creation of modern times' (p. 68).

It is only theologically, against the background of biblical grammar, that the full extent of the irony becomes plain; for in Rorty's liberal utopia the two moral languages are in fact undoubtedly commensurable, but they are certainly not equally valid. As solidarity, justice too becomes the function of self-creation. What Rorty maintains to be a 'shift from epistemology to politics' (p. 68) is in fact the actual retreat from political existence. The fantasy of self-creation, which is derived from the individualist language game, now infects political language too. In order to rationalize his claim, Rorty puts forward a familiar form of 'historical' thinking. The history of progress as the aetiology of liberal society can be described only if the distance from the various epochs makes us able to 'figure out how to use the vocabularies of these movements . . . Christianity did not know that its purpose was the alleviation of cruelty . . . But *we* now know these things, for we latecomers can tell the kind of story of progress which those who are actually making progress cannot' (p. 55).

Here again we see that what may seem plausible on the level of vocabulary cannot stand up to grammatical examination. 'Theology as grammar' fundamentally calls in question patterns of thinking in terms of different epochs. When Rorty associates the invention of the idea of self-creation with an epochal change, in which the Enlightenment and Romanticism invented 'a new kind of human being' (p. 7), we may simply be reminded that the biblical tradition tells us that it was *from the beginning* that human beings strove to go beyond creatureliness. It is not for nothing that the primal history is framed by the motif that the temptation for human beings to strive to be like God, and to know for themselves what good and evil is (Gen. 3: 5 f.), always existed, and that this temptation first found expression in the sphere of the family, and then in the political sphere, as 'rivalling the heavens' (Gen. 11: 1–9).[22]

---

[22] C. Westermann, *Genesis 1–11* (1984), 547 f.

In considering the theological composition of the story of the Tower of Babel, we should note the tensions between the Yahwist's story about the beginning of the tower ('the whole earth had one language and vocabulary') and the previous (J and P) account of the ramification of humanity into many peoples and languages (Gen. 10: 31) which is seen as the result of God's *blessing* after the Flood. According to this, 'Babel' would not be the tragic symbol of the loss of a romantic, primal, unified human language; rather, the unified language about which the story tells would have to be understood as a 'unification' under the aspect of 'self-creation': whose purpose was to 'make a name for themselves'. Thus 'the one language and vocabulary' would have to be interpreted not so much in the sense of a unified 'natural' language, whose variety, as the narrative told us earlier, was the result of blessing, but rather in the sense of what I termed above a 'moral discourse'—a language for which the grammatical dimension is decisive, and the unification of vocabularies of secondary importance. In this light the divine intervention would be all the more understandable as an act of *preservation*.

In this sense this story could be understood as being in a way an aetiology of political existence: the need for communicative endeavour and consensual processes can be perceived in a positive sense as humanity's Babylonian inheritance. According to the Judaeo-Christian view, politics would accordingly begin at the very point where human 'self-creativity' is at an end. So in the perspective of this fundamental contradiction, we would have a counter-aetiology to Rorty's. 'Babel' would also have to be understood as the primal history of liberal society, inasmuch as its forms of life are configured according to the grammar of self-creation. The fact that the open unification of the moral language in 'Babel' reveals itself in 'liberal society' as a hidden commensurability, in the framework of an ironic mobility of vocabulary, makes little difference, substantially speaking. The Judaeo-Christian moral language of 'creature-liness' and 'neighbourliness' cannot be historically superseded by Rorty's 'self-creation and solidarity'; it remains their enduring grammatical antithesis. The biblical language cannot be viewed as the superseded attempt at a linguistic unified model, which bridges actual incommensurabilities (although this is what Rorty's historical sleight of hand would make of it). Instead, it goes to the grammatical heart of the dominating use of vocabulary, and reveals both existing unifying features, which are surrounded by the assertion of incommensurability, as well as existing contrasts, which are concealed under equivocations.

An example of the second case is provided by Charles Taylor with his assertion that in spite of fundamentally different sources of our particular moralities (the appeal to God, nature, reason), we contemporary people are largely in agreement about most of the moral values which are essential in liberal societies. 'We agree surprisingly well, across great differences of theological and metaphysical belief, about the demands of justice and benevolence, and their importance.'[23] It is true that in his book. Taylor certainly distinguishes between moral norms and sources (pp. 495 f.)—that is, in the language used above, between vocabulary and grammar; and he also questions the asserted general assent about moral norms when it comes down to enquiring how these standards can be supported 'ontologically' today in a way that holds more promise for the future than the way they are sustained in the average parasitic, liberal consciousness, which implicitly draws on the great theological or metaphysical concepts which it maintains have been superseded. But for all that, Taylor makes a similar mistake to Rorty—although his error is a mirror image of Rorty's, as it were—since he assumes as a given fact that different sources really can lead to similar norms, to a genuine assent about moral standards which does not rest on a delusion. In this sense Taylor also seems to presuppose a certain contingency between the vocabulary of language and its grammatical dimension which will hardly stand up to closer examination. How can it be really a matter of the same norms when Naturalists, Christians, and positivists talk about justice, the fulfilment of life, or human dignity?[24]

Theological language criticism will assure both Taylor and Rorty that if the fundamental conviction is not the same, values cannot really be the same either; if, on the other hand, the fundamental

[23] Taylor, *Sources of the Self*, 515.
[24] Taylor concedes that there are differences even with standards, giving as example the question of abortion, which, however, is supposed to be the exception which merely proves the rule of 'general agreement' (p. 515). But here the logic seems to have slipped. For differences in the question of abortion are by no means an exception to the general agreement about values. On the contrary, abortion is a real-life test case for the coherence of moral sources and standards. The different judgements about abortion reveal the sources of the standards. They make clear how many meanings one and the same moral term (such as human dignity) can diverge into. Consequently, they do not show the general agreement, as Taylor maintains; they in fact actually show its deceptive character.

conviction agrees, the values will not, indeed, be simply the same, but they will be capable of concurrence (open for a process in which consensus can be arrived at). Consequently, the idea of a 'concurring' ('homologous') form of life which we have developed, an 'ethical identity springing from worship', does not appear simply anachronistic, even in a postmodern world. It rather represents an inescapability which is critically convincing, linguistically speaking, an inescapability which is not revoked in the postmodern world either: the fact that—apart from a pragmatically changeable use of vocabulary—all speak *one* moral language; that we *must* speak one language and *cannot* speak several; that we *can* speak one and do not *have to* speak several. Morally, we are simple beings.[25]

The discussion with Richard Rorty has made clear to us the theologically based inescapability of the grammatical question, above all in the postmodern world, obsessed as it is with vocabulary. In the light of the difference made by the grammatical view, a homology of forms of life emerges which superficial differentiations and unifications conceal, and which has to be laid bare. It is not the words which constitute the identity of a moral language; it is the rules. We have to bear in mind this simplicity of really being able to speak only a single moral language—which also means living it—when we now go on to talk about the multiplicity of role demands which we all encounter today.

'Creature' and 'Neighbour'

These role demands go together with a plurality of role languages. As father I talk in one way, as member of a club or as employer another; and so on. Here we can initially also talk more unreservedly about the different vocabularies we use. Of course here too the grammatical point of view comes into play, if only with the question about the way the different role languages are related to each other. Roles can slide into one another. One person can run a business like a mother, another talks to his friends as if they were a school class, and a third clings to his wife as he did to his mother's

---

[25] In reference to the 'undividedness' of ethical orientation, the psalmist talks about the 'simplicity' of the righteous (Buber's translation of *tanim*), which matches the simplicity of the ways of God (Ps. 18: 27, 32). And we find the same idea in Bonhoeffer as the 'simple obedience' (*einfacher Gehorsam*) which characterizes the discipleship of Christ (see *Discipleship*, 77 ff.).

apron strings. To hold on to one role in the context of others can be the sign of a compulsive personality structure; but for all that, it is basically speaking impossible to dispense with the question about the rank and weight given to different biographical roles. This question is involved in every role conflict. Moreover, we normally recognize that certain roles have an overriding claim—in the case of teachers, for example, or Members of Parliament, or even professional footballers. Here the question whether people 'live up' to their public roles can hardly be restricted to the immediate sphere of their activity in school, Parliament, or stadium. It is rather the case that in acting out their other roles too—as wife, father, or citizen—these people see themselves faced with the demand that their behaviour there must be compatible with their public role as teacher, Member of Parliament, or the nation's outside left. Today role-bearers belonging to these categories often complain about this phenomenon (traditionally summed up under the term 'model'), seeing it as an attack on their personal right to free development. But this tendency reflects the fascination and dazzling power that postmodern accounts such as Rorty's assume is exerted by people in public life. An additional fact is that in the wake of social differentiation the individual role languages tend more and more towards grammatical adaptation to the 'mother tongue' of liberal society, the language of 'self-creation'. The more that roles in society are exposed to changes among the role-players, and are assumed for an ever shorter time and at ever shorter intervals, the less a mature role language (for example, the language of a particular professional ethos) will be able to take hold, since this has to be acquired and passed on only with the passage of time.

For Christians in this situation, however readily they affirm the plurality of roles, living an ethical identity therefore first means a confrontation of a grammatical kind with role languages that are increasingly infiltrated by society's claims and patterns. The task of not losing sight of their role as Christians would have to be fulfilled in terms of moral language if, in their use of the different role language, they never failed to express themselves as 'creatures' and 'neighbours', and not in self-creation in 'solidarity'. It is surely in this form that there is a compelling need today to treat the traditional subject of 'the sanctification of the whole of life'. As we can see from the Pentecost story in Acts 2, the ability of the

Holy Spirit to enter into all languages is the premiss for the conviction that these languages can be confronted and finally transformed.

The Spirit penetrates every language—everyone hears those who are filled with the Spirit speak in his or her own language; but the Spirit is not absorbed by any one of them. It does not merely adopt the different existing languages, but leads to differentiation within their linguistic communities, as the end of the biblical passage shows when it describes the effect of the 'voice': some understand what it is about—the great acts of God—and ask what it means for their own lives; for others, although they speak the same language as their fellow countrymen, the voice of the Spirit is an incomprehensible roaring, and the disciples' confession of faith a drunken babbling (vv. 12 f.) So the Spirit leads to a profound penetration into the moral languages current at any given time. It thrusts into the borderland between grammar and vocabulary. This can certainly only succeed if at the same time the specific linguistic characteristics of the Christian community are cultivated and investigated. How is the moral language of faith learnt? What are the conditions under which it can freely develop? Must there not be a place which protects this development from trivialization? How could the relation to the multifarious levels of communication be so established that it is possible to prove grammatical faithfulness in the use of different role languages?

As I am trying to show, in these questions worship plays a key role. In that practice in worship of the language of creatureliness and neighbourliness makes linguistic criticism of the rhetoric of society possible, it does society an invaluable service. The faithfulness to 'the play' itself which is sustained throughout the multiplicity of roles does not anticipate the end of society's story. This faithfulness is expressed through the repeated question: what play is actually being performed? Although this question is inevitably elenctic in a society which is primarily concerned with producing itself, it nevertheless simultaneously keeps present the economy of God. This is also true of the plays which Richard Rorty thinks of putting on. Over against this, it has become clear that the history of liberal society cannot be told only *in* the language of self-creation; it must also *talk about* that language.

But how ought we to think about the roles assumed in worship, and how are they related to the social roles which Christians have to perform? In the multifarious role demands of the complex conditions in which we live, the 'person' formed in worship (the word *persona* being derived from 'role' and theatrical mask) has to be able to perform his or her role as creature and neighbour in a free and creative way. The role learnt in worship cannot be sustained in the sense of a mere recitation in the different contexts; it must be performed with a certain artistic improvisation, if it is to prove itself in widely differing situations. Of course the work has to be known as thoroughly as possible if the performer is to fulfil his or her role adequately; only a performer who knows the play well and can move freely in it can improvise—only someone who has learnt the part 'by heart' and practised it. Consequently the established language of worship and cultivated forms of interaction, with clearly assigned liturgical roles, are particularly important for the ethical development and culture of Christians.

We shall look at this in more detail in Part III. At this point I may just mention the worship of black congregations in North America as a particularly impressive example of the way in which identity is formed in worship through the specific assumption of roles. The work of James H. Cone brings this out particularly well, with its analyses of liturgical singing, acclamations, prayers, and the experiences specific to these services of worship. Cone describes how the assembly of the congregation reverses the everyday experience of social marginalization, and how the people who have been 'bent low' for six long days can practise an upright walk on the seventh day. What makes this possible is the eschatological experience of a *kairos* which gives them a new definition of their humanity.

This eschatological revolution is not so much a cosmic change as it is a change in the people's identity, wherein they are no longer named by the world but named by the Spirit of Jesus ... The transition from Saturday to Sunday is not just a chronological change from the seventh to the first day of the week. It is rather a rupture in time, a *Kairos*-event which produces a radical transformation in the people's identity. The janitor becomes the chairperson of the Deacons' Board; the maid becomes the president of Stewardess Board Number I. Everybody becomes Mr. and Mrs., or Brother and Sister. The last become first, making a radical change in the perception of self and one's calling in the society. Every person becomes somebody, and one can see the people's recognition of their new found identity by the way they walk and talk and 'carry themselves'.[26]

Of course we can now ask whether the 'counter-experience' of the black congregations which Cone describes is not a flight into an illusory unscathed Sunday world, which may perhaps make life's everyday hardships more endurable, but by doing so also cements them. But the question is: where is life really acted out? Christians in fact assume that the true life comes about in worship, that a *kairos*—the proper time—has more weight than the *chronos*—the chronological moment; and that it is in this *kairos* that they can experience their true identity. In this perspective, what happens in worship would be the intensified reality, as it were, which holds up a mirror to the comedy of real life—a production in which the designated kings and priests act slaves and idolaters; the laughter over this grotesque scene would be the Easter laughter which, on the morning of the new creation, breaks forth from the people who all at once perceive the unreality of what they had previously considered to be real (life unto death, the struggle for existence as life's iron law, and so forth). In this light, it would not be the *persona* formed through worship which would be a retreat from real life. The reverse would be the case: supposedly 'real life' would have to be understood as a retreat from worship and its eschatological reality. The formation of identity in worship does not mean withdrawal into a dream world. It challenges the illusory secular world by refusing to be stabilized by its rituals or provided with significance by its liturgies.

The reverse side of homologous identity, where everything it does, in words or works, is done in the name of the Lord Jesus (Col. 3: 17), is the refusal to view 'identity' as an achievement of integration. Whereas postmodern identity has its epiphany only in its shifting roles, and the individuating person resembles the epic hero who holds together solely through his person the different world and times which he travels, Christian identity is structured in exactly the opposite way. In the Old Testament already, the striking absence of the epic character indicates that it is another

---

[26] J. H. Cone, 'Sanctification, Liberation, and Black Worship', *ThTo* 35 (1978), 140 f.

who holds the narrated story together, not the individuating hero; and similarly, the identity formed in worship is determined by the *story*, not vice versa. As an interpretation of the story of Jesus Christ, it certainly proves itself in different role contexts, but it remains critical towards every demand for integration which has its inception in these contexts and their particular dramaturgies. Kings and priests cannot behave like slaves; white Christians will also stop being 'good whites', just as black Christians cannot simply behave like 'good blacks'. Whereas postmodern morality (like system morality too) decides the quality of an act by its loyalty to its particular social context, a civic identity formed in worship, which continually asks about the law of the Spirit, will be bound to appear as positively amoral; it makes neither a 'good business-man' nor a 'good citizen of the state'; it does not even make a 'good Christian'.

But it must be said, finally, that the homologous identity we have looked at must now be guarded against a natural misunderstanding, and must be more closely defined. Here we may once again take Jesus's exemplary story about the merciful Samaritan. Merciful neighbourliness is not a matter of course. If it were, Jesus would not have had to tell the story. As a social impulse, which embraces the question about its scope, 'solidarity' has always existed. It is not just a modern invention (although it is only in modern times that it has been raised to programmatic rank). Solidarity as a social category, which initially takes its bearings from those close to us, was already presupposed in the Pharisee's question. So we do not have to listen to the story about the Samaritan because we do not act with sufficient solidarity. We are regularly made to listen to this story in worship *just because* we usually act out of solidarity, but ought to act out of mercy; as people who typically turn to those who are in some sense close to us, we are meant to become 'neighbours' instead. This would mean turning upside-down a linguistic progression that has been common coin ever since Nietzsche, who draws a line of moral progress which advances from 'mere mercy' to 'true solidarity'.

If we wish to express the ethical identity of Christians in the language of neighbourliness, it becomes evident from Jesus's story that this identity cannot be understood adequately in the context of the (unavoidable) hierarchy of roles. For one thing, ethical identity does not employ a 'meta-vocabulary'. It does not impose its own

moral vocabulary; it does not push its role through; it does not have
to prove itself by carrying a particular disposition about with it (like
a nagging teacher). According to the rules of Jesus's narrative art,
ethical identity is not 'sustained' at all. Rather, it *comes into being*
through identification, in the course of which one person becomes
the other's neighbour. So neighbourliness does not exist at all as an
ontological category. It does not exist even as identifying criterion
for a Christian ethic. We may *be* people who act more or less in
solidarity with others, but as 'neighbours' we are always still *becoming*. We are not identifiable from the outset as neighbours, as if we
were officially labelled friends and helpers, with the conventional
insignia of peaked caps and uniforms. Neighbours do not march
with a fixed identity through different functional spheres. But they
do enter into these spheres with an ability to perceive the need of
the others, an ability that has to be further refined. Ethically, this
perceptive power makes itself felt as the capacity for identification.
It is formed out of the treasury of biblical and post-biblical grammatically linked 'stories' which, in telling about the Good Samaritan, Elisabeth of Thuringia, Mother Teresa, and unnumbered
local witnesses, speak of strangers such as these who became neighbours to other people.

Because these stories challenge their hearers to identify with the
actors in the stories, or identify the listeners themselves in their own
acts of mercy, people who move in their narrative sphere are empowered to these practical identifications through which the narrative stream is prolonged. They are empowered for something which
they are not capable of, just by themselves. For they do not identify
themselves directly with other people by virtue of their ability to
'enter into' their situation—that would rather be a matter of solidarity. They identify themselves with Christ. This identification
with Christ takes place on many levels. To put it briefly: as people
who are identified by him (Phil. 2: 7; 1 Cor. 8: 2 f.) they are able to
identify others with Christ (Matt. 25: 31–46), so that, as Luther
said, they themselves 'become Christ' for these people. The identification with our neighbour by way of the identification with Christ
is, of course, anything but a detour, complex and complicated
though it may seem. As I shall try to show below in a detailed
analysis of the political meaning of 'entering into' the other, this
Christomorphous mediation is the only way which really
promises that the other will be met *as* another (cf. Chapter 12). In

this process of identification, what the ethical identity of Christians can mean is formed and re-formed.

In this way the reductionist alternative is surmounted, as well as the expansivist one. Jesus's refusal to define our neighbour in advance forbids us to identify neighbourliness with any already existing role. There are no exemplary roles of neighbourliness. The Samaritan was characterized precisely as the one person among all the people who passed by who had no official position. (As a Samaritan, he in fact represented the people who had no 'role' at all in Israel.) For the priest and the Levite, by contrast, their particular roles in the Lord's assembly should especially have laid upon them the need for a merciful act of commitment. But neighbourliness in the sense of Jesus's story evidently means going fundamentally beyond the role profile of the person concerned, and the scope of the expectations bound up with it; it means entering into an identity which is, strictly speaking, not a role identity at all. Neighbourliness is not a defined role, but can be found—discovered—in all roles. Consequently, its supposed closeness to particular socially defined roles, as in the family, teaching, the Church, and so forth, will have to be called in question, as well as its supposed distance from other roles, for example in business or politics. So it is sometimes more difficult to become the neighbour of one's own children, husband, or wife than the neighbour of a colleague or a stranger. The priest and the Levite in Jesus's parable may have been thinking in passing of their 'natural' clientele—perhaps the people in the Temple, whom they did not want to keep waiting. In that case they would have been prevented from becoming the neighbour of the person in need simply because they believed that *they already knew who their neighbours were*. But neighbourliness cannot be made role-specific; it can be neither delegated to particular roles nor kept out of others.

In this sense, as something transcending all roles, neighbourliness must be seen as a political category in which freedom of action is not reduced by role-specific patterns of behaviour. *Homo politicus* is therefore no more a role than is 'the neighbour' or 'the Christian'. For the Christian too, the *homo politicus* is not one of his changing identities; it marks his identity in all his diverse roles. His royal priesthood is a political office. It is not like a costume which he slips into at particular times, only to change into another; it is rather his 'skin' as a Christian citizen. He cannot slough it off, except at the cost of deforming his identity. A Christian does not become a Christian in order to come forward as a Christian citizen now and then. His identity as Christian is already formed politically, and in no other way. He can only become a Christian as a 'fellow citizen with the saints'. Christians will therefore find it worthwhile to pay attention to the conditions in which politics becomes real instead of mere strategies.

8

The Worshipping Congregation
as a True Public

For all that, the faith in political existence which Christians must sometimes maintain *sub specie contrario* is neither heroic nor visionary. It is not the outcome of a 'negative dialectic', a transfer of dissatisfaction with politics as they actually exist to the vision of better politics. Christians have in view a public which is real, not stage-managed; freely constituted, not manufactured; cultivated, not made use of; but all this is rather because in this sense they already experience here and now a public of that kind. In the following chapter we shall turn our attention to the worshipping community as a 'true' public of its own.

8.1 'CHURCH AND PUBLIC' OR THE PUBLIC OF THE CHURCH?

It has become customary, at least in the context of postmodern thinking, to talk about different publics. And as we could see from the theological correlations developed above, it is in fact useful to talk about the Church as a public of its own which is generated in worship.[1] On the other hand, our earlier reflections about 'society' suggest that we must also be cautious about assuming too rashly equivalence to the postmodern syndrome, as if the Church's public could be directly understood in the light of the relationship to other publics as this relationship is defined.

---

[1] Talk about the Church 'as a public *sui generis*' has recently been stressed by Reinhard Hütter, who proposes assigning the public character of the Church to the classic *notae ecclesiae* ('The Church as Public', *Pro Ecclesia* 3, (1994)). Hütter's ideas circle round a structural concept of public, which over against the monopolizing trend of the 'substantial-normative' concept of a single social public has the advantage of seeing a play of different publics. For the Church, as Hütter enumerates, following Luther, it is the central practices of worship (word and sacrament), in association with the canonical doctrinal tradition and the ministry of the Church, of which it can be said that 'they mark and identify the Church as the space of God's *oikonomia*' (p. 354).

Instead, the element of truth in the pre-modern/modern assumption that there is a single public must enter into our examination of a plurality of publics. The modern perspective reminds us that there cannot simply be a number of different publics side by side; there must also, inevitably, be a conflict between them. The truth of the pre-modern view, on the other hand, can be found in its insight into the fundamental character of this conflict. The dispute cannot be seen as a simple clash of interests between publics which are each of them inherently consistent (though this is the way it is viewed in modern and postmodern thinking); the dispute must bring out the true meaning of 'public' in general.[2]

The Public's Truth Claim

In perceiving itself as a public, it is essential for the Church to take account of the different levels of its relationship to other publics, and to ensure that these are not ironed out into one and the same paradigm. This can be summed up in the distinction between a fundamentally critical and a critically constructive relationship. In its fundamentally critical claim, the Church's public is on the same level as society's. But to reject the normative claim of society's public must not at all mean that the Church sets itself up as an alternative 'super-public' with a universal claim to integration.[3] On the contrary, the Church's public can only rightly assume its bilateral, critically *constructive* relationship to the other individual publics if its fundamental conflict with society's public is not glossed over, but is openly maintained. In this perspective, it is then of course no longer individual *sub*-systems in society which encounter one another. Instead, in every such encounter the public as a whole is under discussion. The Church's necessary fundamen-

---

[2] The connection between public and truth must be viewed reciprocally. Just as a public cannot be absolved from asking the question about its truth, so, conversely, it also constitutes the test case for a truth that is asserted: can this be shared and communicated, and thus exposed to criticism? Unlike the postmodern prejudice, according to which there can really be only private truths—truths for you and for me—the public affinity of truth was present in Greek: the true is the unhidden (*a-letheia*); truth thrusts towards public recognition, even if that of course does not make it in any way identical with 'public opinion'.

[3] But it is something different and—in view of the world-wide Church and the self-marginalizing attempt of the churches to understand themselves only over against the State or as part of society—entirely justifiable to talk, as Michael Welker does (*Kirche im Pluralismus* (1995)), about 'the reality of the ecumenical Church as the context for different states and societies' (p. 76).

tal criticism of the concept of society's public *per se* permits the various different publics to appear in a new light as its discussion partners. Now their existence too has to be recognized as posing a question about the true form of a public. The explicitly political character of the Church's public would accordingly emerge especially in its significantly demanding dealings with individual publics—inasmuch as these are allowed and expected to deal with the whole of life. In this way the different publics would not encounter each other primarily as experts for their particular domain (economic, medical, literary, religious, etc.), which close off their spheres of competence against one another; they would also keep themselves open for each other in the still open question about the true form of their public character.

The relational nature of the Church's public is usually seen mainly in the context of its relationship to the State, where it is viewed as the State's opposite number. This concentration may seem historically understandable (and sometimes also entirely appropriate); but today it can nevertheless put perception of the Church's public task on the wrong track. We have seen how the public character of the Church practised in worship was understood from the beginning as a challenge to the public character of the State, in so far as the State came forward with the claim that commitment to 'the common weal' was the primary obligation to which the whole life of its citizens had to be subordinated.

Ever since these beginnings, history has continually been written as a dispute between the claims of these two publics. It is true that history has been shaped on the one hand by attempts of the State to nationalize the Church's public, or to privatize it, and on the other hand by the attempt of the Church to extend its own public to absorb that of the State. But this very attempt on the part of the Church was in fact bound to end up in the precise opposite, and to come down to *a nationalization* of the Church's public: where the Church failed to contrast the total public of the political community with a different *kind* of public, but indiscriminately carried the other's structure into its own public claim. The political character of its own public would thereby be increasingly surrendered, for that cannot be described in terms of the extension of spaces— the model which largely determines thinking about Church and State. But where 'public' is understood in the way that worship enjoins, not as space but rather as a 'field of energy' which is

engendered by a particular form of joint activity, peaceful coexistence with a form of public which purports to be normative is out of
the question.

As long as a political community sees itself as a normative public of
this kind, it will by so doing give the Church's public a fundamentally
critical role. This has continually been the case in history, and is so
still. Yet the Church would be wrong if it were to conclude from its
experiences with the totalitarian state that the critical power of its own
public should be always primarily directed to the public of the State,
or to some other public—perhaps the public of the economy. To do so
would be to deny not merely the possibility of a critically constructive
relationship towards a state reality to whose de-totalization it itself
has effectively contributed in the course of history; it would also
actually deploy and expend its necessary, fundamentally critical potential at the wrong point. For today, as we have seen, this must be
levelled (at least in the political community of the West) against the
total claim of *society*, which has long since also claimed the public of
the State (like the public of the Church and other publics too) as one
of its 'functions'. This absorption of state into society is yet another
way of dissolving the politically fruitful tension between State and
Church. Whereas the tension between the two once shaped society,
this tension is increasingly eliminated through the functional marginalization of them both.

This marginalizing dynamic is apparent not least in the fact that
it has effect within a variety of different frameworks for the relation
of State and Church. For a diminution of the tension between the
two has always throughout history been a motivation accompanying their relationship. Again and again the need to comprehend this
tension theoretically too took the form of a claim to give it a fixed
and final form by way of a theory—and thus practically to reduce it.
Theories of this kind were then translated into political terms,
solutions ranging according to circumstances from concordats to
the constitutional separation of State and Church(es). As far as
the latter solution is concerned, the example of the United States
shows today how the guaranteed freedom of religion can be interpreted to mean a domestication of the gospel in public life. For here
the kind of faith it has to be if it is to enjoy that constitutional
guarantee seems to be already established. It is a question of
that 'mere belief' which, as Thomas Jefferson already said in a
famous dictum, may be pinned to one God or twenty; that is of

no importance, as long as the person neither steals nor injures anyone else.

It is true that even in liberal societies freedom of belief is not simply relegated to the realm of mere freedom of thought; as freedom of religion, the practice of its 'cult' is also protected. Where our association of worship and ethics is concerned, however, the decisive point is to perceive the limitation that is involved here. For the free space given to the cult is conceded only as long as it also acts as a *limitation* of the practice of religion, offering 'mere belief' a protected reserve, shut off from what is outside it. This touches the very heart of political worship, since political worship means precisely a 'celebration of works' (Luther) in the context of the whole of life—worship as a form of life. But we have to see here too that, ultimately speaking, it is society which becomes the factor which decides the outcome of an arrangement between State and Church. Whether this relationship drifts towards a domestication of the Church or a churchifying of the State does not only depend on the arrangement itself—state church, concordat, or separationist— but is influenced by the development of the society too. As for the 'separationist' model of the United States, what the Founding Fathers originally had in mind was freedom of belief in an ecumenical sense—as the peaceful coexistence of different Christian churches, whose respective influences on public life were possible and desired in the framework of the constitutionally prescribed non-preferential treatment of any one of them. After all, the Fathers of that constitution were for the most part Christians of the kind who wished to fulfil their call to contribute to the welfare of society. What was admittedly in tension in the thinking of the Founding Fathers—that is, genuinely liberal and specifically biblical elements—is countered by a one-sided solution brought about by the post-Christian liberal trend of American society, a solution which at the same time promotes the dissolution of the fruitful tension between state and churches. The view of the 'cult' as the reserve for 'the practice of religion' corresponds to the liberal notion of 'mere belief'. So what was once thought of as a limitation of the state, whose neutrality forbids the preferential treatment of any particular denomination, is remoulded into the limitation of the exercise of religion. One might almost say that the social dissolution of the tension between state and churches or religions is pursued as the dissolution of political worship.

The Church as a Social Association or a Contrast Society?

In this way society acts today to a hitherto unknown degree as a catalyst and interpretative authority for the relationship between State and Church(es), a fact which should guard us against concentrating political ethics directly on that relationship. In other words, where the plural relationship of the Church's public (towards the state, society, and other publics) is underrated, the Church remains ultimately dependent on a heuristic paradigm which allows it to fall victim to society's total claim.

This problem also shows itself in the differentiated concept of Church and public with which Wolfgang Huber approaches the latter in his book on Church and public.[4] Huber rightly stresses that simply because of its worship and the public claim of the gospel, the Church cannot be restricted to the private world, but in its public claim is intended and destined to be 'church for others' (pp. 44 f., 616 f.). In saying this, he makes it clear that he is particularly interested in the Church's critical function. But he recognizes that the development of modern society makes it necessary to understand the Church's public as a 'sub-system of society's system as a whole' (p. 633). It is true that theologically he knows that 'the spiritual character' of the Church goes beyond what can be contained in a functional view; but for all that, he believes that the very difference between the Church's eschatological determination and its historical efficacy suggests that in its public activity it should be seen as an 'association' (pp. 635 ff.)—a 'grouping in society which asserts a claim to participate in political processes of decision, and to exert political influence' (p. 29). By accepting the explicitly sociological view of the Church as an 'association', Huber of course tends to reduce the political worship of the Church in its bearing on the public to the articulation of the Church's own concerns. However, in a more recent contribution entitled in translation 'Public Church in Plural Publics',[5] Huber has revised his view at precisely this point, as is evident from the fact that talk about the Church as an association has disappeared. In his essay its place is now taken by the notion that the Church must relate itself equally to the different 'spheres of reference' in public life—the state, the economy, civil

---

[4] W. Huber, *Kirche und Öffentlichkeit*, 2nd edn. (1991). The page numbers in the text refer to this book.

[5] W. Huber, 'Öffentliche Kirche in plurale Öffentlichkeiten', *EvTh* 54 (1994).

society, and cultural communication (p. 177). Huber sees the
Church too as just such an interpretative community, and when it
comes together with other such communities, society's public is
constituted as a 'public made up of publics'.

But what Huber's theory of 'public' does not properly take in,
even in its revised form, is that in actual fact 'society' constitutes
much less of that free space where individual publics interact than
he assumes, and that today the economy especially as a structure-
building force has long since left its status as a 'sphere of reference'
behind. For civil society, just as much as for the economy itself, the
market constitutes the inner logic, which is also followed by the
'public made up of publics', inasmuch as the internal structure of
this sphere is also moulded by the laws of the market: as a contest
between participants competing for an increase of their shares.

Over against this, and in terms of this relationship, how can the
claim of the Church as a public of its own be described? Again, it
must first be remembered here that the Church's claim to find in
itself the model of a true public imposes restrictions upon the
Church itself no less than on other publics. It is not a claim that
can be brought directly into the public of society, as a kind of
'claim upon the public'. It is indissolubly bound to the praxis
of worship, as the church's field of political interaction *par excellence*. No claim derived from this 'public of the Spirit' can be
introduced directly into contemporary political events. For worship
as a political happening always also means the *interruption* of daily
political happening. The Church's claim *as* public (in the performance of its political worship) applies as well—and first of all—to the
ecclesiastical public itself; this, like any other public, has to enter
into argument with rival viewpoints and rely upon the effectiveness
of its argument to carry conviction. Or, to use Wolfgang Huber's
earlier terminology: it is only in this respect—the ecclesiastical
public—that it makes sense to talk about the Church as an 'association'. Here it is not superior to other publics, but remains on the
same footing as all the others. But what the Church must at all
events testify to among them all, and what, again, sets it outside the
rest, is its claim *as* public: the claim of political worship to keep
open in all the different publics (including the ecclesiastical public)
the question about the true meaning of 'public', and to hold within
itself the criterion for answering the question. A large part of the
problem about the relationship of the Church's public, and the

formation of theories about 'church and public', seems to me to lie in the failure to recognize this dialectic in the Church's public character itself. For, on the one hand, it becomes problematical when the Church makes the direct claim that the true (worshipping public) is the organizational and 'associative' public—that leads to clericalism. On the other hand, it is of course no less problematical if the Church sees itself directly as 'associative', and refuses to accept the claim of the worshipping public, let alone passes it on to others. In that case it would certainly be nothing more than 'socially relevant'.

But before we talk about the Church's claim to have a share in the 'wider' public, must we not consider to what extent we can talk at all about a public to which the Church proposes to relate? Is it really capable of relating itself to an already existing 'public made up of different publics'? Who is reached by its public claim? Has 'public' not become largely a fiction stage-managed by the mass media, in which *talk* about public and the pretence of public influence have taken the place of public in the true sense?[6]

Jürgen Habermas describes how the 'structural change in the public' has gone all the way from the public control of hitherto secretive affairs to the secret legitimation of affairs that were hitherto public.[7]

The essential steps in this development may be summed up as follows. The representative public of the feudal phase gives way to the new sphere of 'public' power which emerges with the national and territorial states: a political machinery furnished with the legitimate monopoly in the exercise of power, against which private people initially have their sole function as addressees of the power that is exercised. These private persons, amalgamated into the 'public', then constitute 'bourgeois society', which is critically directed against the arcane character of politics. Here the 'publicity' which is demanded (initially with regard to parliamentary decisions, court proceedings, and the press) mediates between state and society, so that by way of the public control of politics the claim to preserve society's interests through politics can be secured.[8] Press and propaganda contribute largely to the extension

[6] See here M. Welker's section on 'Die massenmediale Realitätsunterstellung und ihre Gefahren', in his *Kirche ohne Kurs?* (1987).
[7] J. Habermas, 'Öffentlichkeit', in *idem, Kultur und Kritik* (1973).
[8] Ibid. 63–5.

of the public beyond the confines of the bourgeoisie, which determines the structural transformation of the public with the consequences we see today.

> The public . . . becomes the field of competing interests in the coarsened forms of violent conflict. Laws which are clearly made under 'pressure from the streets' can hardly be interpreted as resulting from the consensus of the public discussion between private persons; they correspond in more or less undisguised form to the compromise between conflicting private interests . . . The political public of the social state is marked by a curious enfeeblement of its critical functions. Formerly publicity was supposed to subject persons or things to the forum of public reason, and to make political decisions open to revision before the court of public opinion; but today it often enough already becomes the handmaid of hidden political interests—as publicity it procures persons or things which enjoy public prestige, thereby making them open for acclaim in a climate of non-public opinion. The very phrase 'the task of public relations' betrays that a public has first to be manufactured, laboriously and from one case to the next.[9]

The deformed character of what is today presented as political public can be seen from the change of meaning of the 'public' that was once constitutive. Once used for the political participation of the assembled citizenship, in today's usage the term 'public' has been reduced to a spectator's role.[10] It describes the 'consumers' of a political theatre who merely applaud the actors, or withhold their applause. Experience shows that the applause withheld does not greatly stimulate political efforts; it rather activates still further efforts for better 'publicity'. 'The public' becomes the addressee of politics, and public relations the political form of communication. Citizens are no longer trusted to recognize the merits of a policy unless it is sold to them in an appropriate way. This shows how widely suspicion has put its stamp on the way politics is understood and practised today. The invention of society as 'civic public' was already guided by the suspicion that the politics of the powerful perhaps served different interests from those of the society of private property-owners; and this potential of suspicion increased as mass society developed. In principle, everybody sees

---

[9] Ibid. 67 f.
[10] Cf. C. Lasch, *The Culture of Narcissism* (1978), especially the chapter on 'Politics as Spectacle', 78–81.

him or herself as contributing to the formation of a 'critical public'. In fact, such a thing is less and less in evidence, let alone at anyone's disposal; and the public degenerates into a passive audience of political publicity. The awareness of this fact again increases the mistrust of the people concerned, and this in its turn steps up the task of public relations pursued by the political purveyors, so that the hermeneutical circle of suspicion is drawn tighter still.

In view of the questions and questionableness of 'the' public, it seems appropriate to hold back on any insistence that the public claim of the Church means a direct involvement in *this* public. We might rather ask whether the Church should not initially fulfil its public task by making its own 'public spaces' available, as a link with society's public, a place where less disfigured forms of publicity can be fashioned and developed. The insistence that the Church must have that on offer, an idea promoted in the United States today by Robin W. Lovin and others,[11] has contributed not least in Germany to the foundation of academies and conference centres under the auspices of the churches.

But the demand for public facilities of this kind also initially brings us back to the question: with what competence will the Church maintain and establish this 'better public space'? Ultimately it merely points back to the nature of the Church's public, which does not first have to be manufactured but is already present in the praxis of worship. It is therefore necessary before any direct

---

[11] See R. W. Lovin (ed.), *Religion and American Public Life* (1986). Barry A. Harvey has recently offered an interesting account and evaluation of the discussion about public theology. In his essay 'Insanity, Theocracy, and the Public Realm: Public Theology, the Church, and the Politics of Liberal Democracy', *Modern Theology*, 10 (1994), he does not merely present a differentiated analysis of the different types of public theology, but also offers an alternative to the type in general—an alternative which is in some respects related to that which I have developed here. Over against the 'strategic' character, which the 'correlative' (liberal) type of public theology (represented by David Tracy and others) shares with the 'post-liberal' type (represented, e.g., by R. Thiemann), Harvey proposes that the Church should establish a 'tactical' relationship to the different forms of public which would correspond to its 'diasporic existence' in the world. Thus the Church should not look for a firm foundation on which its 'public' relationship might rest, either in the sense of a general rationality (liberal) or as 'middle ground' (post-liberal). It should confine itself to a 'nuanced interplay between participation and nonconformity, simultaneously seeking the welfare of the city wherein God has placed it while acknowledging its status as aliens within that city' (p. 51). Interestingly enough, Harvey sees this alternative, which he—somewhat misleadingly—calls 'theocratic', as 'neither *strategic* nor *sectarian*, but *sacramental*' (p. 50).

reference to other public(s), and also before the Church makes its own sphere of communication available to them, for it to analyse the political meaning of its own public. Here it is necessary to proceed in more detail from the 'counter-ethics' which John Milbank demanded of the Church (cf. section 5.2). In its very existence as worshipping community, the Church stands for the limitation of every claim that the destiny of human beings to live together is to be fulfilled in the world. It thereby marks the limitation of state and society which these themselves cannot provide. Beyond this existential testimony to the limited nature of social concepts, however, we must also remember the idea of the Church as a counter-society, which authors belonging to different denominational traditions have all emphasized in a similar way. Even in its wording, the formula about the counter-*society* is able to include the insight developed above: that it is definitely on the level of society that the Church today must assume responsibility through its critical existence.

Perhaps the most succinct description of this perspective can be found in the work of Eric L. Mascall, whose Anglo-Catholic criticism of Temple's views we already looked at in an earlier passage. So it may be appropriate to quote in some detail what he wrote in 1953: 'The Church has many functions *in* society, but it can never become a mere function *of* society, for it *is* a society—the society of God, the life of the Holy Trinity communicated to men. Before the Church teaches, it lives; and before it teaches about society it lives as a society.' Mascall finds the political individuation of this counter-society explicitly expressed in eucharistic worship: 'The fact that in the sacraments man finds his deepest needs and aspirations satisfied in the context of a social gathering...set[s] before us a picture of society in which both the personal and the social aspects of human nature are united in an ordered harmony of authority and freedom.'[12]

Mascall advances an important step beyond the abstract assertion of a mere counter-force to society by pointing to worship as the concrete place in the life of the Church where the contrast shows itself in concentrated form. This simultaneously identifies the fundamental question of social life, which can find no proper answer in the life of society. Nevertheless, Mascall's formulations betray something of the difficulty in which the idea of the Church as a

---

[12] E. L. Mascall, *Corpus Christi* (1953), 45 f., 44.

counter-society easily gets caught up. The picture of the Church as a counter-society certainly takes on much sharper contours through Mascall's reference to worship and the fundamental question of social life, over against the general affirmation of a counter-society; but for all that, we are still left with the question of *how* the picture put before us in the eucharistic worship of the Church can reach society. The impatient insistence that the Church should relate to the public, all too hastily ignores the *critical* dimension of the Church's life in the sense of a counter-society; but, similarly, the contrast motif is in danger of overlooking the *constructive* dimension in this counter-society. Important though the critically illuminative effect of this contrast may be for society, by allowing it to perceive the limits and deformations of its public, the Church's ministry to the public of state and society must not be restricted to this. If talk about the counter-society is confined simply to holding up the picture of the Church's *societas* to the secular society, this reduction would limit the Church's existence to 'the criticism which makes people aware of something', criticism which is merely able to show the world what it can never become.

This problem emerges, for example, in Stanley Hauerwas's talk about the Church as 'contrast-model' when he says 'that the church first serves the world by helping the world to know what it means to be the world. For without a "contrast-model" the world has no way to know or feel the oddness of its dependence on power for survival. Because of the church the world can feel the strangeness of trying to build a politics that is inherently untruthful.'[13] But must seeking the good of the city not also include the question of how the *counter*-mode can be perceived as a mode of *en*counter too? At the same time, the constructive-communicative relationship seems to me to be already implicit in the idea of the Church as a counter-society, if this is properly understood; we do not have to look for it in more co-operative substitutes for the critical existence that the Church has by virtue of its very existence. It is precisely when people pursue the constructive task of political worship directly that they will miss the mark. But where this constructive task is perceived as the other side of the Church's critical responsibility,[14] it can extend beyond the limits of mere social criticism.

[13] S. Hauerwas, *A Community of Character* (1981), 50.
[14] This is what Robert E. Webber and Rodney Clapp are aiming at when they describe the Church as 'a depth-political community'. In a sub-definition of this, the

8.2. THE DOUBLE BECOMING OF THE WORLD IN WORSHIP

How can the relationship between Church and world, society and counter-society, be described in a way that preserves this integrative character of the critical and constructive relationship? Here we may be helped by a diachronic observation, which brings out the transformations in the understanding of this relationship in the course of the Church's history. So in the following section systematic reflections will have to be interlocked with political observations and comments on liturgical history. For this I should like to start once more from what Hauerwas said in the passage quoted above about the role of the Church as counter-society. We have acknowledged the legitimacy of this idea, and have pin-pointed its limitation. But now, in a more recent essay with the subtitle 'Teaching Ethics as Worship', Hauerwas himself has offered a point of departure which makes it possible to go beyond what he said in the passage we already cited. For in this essay, tucked away in a footnote, he says: 'If the church does not worship rightly how can the world know it is the world exactly to the extent it does not willingly glorify God?'[15]

'World' as the Denial of Worship

This comment is interesting in a number of respects. First of all, it stresses the location where the relationship in its defined form is rooted. Compared with a general theory about Church and world, attention here is directed to the heuristic function of worship. Without that, the relationship becomes cloudy. But now, apart from this greater heuristic precision, the statement does not seem to go beyond what we already heard in the earlier quotations from Hauerwas: that the Church has to show the world that it is world, and nothing else than that. Seen in that light, this would be a matter of enlightenment. The formulation 'how can the world *know* it is the world' seems at first glance to confirm this. But if we add the second half of the sentence, the stress can be placed differently:

Church is viewed as a diacritical community. 'The critic calls attention to something wrong; *the diacritic goes one step beyond criticism and distinguishes an alternative*' (*People of the Truth* (1988), 56).

[15] S. Hauerwas, 'The Liturgical Shape of Christian Life', in *idem, In Good Company* (1995), 250. The following interpretation certainly goes beyond what Hauerwas himself says in the further course of his argument, but it nevertheless, as it seems to me, remains in line with his thinking.

'how can the world know it *is* the world exactly to the extent it does not willingly glorify God'. Here the worship praxis of the Church would be under examination not merely in its illuminative significance for the existing world, but also as an undertaking from which the world can for the first time constitute itself 'as world', so to speak. 'World' in the post-lapsarian sense, distinguished from the creation which 'was very good', would in this light emerge only in and through worship. Where the Creator is worshipped 'in spirit and in truth' (John 4: 4), the created beings who refuse to participate in this worship become in fact 'world'. Worship as the praxis which lives in an elemental sense from God's creative activity, which the worshippers expose themselves to, becomes therefore outwardly efficacious activity, activity which 'brings something about'.[16] For where the one whose acts and words first make sin exist and knowable (John 15: 22–4) manifestly rules, the denial of new life (as well as new life itself) also becomes socially formative: this denial acquires the form of 'the world'.[17] The fact that according to this perspective 'the world' has no being of its own and—as still hostile to God—exists enhypostatically in the Church, as it were, makes it understandable that worship as an activity which brings the 'world' to be world should have been viewed as so dangerous.[18] It was not by chance that 'the world brought into being' in worship was at the same time prepared to forbid Christian worship.

[16] Here I am not of course thinking of creative activity in the strict sense. Augustine also saw worship as the criterion which made Rome *civitas terrena*, in spite of its own claim that it was 'the eternal city'. The righteousness and justice of that *civitas* is hollow, measured against its own claim to fulfil the *suum cuique* ('to each his own'), as the central principle of Roman law; for, as Augustine argues in *The City of God*, since the living God is not worshipped, by no means everyone receives his due (book XIX, 20).

[17] Accordingly 'becoming the world' does not mean a theological judgement alone; it also relates to a social formation, which is pioneered historically in the societal rejection of the worship of the crucified Christ. Seen in this light, the first becoming of the world out of worship is already 'political'. It therefore restores the unanimity of political, judicial, and religious forces which results from the rejection of the *ebed* of God, and which joined together to the common cry 'Crucify him'. Cf. here also M. Welker, *God the Spirit* (1994), 131, 209 f.

[18] Interestingly enough, the need for the world to 'become' is also associated by Hannah Arendt with the theme of belief or the loss of belief. According to her analysis, the obscuring of transcendence in modern times means, not a secularization, but the complete opposite: 'The historical evidence, on the contrary, shows that modern men were not thrown back upon this world but upon themselves... world alienation, and not self-alienation, as Marx thought, has been the hallmark of the modern age' (*The Human Condition* (1958; 2nd edn 1998), 254).

This shows that it is only a perspective like this which shows how talk about the Church as a counter-society can be kept from becoming moralistic. Because it is in worship above all that the Church appears as a Church which both 'produces'—brings about—the world and is challenged by it, we have to reject the idea that, itself uninfluenced, it could tell the world what its status is. It is only when the contrast element is seen to be anchored in worship that a moralistic misunderstanding can be avoided. And for that to be fully achieved, worship must include the birth of the world in two distinct senses.

First, the world becomes the totality of created beings and their activity which do not praise the Creator. But this first becoming of the world, which is really negative, is the pre-condition for a second, salutary, and in the real sense political becoming. By 'producing' the world in the first sense, as the other of itself, worship simultaneously makes it possible for the world to find a different kind of self-understanding, a new identity. This too remains bound to worship. Once the world is brought to know itself as world, it can then also be 'turned around' (and not necessarily in a subsequent process.) Politically, the decisive thing is to see what this transformation leads to. For the transformed world does not enter directly into the heavenly Jerusalem. Nor does it become congruent with the Church.[19] The transformation of the world is not a transubstantiation into the Church which would annihilate it as world. Rather, the world remains world in a certain sense, or rather, it only now truly becomes world. It becomes the world which is no longer hostile to God and now reflects the Creator's original will. It becomes the world which does not desire to abolish worship but recognizes it as necessary for its own existence. So that once again 'in and through' worship the transformation of the world into the world takes place, the transformation of the alleged 'eternal kingdom' into a *saeculum*, a temporal existence.[20]

---

[19] For the Church's goal is 'the eternal city', not the eternal Church, as K. Barth rightly emphasized (see 'The Christian Community and the Civil Community', in *idem, Against the Stream* (1954)).

[20] This second becoming of the world out of worship can accordingly very well be understood as 'secularization'. At the same time, the theological debate about secularization which reached its climax in the 1960s was marked precisely by the failure to realize that the birthplace of the *saeculum* was worship. Because of that, this debate remained to a large degree emancipatorily bound—that is to say, tied to thinking in terms of space and extension ('sacred–profane'); and it is the surmounting of

'World' as saeculum

This transformation, however, required a learning process on both sides, by both the Church and the world, as it still does. For the Church, the real point here was therefore to arrive at a continually deeper understanding of what *leitourgia* means, its customary term to describe its central enterprise. In its secular meaning, the word is used for the service performed by an individual or a community for the benefit of the political commonwealth; and this secular connotation already indicates the direction in which it is now to be understood where the double becoming of the world out of worship is concerned. In the Church there would have to be an increased understanding that, on the one hand, 'world one' (the world hostile to God) can become 'world two' (*saeculum*), but that, on the other hand, 'world two', although it is no longer 'world one', must and may nevertheless remain (only) 'world'. The way of arriving at the first insight emerges if we look at the way the motto 'Seek the welfare of the city' changed its meaning between Jeremiah's letter to the exiles (Jer. 29) and the patristic Church's new assumption of political responsibility in the secular community. Jeremiah justified his exhortation to the exiles to adapt politically to their Babylonian exile by the time that could be expected to elapse before they were liberated. During this period the welfare of the city should therefore be sought, and the city should be prayed for, 'for in its welfare you will find your welfare' (v. 7). This kind of reasoning is also behind the admonition in the First Letter to Timothy to pray for the men in power, 'that we may lead a quiet and peaceable life' (1 Tim. 2: 1 f.).

Here the positive relationship to the political community is motivated primarily by the 'not yet', and is limited to the form of exerting influence for one's own benefit (though this includes the benefit of the 'city' too). It does not envisage a fundamental change in the community itself. In the New Testament the role of the politically powerful is certainly seen in the light of the Creator's desire for order in the world—Paul can even talk about it as God's *leitourgoi*—but its task is still defined in largely negative terms, as the disciplining of evil (Rom. 13: 2–6). This viewpoint changed in the course of the third and fourth centuries. Now what stands at the centre is no longer the 'not yet' of redemption; it is the

this which is actually implicit in the term *saeculum*. For the opposite of 'secular' is not 'sacred' but 'eternal'.

'already' of the reconciliation experienced in the lordship of Christ. Christianity no longer primarily expects 'its share' in the 'orderly' condition of the political community, for which it prays; it asks how the political community can acquire for itself a share in the salutary existence in which the Church already finds itself. In this way the negative definition of the task of government is broken through, and soon baptized rulers are asking—and, as members of the Christian community, are themselves asked by the community and its leaders—how earthly justice can reflect something of the justice and righteousness of God experienced in faith. The famous excommunication of the emperor Theodosius by Bishop Ambrose of Milan in the year 390, on the grounds that the citizens of Thessalonica had been massacred on his orders, acts like a burning-glass, bringing this change of thinking to a point. Until then, rulers' acts of worldly justice were viewed as subject to their own laws, and could at most be relativized by episcopal law into an appeal for pardon, from case to case (which already marked an important step); but now a new notion begins to take shape: the idea that justice by the ruler of a predominantly Christian empire cannot simply mean translating the principle of retaliation; it has to embrace something of the mercy of God himself. 'Justice is to have a new, evangelical content.'[21]

The breakup of the Roman Empire in the first quarter of the fifth century first brought a retarding element into this movement, although in the end the development was again decisively accelerated by the downfall of the Empire. The political influence of Christianity was called in question by the fall of Rome; but the question was given an epoch-making answer in Augustine's vehement apologia, *The City of God*. The difficulty of grasping the way in which the two dimensions of the becoming of the world belong together is reflected both in Augustine's own work and in the antitheses of Augustinian interpretation. As examples of the difficulty of the political evaluation of Augustine's thinking, we may cite the interpretations of John Milbank and William J. Everett. Milbank takes over the Augustinian concept almost in its entirety, and therefore has no difficulty in appreciating to the full the first model of the becoming of the world in worship. It is true that Augustine's

---

[21] O. O'Donovan, *The Desire of the Nations* (1996), 201. O'Donovan works out this connection impressively.

apologia rests on a distinction between the two *civitates*, a model widely accepted in both Stoicism and Neoplatonism. But whereas in these philosophies actually existing political communities (both individually and as a whole) were viewed as more or less imperfect realizations of the cosmic ideal *civitas*, which is ruled by the divine (natural) law itself, Augustine turns this relationship into an antithesis. The *civitas terrena*, the earthly political community, which is determined by self-love, is poles apart from its heavenly counterpart, the *civitas caelestis*, which is governed by *agape*. The difference is qualitative not quantitative, categorial not relative. Consequently the attempt to find rest and true peace (as the *telos* of human life) in the framework of the earthly community or commonwealth is doomed to failure. These goods can be had only with God himself, and in his heavenly *civitas*.

We have seen how Milbank picks up this logic and, like Augustine in his own time, thereby acquires a powerful instrument with which to unmask the arrogant claims of worldly sociality and social theories. But, like Augustine too, Milbank sees himself forced to denounce politics as a means for the godless acquisition of peace. As we have seen, for him politics is an actualization of power ontology, and has to be surmounted in a 'post-political theology' with an Augustinian basis. This was the starting-point of our criticism (see section 5.2). But in my view, Milbank's suspension of political ethics is connected with an unduly constricted interpretation of Augustine. This follows Augustine in the narrower sense, and reduces the unexplored potentialities in his concept. But in the perspective of the idea of a double becoming of the world which we developed above, we can now perceive the possibilities which Augustine's fundamental distinction promoted, even though these were not explicitly unfolded in his concept itself. By changing from an analogy to an antithesis the traditional relation between the 'cosmic commonwealth' (in Christian terms, the *civitas Dei*, or city of God) and the existing political commonwealth, he transferred this 'first becoming of the world' in worship into political categories. In the reversal of worship, the reversed use of practice and enjoyment (*uti* and *frui*), 'world' cannot be understood as a divine emanation, but has manifestly become a world hostile to God. But this de-divinization of the world and its *res publica*, which was still by no means secular, paved the way for a 'second becoming of the world'—now in the truly secular sense. This movement reached its first climax in the course of the fourth century in the Roman Empire, which was in the process of transforming itself more and more into a *saeculum*. At the same time, the turn of events under Constantine had also given rise to an exaggerated optimism in church circles, over against which the shocks at the beginning of the fifth century brought about a new and salutary need for reflection. For Christianity, possibilities for promoting in the world the world's 'second becoming' followed; but Augustine's assimilation and treatment of the Empire's political catastrophe provided the indispensable reminder of the sharp anti-thesis from which the world's first becoming is derived.

Augustine himself, however, hardly went on to grasp conceptually the possibilities of a constructive political efficacy which emerge from the necessity with which the second becoming of the world has to follow the first, if that first is not to be disavowed *a posteriori*. At best he may acknowledge a degree to which the *civitas terrena* has a political task, which is to contribute to earthly peace within its order (reduced though this is in principle) and to create a space for the proclamation of the gospel; but this idea hardly contributes to a concept of how the *civitas terrena* can itself be structurally understood by the proclamation which takes place within its boundaries. Whereas Augustine was certainly aware that the *civitas caelestis* can make an appreciative use of earthly peace, its benefits and institutions, his concept does not include a specifically Christian spelling-out of the way earthly peace is used.[22]

This limitation in Augustine's concept with regard to what I have called the 'second becoming of the world' becomes the centre of William Everett's keen criticism.[23] Everett shows how, in order to counter the republican argument about the collapse of Rome (according to which this was due to the increasing suppression of the republican elements in the Empire), Augustine casts back to an archaic element in Rome's political history. His basic political model is not the republic; it is the royal city: Christ takes the place of Romulus, Rome's founder. But with this model, Everett believes, Augustine would have anticipated medieval paternalism and patriarchalism. The well-administered city is like a well-administered household, in which the unrestricted power of the paterfamilias sees to it that there is peace, order, and unity. Everett

---

[22] This is U. Duchrow's conclusion in his precise account of the doctrine of the two kingdoms in Augustine; see his *Christenheit und Weltverantwortung* (1970), 285.

[23] W. Everett, *God's Federal Republic* (1988).

argues that in the framework of his fixation on familial patterns, Augustine broke down political life into the categories of individual relationships: 'He replaced the search for public glory with a psychology of individual desire...Augustine's psychology not only undermined classical political theory but reinforced the familial models of rule which were to be associated with kingship for the next fifteen hundred years' (pp. 67 f.). In view of present-day challenges with regard to the link between faith and public life, Everett thinks that this legacy has to be surmounted. He would like to replace the hierarchical, patriarchal metaphor of kingship as the main symbol for God's sovereignty by 'God's Federal Republic'. It is this new symbol which has to be put into practice in worship and action.[24]

There is no doubt that by putting his finger on Augustine's microcosmically–macrocosmically structured political orientation towards the power of the paterfamilias over his household, Everett is pointing to a problematical trend; for this may well be the root of the justification of the Donatist persecution, and the religious pressure of the state (*cogite intrare!*—compel them to come in!).[25] But what Everett, for his part, overlooks is the way the second becoming of the world hangs together with the first. Without the eschatological contrast which Augustine stressed in an unsurpassable way, the positive relationship of the two *civitates* would be not Christian but pagan. So it would be no step forward to go behind the 'problematical' Augustine, as Everett proposes, in wishing to make republican (plus federal) elements the political *leitmotif* of a 'public theology'. Instead we must recognize that the kingship of Christ can no more be superseded and replaced than it can be reduced to the paradigm of domestic domination. We do not have to look for a different symbol. We have to show how the double becoming of the world from worship changes the symbols we already have. Here it is the very pluralism of those symbols which is of permanent importance if we wish to understand the special quality of Christ's sovereignty. As we have seen, it is only *the way in which* the political symbols *oikos* and *polis* interlock which makes understanding possible; and this may also be said of the specific outward effect which

---

[24] W. Everett, *God's Federal Republic* (1988), 7 f.
[25] Duchrow, *Christenheit und Weltverantwortung*, 295 ff.

the Church as a household *polis* has on any given secular community.

The possibilities of assuming political responsibility which opened up for the Church through the double becoming of the world, have in fact continually been grasped. This can be shown above all in periods of political crisis such as Augustine's. After the breakdown of the institutions sustaining a political community—whether in the huge Roman Empire at the beginning of the fifth century or in the small German Democratic Republic at the end of the twentieth—the Church has continually stepped into the breach. It could do so only because, as a political community of its own, it had the appropriate institutions and personalities at its disposal; and in the cases we have mentioned it was prepared to do so because it had learnt that it could not be content merely with the becoming of the world in the first sense. So it was Augustine—a man who in the downfall of Rome saw the manifestation of the hostility to God of the *civitas terrena,* and with it the frightful endorsement of the first becoming of the world in worship—who was quite prepared, as representative of the Church's *polis,* to step into the breach which the political catastrophe had torn open. His repeated lamentations about his occupation with the civic tasks which fell to him as the ruling bishop of Hippo during this period, and his frequent comments on political questions in his letters,[26] show that, practically speaking, he was neither willing nor able to shut himself off from the political potentialities arising from 'the second becoming of the world'.

This brings us to the other side of the learning movement we touched on above. The Church, certainly, had to understand how 'world one' can become 'world two'; but the political community had to do so too. If that transformation had its foundation in worship, and was begun there, it nevertheless had to take effect politically as well. It had to take effect in the political community. The second becoming of the world out of worship is then the moment when 'the state' is born. The transformation of the world (world one) into a *saeculum* took place during the process in which the transformed empire became a 'state'. This thesis may at first sight seem surprising, and requires further explanation.

---

[26] Ibid. 280 ff.

Christianity and State: Neither Accommodation nor Occupation

For this it is worth casting a glance at the work of the Oxford moral theologian Oliver O'Donovan, since he is concerned to lead the discussion about 'Christendom' away from a number of reductions.[27] O'Donovan sees himself as largely in agreement with critics of Christendom such as Stanley Hauerwas who believe that today we are living 'After Christendom' (to quote the title of one of Hauerwas's books). But he insists on a more differentiated analysis of Christendom, both as a historical phenomenon and as a concept. Wholesale judgements are generally based on an imprecise use of terms. Consequently, O'Donovan tries to open up terms such as 'Christendom' or 'state' for an inward differentiation which permits their mutual contingency to be perceived. His analysis shows that 'state' was an original Christian concept, a particular way of looking at the political community which allows 'Christendom' to be understood neither as Christianity's accommodation to the secular power, nor as an ecclesial occupation of that power. The term initially indicates, rather, that the attention of the secular power is now directed to the lordship of Christ, which he has already visibly assumed in the Church. 'Christendom . . . is constituted not by the church's seizing alien power, but by the alien powers becoming attentive to the church.'[28] The de-totalizing transformation of the existing political community (the Roman Empire) into a 'state' is the political side of this process. In short, the 'state' emerged from Christendom.

EXCURSUS

O'Donovan points out that this specifically Christian concept is already reflected in the etymology of the term 'state'. Derived from *status regni*, the term betrays the transformation to which it owes itself. Here the continuity of the Empire is no longer thought to be based on its nature as such (Rome as 'the eternal city'). As 'state', it depends in each given case on the *condition* of the political society itself—on the way that society structures its affairs in response to the gospel of Christ, whose sovereignty it acknowledges. It is an essential mark of this Christian invention that the secular proof of the existence of a political rule, the identity of an 'empire', can now be seen in a corpus of law and a particular judicial practice, whose rules also cover the relation of the potentates to their subjects. Every existing political rule is always a 'condition' (*status*) which has to legitimate itself before God,

---

[27] See O'Donovan, *Desire of the Nations*.   [28] Ibid. 195.

who is Lord over the law; it has no eternal claim.[29] In the *saeculum* there is
political rule only as 'state', which as a temporal phenomenon is related to
God's eternal kingdom, towards which it works, while in awareness of its
distinction from that kingdom. O'Donovan shows that it was ideas of this
kind which guided the Christians who founded and fostered the historical
connection between Church and State. 'No account of the pre-Nicene
church can do it justice if it overlooks the extraordinary missionary tri-
umphalism to which this faith gave rise. These Christians saw themselves
riding on the wave of the future, conquering society with the word of truth
and the blood of the martyrs, God's own strategy for success.'[30]

By allowing the voice of the first 'Christendom Christians' to be
heard, O'Donovan frees the phenomenon of Christendom from
some of the impressions which have tarnished it historically and
which influence the political awareness of the churches today to a
not unimportant degree. The reminder of the way those Christians
actually saw themselves can make us more sensitive to the fact that
if this phenomenon is viewed through the lense of modernity, we
are driven to false alternatives. O'Donovan sees one such alternative represented by critics of Christendom like Stanley Hauerwas,
whose frequently wholesale criticism of 'Christendom' corresponds
to the equally wholesale application of the concept of the state
to every conceivable political community in history.[31] For if one

---

[29] Ibid. 232.

[30] Even if O'Donovan does not cite him here, Augustine too can be viewed in a
certain way as the source of the 'Christian invention' of the 'state' in the sense used
above. This becomes clear when in book XIX of his apology he denies that the
political community of the Roman Empire is a *civitas* of this kind—a word which
can here justifiably be translated as 'state'. 'If the state is a matter for the people,
and if the term people includes their unification through a common law, and if law is
only to be found where there is justice, when justice is lacking there can be no talk of
a state. But now justice is the virtue which gives to each his own. But how can one
then talk about justice among men if nothing less than man himself is withdrawn
from the true God and made subject to impure demons' (*City of God*, book XIX,
21). Although Augustine did not develop a political ethics, the novelty of his Christian concept of the state is that he saw that the justice of a community does not
consist in the inclusion of the gods as well, but is dependent on its inclusion in the
justice of God. But where this all-embracing justice becomes the standard, and
where it is from this that a political community experiences its 'status' (irrespective
of its external stability), the later phenomenon 'state' is to all intents and purposes
already envisaged.

[31] O'Donovan, *Desire of the Nations*, 232. But see more recently a chapter of
Hauerwas's with the significant title 'Why Some Remnants of "Constantinianism"
Are, After All, Not Such a Bad Idea', in 'What Could it Mean For the Church to be
Christ's Body?', in *idem, In Good Company*, 19.

assumes, as Hauerwas does, that the essence of the state never changes, Christendom can be understood only as an accommodation to the world. But such sweeping criticism does violence to Christianity's own history, trusting as it does more to the liberal article of faith that all politics are ultimately the power play of interests, than to the self-testimony of Christians belonging to the period in question. This criticism accepts the (modern) interpretation *of* history to a degree which belies the contemporary testimony of the Fathers, their own interpretation of themselves *in* history. As O'Donovan points out, the political order of life which follows the principles of a community of conviction does not have to be fundamentally coercive. That is merely the implication of the liberal doctrine which the Christian critics of Christendom implicitly accept: 'Social doctrine of whatever kind is coercive; those who claim a social identity in terms of unnecessary belief do violence to those who do not share it.' But, 'The story-tellers of Christendom do not celebrate coercion' (p. 223). O'Donovan argues that a political community which supports Christian mission is not therefore bound to exclude people of different beliefs from the state service. Thus he develops the challenging analysis that 'Christendom' does not have to mean either accommodation to the state or ecclesiastical occupation of it, but that the two, Christendom and the state, actually condition one another . 'Christendom' is conceivable only in a political community which sees itself as 'state', and a 'state' is dependent for its part on a Christianity which also lives out its political existence in the Church in the direction of the world.

In this positive evaluation of the two concepts, O'Donovan too, of course, cannot overlook the way in which both have done much in the course of their history to transform this positive view of things into the perspective which has mainly come to prevail in modern times. Of course, 'Christendom' has also again and again existed as accommodation and occupation. This can no more be denied than the observation that there have always been forces to resist these tendencies. What has in essence probably been Christendom's most dangerous temptation can be found not so much in the struggles for power between State and Church as in the notion that the State has to defend the Church. But to act as *defensor fidei et ecclesiae* is not a duty laid on the emperor as representative of state power.[32] Biblical tradition testifies that this is the task of the Spirit, the Advocate (Mark 13: 11). This task—or so Christians understood in the first centuries—is performed by the Spirit in a special way through the witness of the martyrs, who are the Church's true apologists. If the State were to take over this task for itself, it would cease to be 'state' in the proper sense of the word—a community whose activities are limited by the 'politics of God'.

However, O'Donovan is not prepared to see this appreciation of the importance of the martyrs again levelled against Christendom, seen as a positive relationship between State and Church. He recommends the critical and self-critical Christianity of our own time not to cast back to the catacombs as the genuine, true, and pure Christendom. Rather, he sees the testimony of the martyrs as properly vindicated only if the possibilities which their witness has thrown open are seized in their historical consequence; and that means corresponding *as* state and society to the lordship of Christ.[33] In this way 'Christendom' can very well be understood as belonging to the same line of tradition as the martyrs, who gave their lives in resistance to (pre-'state') political power. Of course this certainly does not mean that the political existence of Christianity has to be experienced always and everywhere in the form of 'Christendom'. That is made sufficiently clear by the catacombs, by the so-called missionary churches, and no doubt to an increasing degree by our own present existence in what was historically the sphere of Christendom. It is true that 'Christendom' could be constituted and prove itself only in faithfulness to the martyrs; likewise today, 'after Christendom', what is at state is again faithfulness to what Christianity has inherited from this era of Christendom. Yet this faithfulness cannot be maintained by way of simplistic attempts at a restoration, but first of all simply by refusing to equate the historical phenomenon itself and modern prejudices. We shall hardly be able to arrive at a reasoned assessment of the problem of civil religion, for example, without a differentiated assessment of historical Christendom.

---

[32] S. Luther, 'The Emperor is not the head of the Christian religion nor guardian of the gospel or faith. The Church and faith must have a protector other than emperors and kings' (WA 30 II, 130, 27–30).
[33] O'Donovan, *Desire of the Nations*, 215.

Here another analysis of O'Donovan's is helpful. He shows how 'Christendom' provided itself with a dynamic instrument with whose help it tried to evade the continual temptation towards accommodation and occupation as regards the state, as well as—the other extreme—withdrawal of its character as state from the political community. O'Donovan sees this instrument in the doctrine of the two kingdoms or realms. He describes the changing history of this doctrine since Gelasius I, and comes to the conclusion:

The successive phases of the two-realms doctrine show no kind of historical progress in themselves. If anything, they show a circularity. The thesis of papal supremacy is advanced, prevails, is challenged and withdrawn. The church's authority is claimed for particular ecclesiastical structures; the claim is denied; then it is affirmed again. Secular authority is seen as a force outside the church; it is then seen as belonging within the church; finally, in the most recent post-Christendom era, it is located outside the church again.[34]

O'Donovan sees this hither and thither (like the wise vagueness of Gelasius, who avoids talking about two kingdoms or realms and only speaks unspecifically about 'the two') as displaying a certain thrust which is incumbent on us today too: 'Yet this circularity is not itself pointless. The unsettlement of each successive theoretical foundation corresponds to a new missionary need, laying claim to some aspect of social life that needs to be made subject to Christ's rule. The missionary imperative forces the construction, deconstruction and reconstruction of church–state theories.' So even though we cannot evade the theoretical task of defining the relations between Church and State in some way or other, these attempts should not aim to arrive at a definitive classification. The relevant and appropriate theological theories will accordingly emerge from a sensitive awareness of the given missionary situation. The one and only political theory of Christendom will never exist. It is not least political worship which makes this a certainty.

Stational Liturgy and the Conquest of Space: The City as Church
A glance at the liturgical development of a significant form of worship on the historical threshold of Christendom will help us to

---

[34] This significant formulation is derived, like the one that follows, from the preliminary typographical draft of O'Donovan's book.

capture this ambivalence of the Christendom era in a way which could also offer a key for an evaluation of contemporary phenomena in civil religion. The stational liturgies which grew up in the capital cities of the increasingly Christianized Empire show on the one hand how the sanctification of the cities was a preparation for the specifically Christian understanding of the state. On the other hand, the analysis of the function of these liturgies for civil religion reveals particularly clearly the ambivalent character which was part of Christendom from the outset, an ambivalence without which the political task of Christianity could not have been taken on at all under the missionary conditions of its time.

Stational liturgy is also important in the context of the thesis we developed in the previous chapters about the reconciliation of *oikos* and *polis*, for it shows that it was not only the *oikos*, the Christian life in family and business, which was claimed by the new politics; it was the *polis* too—not merely as concept, but as the centre of public life, the realization of civilization in general. The concentration of Christendom on urban life was not a matter of historical chance. It was a reaction to the structuring of life in the ancient world, where the cities acted as the icons, so to speak, of social life. Accordingly, the Christian claim that the sovereignty of Christ was above all other sovereignties was bound to be concentrated on the cities.

For the following account and interpretation I am able to draw on the work of the American Jesuit John F. Baldovin.[35] In a detailed comparative study of the most important centres of Christianity in late antiquity—Jerusalem, Rome, and Constantinople—Baldovin throws light on the phenomenon of 'stational liturgy' for the first time. In his study, he draws attention to the fact that in the urban context Christian worship was not confined to churches and shrines. 'It was precisely the city as a whole, which was to be the locus of the Church'.[36] One might even say, with a little exaggeration, that in the course of Christendom's development the city was actually to become the *oikos* for the Christian community. It was entirely in line with this that John Chrysostom should have been able to talk about 'the city as church', in the sense that it was the dwelling of the community.[37] And the instrument for this 'conquest of space' was in fact the stational liturgies, which precisely echoed

---

[35] J. F. Baldovin, *The Urban Character of Christian Worship* (1987).
[36] Ibid. 35.
[37] Ibid. 268.

the language of the cities. In the liturgical conquest of space (and time too, since the series of services lasted the whole day), the catholicity of the Church was formed and mirrored in its own particular way. Baldovin defines the typically urban type of worship as follows: 'Stational liturgy is a service of worship at a designated church, shrine, or public place in or near a city or town, on a designated feast, fast, or commemoration, which is presided over by the bishop or his representative and intended as the local church's main liturgical celebration of the day' (p. 37).

The mobile character of the services must be particularly stressed, the stations moving from place to place in the city according to a fixed plan. It was also found that this form of worship as central Christian ceremony in a town or city solved the problem of the variety of places where the Eucharist, the sacrament of unity, was otherwise celebrated in one and the same city. Stational liturgies therefore constituted *per se* the public worship where Christianity in its local form was able to demonstrate both to itself and to the outside world its unity, size, and power. As Baldovin says, these liturgies therefore had a double function: they were 'both prayer and propaganda' (p. 238). And here we have to suppose that there was a two-directional movement. On the one hand, the mobile services of worship, with their public impact, took possession successively of the spaces of the cities. On the other hand, the possibility of celebrating in public places was itself based on the conviction that the city was sanctified through the existence in it of the worshipping community. The stational liturgy followed the presupposed sanctification of the *polis* to the same degree as it strengthened and publicized it. 'It made the *civitas* not only civilization, but also holy civilization, a civilization defended as much by icons and relics and processions as it was by walls and military and political power. Thus, the city as holy civilization was a concept that was expressed above all liturgically.'[38]

Speaking about the processions from one station to another, Baldovin draws attention to one aspect which is of particular interest for our present context. He highlights the simultaneity of the stabilizing and de-stabilizing effect of the stational liturgies. These processions had a strategic effect in that they took up pagan models, which had already played an important public part in urban life in

[38] J. F. Baldovin, *The Urban Character of Christian Worship* (1987), 257.

pre-Christian times. The *pompae triumphalis* and the *pompae circensis* in Rome were centred on particular individuals, while in the Hellenistic area the *panegureis,* which involved the participation of the people, were especially popular. They included games and also cultic sacrifices to the city gods and others. Although Christians distanced themselves from this 'pomp', in assuming the role of civil religion in the Empire they also took over the basic form of the procession, which they modified accordingly.[39] In this way the stational liturgies acted to some extent as politically stabilizing performances laid on by the groups of people who increasingly determined the path of the political community.

On the other hand, however, Baldovin also notes that in the eyes of the rulers the Christian processions had a 'dangerous and eruptive quality'. It is true that their movement had a particular goal, and heightened the sense of participation by leading participants in moving toward that goal. But, conversely, the mobility also suggested the unfinished and fragmentary. The fact that Christian existence largely saw itself from the beginning as a pilgrimage, and hence as a contrast to agrarian and urban culture alike, was bound to be reflected in urban life as well. And this happened through the liturgy. By entirely accepting the circumstances of urban life, the stational liturgy at the same time pointed beyond them, presenting itself as a pilgrimage to 'the eternal city'. In the stational liturgy the viatoric existence of the Christian community was also impressed on believers through continually recurring penitential motifs. The political danger of this kind of unsettledness was soon recognized by the men in power, who tried to checkmate it through legislation.[40] This shows how little this phenomenon, which was typical of Christendom, can be fitted into the pattern of accommodation: the State did not accommodate itself to the Church—for in that case it would not have been able to do anything about the stational liturgy; nor, conversely, did the Church accommodate itself to the State—for in that case the State would not have been forced to step in.

In the perspective of political worship, it is important to appreciate this particular ambivalence—the simultaneous openness of stational liturgy for both the stabilizing and the critical element.

---

[39] Ibid. 234 ff.
[40] Ibid. 268.

For the criterion for an ethical assessment of the character of the stational liturgy as civil religion is to be found at the very point where the *unavoidable* 'civil religion' aspect makes political worship itself *avoidable*; where civil religion itself takes the place of political worship, politicizing political worship in a secondary sense; where the religious celebration is the celebration of the city as such, not of the End-time *polis* to which church and city are on the way; where the political meaning of these services of worship ('community as citizenship') is covered, wholly or largely, by civil religion and is not related to the Church first of all. As the development of stational liturgy shows, Christendom in the cities was undoubtedly exposed to the danger that this form of service, as the climax of the worshipping life, would become a substitute for the real thing. That is clear especially where the celebration of the Eucharist is concerned. This celebration was generally associated with the processions, as their climax. And although the idea was undoubtedly that the assembled crowd would communicate in the full sense, and not simply look on, the danger of a reinterpretation of the Eucharist could not be rejected out of hand. For where the primary experience of the eucharistic fellowship in the local congregational services was missing—as was the case for many people—this *public* worship could in fact actually promote the *privatization* of the Lord's Supper. In that case the political aspect threatened to dissolve into the duality of either civil-religious or individualistic interpretation.

Baldovin explains this apparent paradox:

It was precisely the open and public character of the celebration of the eucharist that eventually encouraged its mysteriological and allegorical interpretation...Moreover, these theological interpretations tended to focus more directly on the hidden meaning of the sacramental actions than on the evident meaning of the gathered *ekklesia* as Christ's body enacting itself in prayer. Thus more attention began to be given to the ritual actors, the assembly began to fade into the theological background. (p. 264)

This sudden need for an 'exegesis' of political worship signalized the way the aspect of civil religion had become paramount. By concentrating more on the elements than on the fellowship of believers, this exegesis encouraged the further privatization of the Eucharist in private masses, a privatization furthered not least by

the monastic reproduction of stational liturgies in individual monasteries and churches with a plurality of altars. A privatization of
this kind could emerge only in a climate in which the political
aspect of worship increasingly shifted in a civil-religious sense
away from citizenship in the church *polis* to citizenship in city or
state.

The Inescapable Challenge of Civil Religion

For an assessment of the elements of civil religion in Christendom
and Christianity today, this means that it is not the actual form of the
stational liturgies and their contemporary equivalents which in itself
provides a basis on which to found an opinion. This is possible only if
we include their interpretation in each case, or—to be more exact—if
we take account of their resonance. Do these elements find an echo in
the sphere of the worshipping community, or do they lose themselves
in the wider spaces of the civil realm? The criterion here must simply
be: does civil religion emerge as a side-effect of Christian worship in
all its diversity, or is worship, conversely, turned into a function of
civil religion? This will continually be a matter of dispute, at least in
individual cases, and the controversy about it in the Church itself is
the essential form which sensibility for the ambivalence takes. These
disputes are unavoidable, because there is no formal criterion for a
preliminary definition of the swing over to civil religion. The criterion is rather the worship situation of the community itself, whose
quality and relation to the public life of society has to be perceived
afresh in each case.[41]

This means that if we ask whether Christian ethics are open to
compromise, the problem of civil religion presents us with a double
answer: 'yes' to compromise as an affirmation of the 'alien' connotations which run parallel to the public praise of God, *as long as*
these connotations do not take on an independent life of their own,
and become idolatry. There are situations in which there can be no

---

[41] In Germany, clergy often 'bless' civic or public buildings (even sometimes
banks, etc.) on their official opening. This practice is controversial, but is a matter
to be decided not by edict of the church authorities, but locally, in the light of the
connection with the worship of the particular local congregation or congregations.
The question is whether this act of worship functions as an extrapolation of the
worship of the congregation—i.e., whether the congregation or local church remains
the determining interpretative community, irrespective of its 'extension' for the
special case.

compromise, and others in which a compromise can responsibly be accepted. But in every case the compromise is part of what we have to exercise our discernment on. It cannot itself be made the fundamental criterion of ethics, as it is in Troeltsch, for example.[42] To invoke terms like 'Christendom' or 'civil religion' is to indicate that discernment is called for, not that discernment has already been exercised. The connotations of civil religion in Christian worship cannot simply be equated with civil religion in the idolatrous sense. So the Church's (justifiable) fear lest it be claimed by civil religion must not lead to an exclusion of the practice of faith in civic affairs. The important thing is to remain vigilant in this respect, and to recognize the changing ways with which civil society employs religion as an instrument for its own self-celebration. In this sense, the task of differentiation must go hand in hand with a constant awareness of the danger of idolatry.

At the same time, however, if out of fear that civil religion can become idolatry, the Church thinks that it must refrain from a public engagement of faith, it incurs the danger of making an idol of itself. It is this which pins down the difficulty of seeing the Church as a counter-society at its theologically most tricky point. The Church would acquire the characteristics of an idol itself if it tried to preserve its purity by refusing to enter into the ambivalence of civil religion which an involvement in the civil and public sphere brings with it.

Today, however, we have in any case to look for the main focus of the movement towards civil religion not so much in connection with the state as in social contexts. And here our perception must be more finely attuned. For these movements are by no means tied

---

[42] E. Troeltsch, *The Social Teaching of the Christian Churches* (1931), sees 'the church type' as the compromising form of the sociological self-formation of the religious idea. Since in his view the Christian ethos cannot live and suffice for itself alone in a permanent world, it is continually and fundamentally dependent on such connotations—'supplements', in the sense of a corresponding cultural ethic. This necessity marks the Christian ethos as a permanent 'adjustment' to different worldly situations (pp. 1001 ff.). Troeltsch places the compromise at the very point where the ambivalence of 'Christendom' would have to stand, an ambivalence which is open to extension in both directions: towards compromise and towards uncompromisingness. Troeltsch, on the other hand, ascribes the latter only to 'the sect', which consequently 'becomes uncultured' (p. 1001). For a differentiated assessment of the compromise motive in ethics, cf. O. O'Donovan, *Resurrection and Moral Order*, 2nd edn. (1994), 93–7.

to church forms any longer. Often they are not religious at all, in the classic sense. Today we find collective identification rituals and cults for the most part in the form of promotions by the mass media, revolving around some aesthetic 'good' ('the adventure society') or some consumer commodity or product ('the designer-jeans society'), or, it may be, games or celebrities (fan clubs).

We have seen from the example of stational liturgy how in its worship the Church did not merely enjoy the fundamental experience which structured in advance its relation to other publics; it was rather that this relation was already constituted in worship itself, as that worship was moved into the public life of the city. Thus Christ's claim not merely to rule the political community of the Church through his Spirit but to subject the forces of this world as well, was carried into the world itself. But at the same time, this turn to the world outside was of considerable importance for the Church's own self-awareness. For it was only by exposing itself to the ambivalence of civil religion—the ambiguity of the way its public involvement was interpreted—that the Church could be kept from making an idol of itself. As a glittering utopian alternative, it would have been no more than a utopia, and its influence on society could only have been secured through the application of a political idealism whose logic is alien to the very nature of the Church (cf. section 5.1).

By carrying its elementally political experience of worship into society, the state, and other public domains, the Church counters idolatry in a double way—and this is so whether it moves its worship into public life directly (as it may occasionally do) or whether it carries that worship into public life by way of the citizens who are familiar with the political experience of worship. It avoids becoming an idol itself, and it offers the same ministry to society. We have also seen that it is only if the Church understands and celebrates its regular services of worship as elementally political that it can retain a secure instinct for the way its special, overtly political worship (with politically orientated orders of service) can tip over into civil religion. In this light, the analysis of the special form of the stational liturgies confirms what we have already said about political worship in its original character.

In the following section we shall look again from another perspective at the importance of the Church's own public for its explicit relation to other publics.

The 'Constituted' Public

Here, as a preliminary, I should like first to pick up an obvious objection. In claiming that 'church' is a public of its own, are we not in danger of cultivating a self-contained and in-turned religious ethics? Two comments may suffice for the moment. In the first place, today's familiar, zealous attempts to assure oneself of the relevance of one's contribution to public life, by demonstrating constant presence and engagement, seems to me to have much to learn from the political culture of late antiquity. There we find a lively awareness of the authority of the cultivated outsider. The model role of the philosopher, as a powerful mediator in political conflicts, was recognized for the very reason that in his self-chosen detachment from the interests and patronage of political society he was able to find the independence and strength which promised that his voice would be heard by those in power. It was by no means chance that, on the threshold to socially influential power, Christendom should have fallen heir to this tradition of *parresia*, or free spokenness, which Christian anchorites, for example, (and later on the bishops) took over, fulfilling the role in their own way.[43] In addition—and remembering what was said above about the criticism levelled by political worship at 'society's' claim to be the foundational pattern—the question about the closed character of the church's public can be given a sharper focus through a critical linguistic reflection. Since political worship, as an essentially non-functional happening, challenges 'society's' systematic claim to integration, it *cannot* be confined to its own insiders' ethos. What has been said about civil religion especially has made it clear that the publics we have talked about are inescapably related to each other in mutual exchange.

Plato was already aware of the explosive political potential of 'stories about the gods', and thought of the politically necessary homogeneity of public voices as being, above all, censorship of 'theology'.[44] Plato did not want to forbid stories about the gods from being told, but was only concerned for them to be in conformity with the state; and similarly, Christian talk about God too was, and is, continually appropriated in the interests of the politics of state or society. It is for that very reason that it is so important to

---

[43] P. Brown, *Power and Persuasion in Late Antiquity* (1992).
[44] Cf. J. Bethke Elshtain, *Public Man, Private Woman*, 2nd edn. (1993), 30.

practise this talk about God in worship, as the Church's own particular 'public'; for it is only that which will allow the Church to remain critical of the way this language is used in the public of state or society. The Church will have to ask who else today could constitute a public that is able to resist the forces of 'publicity' if it is not people who are experienced in publicity of a different kind. Consequently, the Church's own public is not the space to which people can retreat from the public of society. It is the operating base, so to speak, from which the other publics can be reached.

In order better to understand the conditions determining the transmission between the Church's public and the political public (in the narrower sense), it is useful to note a distinction made by Jürgen Habermas in connection with civil society and political public.[45] Politics as the controlling authority in social systems (or in their interest groups as a whole) can fulfil its constitutionally regulated function only if it can refer back to a political public which convincingly fulfils its claim to represent and balance out the interests of all members of the civil community. This public, formed from the communicative network of all those concerned, is of course for its own part now dependent on the supply of themes and problems which, even though socially generated, are still initially articulated and 'pre-digested' in private life, or among a 'literary public'. To the complex of this public, Habermas assigns not only art and literature but religion too. For, according to his view, these sectors dispose over 'an existential language in which socially generated problems can be *biographically assessed*. The problems which are discussed among the political public will first show themselves as a reflection of a social trauma in the mirror reflections of personal experiences. Where these find telling expression in the languages of religion, art and literature, the "literary" public (in the wider sense), whose special field is articulation and the disclosure of the world, is interlocked with the political one.'[46]

In our present context, this concept is interesting in a number of respects. Habermas brings out in his own way the relation between private and public life which we have described as 'the reconciling ministry' of worship. In both perspectives, emergence from private

[45] See J. Habermas, *Faktizität und Geltung*, 3rd edn. (1993) [Eng. trans., *Between Facts and Norms*, 1996; the quotations have been translated directly from the German text, and it is this to which the page numbers refer].

[46] Ibid. 441 f.

existence as the condition for political public life must no longer be understood (as it was in the thinking of the ancient world) as the leaving behind of private life as such. On the contrary, private life is now to be brought into the political sphere. Of course this does not mean simply including private problems and topics as such, but only inasmuch as they reflect social problems, and articulate socially relevant themes. It is also noteworthy that Habermas should recognize the role of religion for society's public as a whole in a way that presupposes religion's character as a public of its own. By neither seeing it as an undefined part of 'the' public as a whole, nor assigning it to the private sphere, but by conceding it a transmitter role, he comes astonishingly close to what was envisaged in our own theological reflections.[47]

Having in this way identified the conditions for constituting the political public, Habermas arrives at a distinction which makes itself felt in a mediated public of this kind. Such a public, once it exists, is open to two kinds of participation, which must be clearly distinguished in the light of the conditions for its constitution. There are participants who were involved in the creation of that public, and who are now concerned to maintain it; and there are others who merely utilize the public as it stands. Habermas is thinking here particularly of the large, well-organized political parties, associations, and interest groups which from the outset have at their disposal organizing power, resources, and the potential for intimidation, and who act on the political system *through the medium* of the public.[48] Although today this collective form of relation to the public is in the foreground under the catchword 'publicity', Habermas reminds us that genetically and generically it can actually only be secondary. It remains dependent on the prior constitution of a public sphere through the communication of the 'primary participants', who form opinion and on whom the public continues to draw. Publicity can undoubtedly manipulate the public formed in this way, but it cannot produce it.

---

[47] At the same time, however, religion comes into question only as one among others in a series of representatives of that 'literary public'. This also makes it clear that the political significance of religion is seen not in its special character—its own particular topics and language—but in a general structural feature which it shares with other members of this same group. What is primarily relevant is not religion's own individuality, but what 'about religion' seems to be possibly applicable in a generalized sense to the 'literary public'.

[48] See Habermas, *Faktizität und Geltung*, 440. [*Between Facts and Norms*].

In this respect the political effect of the two types of participant on the structure and stability of the public differs fundamentally. Although both help to keep the public 'in the picture', the character of that public changes under their respective influence. Whereas the secondary form of influence merely intensifies the fictional character of the public by draining it of substance, Habermas has this to say about the primary participants:

Participants who know that during their conflict of opinions and their struggle for influence they are involved in the *common* undertaking of reconstituting and preserving structures of the public differ from participants who merely make use of the existing forums. By giving their politics a characteristic *double thrust*, through their programme, these former participants exert direct influence on the political system, but at the same time they are concerned to stabilize and extend civil society and public, and to assure themselves of their own identity and ability to act.[49]

Forms of public relations driven by utility are typically accompanied by identifying marks, which derive from the original context of the influencing groups—that is, from their original social function (professional representation, political party, trade union, etc.). As distinct from these, groups who contribute in a constitutive way to the formation and further development of the public have a specific need for 'identity politics'. They must first *engender* their identifying marks, and then have continually to assure themselves of the identity they have thereby discovered.[50]

In language more reminiscent of Hannah Arendt, we might sum this up by saying the following. Whereas in the one case identity is demonstrated by the resources for power given with their functions within the systems (resources which merely have to be employed in order for the public to be influenced), in the other case identity depends on the *formation* of power (in Habermas's vocabulary: communicative potential for conviction, which can then in the regulated channels of a constitutional state transform influence into power). Theologically speaking, there is probably no need to justify further why only the second mode comes into question when asserting the Church's public claim—that is, the mode which has to do with the constitution and regeneration of the public. But in

---

[49] Ibid. 447.
[50] Ibid. 454.

combating the widespread view of the Church as the established
steward of traditional power resources, this can admittedly not be
said without a degree of ecclesial self-criticism.

However, the true identity of the Church in public life can
become visible only if it renounces this utility-driven type of relationship. To use Habermas's vocabulary: this identity consists in its
continual dependence on 'identity politics'. These identity politics
are constituted in worship, where Church becomes Church, and in
this sense ensures its identity. But in doing so it does not merely act
in antithesis to the politics of pressure groups; is also distinguished
(in spite of all the resemblances) from the social movements which
Habermas lists as exponents of the constitutively political type of
civil society. For as pre-condition for (their contribution to) the
formation of a public which cannot be 'manufactured', these are
nevertheless dependent on a moment of self-constitution in which
they legitimate themselves; and this makes their differences from
the Church plain. The Church's identity is not the product of an
identity politics which it itself would have to pursue. On the contrary, it receives that identity in and with the praxis entrusted to it as
God's gift. In the Church, the difference between a 'formed' and a
'manufactured' public which Habermas stresses is actually intrinsic
to the condition of its existence. The Church knows that it is the
creation of the divine Spirit, who gathers it by empowering it to
speak and hear the Word. *Just because* the Church's own public is
the prime example of a 'formed' public, the utility-driven relation
to the political public on the part of the Church is excluded from
the outset—unless it pays the price of forgetting what it is. As a
citizenship at worship, the Church is ever and again reminded that
a public can be a public in the true sense only if it is 'formed'—and
is reminded too that this public is not a secured entity, but needs to
be renewed and restored by 'the founder Spirit'.

Society—Civil Society—State

Karl Barth still saw the political importance of the Church only
over against the state.[51] But the distinction between state and

---

[51] In spite of his own original emphasis, what Barth says in 'The Christian
Community and the Civil Community' (in *Against the Stream* (1954)) is no more
than a variation on the traditional topic. The very first sentence of his famed essay
runs: 'By the "Christian community" we mean what is usually called "the Church"
and by the "civil community" what is usually called "the State"' (p. 15).

society, as well as the internal differentiation of society with regard to its particular civil aspects, opens the way for a more precise theological definition of the political relation of the Church. In a network of relationships like this, a logical order by degrees would seem to be appropriate where the Church (typically) exerts its influence on the state by addressing the public of civil society; and it is in this way that it performs its service to society as a whole. If the Church wanted to influence society without undertaking the laborious work of constitution and restitution in the context of civil society, this would be unrealistic; while to influence society through the connection between Church and State would be beneath the Church's political level.

The Church's influence on the public cannot attempt to bypass the mediating importance of a civil society's public. It would make the attempt only to its own disadvantage, and to the disadvantage of the public too, which cannot, procedurally speaking, win assurance of its reality from its own self: that is the theological objection that must be made to Habermas. Barth claims that the Church is a model or pattern for the state; but if we take up the notion of a formed public, we become aware that the idea of the Church as a model or pattern for the state (as Barth claimed it to be) would also be true of the public of civil society. At the same time it would be clear that the relationship of the two entities would now have to be construed no longer analogically,[52] but by way of their common (even though different) relation to political worship.

[52] The problematical nature of Barth's concept of political ethics as he develops it in 'The Christian Community and the Civil Community' comes out in the tension in which the different elements of the construction are related to each other. For it is much harder than Barth assumed to mediate between the basic notion of two concentric circles with a common centre and the analogical method. For to bring it into line with the geometrical construction of the analogy, the notion really presupposes two tangential spheres, rather than 'an inner circle within a wider circle' (Barth, p. 20, quoting O. Cullmann; see also pp. 32 f.). If we follow this analogy, it is hard to conceive how human and divine politics 'run parallel', as Barth puts it (see p. 32, where the German 'parallel gehe' is, however, mistranslated in the English version as 'can be equated'). Another, similar discrepancy arises when Barth defines the Church's task as being 'to remind' the state of its God-given premisses and limitations—although in another passage he describes this same state as 'unaware' (*unwissend*, p. 16). But a reminder presupposes previous knowledge. This tension can be resolved if the concept of the state is seen in its affinity to the specific secularity of Christendom, as described above. In this light, knowledge of itself and its limitations would indeed be intrinsic to the constitution of the state, and of this it could certainly be reminded.

In the outgoing movement which is implicit here, the public of civil society would have to see itself, like the Church too, as unequivocally at the service of society—which is as far removed from being a 'function' of society as it is from fundamental opposition to the state. An absolutization of the 'civil society' element, the romanticization of citizens' action groups, for example, as the only true mode of political activity, would actually surrender its transmission potential. Instead, it is important to remember that a notion of government is already inherent in criticism of the social process itself; so criticism cannot simply be directed *against* the state; it must be directed *to* it. In the service of society, the state must be discovered afresh as the authority which faces up to the question about control of the social process in the political sense. The state can achieve this only if it is not conceived of as a function of the social process but, as a constitutional state, creates under the rule of law institutional space for the critical forces of society. The participants in civil society too, for their part, are in danger of resignedly viewing the state as a mere function of society; to these the Church has to testify that the state can be understood as a 'benefit' conferred by God, as the Fifth Article of the Barmen Theological Declaration says.

The differentiated view of the complex relationship between state and society, which shows hopeful correspondences in civil society, helps us not to judge the state theologically with either abrupt affirmation or abrupt negation: not simply to preach 'the state' as a fate which requires either obsequious obedience of its 'Christian' subjects or subversive revolutionary activities. If the political counterpart of the Church is seen in a more differentiated way, a more discriminating theological definition of the relation between the public of civil society, the State, and society as a whole will also be possible, in which the reference of the Church to these different publics is not subject to over-hasty conclusions. If the Church were rashly to try to liaise with society, it would lose the state (understood in its original sense). It would either, in left-Hegelian manner, contribute to the dissolution of the state altogether, or it would degrade the state (systems-theoretically) to a mere administrative instrument. If, on the other hand, it were rashly to ally itself with the state, it would give fresh credence to its dubious reputation as a disciplinary institution, a reputation it has acquired for itself from time to time in the course of its history. In either case the Church would lose its character as a public of its own. That of course—and this must now be particularly stressed—would also be the case if it were rashly to associate itself with forces in civil society which are against 'society' and/or the state. As a public established and restored in worship, the Church represents the truth of a 'constituted' public, on which the public of civil society must draw if it is not to be swallowed up in utilitarian modes of relationship.

Habermas's premiss seems to be that men and women are from the outset political beings who need only the right environment (which can be set up through the appropriate procedures) to develop themselves as such. My own perception of a truly political public, however, starts from the assumption that men and women are not born as political beings. In this respect too they need a 'second birth' which leads them to act politically in the world. But the political womb or matrix envisaged here is to be found neither in the family (although this contributes to political socialization) nor even in the political public alone. The conditions for the formation and development of a truly political public cannot be thought of in terms of an evolution,[53] but only as a birth: that is pneumatologically inescapable. Since the Church, as the creation of the Holy Spirit, is the prime case of a self-constituting, non-instrumental public, it can be understood as just such a matrix in its own right, a matrix out of which the human being is born as a political being. But in sociology, talk about the 'second birth' aims at a learning process over time; and in the same way the public constituted in worship, as the school of political life, is of course also effective only if it unremittingly trains its members in the exercise of its specific praxis.

[53] Trusting, at least basically speaking, in evolution, Habermas agrees with Luhmann, even if their emphases differ.

PART III

WORSHIP AS FORMATIVE POWER FOR CHRISTIAN ETHICS

A. HEARING IN COMMUNITY—THE POLITICAL POWER OF THE WORD

Up to now we have seen how the worship of the Christian community breaks down political deadlocks by offering, as the work of the Spirit, a citizenship where people learn to be citizens in the true sense—beyond the frontiers of the Church's *polis* as well. Political worship is not a programme of education. It is an elemental experience of citizenship which bears out what Karl Barth once called for: 'Let us pray that the Church may supply the State with such Christians, such citizens, such political men and women in the primary meaning of the word!'[1] How can this requirement be interpreted in the light of political worship? In the main section that follows I shall try to find an answer, which I may already sum up here by saying the following. Christians make their specifically political contribution, moulded as it is by the experience of worship, when they speak and act publicly as people who have learnt to trust the power of the Word instead of relying on the effect of slogans—as people who are practised in eirenic listening and speaking.

---

[1] Karl Barth, 'The Christian Community and the Civil Community', in *idem, Against the Stream* (1954), 50.

9
Trust in the Word: Unlearning the Hermeneutics of Suspicion

In this first section (A), therefore, our discussion will centre on the political power of the Word. Here we shall try to show how the hermeneutics of mistrust, which has so disastrous a political effect, can be thrown off if people listen together to a Word in which there is no deception. In a further step, we shall work out the political importance of the Church's commitment to a 'conciliar consensus', which is the consequence—how what is deserving of consensus can be distinguished from affairs which simply have to be decided in one way or another, and what it means to avoid breaking off prematurely the joint struggle for consensus. In this connection we shall have to assess the part played by forgiveness, since this frees action from the vicious circle of mere reaction, and makes it possible for people to make a fresh start with one another. The fact that these fundamentally political gifts certainly have to be carefully cultivated in the Church becomes evident—to take one example—from my discussions of homiletics as a preliminary political study. These discussions centre on the question: how can the proclamation be based entirely on the power of the Word and the Word only, in the face of the subtle temptations of forcibly elicited agreement? And what can political rhetoric learn from this?

In the section that follows (B) we shall again concentrate on the special character of an ethics springing from political worship. This is an ethics drawn from the fullness of God's gifts. That is shown by analyses of the basic problem posed by the political theory of 'putting oneself in the other person's place'. For this can only happen without appropriation of the other person if what rules our lives is not predominantly scarcity (and hence rivalry and mistrust), but the wealth of good gifts. The aim of these reflections is to show the way these gifts are received in worship and, in intercession, are thrown open for one another in an exemplary way as the mutual transposing of Church and world.

The book closes with a chapter on 'Celebrating from his Works'.[1] This tries to show how the sanctification of 'the Sabbath' and the whole range of human responsibility go together—how contemplation of God's works empowers us for political life by letting us see what has to be done, and what must not be done.

But let us first turn our attention to the 'listening'.

The Sanctification of the Spoken Word

Why listening? Of course worship can be understood as a total aesthetic enterprise in which multifarious sensory and rational components come together and interact. The visual factors in symbolic communication especially have received growing attention. The reason why I am nevertheless focusing especially on hearing is the present context itself, in which we are trying to elucidate the *political* dimension of worship. Israel's worship— above all in its bearing on her political existence (in the social structure of life ordered by God's Torah)—could be understood as being in the widest sense 'listening to YHWH's voice'; just as, conversely, false worship was identified through the complaint: 'They do not listen to me' (Jer. 7: 26a; Deut. 9: 23b; and elsewhere).[2]

Hearing is the real political sense. Everyday speech shows the awareness that, in a quite basic sense, the politics pursued in any given case lose their footing if they cease to listen to 'the voice of the people'—for the fundamental experience of 'obtaining a hearing' for my concern is even more important in some cases than the acknowledgement of its justice. Hearing precedes seeing, especially at the period when human trust and the ability to trust are basically formed. In the womb, and in our first days on earth, we can see only very indistinctly. We do not initially identify our mother visually at all; we get to know her when she talks to us. It is true that later the visual skills, in their ability to differentiate, fall into line with the sense of hearing; but the two senses continue to structure different fields of perception. Whereas seeing provides an overview and makes possible the strategic mastery of the circumstances in which we live, the world of hearing remains structured

---

[1] This is how Martin Buber translates Gen. 2: 2.

[2] Cf. B.-J. Diebner, 'Gottesdienst II', *TRE* 14 (1985), 14 f.; on Israel's worship as a whole cf. H.-J. Kraus, 'Gottesdienst im alten und neuen Bund', *EvTh* 25 (1965).

towards an event and is dependent on direct communication. We see space, but we hear in time. We become all the more conscious of the difference when our perception is reduced by the loss of one of the two senses. A blind person perceives directly; he perceives the other 'within' the word, so to speak, with which the other person addresses him. The sighted, person, on the other hand, sees the other person coming in advance. So he has time to react strategically. He can consider beforehand what the other person in all probability wants of him, and he can then match this prejudgement against what the person actually says once he has arrived. The strategic potential of seeing promotes the distinction between saying and meaning, which forms the fundamental type of the hermeneutics of suspicion, the surmounting of which we are about to discuss.[3]

If we are to begin at the proper point, we have to be aware here of the political effect of the hierarchy assigned to the senses[4] in the modern world of the media. The unlimited visualization of life outplays the sense of hearing, and corresponds to a far-reaching political anaesthesia in which politics can only be understood strategically. To be seen is more important than to be listened to. We can see this from the struggle of political functionaries to appear on television, to be properly 'part of the scene', as well as from the colossal electioneering posters, with their indistinguishable slogans. But of course other members of the community are subject to the hegemony of the visual too. This does not emerge only when they allow their votes to be influenced by visual presentations of this kind; the not unjustified suspicion that reality does not correspond

---

[3] The precedence of hearing does not imply a dualism of the senses in principle. What is meant—that the other is not absorbed strategically within our horizon as he approaches us—can also be expressed in visual metaphors, as Emmanuel Lévinas shows in his 'philosophy of the other'. The direct active 'meaning' of the other (as distinct from the discovery of his meaning) is 'the epiphany of his face'. But epiphany means precisely that his appearance cannot be grasped; it is not a 'picture' which one could make of the other, and which would thereby melt his difference into one's own being. It is worth noting that at this point Lévinas is compelled to press his language beyond the visual metaphors. 'The face speaks. The appearance of the face is the first utterance' (*Otherwise than Being* (1981)). In another contribution Lévinas is even more precise, asking from the perspective of his criticism of ontology: 'How is the vision of the face no longer vision, but *hearing and speech*?' ('Is Ontology Fundamental?', in *Entre Nous* (1998), 11).

[4] Michel Foucault's *Discipline and Punish* (1977) offers an acute criticism of Western 'panopticism', in which the modern obsession with theory turns the world into a gigantic surveillance institution.

to the pictures of it which are presented to us is especially easily stylized into a permanent turn of mind[5] in which the distancing engendered by the visual paradigm contributes to the practical suspension of political trust and engagement. In Israel, by contrast, the political importance of listening was well known. The young Solomon, for example, on the threshold of his assumption of political rule, does not ask YHWH for the instruments of power. He prays: 'Give thy servant a hearing heart to govern thy people, that I may discern between good and evil' (I Kgs. 3: 9).

The loss of the ability to listen is often lamented today, but where should this ability be recovered? In this respect the Christian proclamation creates a unique situation; for the shared hearing of public preaching overcomes the subjectivism and individualism which otherwise belong intrinsically to a manufactured public, and as such conditions its often fictitious character.

In the act of shared, public listening—as distinct from the solitary conversation of the soul with its impressions, but as distinct even more from talk between human beings who are not at one in their listening, who diverge increasingly from each other through the imposition of their opinions, and thereby arbitrarily restrict publicity (instead, as it seems, of expanding and deepening it through the variety of the opinions held)—in this act of unforced ability to listen, the common ground shared by people before God is expressed.[6]

But this common ground does not mean a levelling out of the differences.

EXCURSUS

The story about the descent of the Spirit at Pentecost shows impressively that the concord which the Spirit induces in its listeners does not do away with their different cultural identities. The Spirit rests on every individual disciple, and in the same way the individual nations and ethnic groups hear each in their own language, and yet the preaching they hear is the same. The differences remain, but they are transformed. They lose their divisive character. Through his quotation from the prophet Joel, Peter's interpretation of this event in the sermon that follows extends the horizon still

[5] Cf. my essay 'Der liberale Zwiespalt: politische Nebelfelder zwischen Wertkonservativen und Habitualkritikern', *LM* 3 (1994).

[6] G. Sauter, 'Die Kirche in der Krisis des Geistes', in W. Kasper and G. Sauter, *Kirche—Ort des Geistes* (1976), 84.

further, beyond the surmounting of social and political frontiers. Where the Spirit is poured out on 'all flesh', what have hitherto been experiences of profound division are gathered together and named in a single breath: 'Your sons and daughters shall be prophets, your young men shall see visions and your old men shall dream dreams. And on my menservants and my maidservants in those days I will pour out my Spirit' (Acts 2: 17 f.). The cultural identities are not dissolved in some superstructure, but the different peoples are united in the experience of their shared listening; and similarly, the divisions between sexes, generations, and social classes are not simply said to have been overcome, but are surmounted through the endowment with the Word: 'They shall be prophets.' The Pentecost miracle of tongues means both these things at once; for the 'frank'—that is the open, fearless, and public—proclamation of the Word is as much a fruit of the Spirit as the new community in the hearing of that Word. In this way the Pentecost event 'produces a powerful public in which there is the possibility and the reality of *diverse* experiences of the removal of isolation and of individual and collective separation coupled with the preservation of cultural, historical, and linguistic diversity'.[7]

The political significance of this new language community can be seen in the fact that it can function as a paradigmatic 'discourse community'. In the shared listening to the same 'story', a coherent space for discourse is established, in which dispute about the proper path to be pursued by the Church *polis* is not blocked *a priori* through the equivocations of (moral) terms, in the way that seems to be unavoidable for discourse in a fragmented society.[8] But what seems to me even more fundamental is the empowerment to listen which Christian tradition acknowledges as an efficacy of the Word itself. The Word creates its hearers for itself. As creatures of the Word, these listeners are empowered for the 'peaceful hearing' which may be considered the most political of all the virtues. It means holding sacred the spoken Word which encounters us; it means the power to resist the temptation forcibly to trace back the encountering Word to the paradigm of the pursuit of already familiar interests: 'As a

---

[7] M. Welker, *God the Spirit* (1994), 235.

[8] On the crisis of modern discourse, which has left us with 'the fragments of a conceptual scheme, parts which now lack those contexts from which their significance derived', see A. MacIntyre, *After Virtue*, 2nd edn. (1984/5), in particular the famous opening paragraph just quoted (from p. 2). For the concept of the Church as discourse community (especially in relation to the thinking of Stanley Hauerwas), cf. R. Hütter, *Evangelische Ethik als kirchliches Zeugnis* (1993), 254–65.

right-winger or a left-winger, as a business man or a worker, as a man or a woman ... he or she *is bound* to talk like this.'

The Greek political model was based on the presupposition that people can be split up into groups, most of them being assigned to the category of the 'wordless'. And today's fashion of fitting everything and everyone into already existing categories may well serve the same purpose: defence against the authority of the spoken or written but always encountering Word. But in worship the renunciation of classifications of this kind is practised, which frees us to see things and people just as they are. And without that pre-condition, politics cannot begin to be true politics.

Inasmuch as the worshipping community makes it possible to unlearn the hermeneutics of suspicion, its political significance can hardly be overestimated.[9] For this hermeneutics is the foundation of that crypto-Machiavellian understanding of policy-making under which politics as we know them today suffers. For Machiavelli, moral rules are the technical instrument for preserving power; and it is not by chance that he takes as explicit premiss for this concept the 'fact' that everyone is corrupt, or at least corruptible.[10]

Meaning in the Head: The Metaphysics of Suspicion

As Wittgenstein's later philosophy[11] shows, this hermeneutics of suspicion is nurtured by a metaphysics in which a hidden 'meaning' in the head is assumed, a meaning which is obscured by the body, and hence has to be brought to light through hermeneutical oper-

---

[9] Karl Barth already detected this connection, saying of the Christian community, which itself knows that it is founded and nurtured by the Word of God: 'By a process of analogy, it has to risk attributing a positive and constructive meaning to the free human word in the political sphere. If it trusts the word of man in one sphere it cannot mistrust it on principle in the other. It will believe that human words are not bound to be empty or useless or even dangerous, but that the right words can clarify and control great decisions' ('Christian Community and the Civil Community', 39–40). However, Barth used the theme of trust in the Word only as one of his many examples of the capacity of the Church to be a parable for the state. He did not develop the idea in its fundamental significance for political ethics as a whole.

[10] Cf. the account in A. MacIntyre, *A Short History of Ethics* (1966), 127 ff. But, as I shall go on to show in the present chapter, to view Machiavelli as 'the Luther of secular power' (p. 127) is of course pure nonsense, especially where the attitude to suspicion is concerned.

[11] Especially in the *Philosophical Investigations*, written between 1945 and 1949, which appeared in English in 1953. The numbers in the text refer to the sections into which Wittgenstein divided the first part. The second part is not so divided, and page numbers are given in each case.

ations. The centre of Wittgenstein's criticism is the fundamental attitude of suspicion which finds expression in the distinction made between saying and meaning: 'So you really wanted to say...' (§334). Wittgenstein points out that the premiss implied in this type of statement is that 'what he really "wanted to say", what he "meant", was already *present somewhere* in his mind' (ibid.). But it is just this epistemological precedence of thinking before speaking which, says Wittgenstein, cannot be maintained in the practical world of everyday. Even when 'the hermit in the head'[12] goes shopping, it becomes clear how the act of naming things is bound up with other activities (§1).

Over against the illusory search for a pure, logical, fundamental form of language, in the sense of a theory of meaning—the search which still informed the *Tractatus*—Wittgenstein now perceives the indissoluble link between the grammatical and the performative elements of language. The thought never exists in detachment from its linguistic expression. 'When I think in language, there aren't "meanings" going through my mind in addition to the verbal expressions: the language is itself the vehicle of thought' (§329). Whereas 'the meaning of a word is its use in the language' (§43), and only that, and is embedded in a wealth of language games and forms of human life, the distinction between saying and meaning rests on one of what Wittgenstein called one of the most dangerous philosophical notions: that we think with or in our heads.[13] Linked as it is with the assumption of a quasi gas-like condition of the mind, thinking in the head becomes a mysterious and secret affair,[14] the meaning of which has first to be disclosed. This disclosure can take the form of speech utterances—or so this kind of thinking concludes. But since speaking as a physical occurrence often reproduces the purely mental occurrence of thinking only imperfectly (if not even deliberately modifying it), the laying bare of 'the real meaning' of what is said, in the sense of the reconstruction of its original form in what was thought, still has to be undertaken. (Here Wittgenstein touches on the metaphysical presuppositions of the hermeneutical tradition.) Thus the mind

---

[12] This is the phrase with which Fergus Kerr characterizes the epistemological solitariness of the mind which Wittgenstein disputed. See the lucid Wittgenstein interpretation in F. Kerr, *Theology after Wittgenstein* (1986), 57.

[13] L. Wittgenstein, *Philosophical Grammar* (1974), 106.

[14] Ibid. 100; *idem*, *Zettel* (1967), §§605 f.

appears in epistemological solitariness, detached from the body, which gets in the way of understanding.

As Wittgenstein shows, this metaphysical divorce takes no account of life's complexity. Even 'pure' thinking can only be grasped in language. It is like a conversation with oneself which grows out of the experiences of speech which we have had in a particular language community. It is obvious that Wittgenstein's criticism is aimed at the intellectual tradition which finds concentrated form in the Cartesian view, where all reality is secured to the *res cogitans*, which must be kept unsullied by every influence of the *res extensae*. Wittgenstein, in contrast, insists that men and women as physical beings can be assured of themselves and of others. The body is not to be seen as a hindrance to communication, but actually as a communicator. Wittgenstein demonstrates this especially in his extensive reflections on the way human pain is expressed, a point to which he reverts again and again in different places. In the course of these reflections he dismantles, piece by piece, the fantasy of a 'private language' which assumes that feelings—at least such as pain—are radically private and cannot be adequately communicated. But Wittgenstein shows how, over against our initial crying, learning to talk 'about' one's pain is really only a different way of expressing the pain itself. '[T]he verbal expression of pain replaces crying and does not describe it' (§244). '[H]ow can I go so far as to try to use language to get between pain and its expression?' (§245).

If we mistrust the way another person expresses his pain, saying 'it can't be as bad as all that', we are not really saying something about the other; we are saying something about ourselves. If someone makes a remark like this, he is making it clear that 'He believes in something behind the outward expression of pain'. 'His attitude is a proof of his attitude' (§310). Statements of this kind therefore show a person's general attitude, or the specific relationship to someone else. They do not demonstrate the fact that one person cannot know what another person is feeling.

Similarly, Wittgenstein does not trace the experience that there are people who seem to us 'not transparent' directly back to *their* possible lack of 'authenticity' (which would give countenance to the suspicion that they do not show their 'true face'). If other people are for us 'not transparent', it is not because we cannot hear what they are inwardly saying; it is because, as Wittgenstein says, 'we cannot find our feet in them'. It is as if we were in a foreign country whose traditions we do not know. Because their customs are strange, we don't understand them even if we know their language (p. 223ᵉ).

The question about understanding, therefore—the question about the reason for mistrust or trust—would seem to be mainly a question about shared forms of life. But, politically speaking, the dominance of the hermeneutics of suspicion then means the refusal to participate in shared life, the refusal to communicate the form of life in question. It is this that constitutes its fundamentally anti-political character. Incidentally, this again explains afresh how appropriate it was that Marx should have linked his anti-political theory of society with suspicion of language, which he saw as an instrument of deception.

Unlike Marx, however, Wittgenstein insists that life in its everyday relations is factually guided by basic trust. His sequence about 'the following of a rule' demonstrates how human beings always do precisely this in the language games and forms of life in which they are at home—they follow a rule, and do not decide from case to case whether they should do so; even less do they invent the rule first of all. The confidence that it is the rule and not the exception which makes the game work, is primary (§§199–202). Consequently, it is not mistrust that is 'healthy', as the hermeneutics of suspicion which has thrust its way into everyday language would have us believe. Indeed, this hermeneutics must itself be viewed as being in a way a pathological phenomenon, inasmuch as it would like to make a traumatic experience—the experience of misused trust—the basis for normal behaviour. Fergus Kerr rightly says of this: 'The metaphysics of solipsism may well feed on the realities of madness.'[15] It is not by chance that the dualist view about the mind/soul imprisoned in the body was theologically rejected by the Second Council of Constantinople in 553, in the context of its condemnation of some of Origen's opinions. And Augustine had already emphasized the political character of trust in the senses created by God, contrary to 'the addiction to doubt' of the second Academy. Accordingly, it is actually the City of God about which we can say: 'It also trusts in all matters the evidence of the senses, which the mind uses through the agency of the body; for wretchedly deceived is he who supposed that they should never be trusted.'[16]

---

[15] Kerr, *Theology after Wittgenstein*, 72.
[16] Augustine, *City of God*, Book XIX, 18.

Today theology has again every reason to rid itself of the metaphysics which Wittgenstein attacked philosophically: the denial of the bodiliness of meaning and mind. Can a more powerful therapy for this be conceived than the sensory hearing of 'the bodily Word' of the God who himself took bodily form?

The assumption that we cannot trust what we perceive through the senses may have its origin in the conflicting experience of our selves. That is at least suggested by the lasting dominance in this respect of the Cartesian legacy. Descartes's break through to his discovery of a new scientific method which revolutionized everything began, as we know, with doubt about the evidence of his own senses: can I trust them, or do they not rather expose me to the prank of a cheating spirit? If we are not clear about ourselves, it is but a short step to encountering other people too with fundamental mistrust—an attitude which at the same time 'objectifies' these others: what *about* them, and what *about* the things they bring to meet us, is genuine, and what not? Here the uncertainties reinforce each other mutually, and drive suspicion even more deeply into the self-consciousness. Neither our perception of ourselves nor the way we perceive others seems any longer to go hand in hand with any certainty.

'Who am I?' Dietrich Bonhoeffer's 'Suspicion of Suspicion'

Dietrich Bonhoeffer's famous poem 'Who am I?', written in his prison cell in Tegel, offers an impressive example of this vicious circle of suspicion.[17] In the course of the preceding letter to Eberhard Bethge (of 8 July 1944), Bonhoeffer complains of the tendency to ferret out a person's most intimate and interior thoughts, as if what is 'really' interesting is to be found only in what is concealed. In close similarity to Nietzsche, Bonhoeffer calls this urge to pursue people's weaknesses 'a revolt of inferiority', in which 'mistrust is the dominant motive in [the] judgment of other people' (344 f.). Bonhoeffer believes that a good part of contemporary theology

[17] See D. Bonhoeffer, *Letters and Papers from Prison*, (4th enlarged edn. (1971). The poem 'Was bin ich?' ('Who am I?') has been translated directly from the German [Trans.]. As far as I know, it was Rowan Williams who first pointed to the connection with the 'hermeneutics of suspicion'; see 'The Suspicion of Suspicion: Wittgenstein and Bonhoeffer', in R. H. Bell (ed.), *The Grammar of the Heart* (1988). This essay stimulated my interpretation here, although this belongs within the context of a different question.

subscribes to this hermeneutics of suspicion. This theology has indecently concentrated on the 'personal', the 'inner' and 'private' spheres, where—God now having been driven out of the world and public life—it hopes to keep for itself an enclave in which its authority is still in demand.[18] In biting words, Bonhoeffer lashes out at this parasitic attitude, focused as it is on existential philosophy and psychotherapy, which instead of facing up to the strengths of a world that has come of age, makes free with its hidden weaknesses; a Church which uncovers the wounds of the world and 'nurses' them, in order to protect its own therapeutic relevance. At the same time, Bonhoeffer's poem betrays that, where he himself is concerned, he too cannot entirely evade the morbid attraction of this attitude in its mistrustful questioning about the 'true self'.

'Who am I?' Bonhoeffer pursues the question first of all by thinking about what his fellow prisoners perceive. 'They often tell me I step from my cell tranquil and cheerful and firm.' But mistrust is the dominant theme: 'Am I really that which others say that I am?' As answer, Bonhoeffer puts forward his own self-perception: 'Or am I just what I know that I am? Restless, longing and sick.' But then mistrust of the perception of others turns even against itself: 'suspicion of suspicion': Bonhoeffer finds his own suspicion suspicious too. 'Who am I? This one or that? Am I this one today, and tomorrow another? Am I both these at once? Before others a hypocrite, to myself a whining, contemptible weakling?' It appears that even the suspicion of suspicion cannot put suspicion to rest. Even though suspicion is at first a relief ('seen through!'), in the end it leads into a tragic circularity. The chain of suspicion can find no end just because it so easily finds credence.

'Who am I? Lonely questioning mocks me.' Isolation is the code word for the circle that leads into self-doubt and despair. The loneliness which Bonhoeffer often complains of in Tegel as the absence of friends, engenders the attitude which throws itself into concern with 'the inner self', and which can then be so easily detected in others too. Primal mistrust is the hermeneutics of the

[18] Here Bonhoeffer's wording is astonishingly close to Wittgenstein's. In the same letter to Bethge (of 8 July 1944), Bonhoeffer writes '. . . it is thought that a man's essential nature consists of his inmost and most intimate background; that is defined as his "inner life"; and it is precisely in those secret human places that God is to have his domain!' (p. 345). Wittgenstein says: 'Only God sees the most secret thoughts. But why should these be all that important?' (*Zettel*, §560).

solitary, sick bird, 'fighting for breath to live, as if I were being throttled, hungering for colours, for flowers, for birdsong, thirsty for kind words, for human nearness . . . helplessly fearing for friends so endlessly far away'. But the 'kind word' and 'the human nearness' themselves are actually thrown away in the suspicion from which there seems to be no escape: 'shaking with anger at spite and pettiest insults'.

The poem ends simply: 'Whoever I am, you know me, I am yours, O God.' Bonhoeffer positively takes flight from this depressive mistrust. But of course the conclusion of the poem is not a solution. The question that torments him is still unanswered. And yet the vanishing-point is the key point too, the fulcrum which can lever the questioner out of the vicious circle of the hermeneutics of suspicion. Here the movement in the language is as important as its content, and itself already shows how the circle is broken through. The 'lonely questioning' of the soliloquy becomes an address. We are familiar with this speech movement from the psalms to which form-criticism gives the name of 'individual lament'. Here too, in a change of mood without preparation, the complaining description of distress switches over into a confession of faith (whether it be a song of thanksgiving, a grateful vow, or an expression of assurance). Was this confession of faith always uttered only retrospectively (as the psalmist looked back to the deliverance he has experienced)? That is a matter of dispute. It is just as conceivable that in the very midst of his distress the psalmist takes flight into the language of faith's acknowledgement, with which he is familiar from his people's experiences of deliverance, and which he trustfully anticipates in his lament.[19] Bonhoeffer's psalm of lament too does not introduce 'God' *into* his soliloquy as the solution; it leads the solitary questioning '*out*' to God, in whom all questions are absorbed and ended.

Here another related point emerges at the same time. Mistrust makes the question 'Who am I?' an endless affair. It makes every answer suspicious, while at the same time holding fast to the possibility and necessity of decoding 'the inward self'; but the speech movement towards the invocation of God can be recognized as trust by the very fact that no such decoding is expected. Bon-

---

[19] Cf. J. Becker, *Wege der Psalmenexegese* (1975), especially the chapter called 'Der Stimmungsumschwung in den Klageliedern des Einzelnen', 59 ff.

hoeffer does not expect of God the final unveiling of his true self, an outbidding, so to speak, of the mistrust which has not up to now been radically enough practised. Instead, the flight into trust in God is itself the solution of the hermeneutical circle: 'Whoever I am . . . '

The formal parallels to some of Israel's hymns again points us to a fact with which we have had to grapple again and again in the course of our whole investigation. The essential movements in speech and life are not instinctive; they have to be learnt. If Bonhoeffer was able to break through to the vanishing point of the invocation of God, it was not because of his 'natural religious sense', not even simply because of the 'crying need' which caused him to cry out; it was mainly because he was at home in Israel's psalms. Their language and their formal dynamic (the change of mood) were available to him because he was practised in them, having used them again and again in the worship of the community and in personal meditation.[20] In this tradition, its language and form, he could find refuge, as someone who had felt himself to be too 'tired and empty to pray, to think, to do.' That is why, in Bonhoeffer's case, the role played by the invocation of God is not an antithesis to the primacy of hearing, which we stressed above as being the pre-eminent form of therapy for the hermeneutics of suspicion. For the invocation of God grows out of hearing. The experiences of hearers in worship provided the necessary background for the speech movement which led Bonhoeffer out of the disastrous circularity of the hermeneutics of suspicion.

Learning to Take God at his Word

The language of praise is a threat to the hegemony of the hermeneutics of suspicion, but the reverse is also true. And here it will hardly be by chance that the three masters of suspicion, Nietzsche, Marx, and Freud, all had little use either for politics or for religion.

---

[20] During his time in the Finkenwald preaching seminary and fraternity, the psalter, as 'the prayer book of the Bible', became increasingly important for Bonhoeffer. Eberhard Bethge writes that it was Bonhoeffer's concentrated extemporary prayer which motivated the other members to adopt his 'Exercises', which are recognizably influenced by the language of the psalms. Bonhoeffer was convinced 'that the language used in prayer should as a rule be modelled on that of the Psalms, with which it should in any case harmonize' (E. Bethge, *Dietrich Bonhoeffer* (2000), 383).

Their particular forms of mistrust were, and still are, well suited to undermine both equally. After the collapse of 'socialism as it really exists' in the countries of Eastern Europe, and in spite of an impassioned Nietzsche renaissance in recent years, the Freudian variant may probably be viewed as the most influential form of the hermeneutics of suspicion, and to have the widest impact. In liberal societies such as the United States, the popularization of psychoanalysis in the last forty years has changed the feeling about life to a degree which makes it permissible to talk about 'the triumph of the therapeutic'.[21] This therapeutic culture is not anti-political just because its concentration on the interests of individual well-being diminishes the readiness for public engagement and for activity on behalf of the general good. It is more than that. For therapeutic thinking, politics is suspect as such.

As the team with whom Robert Bellah worked in his important study *Habits of the Heart*[22] brought out in the context of American (US) society, politics is bound to become a problem wherever the *relativity* of morality is made the principle of free self-fulfilment. Once moral convictions are viewed as subjective phenomena (not as good or evil, but as 'right or wrong *for me*')—subjective factors which seem to be virtually incommunicable even in the sphere of private relationships—politics as a matter of the joint formation of conviction in the public sphere must inescapably fail to enjoy supreme value in the culture concerned. Politics is 'inauthentic'.[23] Bellah's team therefore summed up by saying: 'For... many of the therapeutically minded, lacking the notion of a common language of moral discourse in terms of which public debate can reach at least occasional consensus, there are only the authentic, but ineffectual, voices of countless individuals on the one hand and the inauthentic, but necessary, assertion of one right way on the other.'[24] That explains why in this perspective everyone who gets involved in politics is initially suspect: what could possibly motivate him except the will to power?

<hr />

[21] Thus the title of Philip Rieff's well-known book, published in 1966.
[22] Robert Bellah *et al.*, *Habits of the Heart* (1985; rev. edn., 1996); see especially the chapter on 'Therapy and Politics', 130–3. Cf. also M. Berman, *The Politics of Authenticity* (1980).
[23] Bellah *et al.*, *Habits of the Heart*, 130 ff.
[24] Ibid. 133.

EXCURSUS

This conviction was already at the root of Wilhelm Reich's explicitly anti-political vision of a psychological revolution. Reich interpreted all power as pathological. His Freudian–Marxist analysis of politics declared it to be the most severe symptom of a sick society, a symptom which reached its most virulent peak in Hitler, as the incarnation of political genius. This analysis ultimately took on a decidedly religious form—politics as Anti-christ. Philip Rieff sees this twist as an outcome of Reich's chosen way of life: 'More precisely, it is religiosity, faith cut loose from all institutional connections and disciplines, that has become the established Western way of retreat from politics. In practice, Reich retreated into his therapeutic community, to await the fall of the world as it stands.'[25] In this respect too Reich probably anticipated to a large extent what everyday therapeutic culture copies. The flight from politics is practised with a positively religious drive. This is illustrated by the retreat of many political radicals of the 1960s into the concern for personal psycho-hygiene which came to the fore in the 1970s,[26] and which in the 1980s was extended 'holistically' to bodily health in general. But this line of development is really obvious enough where therapy as institution has established itself as religion's successor.

Since from the nineteenth century onwards, religion became increasingly familialized and feminized—which means de-publicized—it came to act as a refuge from the cold functional world—the very role, in fact, which today it has passed on as a legacy to therapism. It can by no means be said that the threat to political worship posed by therapeutical culture has an entirely new quality, for in fact it acts as a secular projection of political wor-ship's own deformation; but it can hardly be denied that this culture can painfully affect the development or rediscovery of political worship. The therapeutic attitude of mind has long since infected churches and congregational members in the societies it has infil-trated. Worship itself is then judged and fashioned according to the criterion of the degree to which it increases individual well-being; while the missionary activity of the churches now adopts the characteristics of advertising campaigns ('Everything's easier with Jesus!'). 'The triumph of the therapeutic' does not stop at the

---

[25] Rieff, *Triumph of the Therapeutic*, 177.
[26] Cf. C. Lasch, *The Culture of Narcisism* (1978), esp. 14–16: 'From Politics to Self-Examination'.

church's doors either,[27] and is well placed to marginalize its political worship in a way that no explicitly a-political theology ever
succeeded in doing.

But another possibility is also inherent in this conflict. In worship, politically efficacious resistance to the pull of therapism can be
formed and re-formed. In worship the hermeneutics of suspicion
can be unlearnt. This is of course not because people are more
'authentic' face to face with God, but because in worship they
encounter a perfectly trustworthy counterpart, in whose Word
there is no deception. So they learn what it means to take someone
literally at their word—to receive the audible Word as an event
which communicates the essential, and does not conceal it. The
Word of God makes the distinction between saying and meaning
inapplicable. And the cogency of this argument by no means
depends on an answer to the question to what extent and in what
way the biblical word expounded in preaching can be understood as
the Word of God.

What must be appreciated here is first, and quite simply, the
phenomenologically unequivocal fact that trust in this Word is
inherent in the practice of worship as such. Worship gathers people
together around a Word which they trust.[28] There is no such thing
as hearing without presuppositions. But the multifarious components of a hearer's situation can be traced back structurally to the
alternative: trust or mistrust—the authority of the Word or the
authority of the hearer. What is primary? Do I encounter as exposi-
tory authority the encountering Word, do I look behind what is
heard for its 'true meaning', or do I let myself be interpreted by that

---

[27] The influence of therapeutic thinking can be found in both 'liberal' and
evangelical churches, and not merely in the United States. As James D. Hunter
has analysed, on the basis of the publications of the biggest evangelical publishers,
the phenomenon of a 'psychological Christocentricism', which cropped up in the
1960s, has since become the determining trend. Here a flexible expressivism has
replaced the old ascetic morality of conservative Protestantism; see J. D. Hunter,
American Evangelicalism (1983), 91–101. On the infection of churches and theology
with the 'gospel of self-fulfilment', cf. also Rieff, *Triumph of the Therapeutic*, 251–61.

[28] It is along these lines that Paul Ricoeur has described the situation of hearing in
worship as a deliberate breach with the vision of a 'dialogue without presuppositions'. 'It is therefore only with a definite presupposition that I adhere to the position
of a hearer of the Christian proclamation. I am presupposing that this speech is
useful, that it is worth investigating, and that its investigation can accompany and
guide the transference of the text into life, in which it will comprehensively prove
itself' ('Nommer Dieu', *Études théologiques et religieuses*, 52 (1977)).

Word? Political worship presupposes that the hearing of the Word in the latter sense takes place intra-textually and not extra-textually.[29] Consequently the meaning reaches the hearer in the sensorily heard Word itself, and is not looked for outside the wording, neither in the sense of an external, propositionally grasp-able theorem, nor in some primal religious experience in the human heart, which would merely 'find expression' in the concrete Word. Denied the search for hidden meaning behind, above, and beneath the Word uttered (and here Luther's theology agrees with Wittgen-stein's philosophical ideas), the hermeneutics of suspicion is shown the door. It is replaced by an elemental trust which starts from the assumption 'that the Words of God are more understandable and more sure than all the words . . . of men; so that they are not taught, tested, expounded and strengthened by the words of men, but the words of men through them'.[30] Accordingly, it is only if an elemen-tal trust in the Word is developed, and only in that framework, that the paradigm change in political hermeneutics can begin: as resist-ance to the disembodying of human communication in the attitude of suspicion.

[29] 'Intratextual theology redescribes reality within the scriptural framework rather than translating Scripture into extrascriptural categories. It is the text, so to speak, which absorbs the world, rather than the world the text' (G. Lindbeck, *The Nature of Doctrine* (1984), 118).

[30] Luther, WA 7, 98, 11–13.

10

Consensus and Forgiveness

The Church's special perception of itself as a body made up of many members corresponds to the bodiliness of its elemental act of communication, the sensory communication of the bodily Word in proclamation and sacrament. And the unavoidable consequence of the life of the Church as the Body of Christ—a life effected by the Spirit—is the principle of consensus in decision making. The mutual recognition of the different members in their importance for the life of the body knows no exception, and the shared citizenship of all who belong to the Church's *polis* does not permit any to be excluded *on principle* from decision processes. For here there is no division into politically important and politically unimportant, 'lesser' members (1 Cor. 12: 12 ff.). In processes of decision in Church politics, unanimity has not always, will not always, and cannot always be attained; yet it is this which the Church as 'body' is in duty bound to strive for. The model for the political process is still the council of the apostles in Jerusalem, the result of which James could announce by saying: 'It has seemed good to the Holy Spirit and to us . . . ' (Acts 15: 28).

This obligation to arrive at a consensus may certainly be incorporated in democratically constituted ways of striving for agreement, but it must also involve a critical reserve towards a complete take-over of the parliamentary democratic principle in the Church. In the parliamentary model, the formation of political opinion is often not much more than the discursive reflection of existing majorities. But in the Church, in the essential questions of its faith and life, it is a matter of arriving at a true consensus. And this is bound to prevent a premature curtailment of the process of arriving at a shared conviction, an artificial cut-off that must continually be employed in the parliamentary model. There, the decisions made then reflect the majorities that obtain, rather than a path pursued in common in debate.

Conciliar Obligation

In contrast to this, the irreplaceable political service which the Church can offer to the 'body politic' (in the literal sense) is to show how in a political organism joint ways of arriving at convictions can be pursued and carried through to an end. As we have said, this aim will by no means always be attained in the Church. But a distinction must be made between decisions which have to be swiftly and pragmatically made and those where the discussion has to be continued until the Church finds itself in a consensus that can be formulated.[1] But where the Church gives way in its own procedures to the forces which enslave politics in the wider world (the pressure to reach a decision, the need to act, and so forth), it will do the political culture by which it is surrounded no service, however busily it labours to acquire public influence. So if church bodies were to strive too deliberately for procedural democracy in their deliberations, with the enforcement of majority opinions, this would testify rather to a lack of political orientation.

As early as 1935, in his perspicacious book *Liturgy and Society*, Gabriel Hebert worked out the critical distinction between council and parliament in its bearing on the way the Church's decision-making bodies see themselves.[2] Admittedly, history shows that the Church's councils were by no means homogeneous in this respect. Experiences of surprising agreement stand side by side with others arrived at through more or less velvet-gloved pressure. Consequently, although historically the consensus principle went hand in hand with conciliarism, the two are not identical. This was emphatically pointed out by the Reformation especially, whose motto 'Councils can err' was enunciated precisely in the name of a consensus arrived at in a different way. This meant that, from the very beginning, to cultivate ways of arriving at a consensus was a pressing concern for the churches of the Reformation; for where conformity with the gospel was in question, there could be no other way of arriving at binding formulations. The Lutheran Formula of Concord

---

[1] Among these are questions of fundamental importance, in which what has hitherto been doctrinal or ethical consensus is called in question, or where a consensus has first to be formulated because of the emergence of new problems. One example is the present discussion about homosexuality. This reflects in all its facets the uncertainty in the churches about the appropriate way of forming a conviction and arriving at a decision. The question is of such paradigmatic importance for Christian ethics that the process of reaching a consensus must not be cut short by majority decisions in church 'parliaments' before the discussion has properly got going. Cf. my discourse-critical comments in 'Das "Natürliche" und die "Moral"', *ZEE* 38 (1994).

[2] A. G. Hebert, *Liturgy and Society* (1935), 232 ff. As an introduction, cf. Part I, 5.

and the Barmen Theological Declaration are examples, and all the more important because of the different ways in which they came into being.[3]

The essential point here is that consensus as an obligation laid on the Body of Christ cannot be identified with the normative practice of any particular political procedure. To utilize this liberty productively, of course, does not mean settling down into a politically amorphous condition, and waiting for the intervention of the Spirit as a kind of *deus ex machina*. As we shall see in more detail below, waiting for 'unity in the Spirit' requires the closest attention to political procedures. The conditions under which agreement is sought, like the praxis of communication itself, belong to the category of the *endeavour* of the communicating community. At the same time, this endeavour to find the appropriate procedural conditions remains open for different possibilities, and cannot be pinned down to any historical model. This also applies to the affinity with parliamentary democracy, which is often invoked.

The 'conciliar' obligation to arrive at a consensus which is discerned in political worship offers the basic clue to political life in its widest sense. For the consensus principle by no means applies only to the Church. It can claim validity in secular politics too, and in parliamentary democracy especially. Secular politics must also make this obligation its lodestone, even though—and especially because—it is not wholly attainable.[4] If the questions which are on the agenda are not, at least as far as possible, put on the road that leads to the formation of a common conviction which does not *a priori* exclude consensus ('hermeneutics of suspicion'), parliamentary debates become merely play acting, a stage-managed show of democracy. It is only the presence of a body politic which lives out the joint formation of intent as the link between the expectation of consensus and its attainment which is therefore in a position to guarantee the reality of political life, especially under the circumstances of policy making as it exists at present. Of course,

---

[3] For more detail cf. here G. Sauter, 'Was ist Wahrheit in der Theologie?', in *idem*, *In der Freiheit des Geistes* (1988), 61–71.

[4] That is why I am using the word 'clue' and not 'model' or 'archetype' for the relation to politics. The Church's consensus policy is not a 'model' for secular politics, because the one cannot simply be transferred to the other. It is not the 'archetype', because it does not of itself transfer the form of its activity to secular politics. As 'clue', the politics of the Church is productive for secular politics precisely because it is experienced differently.

biblical 'unity in the Spirit' must be distinguished from experiences of consensus in political decision processes. The pattern of ecclesial consensus cannot necessarily be transferred as model ('prototype') to state and society. But for that very reason state and society are all the more dependent on the existence of a political sociality which lives in expectation of such a consensus.

What consensus means in the Church, however, cannot be generalized into 'the idea of consensus' which, in the form of 'ideal politics', could be made the transcendental presupposition ('archetype') for practical politics. The idea cannot be mediated by way of the abstraction 'is and ought', for with Christian citizens the political public has to do with real people, who live and act in both contexts as those who are equipped with experiences of consensus. These guarantee that consensus does not become a mere airy notion, and that the striving for it does not become political mimicry. In the business of politics they are a reminder that politics must not lose its structural relation to the question of truth. The experiences of consensus in the Church's public train people to resist the plebiscitary tendency to view consensus simply as the social recognition of particular opinion quotients (lowest or highest common multiple). At the beginning of the fifth century, Severian of Gabala enunciated the maxim that *ubi namque veritas sese prodit, omnia consentiunt*—'if truth is seen, all agree'.[5] But this maxim is not reversible. An avoidance of this pitfall, however, depends on the experience that the maxim is in tendency correct. Consequently, in the differing political contexts, people are needed who can contribute the experience that in consensus what has validity is not simply *contrived* but a truth which shows itself to be such is *apprehended* (in both senses of the word). This goes together with the no less important experience that truth does show itself, and that it really can be apprehended—and that to arrive at a consensus does not have to mean entering into a process which is in principle open-ended.

Consequently, the expectation of consensus can preserve the process of jointly forming a judgement from the aporetic alternative: decisionism or reflection without end. For, on the one hand, the Spirit that lends assurance gives the openness which is required for a really free discourse. Its ecstatic mode of efficacy breaks down

[5] Cited in Sauter, 'Was ist Wahrheit in der Theologie?', 62.

hard and fast positions, and permits new, unwonted experiences. Of course this openness always has its necessary frontiers too; but their position cannot be discovered in advance. To perceive where the frontiers run in each given case requires practice in judging. Here the Spirit also enables discussions to find an end, because it makes it possible to say what the politics of a community can be, and what not: where the limits lie—the limits of whatever empowers an expectant life together, or hinders it. The conviction that the Church is called to mediate these experiences, and the extent to which it can do so, again depends on its perception of its corporate identity. Hebert pins this down as follows:

> But the Church is by nature a Body, and is thus impelled, in so far as it is true to itself, to seek a common mind; and this is possible because the Church's existence is based on a common faith. It is thus that the Church has the power to create a social life, not through mere organization but through the actualization of the organic life of the Body. Can anything but this common faith and this organic life re-create our secular politics?[6]

What Hebert describes here is nothing other than the power of political worship. To empower the joint formation of opinion in the political questions of the Church is the work of the Spirit. The common mind springs from the common faith. And the common faith grows out of the shared hearing in worship. Here members learn to speak 'with one tongue'. They learn a language in which the search for consensus is meaningful, and the formulation of a consensus possible. In worship what Hebert calls 'the actualization of the organic life of the Body' also comes about in a primary way, and this leads to the re-creation of political existence. For the multitude of believers experience themselves as the Body of Christ when they are gathered together: in hearing and in the tasting of God's bodily Logos. Without these sensory experiences in worship, to have recourse to the metaphor of the body would be mere political romanticism. It is precisely this connection which Gerhard Sauter formulates when he talks about the primary conditions of consensus.

> 'Consensus' means discerning the place where we perceive the community created and vouched for by God, and arrive at a shared life in this unity.

---

[6] G. Hebert, *Liturgy and Society*, 234.

Because of that, theological consensus is always ultimately rooted in worship . . . Consequently the forms of action in worship are also paradigmatic for the way in which a consensus comes into being, and the ways in which it can be expressed and followed up. This means that the public expression of consensus and its transmission belong to the fundamental acts of the liturgy.[7]

Anticipating the homiletic reflections which we shall go on to presently, it may be said here that the original praxis of communication in the Church, the proclamation as communicative process in the freedom of the Spirit, clearly shows how a consensus can be found; how an agreement can be reached which is neither contrived, nor splits participants in the debate into winners and losers. Politically speaking, the essential point here is a proper appreciation of the significance of the procedural aspect. It can hardly be stressed too strongly that the attempt at understanding is an enterprise. Here there are premises which can be clearly determined, correct patterns of behaviour that have to be practised, and wrong patterns that have to be avoided, rules and limits that have to be observed. But the thing about these limits is the very fact that the goal of the whole undertaking—agreement—must be kept out of the procedural sphere. In expecting that a consensus will be found, we must avoid trying to bring it about by methods and procedures. Although the anticipation of the consensus is necessary, in the form of confidence, it is politically deadly to snatch covetously at the consensus, in a forcible seizure. Because the end—the consensus—is not declared to be the purpose of the political means, the political aspect remains free—it remains, in fact, political.

Thus the consensus which politics must always have in mind as possibility is the most powerful indication of the 'enhypostatic' character of secular politics. For the sake of its own liberty, in order not to be instrumental, politics cannot stop short at itself. In just this sense worship, as a non-utilitarian act *par excellence*, sets political existence in the presence of the Spirit. It constitutes the 'clue' to political existence, since in talking about the Spirit, talk which becomes immediate as address ('Come, Holy Spirit'), it takes up in its explicit liturgical enactment and permits the communication of that which must be inherent in the *finding* of every

---

[7] Sauter, 'Was ist Wahrheit in der Theologie?', 79.

consensus. To take a somewhat daring image: a consensus is be-
gotten, not made. The fact that it comes into the world is not
independent of the begetting, but the begetting is not yet the
birth. The begetting of a mutual assent, an agreement, is an act of
passionate endeavour for understanding, which follows its own
rules, both pleasurable and strenuous. But the consensus is born
at its proper time, a time which is incalculable. In the words of the
Augsburg Confession (Article V), it is born *ubi et quando visum est
Deo*—'where and when it pleases God'.

Worship and the Culture of Dispute

As the practice of a shared language, worship makes possible the
political formation of conviction in the direction of consensus. It
does so in a way which is barely conceivable in the present confu-
sion of incommensurable moral languages. But here there is a
surprising point. The univocity which worship makes possible
does not make the discourse harmonious; it actually furthers the
dispute. Because it envisages consensus as a genuine option, it
makes dispute really possible for the first time—possible and also
real. For conversely—on the basis of equivocations—it is impossible really to dispute. Where the dispute about terms cannot be
decided, and is therefore either perpetuated or swept under the
carpet, the dispute about the point in question never really gets
going. But the language community of worship is able to pursue the
search for a consensus as a true dispute about substantial questions,[8] a dispute which is able to distinguish a genuine consensus
from a false one. False consensuses have fallen victim to the spell of
dazzling equivocations, which have not been seen for what they are.

By developing a unified moral language, however, worship does
not only provide the material which helps a consensus to be accomplished. It also develops the specific living conditions in which this
path can be followed, through all its crises and difficulties. So one of
the essential contributions which worship makes to political life is
the circumstance that people who are engaged in a dispute with one
another can worship together. And here stress is not on the fact that
these people can *nevertheless* worship together; the emphasis is

---

[8] See S. Sykes, 'The context of communal worship permits doctrinal dispute', in
idem, The Identity of Christianity (1984), 286.

precisely reversed: *as long as* people can worship together, they can dispute freely with each other.

It is in fact the shared celebration of worship which actually guarantees the political form of the dispute. Here the disputants turn again and again to the common foundation on which the dispute takes place. Communal hearing leads to the *magnus consensus* which makes the search for consensus in individual questions promising. The search for a 'second order' of consensus is accompanied and framed by experiences of the 'first-order' consensus: coming from the articulation of that, and moving towards its next expression, the search is unremitting. 'May the God of steadfastness and encouragement grant you to live in the harmony with one another which accords with Christ Jesus, so that together you may with one voice glorify the God and Father of our Lord Jesus Christ' (Rom. 15: 5 f.). In chiming in with the creed, and in the praise of God, the power of the hermeneutics of suspicion is broken, and with that its basic assumption that no real and unforced agreement will in any case be reached. Where the strong and the weak see themselves as all equally in need of the Word, and as continually having to learn afresh from their common praxis, the course of the discussion cannot be determined by force—perhaps in the form of a demonstration of rhetorical superiority. Peaceable hearing is sensitive to soft voices. Attuned through worship, the discourse will be truly political, *sine vi sed verbo*—'through the word, not through force'. The form it takes is, to use a grammatical metaphor, the continuous form of trust in the power of the Word, which is able to dispense with the use of force, either verbal or non-verbal.

At this point, certainly, an obvious objection may be raised. Unless it is confined simply to the Word of God and the proclamation, doesn't trust of this kind in the authority of the spoken word (if it is supposed to mould the political discussion context as a whole) forge a highly uncritical attitude of mind? Would a 'hermeneutics of trust' not inevitably end up in political naïvety? Is it not trustworthiness which constitutes the infinite qualitative difference between God's Word and the words of human beings? Viewed phenomenologically, however, the matter looks different. What distinguishes criticism from mere *ad hoc* negation? Surely the fact that criticism is dependent on attention to what is said. Real criticism can only start from, and be effected by, the word that has been heard. It is the very ability to criticize which requires us to talk about the 'authority' of the word—of every word spoken by a human being.[9] This does not mean ignoring the qualitative difference between human words and the Word of God. But the difference makes itself felt not as the dividing line between trust and mistrust, but in the sphere *where trust is constituted.*

The fact that the political arena is not itself the ideal place for learning to trust the words of other people must not blind us to the fact that this arena is, for all that, dependent on this trust in words. Consequently, it is essential for political culture to find places where trust in the word can be learnt, where words can be found to count and not to deceive. To put it differently: the distinction between the trustworthy Word of God and the words of human beings is essential just because it allows a fundamental trust in the word to be developed in worship which can still be potent in the realm of human words too. But this trust is effective because of the fact that it cannot easily be deceived. Only trust which is open for the communication in the spoken word ultimately makes criticism possible—because it takes others 'at their word' and if necessary challenges them by reminding them of that word.[10] Thus the trust in the word which we bring into communication with another can also provide self-criticism on the other's part, by showing what it would mean—what would happen—if the word he uttered were taken seriously, or perhaps by showing that he himself has not taken it seriously enough.

At times when mistrust is dominant, the political exposition of the power conferred by trust in the word will typically take the form of surprise. And particularly as surprise, it can become salutary criticism. What could make us surrender so deep-seated an attitude as suspicion except the experience of being taken at our word, and hence being taken more seriously than, as a rule, we take ourselves? The hermeneutics of suspicion cannot simply be contradicted, for the very reason that everything seems to speak in its favour; as a

---

[9] Illuminating here are O. Bayer, *Autorität und Kritik* (1991), 65 ff., and M. Polanyi, *Personal Knowledge* (1958), 269–98.

[10] Biblical tradition knows criticism like this as criticism of God too especially in the form of a complaint which holds up to God his own Word, which he has not yet fulfilled. Here the important point is to see that the complaint is itself an expression of trust, not mistrust, since it remains within the relationship of address. Mistrust dominates only in the 'theoretical' form of theodicy, where speculation about God's existence (because of the suffering in the world) has already departed from the relationship of address.

primal sensory phenomenon, it cannot be confuted through argument, even though there are sound arguments against it. It can only be broken through like a hard shell—through surprising experiences of trust in the word, which burst open the armour of mistrust.

The path the argument has taken up to now will perhaps have made it plain why the trustful hearing of the word is so important politically. The person who has learnt to hear in this way takes the other at his word, the word which communicates something—which does something to the person who hears it. But this means taking the other person seriously as someone who is really capable of acting. Only trust in the word like this meets the other person as a political being who can give a new impetus and who is capable of 'beginning'. Trust does not reduce the other person to mere behaviour, by hearing in his words only what we expected of them, in the light of our predetermined view of him (as right-wing, or left-wing, and so forth). It does not pin him down to a particular role, and does not degrade the political discourse to the mechanism of provocation-reaction. As we have seen, trust leads to the movement towards consensus, to the common search for sustainable conditions of social life. It makes it possible for people to act together.

Forgiveness as a Political Virtue

It is one of the dilemmas of politics in our time that it is often unable to get beyond the level of mere reaction. Consequently, the Christian practice of forgiveness constitutes a political virtue of the first order. For the hermeneutics of suspicion is not a creation out of nothing. It is the result of countless processes of assimilating experiences of abused trust. This means that practically speaking this hermeneutics can only be replaced through the forgiveness of 'those who trespass against us'. As Christians learn from the Lord's Prayer, the prayer for *God's* forgiveness precedes the rest. The forgiveness received which people experience in worship then makes it possible for them to be led out of the vicious circle of mere reaction. The forgiveness of God that has been received frees people from the iron law of retaliation, and this in its turn also frees the other people concerned for action. For they then have to respond to something new, an initial act, instead of having to prolong the feedback system of reaction. Forgiveness is the empowerment for a new beginning. This is the continually new 'discovery of political existence': that people can make a new beginning in getting along together. In worship, the empowerment for action and the acting together are intertwined. So reconciliation in the kiss of peace is followed directly by fellowship at the table in the Lord's Supper.

It was Hannah Arendt who, picking up what Aristotle had already said, impressed on us that political existence means both a beginning and an assenting acting together. And it was Hannah Arendt too who was able to appreciate the importance of forgiveness in political theory. She understands 'the faculty of forgiving' as 'the possible redemption from the predicament of irreversibility'— the irreversibility of what has been done. 'Without being forgiven, released from the consequences of what we have done, our capacity to act would, as it were, be confined to one single deed from which we could never recover; we would remain the victims of its consequences forever, not unlike the sorcerer's apprentice who lacked the magic formula to break the spell.'[11] Arendt also stresses that forgiveness acts as a release from the circularity of retaliation, and associates this potency with the fact that because we cannot reckon with forgiveness it must be a primal act. 'Forgiving ... is the only reaction that acts in an unexpected way and thus retains, though being a reaction, something of the original character of action.'[12] But in contrast to what we have developed here, Arendt assumes that the ability to forgive is rooted in the ability to act itself.

Here Arendt, in explicit antithesis to Christianity, once more picks up the tradition of the ancient world. It is not just love that makes forgiveness possible, as the Christian faith believes. For Arendt, love, as an 'unworldly' phenomenon, as 'the most powerful of all antipolitical human forces', is at home only in a 'narrowly circumscribed sphere'; for in the political world, 'the larger domain of human affairs', *respect* (in the sense of the Aristotelian *philia politike*, 'political friendship', 'a kind of "friendship" without intimacy and without closeness') takes the place of love. This is 'quite sufficient to prompt forgiving'.[13]

A dispute about terms is not particularly fruitful here. Perhaps Arendt's concept of 'respect' is closer than she thinks to the sober biblical idea of love, as the efficacy of faith which respects our

---

[11] H. Arendt, *The Human Condition* (1958; 2nd edn. 1998), 237.
[12] Ibid. 241.
[13] Ibid. 242–3.

neighbour as someone created by God. But the real crux here is the question of how we can summon up the power to forgive. And in my view, Arendt considerably underestimates the circularity of retaliation and its power. Can people who are actually imprisoned in this circularity really summon up the power to escape from it, just by themselves? Must this overmastering force not be overcome by another force that is still more overmastering? Must forgiveness not first be learnt through the overwhelming experience of its own power, as an unexpected gift of grace? At the end of her reflections, Arendt breaks into new terrain when she writes that 'nobody can forgive himself'.[14] But the source of this experience of forgiveness as something received remains for her undetermined. Where is '[the world around us which forgives our guilt']?[15] It would certainly be impossible to maintain that forgiveness is given only in worship, and is an act performed only by Christians. But, going a step beyond Arendt, one might say theologically that 'the people around us', the accompanying world of God's forgiveness, are in a primal way the fellowship of pardoned sinners assembled for worship. Here what prevails is the forgiving love which creates political 'respect' in the first place.

Now we had of course to look critically at Hannah Arendt's option, which was to see the ability to forgive as already included in the action, as this ability is based not on acting but on receiving. Yet if we remember this difference, we can arrive at a new appreciation of the elements of truth in what Arendt maintains. It is not the *ability* to forgive which is an intrinsic part of the political context; it is the *necessity* of forgiveness. Since this first emerges together with the political situation (our communicative responsibility for each other), we can also say in a derived sense that forgiveness is possible only in the political sphere. It is there only that forgiveness is necessary and possible, because it is there that we find rules for living together which require free assent and which can also be rejected. A social group only becomes a political community

---

[14] Ibid. 243.
[15] 'eine Mitwelt, die unsere Schuld vergibt': this phrase at the end of ch. 33 of the German text of Arendt's book does not appear in the English version. In the German version (p. 238), the final sentence, translated, runs: 'Were there not a world around us which forgives our guilt as we forgive those who trespass against us, we too could not forgive ourselves for any failing or transgression because, closed within ourselves, we would lack the experience of the person who is more than the wrong he did.'

through the law which lifts the consequences of an act above the individual sphere into the public one. So in the political community, other than in an anarchistic group, an act is always doubly codified. Its consequences must be dealt with both privately and publicly. So the need for forgiveness always has this double reference, since in order to be fully resocialized, the perpetrator must be released from the consequences of his act in the field of personal relationships and in the *civitas* too.

Because the Church has always understood itself as a political community, it was bound from the beginning to be aware of the connection between personal and public forgiveness. Forgiveness is therefore politically codified in a double sense. Its possibility and its necessity are given only in a community 'under rule', whose public is fenced round by a certain set of ordinances,[16] and its *telos* is the reintegration of the community itself, to which the integration of the transgressors ministers (Matt. 18: 12–18). So forgiveness is also political inasmuch as the resocialization of the perpetrator is not conferred upon the individual like a sovereign act of grace. Rather, it emanates from the need of the forgiving community, which would not be complete without the one who has transgressed.[17] So the political character of forgiveness is at the root of all individual forgiving acts. This was brought out particularly in the rite of public repentance, where penitents and congregation together experienced forgiveness as a socially identifiable change of status which took place in worship. In contrast, the unabated trend to reduce forgiveness in worship to the private or collective (but still individually centred) act of repentance tends to obscure the full political meaning of forgiveness.

---

[16] The restricted space is one of the structural conditions of a 'public'. As Reinhard Hütter has established, this political space—constituted for the *polis* of antiquity by city walls and by laws, and for Israel defined by the Torah—is determined for the Church by its doctrine and its central practices. See R. Hütter, 'The Church as Public: Dogma, Practice, and the Holy Spirit', *Pro Ecclesia* 3 (1994).

[17] Thus forgiveness does not merely serve the integration and reintegration of a community; its political character also contains a centrifugal aspect, in which the community keeps its frontiers open for the perpetrator. This has been perceived by James W. McClendon jun.: 'It is exactly this skill of forgiveness that is the divine gift enabling disciple communities to cope with the looming power of their own practice of community, otherwise so oppressive, so centripetally destructive. Without forgiveness, the social power of a closed circle may crush its members, soil itself, and sour its social world.' See his *Ethics: Systematic Theology*, i (1986), 229. Cf. also L. G. Jones, *Embodying Forgiveness* (1995).

The role of forgiveness can now be more clearly grasped in its relevance for our wider context, which is the political importance of trust in the word in the hearing of it. Forgiveness prevents trust which has been disappointed from mutating either into naïvety or into the hermeneutics of suspicion. For it neither filters out the reality of disappointed trust (naïvety) nor does it consider disappointed trust to be the all-determining reality (mistrust as a principle). Instead, forgiveness acts as the place where these experiences can be assimilated, while forgiveness itself springs from trust in the word. For only what is assumed can be redeemed: only the one who is taken at his word (or act) can become the 'transgressor' who can be forgiven. Likewise for him, forgiveness makes possible a new word, and a new hearing, and as it does so re-establishes the community of the hearers.

EXCURSUS

The political significance of forgiveness can be seen in the sphere of international relations too. It would be easy to demonstrate this from the many cases where forgiveness is lacking; but that makes the positive examples all the more important. We may cite just a few examples. The integration of the German churches in the ecumenical community played a pioneer role in the process of reintegrating post-war Germany into the community of nations. This can also be described as a process of forgiveness. We may think here of the Stuttgart Declaration.[18] And how else should we see Chancellor Willi Brandt's gesture in falling on his knees in the Warsaw ghetto, an act which at the time gave the political impetus for a new policy towards the countries of Eastern Europe?

On the fiftieth anniversary of the 1944 Warsaw rising against German occupation, the then German president, Roman Herzog, could pick up this tradition, saying: 'I ask forgiveness for what the Germans did to you.' The Polish writer Andrzej Szczypiorski responded by paying tribute to the importance of these words, for which no treaty could be a substitute: 'For these words the Polish people have waited for forty years.'

Examples like these are well suited to show the importance practically ascribed to forgiveness in the relationships between political communities. But it must be said that this hardly explains the real significance of forgiveness, or the emphases of what is said. The

---

[18] This was a declaration, or admission, of guilt laid before a delegation of the World Council of Churches in 1945 by the provisional Council of the Evangelical Churches in Germany (EKD).

questions here are too diverse and, if we look at Herzog's plea, leave
too much unexplained. Who is supposed to forgive? The Polish
people? God? Who is to be forgiven? The German people? Those
who at that time simply went along with what was happening, or the
active perpetrators? What does forgiveness involve? Does it mean
the establishment of normal relations? Or the non-imputation of
guilt to the second and third generation? A clarifying answer to
these questions, and others like them, is urgently required in the
framework of an ethics of political relationships.

Trust: Theoretical Necessity or Creative Passion?

Not least, forgiveness as the restoration of trust is a reminder that
people have to be empowered for political action. No one comes
into the world as a political being. But everybody can become one.
In order for this empowerment to come about, however, the hermeneutics of suspicion must be unlearnt through the development
of a basic trust. This can be the outcome of the development of a
basic trust in the word in speech situations which are trustworthy.
This trust is the political basis for which there is no substitute,
either through a constitutional guarantee of participatory rights,
or through the procedural provision of ideal communicative conditions, such as is demanded in the discourse ethics of Jürgen Habermas and Karl-Otto Apel.[19] In this concept of political ethics, trust
also plays an essential part; and that makes the comparison interesting. To begin by summing up briefly my objection to this discourse ethics: trust in the ontogenetic evolution of moral
consciousness in the direction of an 'autonomous morality' cannot
replace the basic trust in words which has been lost.

EXCURSUS

Trust in the ontogenetic correspondence to the phylogenetic evolution of
the moral consciousness, which finds expression in the formulations of
human rights, for example, or in the consensually moulded constitutions
of democratic states,[20] is a fundamental presupposition which discourse
ethics shares with the work of Lawrence Kohlberg. Now Apel of course sees

---

[19] See J. Habermas, *Moral Consciousness and Communicative Action* (1990); also
idem, *Erläuterungen zur Diskursethik*, 2nd edn. (1992). However, the following discussion takes as its starting-point K.-O. Apel, *Diskurs und Verantwortung*, 2nd edn.
(1992), since Habermas's concept also has a reference to Apel's work.
[20] Apel, *Diskurs und Verantwortung*, 364.

the problem here. The categorical imperative of this ethics: 'act as if you were the member of an ideal communicative community', would be universally valid only if a new beginning were possible in this world in the sense of a discourse ethics; a state in which all human beings were able and willing to act in accordance with the sixth stage of Kohlberg's model of moral development, 'reversible role-taking'.[21] But in reality only about 5 per cent of the population, even in enlightened states, can be assumed to have reached this stage; and that unmasks as an impermissible abstraction the 'Kantian' assertions of a universal moral principle, inasmuch as these assertions proceeded from the premiss that the moral competence to judge is in principle the same in everybody.

At this very point, however, Apel makes a virtue of necessity by incorporating it into the reflective stock of his ethical concept. He tries to show that the functioning of a political communicative community is logically dependent on each of its potential members being treated *as if* he or she had already reached this stage. For a fatalistic acceptance of the incongruent reality would actually lead to the dissolution of truly democratic, consensual processes. So in Apel's system, trust assumes a central role: it is the 'cognitive premiss', as Apel explicitly stresses.[22] Trust in the self-implementation of the evolutionary process, morally speaking, is necessarily articulated as trust in the individual participants in the discourse, to whose state of moral consciousness more is conceded than as individuals they have actually reached, in any given case.

Here trust is introduced as a fundamental *theoretical* premiss, and Apel views this as the actual strength of his argument, making it, he believes, universally convincing and cogent. It provides an ultimate logical foundation for a morality superior to all others, whether they be Aristotelian, religious, or whatever.[23] Apel is certainly able to show the necessity of trust for a politics which can meet its own claim. But the real predicament of the extensive occupation of political existence by the hermeneutics of suspicion (in Apel's terminology: a consciousness whose premiss is the moral non-homogeneity of the participants) cannot be solved theoretically. The awareness of the need for trust does not in itself create the trust needed. In other words, the hermeneutics of suspicion cannot be superseded simply by a rational operation. The problem cannot be solved theoretically, because trust is not primarily a matter of the consciousness. Whereas suspicion is a secondary

---

[21] Ibid. 358.   [22] Ibid. 367.   [23] Ibid. 346–9.

phenomenon,[24] trust must be based on experiences in everyday life. 'For finally social and political theory depends on people having the experience of trust rather than the idea of trust.'[25] It is impossible to circumvent the sensory character of trust, and this prevents it from being stylized into a quantity that can be universalized.

Trust must also be understood as 'pathos', in the literal sense of the word. Pathos goes beyond the receptive character of trust (as a response to an act of address), for the possibility of rejection and suffering cannot be banished from trust. Of course the passive aspect of trust does not contradict our understanding of its creative aspect, but provides a necessary complement to it. In this sense the biblical narratives can be understood as the history of God's passion: the passionate God who invests trust in those he has created and seeks their trust; the suffering God who finally entrusts his own life to human beings, and by doing so frees them for trust. The connection between suffering and trust has found an existential testimony in the historic peace churches. An appreciation of their contribution to political theory is still largely lacking. But their resistance, in the form of suffering, to the politics of violence testifies to the political importance of trust as neither knowledge nor ignorance, neither certainty nor naïvety.

But it is not just today that we are faced for the first time with the problem that it is trust in the word above all which is politically played out. As Wittgenstein demonstrated, trust undoubtedly exists on the level of everyday life, which would cease to function at all without it. But this usually changes once allegedly 'higher' levels such as the political one come into play. There we find the hermeneutics of suspicion commended as the 'art' of politics; and this is already the case even on the level of clubs, inter-school student councils, or in the formation of citizens' action groups. This creeping paradigm change explains both the experience of detachment from politics, which is so often complained of today, and the general disenchantment with politics, which goes with it. This hermeneutical process of assimilation is certainly free: no one is compelled to adopt an attitude of suspicion; and yet it is still in a way compulsive, since it is enforced by the lack of alternative

[24] L. Wittgenstein, 'A child has much to learn before it can pretend. (A dog cannot be a hypocrite, but neither can he be sincere)' (*Philosophical Investigations* (1967), p. 229^e).
[25] S. Hauerwas, *A Community of Character* (1981), 86.

experiences in the political sphere itself. The reconciliation of *oikos* and *polis* in worship—the reconciliation of these allegedly lower and higher spheres—gives new force to the question whether politics can legitimately be contrasted with everyday life in this way. And yet—so we might ask—would not a politics of trust, conversely, be idealistically and dangerously overstrained if it attempted to win acceptance in the world of major politics? A 'politics of trust' in which trust is applied as principle would probably not be able to evade this suspicion. But what would happen if more and more people practised in peaceable hearing were to play a part *as such* in the political sphere? Would that not make 'major' politics seem rather minor—and then accordingly subvert them—for the better?

If we believe that a paradigm change in political hermeneutics is required, it must of course be pointed out that the direction of this change is already latent in the perceptions without which politics could not get along at all on any level. One essential perception of this kind is the importance of confidence-building measures. This insight comes into its own in the conduct of negotiations. Negotiations are among the most important confidence-building measures.[26] In the negotiation process, if it takes a successful course, political hermeneutics can be modified, and their relationship to trust reversed. If negotiations are begun instrumentally in the first place, with the purpose of building confidence (without, perhaps, those concerned being able to conceive in advance even the faintest chance of a consensus), the trust that can grow up in the course of the negotiation process may then bring the negotiations themselves into a dimension where what is possible exceeds all expectations.

[26] Hannah Arendt put the ability to promise side by side with the ability to forgive as among the principles of action which derive from political existence itself and remain the necessary presupposition for its implementation. 'The power of promise' is therefore for her a basic condition for political power in general. Whereas power is formed when people assemble for joint action, power's continuance depends on promise: 'The force that keeps them together... is the force of mutual promise or contract' *Human Condition*, 236–47, quote on pp. 244 f; cf. here Habermas's criticism 'Hannah Arendts Begriff der Macht', in *idem, Politik, Kunst, Religion* (1989). But in my view Habermas rests his criticism too much on the element of contract, which in Arendt does not in fact marginalize the communicative praxis but presupposes it. He overlooks the way in which, for Arendt, promising and forgiving only assume their fundamental political importance when they are together. However, Arendt falls short when she describes both as 'natural' abilities possessed by the *zoon politikon*. Perhaps the reflections above may take us a step further, inasmuch as they show how both forgiving and promising are categorially related to trust.

The fact that a mere return to the negotiating table is often lauded as a political triumph shows that the different thrust of the rival hermeneutics is not foreign to the political process itself. Unfortunately, all too often this insight is taken on board only as a last, ultimate resort: when the notorious cultivation of the hermeneutics of suspicion has disclosed all too clearly its lamentable and murderous consequences. The distance from trust to mistrust is as short as the distance from mistrust to trust is long.

Can this relation be reversed? It is true that, as we have seen, trust cannot be thought and experienced without suffering. But the primacy of mistrust leads political life into devious paths which involve suffering that is unnecessary. The suffering of trust may lead the trusting person to his or her own suffering: this can be part of political worship. But the hermeneutics of suspicion *always* draws other people too into suffering that is unnecessary. So that this hermeneutics can be surmounted before it leads to death, taking the people concerned with it, spaces for learning are required in which trust in the power of the word can grow up without coercion, and without being destroyed by misuse. The worship of the Christian community is excellently designed to be a learning space of this kind. Admittedly, it cannot directly maintain this claim to outsiders; it must first face up to it internally, in forming its own praxis. In the following chapter we shall look at the way in which this can happen, taking preaching as an example.

11

Homiletics as Political Propaedeutics

In the perspective of what has been said, it will be clear why homiletics particularly presents a highly political discipline. For every individual act of proclamation is a test case of the alternative hermeneutics of trust in the word. Each time it raises anew the question whether the structure and 'performance' of the proclamation is adapted to build trust of this kind or, rather, to hinder it.

Authority in the Word

Here we have to consider what it means to trust wholly in the power of the Word instead of trying to secure its efficacy in other ways. It is therefore essential not to circumvent the freedom of the Spirit where agreement with the Word is aimed at; but it is also necessary to highlight what corresponds to that, as the attempt at communication, where the attention of the community to the procedure cannot be too great. This specific interaction between waiting for the Spirit, who engenders consensus, and the passionate endeavour for communication, without which the Spirit will not bring it about, must be acknowledged in its fundamentally political significance, and in comparison with the principles of political rhetoric too. But we must first note the way the Christian proclamation is described in the New Testament. This may be summed up under the heading 'the power of the Word in the liberty of the Spirit'.

In the opening passage of the First Epistle to the Corinthians, Paul brings out the contrast which is the real point at issue: 'And my speech and my message were not in plausible words of wisdom, but in demonstration of the Spirit and of power, that your faith might not rest in the wisdom of men but in the power of God' (1 Cor. 2: 4 f.). Here Paul uses a number of technical terms belonging to the rhetoric of the ancient world (*peitho, apodeixis*), using them to differentiate what he is saying from particular rhetorical and sophistic practices and ideas.[1] For Paul, the 'demonstration' he is

---

[1] W. Schrage, *Der erste Brief an die Korinther*, I/1 (1991), 232.

concerned with does not consist in the *inherent* plausibility of what
is said, which therefore has an inescapably cogent effect. He understands the demonstration of the Spirit and the power of his proclamation directly in the light of its effect on the Corinthians, who
have trustfully accepted the word about the *foolishness* of the cross
as a word characterized precisely by its renunciation of 'persuasion'
and the plausibility of human wisdom (v. 1). God's Spirit and his
power themselves provide the proof of Paul's message, as the gospel
which is efficacious in its very weakness (v. 4), and which wins the
trust of its hearers.

This powerful weakness by no means presents itself with irresistible force. For Paul, irresistibility is the very sign of dumb, heathen
idols: 'Now concerning spiritual gifts, brethren, I do not want you
to be uninformed. You know that when you were heathen, you were
led with irresistible force to dumb idols' (1 Cor. 12: 1 f.). Whereas
the irresistible force of dumb idols perhaps rested on their very
speechlessness, Paul is concerned to give outsiders too the chance
for a comprehending assent, through the comprehensibility of the
proclamation.[2]

For our present context, political worship, the consequences of
the New Testament view of the event of proclamation are obvious.
The less trust in the word is deliberately striven for through 'attendant measures', which are designed to provide outward or inward
evidence for the word that is to be communicated, the more that
trust can grow. Even where a 'support' of this kind for the word is
not deliberately manipulative, its undermining effect grows under
the surface. In this way the seed of the hermeneutics of suspicion is
planted, and grows with every kind of forcibly elicited agreement.
But where the proclamation relies solely on the power of the Word,
a perception is initiated and practically impressed which can hardly
be exaggerated, politically speaking—the perception that although
consensus processes cannot be forcibly 'contrived', but are the
work of the Spirit, they are nevertheless dependent on certain
conditions which have to be observed. The essential question that
arises here is, in what way can the proclamation be grasped as a
responsibility of the whole congregation? The answer will be: if it is
understood as a mutual testing of the spirits, as a mutual entering
into one another through the Holy Spirit. If we wish to comprehend

---

[2] H. Weder, *Neutestamentliche Hermeneutik* (1986), 42.

what this means, a helpful distinction can be made between communication (illocutionary) and agreement (perlocutionary—i.e., from the viewpoint of the effect actually achieved). In preaching, the two must be carefully differentiated.

On the communication level, hermeneutical and rhetorical work is required of the preacher. Here, in the context of the illocutionary role, what the preacher intends to do through his or her speech act (console, admonish, ask, etc.) has to be worked out *etsi Spiritus Sanctus non daretur*—as if there were no Holy Spirit to help over the hurdles of even unsuccessful attempts at communication. The other side, which necessarily complements the definition of the illocutionary role as the sphere in which the preacher operates, is of course his or her perlocutionary abstinence. The preacher is barred from trying to win listeners' assent without attempting to communicate with them—from striving directly for the perlocutionary effect of an utterance without making the illocutionary role plain. This is inadmissible, as an intrusion into the liberty of God's Spirit and the spirit of the listeners as well. Here it must always be remembered that the Spirit is not tied to the intention of the preacher, coupled as it is with the illocutionary role. However inept the word, the Spirit can still let it be verified as gospel and permit the address of the Christian message itself to arrive at its goal (the Spirit's intention) even in an emotional, polemical, or ideological interpretation.

The Spirit's freedom from the intention of the preacher, as it is seen in the differentiated relation between the illocutionary and the perlocutionary roles, clears the way for the 'distinguishing' (*diakrinein*) which Paul declares to be a task for the assembled congregation (1 Cor. 14: 29). It is only when this judgement is freely exercised that the hermeneutics of suspicion will find no fertile ground. Trust in the Word grows with the testing of the spirits. For the testing of the spirits is the work of the same Spirit who constitutes the community of listeners. But politically, this connection is only fully comprehended if the distinction is perceived to be a reciprocal one: through preaching, the spirit of its hearers is tested, and through the hearers, the spirit of preacher and preaching. In this way believers help one another to an understanding of the gospel, to agreement with it, and to a common assent in the Amen—'so be it'. This describes the power of the Spirit to let the one enter into the other. The communication which takes place in worship, brought to agreement by the Spirit, transposes the participants in the event of proclamation into one another. To be more exact: the mutual transposition is the way in which the Spirit guides attempts at communication in the direction of agreement. Homiletic tradition has always enjoined the need to enter into other people, as a requirement for both preacher and listeners.[3]

Political Rhetoric: Between Sales Talk and Personal Accounting

Before we look further at what mutual transposition means for political ethics, we must go more deeply into what political rhetoric can learn from homiletics. For the two belong to the same problem context, as we can see from the dilemma of the Platonic dialogues. Plato certainly inveighs against the instrumental rhetoric of the Sophists, who talk about things they do not understand, but in a way he merely applies the same rhetoric more persuasively; for although 'he does not know', in the end he still emerges as victor.[4] Discomfort over the compelling vehemence of 'the art of persuasion' does not in itself make available a new ability to form a conviction in a free exchange of arguments.

We have stressed that the doctrine of preaching (homiletics) takes its bearings from the praxis of the Pauline proclamation, which proved itself as aware of the Spirit precisely through its renunciation of linguistic and non-linguistic amplifiers.

EXCURSUS

Thus a hearing is lent the Spirit which blows like a gentle breeze, and does not go together with attendant circumstances which seize complete possession of the senses, and which were accordingly so much valued by the rhetoricians: stormy, fiery, shattering (1 Kgs. 19: 11 ff.). Biblical tradition turns in the sharpest terms against the manipulative power of instrumental rhetoric: 'Let him blot out all smooth lips, the bombastic tongues, those who say "with our tongues we have the best of it; our lips are with us, who is our master?" '(Ps. 12: 3 ff., following Martin Buber's translation). Because

---

[3] Cf. R. Bohren: 'The "alien" character of the listeners expands the preacher's own existence. The process is parallel and in both cases is mediated through Jesus, present in the Spirit. The listener is absorbed into the preacher as subject. The preacher goes out of himself and enters into the other, and allows the other a space in his own existence. The fatal thing about the customary "preaching to" people is that those preached to remain outside the preacher himself' (*Predigtlehre* (1971), 460 f.).

[4] Cf. here T. W. Adorno, 'Kritik der Ursprungsphilosophie' in *idem, Philosophie und Gesellschaft* (1984), 60 f. (see *Against Epistemology* (1982)).

of this, Jesus is seen and known (Matt. 12: 18 ff.) as the primal bearer of the Spirit, about whom the Servant Song in Isaiah 42 writes: 'He does not cry and lift up his voice, or make it heard in the streets' (v. 2). As Michael Welker aptly remarks, the bearer of the Spirit is characterized by the very fact that he renounces the usual strategies for winning attention and loyalty 'from above and from below'. He pursues neither 'power politics' nor 'opposition politics'. 'The bearer of the Spirit does not make himself and his action prevail by means of a public relations campaign. He does not "plug" himself and his actions.'[5] Yet in him people see the Messiah, on whom the Spirit 'of counsel' rests, who wins justice for the poor and 'slays the wicked with the breath of his mouth' (Isa. 11: 2, 4).

If we compare this specific view of the power of the mere word with the political rhetoric of our own time, the difference is patent. Political rhetoric has increasingly become sales talk. 'Politics' is extolled like a product created by professional manufacturers ('the political class'), which must be sold to 'the public' by the same agency. Lost elections are put down to a deficient sales strategy—which diminishes the value of politics even more: for according to this line of thought, the product 'politics' is defined not by its actual utility to the citizen but by its market value—which again depends on the degree of success achieved by the sales rhetoric. Here we find in actual practice the economizing of political existence which Plato ideally conceived of when he wanted to introduce into the structure of the political community the separation which was typical for the *oikos*, the separation between knowing and doing, between the one who knows (the father of the household) and those who obey (the members of the household) (see Section 5.1). In the degree to which politics today is understood as a material for knowledge, and no longer as an undertaking dependent on mutuality, the radical Platonic differentiation of the political roles into experts and lay also gains admittance, in the corresponding form of the differentiation between 'producers' and 'consumers'.

In the light of the communication practice of political worship, the difference between political and economized-political language is characterized as the difference between accountability and (self-) justification. Whereas the justification of a certain policy knows *the public only as addressee*, the political rendering of an account subjects itself to the *judgement* of the *citizens* represented. Admittedly, the

[5] M. Welker, *God the Spirit* (1994), 125.

rendering of an account is one of the recognized marks of political structure today, and in a democracy especially; but it presupposes a freedom which cannot always be assumed to exist, even in a democracy. This freedom is the freedom from the urge for self-justification, which is by no means built up and imposed only from outside. For the less politics is viewed as an 'intermediary phenomenon', as a matter which always exists and comes into being *between* people who act together, and the more it is seen as a product bound to its producer, the less we may expect there to be freedom from the pressure for justification. Where, on the basis of economized-political logic, the matter of politics is so closely linked with persons (or party, as *persona magna*) and their careers, more is at stake in any given case than can be settled through the objective rendering of an account.

In order to break the fateful, mutually potentializing effect of the economization and the over-personalization of politics, the experience of citizens who have learnt to keep accountability and justification apart is therefore of vital importance. These people know that their justification through God as persons makes them free to give an account of their actions—actions which give expression to the hope that is in them (1 Pet. 3: 15b). Unless that distinction proves itself in the praxis of political accountability, the procedural securities of this fundamental element of political culture will also be increasingly circumvented, so that the 'legitimacy of the procedure' (N. Luhmann)—free elections, for example—can be viewed as political accountability only in a qualified sense. Ultimately, the free rendering of an account, which submits itself to the judgement of others, can only be *warranted* through God's Spirit. Thus Jesus, the bearer of the Spirit, is characterized by the fact that he does not want to witness to himself—he puts on no show to justify himself (John 5: 31; Matt. 27: 14). Though he is free to render an account of his acts and his mission (Mark 3: 22 ff.; John 18: 37), another must bear witness to him: the Spirit. For it is the function of the Spirit to witness to another—to Jesus, as the Christ (John 15: 20)—and not (like Hegel's 'Spirit') always to witness only to himself (cf. Chapter 3). To put it in dogmatic terms: God's Spirit is the Spirit of accountability. In Jesus as the Christ we are justified—in the Spirit we are freed for accountability.

But as the central aspect of political life, the rendering of an account presupposes that it is not only the reasons for doing something which are stated. It is the background to what is done as well—the political 'good' which determines the reasons for acting, and which belongs to the idea of 'the good life'. From this aspect, political responsibility always includes an account of the 'hope' which prompts those who converse about a particular way of acting. The premiss here, of course, is that there is a common good which can be grasped in consensus. Otherwise the account rendered would be conceivable as at most an explanation of (incommensurable) personal reasons for acting; it would not be the rendering of a *political* account, which submits to the judgement of other people. If the premiss were not a common good, the communication of which can lead to common judgement and action, 'politics' would indeed be no more than a 'continuation of war by other means'.

However, the disproportionate importance of the political parties tends more and more to abolish or absorb—*aufheben,* in Hegelian parlance—the practice of political accountability. Of course, communication about the common good is particularly necessary in the formation of parties; but there is a lurking danger that in the course of time this common good will increasingly be identified with the party programme. Then the political debate will no longer be conducted by citizens on the one hand and their representatives on the other, but by representatives of the various parties and programmes, or other interest groups. If a discussion about the common good which oversteps party politics ever shows signs of getting under way, it is firmly quashed, because it upsets the political 'order' of things, pre-eminently symbolized as that is by the predictability of the different stances.

It is this very order to which political rhetoric ministers. This rhetoric is free of surprises,[6] and is sometimes more reminiscent of a stimulus–reaction determinism than a free discourse. Yet the

---

[6] The high degree of formalization and ritualization is not a new component in political rhetoric. In the ancient world it was already a mark of this form of speech which, out of a limited store of terms, quotations, turns of speech, historical and mythological allusions, developed a customary code, in which the élite could communicate and mutually support their own position. It was identified as instrumental political speech by its very predictability. As Peter Brown shows in his discussion of late antiquity, 'The formalized speech of the upper classes was not designed to express sudden challenges and novel sentiments, and still less to indulge in unwelcome plain speaking. This was its principal social and political advantage, for if the utterance of a speaker predicts what sort of thing he will say, it also predicts the answer of the other person so long as this person is also accepting the code' (P. Brown, *Power and Persuasion in Late Antiquity* (1992), 41 ff., quotation on p. 42, citing M. Bloch).

political consumers demand security; and in that respect the importance of economized politics and the rhetoric that goes with it must not be underestimated. The calculability of the debates can also give people a sense of security: politics are jogging along, and moving in the familiar grooves; so they cannot run amok. Nothing is ever begun; things just go on as before.

In the ancient world, political rhetoric was already characterized by the bond—intensified today—between élitism and predictability: a means whose end is to preserve the power of the ruling élites. But in the experience of the Spirit in worship, this connection has been broken through in respect of both élitism and predictability. Peter's Pentecost sermon is concerned as a whole to trace the entirely unpredictable way God acts (Acts 2: 17–21); and the inclusion of the quotation from the prophet Joel (Joel 2: 28–32) shows emphatically that God's Spirit breaks with common political patterns. The outpouring of the Spirit does not let itself be confined by the limitations laid down by human beings, any more than does the rain. According to the prophetic sayings, the Spirit also and especially comes to those who are otherwise considered not to be 'of age', politically speaking, or to be no longer politically responsible—the young and the old, 'menservants and maidservants'. Now the voice of people who are otherwise condemned to silence, or who have been silenced forcibly, can be heard. The old are no longer viewed as people whose experience is of merely historical interest, and the young do not only win a public hearing and prove themselves politically competent by adopting the predictable patterns of political rhetoric. The people at the bottom of the social ladder, the 'menservants and maidservants', hitherto politically negligible and wordless (*aneu logou*), will 'speak prophetically'. All these people will see and express 'the new thing' which comes to human beings from God. The Spirit brings about a situation in which the voices of men and women are no longer heard in accordance with their 'political importance'; now the importance of political existence (the truth of a citizenship) is decided according to the extent to which the voices of all these people can be heard.

Here the Spirit does not just become the 'advocate' of those who are not mature, in the sense that he speaks on their behalf. On the contrary, he makes them mature themselves (the German word for mature, *mündig*, means literally having a mouth). They themselves are to open their mouths and speak prophetically. Ever since then,

the Church has had to accept this new standard of political existence, which is met only if everyone can raise his or her voice and
find a hearing[7]—if the central political event of the Church, its
worship, is complete because it also includes the voices of 'babes
and sucklings' (Ps. 8: 2; cf. Section 6.3). There is evidence enough
that the training and practice in worship of the individual voices of
many Christian citizens also made citizens for city and state, who in
that context too did not, and do not, fail to make their voices
heard.[8]

And yet, in the wandering citizenship of God the Spirit is necessarily still the *parakletos* too, the one who speaks *on behalf of* others
and intercedes *for* them, until the entry into the eschatological city.
As long as not all have taken their place in this citizenship, exercis-
ing their citizens' rights and their 'vote', the priestly ministry
remains one of the essential marks of the church (cf. Chapter 12).
In this way the Church lends its voice to those who are voiceless,
whether voluntarily or involuntarily. It intercedes before God for
those whose voices are missing in worship, and it raises its own
voice (in intercession and beyond) for those who still have no say in
the world.

But that is to anticipate the chapter that follows.

---

[7] The central problem of political theory, reversibility, which we shall look at in
the following chapter, is intrinsically connected with the question whether the voice
of the other can be heard. That this cannot be guaranteed through formal criteria of
'fairness' has been emphasized by feminist writers especially. Cf., e.g., Seyla Benhabib, *Situating the Self* (1992): 'Neither the concreteness nor the otherness of the
"concrete other" can be the norm in the absence of the *voice* of the other' (p. 168).
[8] I may give three examples: first, the Leipzig prayers for peace, out of which the
Monday demonstrations issued (in the quite literal sense), and which contributed
not inconsiderably to the fall of the Wall in 1989; second, the experience of African
and other women in the Two-Thirds World, who through the roles they assume in
worship have achieved a voice which as a whole can hardly now be suppressed, in
social life as well; and third, phenomenologically, the importance of the Church's
liturgy, with its choral speaking, for the formation of 'the voice of the people' in
antiquity. Cf. here Brown, *Power and Persuasion*, 149–50.

B. LIFE OUT OF ABUNDANCE

12

The Transposing Power of the Spirit

The idea about transposing oneself into others is an element in the proclamation of the gospel which goes back to apostolic times, when Paul 'for the sake of the gospel' was prepared to be a Jew to the Jews, a Greek to the Greeks, and weak to the weak (1 Cor. 9: 19 ff.). But Luther especially gave this idea a new conceptual depth which helps to bring out its political importance.

Transposition and Otherness

Luther explicitly uses this notion as a 'hinge'—as an idea with the help of which he can make clear the connection between faith and life, worship and ethics. In his 1520 treatise on *The Freedom of a Christian*, Luther reduced spiritual transposition to a succinct and unsurpassed formula: 'We conclude, therefore, that a Christian lives not in himself, but in Christ and in his neighbour. Otherwise he is not a Christian. He lives in Christ through faith, in his neighbour through love.'[1] How does Luther arrive at this formulation? The most important thing is the Word. The human being (Luther says 'the soul') can do without everything except the Word. That is enough, and more than enough. 'If it [the soul] has the Word of God it is rich and lacks nothing since it is the Word of life, truth, light, peace, righteousness, salvation, joy, liberty, wisdom, power, grace, glory, and of every incalculable blessing.'[2] The soul possesses everything in the Word, because the Word, heard in faith, binds it to Christ—'weds it' to him, as Luther puts it. In this bridal union with Christ, a marvellous exchange occurs. The 'community of goods' in the marriage with Christ ('everything they have they hold in common') means that goods and attributes are mutually

---

[1] M. Luther, *The Freedom of a Christian* (1520), in *Luther's Works*, vol. 31 (1957), 371.

[2] Ibid. 345.

conferred, as a communication of idioms which is of saving grace for the human being.[3]

Thus faith as the work of the Holy Spirit[4] transposes 'into Christ' (in whom God has transposed himself into human beings), and makes all the good things that can be said of Christ and his Word the property of the Christian too. This transposition process (of 'the inner man') finds its precise correspondence in another (the transposition of the 'outward man'): the good that has been received is passed on to the Christian's neighbour. Thus Luther (following Phil. 2: 1–3) formulates as ethical rule—the law according to which the Christian must act—'Here we see clearly that the apostle has prescribed this rule for the life of Christians, namely, that we should devote all our works to the welfare of others, since each has such abundant riches in his faith that all his other works and his whole life are a surplus with which he can by voluntary benevolence serve and do good to his neighbor.'[5] To follow this rule, the rule of Christ, then means what Luther describes in another famous formulation as becoming Christ for the other person: 'Just as our neighbour is in need and lacks that in which we abound, so we were in need before God and lacked his mercy. Hence, as our heavenly Father has in Christ freely come to our aid, we also ought freely to help our neighbor through our body and its works, and each one should become as it were a Christ to the other that we may be Christs to one another and Christ may be the same in all, that is, that we may be truly Christians.'[6]

We shall leave here for the moment our analysis of what Luther has to say in this respect, although we shall return to it later. It will help us to a better understanding of the political importance of the transposing power of the Spirit if we first outline the problem for political philosophy with which the idea about mutual transposition is connected. This idea turns up in different frameworks and in different forms. Picking up Kant's ideal of an 'enlarged mentality', elevated above the subjective and private sphere, Hannah Arendt

---

[3] Ibid. 351 f.

[4] Luther sees it as actually the 'calling' of the Spirit to transpose: to transpose the Word into 'the bosom' of the human being (*BSLK* 654, 26 f.) and the human being into the bosom of the Church (*BSLK* 654, 15 f.).

[5] *Freedom of a Christian*, 365.

[6] Ibid. 367 f.

sees it as the foundation for the human being's political potentiality, his power of judgement.[7]

This notion also plays a central part in so-called discourse ethics in the form of 'reversible role-taking' (which, according to Lawrence Kohlberg, is the highest stage of moral consciousness) or in John Rawls's 'theory of justice', in the sense of the recourse to an assumed 'original state'. The essential problem about this schema, and one with which all its modes of application have to struggle in some way or another, is a hermeneutical one. The difficulty, to put it briefly, is that the attempt to transpose oneself into the other almost unavoidably means transferring the other into oneself. And in this hermeneutical procedure, the other's difference all too easily gets lost along the way. Feeling one's way into the other person can become an attempt to overcome his 'strangeness', if in interpreting the (linguistic) information I receive from him I start from my own feelings, which I then transfer to him.[8] The problem that presents itself here arises from elements in Romantic hermeneutics, which were developed by Schleiermacher particularly.

Their very point of departure already shows their close connection with the hermeneutics of suspicion. For Schleiermacher, the foundation of his viewpoint is the assumed fact that 'misunderstanding results as a matter of course'.[9] That is why hermeneutics is an 'art', a skill which always has to bring understanding into being—has to originate it. Since for Schleiermacher 'speaking is only the external side of thought',[10] the communicative task of understanding is structured on the model of the 'inner conversation' of the author with himself. The hermeneutical act reconstructs this inner soliloquy. This essential element of 'psychological interpretation' as the reconstruction of the motivating level—the decoding of the author's essential 'core intention'—is called by Schleiermacher 'divination'.

'The *divinatory* method is the one in which one, so to speak, transforms oneself into the other person and tries to understand the

---

[7] H. Arendt, 'The Crisis in Culture', in *idem, Between Past and Future* (1961; rev. edn. 1968), 220.

[8] L. Wittgenstein, *Philosophical Investigations* (1967), §350: ' "But if I suppose that someone has a pain, then I am simply supposing that he has just the same as I have so often had"—That gets us no further.'

[9] F. D. E. Schleiermacher, *Hermeneutics and Criticism* (1998), 21 [trans. altered].

[10] Ibid. 7.

individual element directly.'[11] The 'real thing', the meaning of the communication, is therefore not sought in the word but behind the word, in the unique movement of the author's thought. The result is that the word's encounter is no longer direct, in the form of address; instead it becomes the *object* of the art of interpretation. The interpreter becomes, roughly speaking, the only true determining subject of the process of understanding. The supposedly non-disposable element in this process of divination, the congenial discovery, the putting oneself into the other person, actually becomes the quintessence of the virtuoso productivity of the interpreter. But as Wittgenstein continually stressed (though without explicit reference to Schleiermacher), this ultimately makes the hermeneutical process counter-productive. It does not really lead to the understanding of the other *as* another, since the 'grasp' of his otherness is limited in the methodologically essential act to that which one's own experience comprehends. 'Divination', says Schleiermacher, 'is consequently excited by comparison with oneself.'[12]

But in this way hermeneutics, precisely as the doctrine of understanding, actually serves to distance the other from ourselves, as a protection against the demand of the other,[13] the pressure of what he communicates.

---

[11] Ibid. 92.

[12] Ibid. 93. Schleiermacher did not completely overlook this danger, however. At one point he formulates the counterbalancing idea, according to which 'as soon as in the attempt to understand the direction towards our own ideas is dominant', a 'complete understanding' becomes impossible. 'But if the task is to understand completely the ideas of another as his own production, we must detach ourselves from ourselves' (ibid. 213). Consequently, Schleiermacher seeks in the 'grammatical interpretation', which is well practised in the art of composition, a counterweight to the 'psychological interpretation', although that does not put an end to the problematical nature of that interpretation.

[13] Emmanuel Lévinas particularly has stressed that understanding always includes an element of violence. Understanding becomes a 'ruse' when it is developed solely within the horizon of my own ideas, which sets the scene in which the other is 'grasped' and 'fitted in' ('Is Ontology Fundamental?', in *idem, Entre Nous* (1998), 9 f.). In contrast, the visitation of the self by the other is never merely an apprehending, but always an 'appeal' in complete immediacy as well. Whereas the mythical father of all ontology and hermeneutics is Odysseus, who is on the eternal return home to Ithaca, Lévinas's philosophy rests rather on the patriarch Abraham, who is called into the foreign land in order to remain there (*Otherwise than Being* (1981)). For this 'movement towards the other without a return', Lévinas finds no more adequate term than 'liturgy'. This has its place 'not as cult, parallel to works and ethics. *It is ethics itself*' (ibid. 218, my italics).

Living 'as Christ' in One's Neighbour

Whereas in Schleiermacher's hermeneutics 'divination' is supposed to contribute to 'a *direct* grasp of what is individual' (my italics), the purpose of what Luther has to say has a peculiar indirectness. The Christian does not find himself 'in' his neighbour because he has transposed himself into him, but because for that neighbour he has become 'a Christ'. He is in the other not directly as himself, but 'as' a Christ.[14] And in order to reach the other, he must first become 'in the likeness of Christ' (2 Cor. 3: 18).

The remarkable thing about this is, first, that Luther evidently does not see the transposition into the other person simply as a natural ability belonging to the human being as 'a social being', as has been usual ever since the Scottish moral philosophy of the eighteenth century. Neither can the special endowment with a natural sensitivity be immediately equated with that 'enlarged mentality' which is able really to embrace the other's standpoint.[15] For it might be precisely the empathic potential of sensitive people which makes it particularly difficult for them in any given case to draw the line between themselves and the other clearly enough. But the insight that transposition into the other under the given (hermeneutical) conditions threatens to become, practically speaking, a distancing from the other, is only a first indication of the political dilemma. For without this idea, politics cannot get along at all.

EXCURSUS

This dilemma is reflected, for example, in John Rawls's concept of justice as 'fairness'. His recourse to a fictitious 'original position' ('the state of nature') recognizes both the necessity of the mutual transposition and the practical problems involved. On the one hand, the purpose of this recourse is to make it possible for everyone to transpose themselves into everyone. That is to say, the idea is universalized. On the other hand, a 'veil of ignorance' must be drawn around this state of things, ignorance which relates especially to knowledge about one's own possibilities—so that no one out of an assessment of his own possibilities can plant the germ of the promotion of his own advantage into the idea of justice, which has to be

---

[14] Here too there is a parallel to Lévinas. His talk about 'illeity' is the attempt to state that from which the 'face' of the other comes, a 'beyond' on the far side of hiddenness and unveiling. 'Beyond being, there is a third person ...' (*Die Spur des Anderen*, pp. 228 ff., quote on p. 229; see *Otherwise than Being*).

[15] Arendt, 'Crisis in Culture', in *Between Past and Future*, 220 ff.

negotiated in common.[16] It is only if the capacity for empathy is purified from the tendency to appropriation through *abstraction* (the separation from everything concrete, both in regard to oneself as well as the other person) that it is suited, as it seems, to serve as the seminal idea for a political theory of justice.

Thus mistrust remains the fundamental category at the very point where it is supposed to be methodologically suspended. And the fundamental political schema, 'transposition into the other', remains embedded in the unhappy dialectic of appropriation and detachment.[17] Yet, as I believe, this is precisely the only way of overcoming this dialectic, which is disregarded in both paradigms of this schema, the hermeneutical (Schleiermacher's) and the procedural-ethical (Rawls's). Transposition into the other, if it is both to respect him as another as well as truly to arrive at its goal *in* him, must be without reserve. But practical surrender is possible neither for the interpreter—since his activity is ultimately solitary and reconstructive—nor for the procedural-ethical theorist, since he aims to make available procedural conditions in which justice is no longer dependent on the actual transposition into the other.

What Luther, on the other hand, says about transposition 'as Christ' into the neighbour, bursts apart the dialectic of detachment and appropriation. As 'Christ', the one will neither remain for the other an ultimately untouched and detached person, nor will the one forcibly invade the other. How can this happen? Here the bestowal of Christ's benefits and attributes is brought to bear. This takes place in 'the merry exchange' through trust in his Word. It is this which makes a person able to make the *need* of the other person his own, and not just 'the person' in a diffused sense.[18]

---

[16] J. Rawls, *A Theory of Justice* (1999), 118 ff., and esp. 136 ff.

[17] This is also the thrust of Seyla Benhabib's criticism of Rawls's concept and its adoption by Kohlberg. Where the idea of reversibility is identified with the perspective of the detached, disembodied, general other, it becomes incapable of fulfilment. Accordingly, the other in the general sense (defined through what all have in common, as distinct from the 'specific other' who would be perceived in his special character) is not allowed true reversibility. 'Definitional identity leads to *incomplete reversibility*, for the primary requisite of reversibility, namely, a coherent distinction between me and you, the self and the other, cannot be sustained under these circumstances. Under conditions of the veil of ignorance the other disappears' (*Situating the Self* (1992), 162).

[18] In Lévinas's thinking, again, a very similar fact is termed the 'nakedness' of the other's countenance. This means first of all that the other directly appeals to me, without any given form which would enable me to 'seize' him. It is just this pre-hermeneutical directness of appeal, in which no 'understanding' comes between me and the other, which allows the ethical dimension of the encounter to be perceived. I

This special kind of transposition into the other is made possible through both the quality and the quantity of the specific 'good things' and attributes of Christ. On the one hand, their quality is determined by the self-surrendering love of the Christ who took the shape of human beings upon him in such a way that he assumed their predicament itself, their way of life and their fate, including the fate of death (Phil. 2: 7 f.). On the other hand, it is the quantity of Christ's 'good things' which sees to it that the Christian who has been transposed into his neighbour is saved from an appropriation of the other (apart from his necessity).

What keeps the person who is living 'in his neighbour' from the covetous seizure of the other, and preserves the other from being pillaged, is the abundance which faith experiences. When Luther talks about becoming Christ for one's neighbour, the motif he always employs is the overflowing wealth of all good things given through faith; and this is more than fortuitous. 'I will therefore give myself as a Christ to my neighbour, just as Christ offered himself to me; I will do nothing in this life except what I see is necessary, profitable, and salutary to my neighbour, since through faith I have an abundance of all good things in Christ.'[19] The purpose is more than simply to pass on what has been received. Luther is saying at the same time that the giver must not himself control, measure out, or condition the giving in order to protect himself from loss of self. In his giving, he is freed at the same time from the compulsion to secure future conditions of the giving and commitment to his neighbour.

It is precisely this, however, which pin-points the central problem of political philosophy, which the figure about transposition into the other tries to solve but cannot yet achieve as long as the reason for the problem is still determinative within this schema. For where the question about justice is seen as a problem about the distribution of goods or opportunities, and where politics is viewed as the management of the distribution struggle, the fundamental point of departure is the deficiency. But deficiency makes the other in a

---

cannot escape the countenance of the other, it becomes a 'command'. 'His form stripped bare, the countenance is nakedness through and through. The countenance is necessity. The nakedness of the countenance is necessity, and in the directness which points to me it is already an urgent beseeching ... and in this way the ethical dimension of the visitation is heralded' (*Spur des Anderen*, pp. 222 f.; see *Otherwise than Being*).

[19] Luther, *Freedom of a Christian*, 367.

threateningly primary way a competitor for restricted goods, and someone who can therefore only in a secondary way become a partner (or accomplice).

It is only where abundance 'rules' (in the literal sense) that the other is not a threat. He can be perceived as the other, as the one who he is, without from the outset being assigned to a strategic relationship in which *his* necessity becomes a threat to *me*. It is only through the abundance from which the one to be transposed can draw, that the relationship remains free—remains political or becomes so. As we saw above in connection with the event of proclamation, the transposition of the one into the other which is consummated in the freedom of the super-abounding Spirit liberates the relationship from the compulsion which an immediate, non-pneumatological transposition would merely sublimate and ultimately heighten. Accordingly, Luther sees love, as the continuous form of being-in-one's-neighbour, as explicitly bound up with the freedom of the Spirit, a 'free Spirit', which he characterizes as follows: 'Behold, from faith thus flow forth love and joy in the Lord, and from love a joyful, willing, and free mind that serves one's neighbor willingly and takes no account of gratitude or ingratitude, of praise or blame, of gain or loss. For a man does not serve that he may put men under obligations, he does not distinguish between friends and enemies or anticipate their thankfulness, but he most freely and most willingly spends himself and all that he has.'[20] It is

---

[20] Ibid. John Milbank has stressed that abundance is a mark of Christian ethics; see his essay 'Can Morality be Christian?', in *idem, The Word Made Strange* (1997). Answering his question in the negative, he sets five characteristics of morality and Christian ethics over against each other. Whereas 'morality' is characterized by the concepts reaction, sacrifice, complicity with death, scarcity, and generality, Christian ethics take their stand on the opposite in each case: gift, abolition of sacrifice, resurrection, plenitude, and confidence. Here it is not by chance that for gift, plenitude, and confidence especially Milbank appeals largely to Luther, who does not play much part in his *Theology and Social Theory*. But at the same time, Milbank's view of abundance is still invested with a distancing element. Thus he says that Christians will act in spite of the existing deficiency '*as if* there were only abundance and no death' (p. 55). But for Luther, to whom he appeals at this point, abundance and action are not connected by any 'as if'—by an intellectual disposition. Luther makes so tight a connection—'life *out of* abundance'—that nothing can come between the two: no disposition ('gratitude'), no heroism ('in spite of everything'), no optimism ('the glass is half full, not half empty)', and no eschatological proviso either. Even the famous Pauline *hos me* (1 Cor. 7: 29–31) is not an 'as if', but describes the specific form in which the 'already' is perceived, the 'eschatological aesthetic' of life lived out of abundance; cf. B. Wannenwetsch, 'Die Freiheit der Ehe', *Evangelium und Ethik*, 2 (1993).

only here, by way of the detour of transposition into Christ, as it were, that the political significance of the transposition into one's neighbour can be perceived without distortion.

Overflow into the Other and the Perfection of Works

We find this endorsed if we remember that the ethical form of the Christian life in creatureliness and neighbourliness (cf. Section 7.2) could be especially characterized by the term 'mercy'. The ecstatic event of *miseri-cordia*, which literally has its 'heart with the poor' and not with itself, is a highly perilous affair, in two respects. For one thing, as we have seen from Jesus's exemplary story about the merciful foreigner (the Samaritan), this passion for the neighbour is distinguished by a specific limitlessness. Since it can accept no limitations as norm for itself, it cannot be politically 'domesticated' either; it retains a potentially antinomistic element, which was, for example, demonstrated when Jews were helped to escape during the Third Reich.

But this political risk is preceded by another. It is bound to seem as though the unreserved commitment to the other, the transposition of 'the heart' into the other, is always threatened with loss of the self. A soft heart is vulnerable. That is why the Stoic already guarded himself against the emotions: he was inevitably afraid that he would not remain master of himself, but would be carried away by compassion, or the like. That is why Nietzsche despised pity. When, unlike these others, Paul can tell his readers to weep with those who weep (Rom. 12: 15), when the synoptic gospels tell us that 'having compassion' was Jesus's chief emotion, this, conversely, can only be because mercy is assumed not to involve a threat of loss of the self. In the perspective of Jewish–Christian thinking, fear of loss of the self does not have to be the law determining action, because life is not lived in the mode of self-having, but enhypostatically *in* God, or—which is the same thing—it is life lived *out of* the fullness of God.

EXCURSUS

Accordingly Paul can, for example, discuss the collection in the Macedonian congregations for the mother community in Jerusalem under the significant term *perisseuein*, 'overflow'. Paul does not put the privation of the poorer congregation in Jerusalem at the centre of his argument in 2

Corinthians 9. His main point is the superfluity of God's gifts to the congregations who are the givers (v. 8), and their overflow to others (v. 11), as well as their 'reflux' in the exuberant thanks of the recipients (vv. 12, 14). 'God is able to provide you with every blessing in abundance, so that you may always have enough of everything and may provide in abundance for every good work' (v. 8). Here Paul picks up the baseline of the biblical ethics of abundance, whose first word is 'You may freely take and eat' (Gen. 2: 16) and its last: 'Behold, everything is prepared'. Oswald Bayer concludes from this that the first sin committed by human beings was first and foremost contempt for what was put before them.[21] And it is true that according to the story in the Bible, the plight of these first human beings begins with the sceptical questioning of the sufficiency: 'Is God supposed to have said "You shall *not* eat of *all* the trees in the garden"?' (Gen. 3: 1).

If the first sin lay in the suspicion of deficiency, in the 'hermeneutics of suspicion' towards the abundance of God's gifts, then of course the reverse can also be true: to act out of the abundance of God makes every act perfect.[22] The good deed, however unimportant it appears—the gesture of commitment, however small it be—the stammered word of consolation and the clumsy gesture of tenderness: all these can be called *teleios*, complete. Nothing is lacking for their perfection. In this perspective, judgement about the quality of an action is therefore determined neither by its intention (as in dispositional ethics), nor by its results (as in the ethics of responsibility),[23] but by its source—by the thing it represents or from which it springs (Eph. 2: 10). Does it represent the deficiency which it is combating, or the abundance which overflows in it?

In his 'Sermon on Good Works' Luther sums all this up under the alternative between 'confidence' and 'uncertainty'. If the works are 'sure'—if, that is, they derive from the faith that gives confidence—then they are good and well pleasing to God.[24] But of

---

[21] O. Bayer, 'Kategorischer Imperativ oder kategoriale Gabe', in *idem, Freiheit als Antwort* (1995), 14 (see also the forthcoming translation *Responsive Freedom*).

[22] This connection can also be understood linguistically in the admonition of Jesus in the Sermon on the Mount to love our enemy (Matt. 5: 47 f.). The perfection demanded of the disciples ('Be perfect as your heavenly Father is perfect') is connected with the semantic of the *perisseuein*. It consists in the *perisson*, in the overflowing act, the 'extraordinary, irregular, not self-evident' (Bonhoeffer's rendering of the word in *Discipleship*, 144).

[23] According to Max Weber's seminal distinction between *Gesinnungsethik* and *Verantwortungsethik*.

[24] 'If he finds his heart confident that it pleases God, then the work is good, even if it were so small a thing as picking up a straw. If the confidence is not there, or if he

course if they are not sure—if they are full of doubt about themselves and the person of the doer, who mistrusts his justification through God just because of what he feels to be the meagreness of the works—then the works 'are nothing and wholly dead' however much they 'glitter'. Whilst Luther here picks up Paul's dictum that 'whatever does not proceed from faith is sin' (Rom. 14: 23), he also accepts the validity of the converse: all works of faith are good, since faith is 'the first, the highest and the best' work, 'from which all others flow'. This is not true merely in the sense of a 'forensic' act of God's, an act in which he accepts the works 'for the sake of the faith', thereby overlooking their actual ambivalence, so to speak. No: 'The works are not well pleasing for their own sake, but because of the faith, which *is efficacious* and lives equally and without distinction in all and every work' (my italics). Here Luther's talk about faith *as a work* must not be underrated. For faith, understood as God's work in the human being, means for Luther 'efficacious' faith, the faith which can 'never grow idle', the faith which *makes* the works and makes them really *good* works. The goodness of the works is faith's effect on them, and not merely their effect on God, who accepts them 'in spite of everything'.

The logic of life out of the abundance which knows perfect deeds may also provide the deeper reason why Luther's ethics (and Lutheran ethics too) had such difficulty with the idea of an *ordo sanctificationis*, progress in sanctification. For sanctification 'models' based on this concept tend to deny the perfection of good works, inasmuch as they postpone that perfection until the final goal of the process of sanctification has been reached. The fact that they also tend idealistically to overvalue the moral capacity of the human being and to underestimate the sinfulness of the same being (Luther: 'simul iustus *ac peccator*') is only at first sight a paradox. For there is in fact a fundamental connection between the two movements. Just because a linear model of sanctification denies the perfection of works, it results in the problematical assertion of a perfection that lies ahead, and a progressive perfecting on the way. In this case the goodness of an action ultimately appears once again to depend on a potentiality in the human being: his

has any doubt about it, then the work is not good, even if the work were to raise the dead and if the man were to give his body to be burned' (Luther, *Treatise on Good Works* (1520), trans. W. A. Lambert, in *Luther's Works*, vol. 44 (1966), 25).

reason as a Christian, his maturity, or the virtue which he has wrested from a deficient initial disposition (even if it was with God's help).

Now, life out of abundance does not consist merely of giving—of passing on; it consists primarily in receiving. This is of course not a 'pre-ethical' pre-condition for the giving-further, but is itself already to be understood in its political dimension. Politically, the reception of the gifts of the other is no less important than the passing on; the overflow to the other only remains in the context of transposition in the Spirit if it also permits the overflow *from* the other. Just as I can only reach the other if his necessity becomes my own, so the other can only reach me if his gift becomes mine. And it must be said that his gift is no easier a matter than his necessity.[25] To be open for the gifts of the other—and this means recognizing one's own neediness—also presupposes living out of the abundance of God's gifts: that is, seeing the gifts of the other person as good gifts with which he enriches me. Otherwise the gifts of the other would rapidly become suspect; like his deficiency—and even more so—they could be experienced as a threat. Can I keep pace with them? Will they not put me in the shade? At all events, the suspicion of deficiency leads to the inability to perceive and accept the other *as* another: I cannot perceive him as other—that is, with his necessities and his gifts—because behind them I always see my own deficiencies and my own gifts, and compare them with his. To live out of the abundance of God, on the other hand, means seeing my deficiencies against the background of the gifts of the other (and not his deficiency), and my gifts against the background of the other's deficiency (and not his gifts).

What that means politically for life in the citizenship of God was brought out by Paul in the image of the body made up of many members, in which 'everyone is a member of another' (Rom. 12: 5). Because this transposition into the other is not a matter of a special skill, but is a phenomenon springing from abundance, Paul can also speak quite unreservedly about an *emotional* indwelling in the other: 'If one member suffers, all suffer together with him; if one member is honoured, all rejoice together with him' (1 Cor. 12: 26). If this were not to spring directly from the specific relationship between

---

[25] See my essay 'Members of One Another', in G. Bartholomew *et al.* (eds.), *A Royal Priesthood* (2002).

deficiency and fullness, mine and thine, which we described above—if, instead of that, it were practised as what has been seen to be the proper behaviour—then we should not be too far removed from Nietzsche; then the shared joy would be opportunistic, and the pity humiliating; at least both would never be free from such a suspicion.

EXCURSUS

I should like to make this clear through an example. What does it mean for the Church's catechetical task to live from the abundance of God, with the good gifts of the other and all the many and varied charismata? What we have said seems to me to be a pressing reason not to be content with the description of catechesis as religious or ecclesial *socialization*, which we increasingly hear in the Church as well. This idea is based on thinking in terms of society. A society (in the modern functional sense) requires a whole complex of abilities and characteristics (mobility, flexibility, independence, etc.) which define its requirement for socialization. It develops the appropriate mechanisms, establishes the appropriate agencies, or influences those that already exist (the family, for instance) in the interest of the primary task of socialization: to make men and women efficiently functioning members of society—to make them 'socially competent'.

The Church, on the other hand, since it reckons with the *abundance* of the gifts, cannot set up any normative catalogue which its members have to live up to. Of course the subject-matter of the catechumenate is always the communication of authoritative Christian doctrine too, but this cannot simply mean that its purpose is to make the new members of the Christian citizenship 'acceptable' to the Church. If it starts from the *abundance* of the gifts, the Christian catechumenate will always also see itself as an experimental space within the Church, where it can see what it can become once the new members contribute their charismata. Accordingly, at baptism the Church does not merely accept responsibility *for* the person baptized. Equally, it accepts the responsibility *of* the baptized person: it agrees to share its power through the empowerment of the 'outsider', the new member of the body, who is given responsibility in the Church and for it, although the Church is given no guarantee about the new member's future behaviour.

Living out of abundance is not a question of 'attitude'. It does not mean going through life with the right attitude, living *as if* there were abundance, regardless of whether or not we can see it. Ethics out of abundance is no such cunning trick played on life, no higher pragmatism which rewards the convictions which make living easiest, while leaving their truth on one side. And this is so because this ethics out of abundance is an ethics *springing from worship*. In worship, the abundance of God's gifts is actually present, in such a way that they can be apprehended with eyes and ears and all the senses—in such a way that the senses let us hear, taste, and see that the Lord is good, and his goodness abounding. At the Lord's Table there are no quotas; the gifts of God are present in the charismata of the others too: they too can allow themselves to be heard and seen. The abundance of God is present in the hymns and doxologies and, properly looked at, in all the elements of worship. The doxology especially offers a positive phenomenology of overflow.[26]

Here the abundance is present not merely as background phenomenon in the experience of particular acts performed, but as an 'object' of perception in its own right. The abundance is *expressed*; here the doxological language does not just approximate to what is in any case outside the bounds of language. Rather, it assumes the features of that which it expresses. Doxology is not merely the home of exalted and exalting language. The language of praise reaches out beyond the frontiers of all identifiable speech. In the ecstatic phenomenon of glossolalia, language itself overflows. Even though Paul also warns against attaching too much importance to this element, and sets it over against comprehensible speech for the building up of the congregation (1 Cor. 14: 4), it should nevertheless not be overlooked that the two are ultimately rooted in the same fact: the overflow of the heart into words (Matt. 12: 34) and the overflow of language itself are both a phenomenon of abundance—like 'the greatest of all' the gifts, love (1 Cor. 13: 7).

Intercession as the Transposition of Church and World

Whereas doxology is the form of worship in which abundance is immediately perceived, it is intercession—apart from the proclamation—in which transposition into the other becomes most vividly plain. In closing we shall think once more about the political importance of this praxis. Even though there is no special term for it in either Hebrew or Greek, the practice itself can be clearly identified in both the Old and the New Testaments.[27]

[26] This 'logic of overflow' is stressed by Daniel W. Hardy and David Ford in their book *Jubilate: Theology in Praise* (1984); see, e.g., 19.

[27] Cf. G. Friedrich, 'Die Fürbitte im NeuenTestament', in *idem, Auf das Wort kommt es an* (1978).

According to the Old Testament, it was at first the task of the prophets to intercede for others with God (Gen. 20: 7; Exod. 8: 8, 29 f.; Deut. 9: 20; 1 Sam. 7: 5; Amos 7: 2; Ezek. 9: 8). Later this became the function of the priests (Num. 16: 22; Ps. 99: 6; Joel 2: 17). Finally it also came to be seen as a matter for the whole people (Jer. 29: 7). This is taken up in the New Testament, where this last aspect is clearly intensified. There too, the great intercessors for human beings before God are duly acknowledged—Christ (John 17; Heb. 9: 24; Rom. 8: 34), the Spirit (Matt. 10: 19 f.; Rom. 8: 26), and the apostles (Rom. 1: 9; Phil. 1: 4; Philem. 4). Nevertheless, the community is seen from the beginning, and, as a matter of course, as intercessor—for the apostle too (1 Thess. 5: 25; Rom. 15: 30). The congregation is to remember in prayer not only its own affairs or the apostle, but 'all the saints' (Eph. 6: 18) and even 'all men' (1 Tim. 2: 1), especially those who exercise power and responsibility over other human beings (1 Tim. 2: 2).

In spite of this pointer to prayer for the political power-holders, it seems to me useful initially to approach the political importance of intercession from a general standpoint—from the fact that for the phenomenon there is also a genuinely political *Sitz im Leben*. It was already important in the imperial period for citizens to have intercessors (advocates, generally dignitaries) who had the ear of the political power-holders,[28] and the connection between citizen and advocate is more evident still in democratic states. For the democratic ideal that every citizen should have a 'vote' does not merely mean the citizen's right to 'give up' his vote (as the German idiom for voting seems to suggest); for in fact he does not 'give it up' in the sense that he surrenders it; rather he gives his vote to someone else, hands it over to an advocate who, as representative of the people or a particular group of voters, is supposed to make their voice heard in Parliament. Here there is no need for us to consider the familiar problems: that there ought not to be a binding mandate; that Members of Parliament are often remote from 'the voice of the people' and prefer to listen to the voice of their party; and so on and so forth. Here we need only remember that the cry 'Every vote counts' is as abstract as it is undeniable. Advocacy cannot be constitutionally complied with (at least not completely); it cannot be delegated to a professional élite. In every political community

---

[28] Cf. P. Brown, *Power and Persuasion in Late Antiquity* (1992).

people will be required who come forward as advocates for others, unasked and uninhibited, unawaited and even, it may be, unwanted. The commandment 'Open your mouth for the dumb' (Prov. 31: 8) therefore designates a permanent political task for Christians, in whatever political situation or constitution they may be living.

Advocacy of this kind certainly begins in worship, where people learn to lend their mouths to other people—in principle unasked. Advocacy does not consist primarily of spectacular actions which generally peter out quite quickly; it means speaking up 'perseveringly' on behalf of others, as is to be the case in intercession (Eph. 6: 18). Advocacy of this kind is not a natural potentiality—'we do not know how to pray as we ought'; it must be learnt. And the Spirit as the *parakletos*, the advocate *per se*, represents believers (Rom. 8: 26) and teaches them as it does so. Advocacy must be learnt in the intercessory practice of the community, but it can also be a guide to mediation, to 'good offices' apart from prayer. Anyone who before God opens his mouth for the dumb can also raise his voice before the world and the powerful on behalf of the people who have no voice of their own, or whose voices are not listened to. For this reason too it is highly desirable that intercession in our worship should be restored as a *congregational* ministry, which is what it was in the early Church; it is important that intercessions should be formulated by members of the congregation, and spoken by members of the congregation, and should not be treated as if they were a function of the 'professional' ministry. Otherwise there is a danger that the Church will disregard its own special political character, and will do just what the state does when it organizes 'advocacy' professionally, thus in a way domesticating it.

Now it would of course be a gross misunderstanding if we were to deduce from the connection between intercession in worship and advocacy in the world that the one is simply there to prepare for the other and to get it going. Another point is at least as important as the extension of intercession into advocacy for others in the world and into action on their behalf. This is the recognition that prayerful intercession for others is both an admission of the limitations of action, and an acknowledgement of the limitlessness of compassion. On the one hand, we recognize in intercession the limitations of our active transposition into the other. Here it is not just a question of the limited scope of what we can do for other people; in the emotional dimension as well, we all too soon come up against the limits of our concern and our capacity for sympathy (in the literal sense of co-suffering). This is especially true in a telegenically expanded world, in which our concern becomes more and more anaesthetized. In the logic of prayer, the recognition of the limits of what we can *do* for others is always implicit, since God is asked to do what we are not capable of doing. (A requirement to ourselves, expressed in the form of a prayer, 'Help us to share with the poor . . .' is then not really a prayer at all, common though this formulation is.)

Yet in intercessory prayer, accepting responsibility for the world goes fundamentally beyond anything that could be met by corresponding action. Intercessory prayer, while recognizing the limits of what we can do, always keeps alive the awareness that God wants *all* human beings to be helped (1 Tim. 2: 4). In other words, the practice of intercession vouches for the truth of compassion. Under the conditions of our limitations, it insists on the *practical* limitlessness of compassion, which should not be transformed into mere solidarity because of our experience of these limitations (on the distinction between compassion and solidarity cf. section 7.2). If compassion were limitless only in principle, in the sense that, although it potentially means everyone, it could practically speaking just as well pass everyone by, solidarity would of course have to be preferred; for although it limits its own application in principle, within these limitations it is nevertheless *efficacious*. Under the conditions of creatureliness, neighbourliness in the sense of direct action on our neighbour's behalf is limited. But in its own, *priestly* form of action, the praying community intercedes 'for all men' in a way which anticipates the eschatological dissolution of these limitations.

In the unrestricted, outward-looking intercessory remembrance of the world, Luther saw an infallible mark of the Church as such, one which distinguishes it from those religious groups which only pray 'looking inwards'.[29] In 1529, in the face of the Turkish danger, he again introduced the Litany in Wittenberg, thus emphasizing the priestly character of prayer (Luther talks explicitly about 'the sacrifice of prayer'): 'By taking on itself the sins of the people in repent-

---

[29] V. Vajta, *Die Theologie des Gottesdienstes bei Luther* (1952), 306 f.

ance and intercession, and coming before the face of God in this way, the Christian community performs its priestly sacrificial ministry.'[30] In the face of the unlimited outreach of the Church's intercessory practice, we can very well talk about a 'transposition of Church and world'. The world is (re)presented and brought before God in the worship of the Church, and the Church is sent into the world so that it may bring the world's necessities into its own worship.

But the political importance of the range of the Church's intercessory practice only fully emerges if we appreciate not only its breadth, but the fact that its prayers include intercession for enemies. It is in the light of this unheard-of demand of Jesus's in the Sermon on the Mount (Matt. 5: 44) that we also have to understand the exhortation in the First Epistle of Timothy (1 Tim. 2: 2) to pray for the men in power. This exhortation was formulated at a time in which the congregations were looking back to phases of persecution and repression by the powerful; in some parts of the Empire they were still under pressure. In view of this background, the admonition is more explosive politically than the final phrase 'that we may lead a quiet and peaceable life' would suggest.[31] When Christians pray for those with political power, the underlying premiss is the *need* of the powerful. The mighty of this world also belong to the people[32] who should be 'helped' and who are to come to

---

[30] Ibid. 304.

[31] The connection between rulers and enemies is explicitly brought out in the appeals for intercession made by the almost contemporary Apostolic Fathers. The invitation in the Epistle of Polycarp runs (12. 3): 'Pray for all saints. Pray too for the emperor, power-holders and princes as well as for those who persecute you and hate you, and for the enemies of the cross, so that your fruit may be manifest to all and that you may be perfect in it.' This by no means necessarily documents an a-political attitude, but could be understood as being itself a political assignment—as a specific contribution made by Christians to the *salus publica*. That is made evident, for example, when this Christian obligation to pray for the *res publica* is laid down in the Toleration Edict of Galerius (AD 311): 'Unde iuxta hanc indulgentiam nostram debebunt Deum suum orare pro salute nostra et rei publicae ac sua, ut undique versum res publica perstet incolumis et securi vivere in sedibus suis possint.'

[32] It should be emphasized here that it is *individual human beings* who have had political responsibility laid on them who should be prayed for, not, for example, political parties or systems. It is only in this way that the universality of intercessory prayer—and therefore of Christian mercy—can be complied with. Unless intercession were to reach out beyond the competition between parties and political systems, there would only be partisan prayer, which for its part would rest on political decisions that had already been made.

knowledge of the truth (v. 4). Or, as Berthold Brecht says, no one is so great that he doesn't fit into a prayer.

Intercession for the powerful, then, looked at correctly, also includes a critical impulse towards the politics of the day. These are certainly not to be considered from the outset as sacrosanct. But at the same time, for the Christian community intercessory praxis means that the role of a 'fundamental opposition' has to be rejected. The people in power (or others who are prayed for) may *be* enemies. But if they are included in the intercessions of the community, they cannot of course simply *remain* enemies (even if they go on behaving as if they were). As we saw above in Luther's ethics, transposition into the other does away with the friend– enemy category altogether.[33] Instead of cultivating these categories and the readiness for violence which goes with them, the practice of intercession is the preparation for a peaceable relationship. From the beginning of their history, Christians learnt to pray for hostile rulers, and not merely for their own partisans. This praxis (at least to the extent to which it was followed) was the pre-condition which closed the door to the most dangerous potential of an anti-political politics of violence: the violence which is legitimated in the name of 'a higher reason' or of 'supreme values' (even if they are Christian ones), or is even employed in the name of God himself.

---

[33] Thus Luther says about the spirit of the Christian freedom to be in the other through love: 'For a man does not seek to put men under obligations *nor does he distinguish between friends and enemies*, nor look if they be thankful or unthankful, but he most freely and willingly spends himself and all that he has' (*Freedom of a Christian*, 117, my italics (trans. altered)).

13
'Celebrating from his Works':
Sabbath and Responsibility

In closing, let us turn to the time of worship. Worship does not merely *have* its time (just as it has its place); it *is* a temporal phenomenon in a particular way; and we now have to consider the ethical dimension of this fact. These reflections can find a focus in the question about the scope of human responsibility. Talk about responsibility is designed to bring out once more what characterizes ethics springing from political worship, and what distinguishes it from common conceptions. Since the sanctification of the sabbath is something demanded of us, the sanctification of the sabbath itself belongs to ethics. It by no means marks the point where ethics arrive at its limits. Seen in this light, the sanctification of the sabbath is part of the sanctification of the human being as a whole. The sanctification of our lives *grows out of* the sanctification of the sabbath. Here we contemplate the completed works of God which let our own work 'stand'.[1] Here, on the day free of work, the good works 'which God has prepared beforehand so that we should walk in them' (Eph. 2: 10) are before our eyes, ears, and hands.

Sharing the Sabbath

'On the seventh day God finished the work which he had done, and on the seventh day *celebrated from all his work* ('feierte von all seiner Arbeit') that he had done. God blessed the seventh day and sanctified it, for on that day he celebrated from all his work which God, making, had created' (Gen. 2: 2 f.). That is the way Buber and Rosenzweig translate the close of the Priestly Writing's acknowledgement of creation. The curious phraseology 'God *celebrated from* all his work' (Luther, the 1611 and other English Bibles say: 'And God *rested* from his work') draws us into the depths of the

---

[1] 'On his work must thou look / if thy work is to stand' ('Auf sein Werk mußt du schauen / wenn dein Werk soll bestehen': Paul Gerhardt, in his hymn 'Befiehl du deine Wege').

sabbath mystery. The relation between work and rest, works and the freedom from works, ethics and liturgy, life and worship, is here removed from all the directness of an 'in order to'. God does not celebrate his works directly, as if he were nothing without them. Nor does he simply rest *from* them, as if he were only his true self apart from his working. The 'celebrating from the works' evidently cuts right across the way we are accustomed to relate working time and free time to one another.

Apart from the genuine logic of the sabbath, it seems positively impossible not to view and practise the relationship in the instrumental sense. We either relax so that we can work, or work so that we can relax. If we follow Karl Marx, we assume that it is only work that makes us human beings;[2] according to Ernst Bloch, it is only in the cultivation of continuous free time that we fulfil our true selves.[3] In the first case, on the sabbath we are revitalized and acquire new ability to perform efficiently; in the second case we work towards the evening, the weekend, and our holidays. But of course in both cases it can only be a question of 'free time'—of 'vacations'—*empty* days, never holidays in their true sense of 'holy days'. Whereas these holy days were understood from the beginning as 'fulfilled time', as days which bring their fullness with them; the 'empty' days depend on what we do with them—whether we know how to give them content and to make them meaningful, or not.

If in our free time we always have to have some business on hand, or have to 'treat ourselves' to something, then our everyday language betrays that the consumer-bourgeois versions of the instrumentalization of work for the sake of free time also remains imprisoned within the economic logic which determines the reverse vision of 'live to labour'. Just as in this logic the holiday becomes free time, and the Sunday part of the 'week-end', so the profession—the 'calling'—disappears behind 'the job'. For there can only be a profession if there is also a holy day which manifests the *telos* which is the only thing that makes work a calling. Admittedly, theological ethics also finds it difficult not to draw the 'celebration from the works' into the functional logic which dominates us. Even

---

[2] Picking up Hegel, Marx could see work as 'the nature of the human being', as the medium of his 'self-creation' ('Nationalökonomie und Philosophie' in K. Marx, *Die Frühschriften*, ed. S. Landshut (1971), 269 f.).

[3] For a discussion of Bloch's utopia of 'the earthly paradise of active leisure' cf. H. Jonas, *The Imperative of Responsibility* (1984), 194 ff.

Philo of Alexandria already defended the sabbath against the Hellenistic 'enlightenment' by way of a 'recreation' rationale, and Wilhelm Herrmann, for example, closes his *Ethics* with a chapter on the 'the morally permitted recreation' which promises to win for us 'new capacities and new powers for the moral struggle'.[4]

If we ask what the sabbath is there *for*, we are asking about two different things. It is one thing to ask about its function, and another to ask what is meant by its 'blessing'. (It is only in this sense that we can ask about a commandment.) What does it mean for us when God 'blessed' the seventh day? In the way the story of creation is told, it may first of all strike us that the human being celebrates the first sabbath *before* he himself has performed any work. So he shares God's rest, not *like* God, by 'celebrating from his (own human) works', but by celebrating *with* God 'from *his* (divine) works'. For the human being himself has as yet no works which he could contemplate. This relativity and relatedness remain the secret of the sabbath even after the human being has gone to work himself. The sabbath does not acquire its meaning from the act of working. It does not just belong to the people who have work. It belongs to all human beings. On the sabbath, human beings do not look at their own work, at least not primarily. Every sabbath is supposed to be like the human being's first sabbath, when he had as yet no work of his own at which he could have looked back. The rest which is meant for human beings is to be found in the contemplation of God's works, from which they live. If a person looks at these, his gaze becomes free. It is neither drawn downwards, because it is fixed on the part-work of his own hands, nor upwards at the success of his work, which elevates him above other people.[5] It is not the fragments of what he does that he sees, and not the question of how he could perfect them; what he has before him are the perfect works of God.

As Augustine knew, the human heart can only find the rest it craves—fulfilled rest—by entering into God's rest, in the 'enjoyment' of God and his works. For our own works do not create any

---

[4] W. Herrmann, *Ethik*, 4th edn. (1909), 227.

[5] To turn away from one's own works does not merely let us 'breathe' but is also extremely difficult for human beings to practise. This was stressed by Luther in his exposition of the Third Commandment in his *Treatise on Good Works*: 'It is a bitter holy day for nature to cease from its own works and be dead' (*Works*, vol. 44 (1966), 78). The 'proper sabbath rest' is always at the same time a remembrance of baptism and with the crucified Christ leads to the dying to works. Cf. V. Vajta, *Theologie des Gottesdienstes bei Luther* (1952), 238 f.

true rest. The rest given by the contemplation of our own works is the deceptive peace with which 'the rich fool' tried to silence his own soul, the inner malcontent ('Soul . . . take your ease', Luke 12: 19). The proper sanctification of the sabbath is different: as Luther says, it can only mean 'allowing room for God to do his works' (WA 6, 249, 6). Now, the interpreters are undoubtedly right when they continually stress that the sabbath rest does not mean the depreciation of work and works, but that through the sabbath the human being is 'put to work'. This is especially evident in the Christian relocation of the day of rest to Sunday.

The meaning of this shift to Sunday as the *beginning* of the week (1 Cor. 16: 2; Acts 20: 7), the day following the Jewish sabbath, must certainly be fully appreciated. Just as the sabbath represents a work of creation of its own,[6] and not merely the 'end' of God's six days' work, so Sunday was understood as the morning of the *new* creation, which had dawned with Christ's resurrection. But we should not construct an antithesis to Judaism at this point, since, according to the creation story, the last day of God's creation was the *first* day for the human being. So according to Jewish interpretation, it is by no means a question of working towards the sabbath rest, let alone earning it. In any case, the regularity which is an essential characteristic of the sanctification of the sabbath provides no occasion for a dispute about the direction of the movement, either away from the sabbath or towards it. It is much more important to perceive the meaning of the day's *presence*. We do not achieve this rest for ourselves by ourselves. For we are told that 'a rest *is present* for the people of God' (Heb. 4: 9). What is said here in respect of the final, the eschatological rest, sabbath and Sunday bring into the rhythm of life: it is God's rest, into which we can enter. As a work of creation, the sabbath is 'there'. We do not have first to extract a time of this kind for ourselves—'*take* a day off'—in order to arrive at rest; the sabbath comes to us of itself, reliably and regularly. It comes to visit us like a beloved, honoured guest, and takes us into its own time.

The special relationship to time into which the sabbath moves those who celebrate it has been impressively worked out by the

---

[6] The 'rest' must be specifically created; as the *telos* or crown of creation, it is not merely a negation of activity but, as rabbinic tradition says, a 'personality' of its own. In this way the sabbath can be seen as Israel's 'bride', and the ceremony on the eve of the sabbath is observed like a marriage feast. Cf. A. J. Heschel, *The Sabbath* (1951).

Jewish religious philosopher Abraham Heschel, in his meditations on the sabbath: 'The meaning of the Sabbath is to celebrate time rather than space. Six days a week we live under the tyranny of things of space; on the sabbath we try to become attuned to *holiness in time*.'[7] Whereas we move about in space in order to win space through the use of technology, and in order to deal with the 'thingness' of space, the goal in the realm of time is not to have but to be.[8] The religions of 'the nations' concentrate on sacred places and sites. But 'Judaism is a *religion of time* aiming at *the sanctification of time*'.[9] The sanctification of time is not a disparagement of space. Both the conquest of space and the sanctification of time are part of the task assigned to human beings. But the sanctification of time has to be a commandment of its own, since it does not impose itself of itself, like the conquest of space. It is the necessary counterweight to the life that usurps space, because it calls a halt to the threatening enslavement of the human being to technological civilization. So on the sabbath the tools which can so easily be beaten into weapons are laid aside, money dealings are avoided, and in the midst of the struggle for existence which seems so omnipresent, we can find an island of peace in which to live.

What is particularly important for the political worship which is our concern here is the conclusion which Heschel draws about the bearing of the sanctification of time on the coexistence of human beings. He points out that the Third Commandment is, as it were, the pre-condition for the observance of the last two commandments, the commandments about not coveting, because it puts desire for the gifts of time in place of the coveting of the things of space.[10] So Heschel sums up the ethical meaning of the sabbath as follows: 'Every one of us occupies a portion of space. He takes it up exclusively. The portion of space which my body occupies is taken up by myself in exclusion of anyone else. Yet, no one possesses time. There is no moment which I possess exclusively... We share time, we own space. Through my ownership of space, I am a rival of all other beings; through my living in time, I am a contemporary of all other beings.'[11]

What Heschel says here about the sabbath fits in very well with what we have already said about 'ethics out of abundance'. For

---

[7] Ibid. 10.   [8] Ibid. 3 ff.   [9] Ibid. 8.
[10] Ibid. 90 f.   [11] Ibid. 99.

there is abundance only in the experience of time, and not in space, which always has a particular and limited extension. Because we compete for space, the suspicion of deficiency—the suspicion that we are outdone—may touch us more closely than does our neighbour. But we cannot steal time for ourselves. We 'have' time only to the degree in which we give it away. (And when we say that someone has stolen our time, we really mean that the time we gave was not accepted.) Just because time permits no mode of 'having', the sanctification of time can open the door into political life; for political life, a free acting-together in public matters, can only be achieved among true contemporaries, sharing in time instead of competing in space. In this light, we can already see how in the Old Testament the sabbath commandment continually breaks through the mode of having, and how the sabbath order can almost be called the 'Programme of Social Ethics: The Balancing Out of Poor and Rich'.[12]

EXCURSUS

In the Decalogue the sabbath commandment is already so formulated that the sabbath rest is a command for masters and servants, parents and children, the indigenous people and strangers equally. In this way it makes them all contemporaries and nothing but that, however different their social status may be (Exod. 20: 10). But the Priestly Law of Holiness draws up a whole social order in accordance with the sabbath (Lev. 25). As well as fallowing in the seventh year (vv. 1–7), particularly illuminating regulations are connected with the institution of the 'Year of Jubilee', dealing with the possession of land and with debt slavery. According to these enactments, every fifty years land which has been impounded or sold must be given back, since the land belongs to God, and can therefore be only a loan (vv. 23, 28). In addition, anyone who has been enslaved because of his debts is to be freed (vv. 39–46). The slave-owner is admonished that the person who has been sold to him because he had fallen into debt 'shall go out from you . . . and return to the possession of his fathers. For they are my servants, whom I brought forth out of the land of Egypt; they shall not be sold as slaves. You shall not rule over him with harshness, but shall fear your God' (vv. 41–3). The sabbath order (in this case the order for the Year of Jubilee) forbids anyone to shape relationships among the children of Israel according to the mode of having. The person who has become a slave because he has fallen into debt must not be kept like a slave, but must be treated as a hired servant, and in the end be given his freedom.

---

[12] E. Otto, *Theologische Ethik des AltenTestaments* (1994), 249.

Although these enactments may well have remained more of a programme for the most part, they nevertheless make one thing clear: the paradigm of Israel's social order was not constructed on the basis of a relationship of rule founded on economic inequality. What shaped the paradigm was the fact that the sabbath created contemporaries, brothers, and allowed conditions to be adopted without compulsion—one might almost say: politically. Accordingly, this section of the book of Leviticus closes as follows: 'Over your brethren, the people of Israel, you shall not rule, one over another, with force' (v. 46).

Power and Responsibility

The temporal logic of the sabbath brought out here also lets us see the concept of responsibility in a way which is bound to remain hidden if it is spatial thinking that is dominant. Here, in his studies on the responsibility which emerges with the face of the other, Lévinas especially has pin-pointed important insights. In his lecture on 'Diachrony and Representation',[13] he shows how responsibility for the other must be viewed as a fundamentally temporal phenomenon. Two of his comments make this point: 'In the depths of the concreteness of the time that is that of my responsibility for the other, there is the dia-chrony of a past that cannot be gathered into re-presentation.'[14] And then: 'Responsibility for the other man . . . this way of being devoted—or this devotion—*is time*' (my italics).[15]

However, the radicalism of this responsibility for the life of the other person, to the point of dying for him,[16] goes together with a specific view of time, in which time cannot be formalized and represented (we might also say: where time is not after all still structured according to spatial categories, in that past, present, and future are separated from each other and related to each other as if they were spaces of time). It is precisely the diachrony of time, which is not represented through remembrance (of the moral resolve) or anticipation (of the auspicious action) in which the face of the other appears, and which enjoins responsibility with absolute authority. In the light of what we have said about the

[13] E. Lévinas, 'Diachrony and Representation', in *idem, Entre Nous* (1998), 159–77.
[14] Ibid. 171.
[15] Ibid. 173.
[16] Ibid. 211.

sanctification of the sabbath, we can say here that the ethically fundamental view of time, of the kind Lévinas envisages here, is the temporality of the sabbath—a time which makes people contemporaries through their participation in God's rest. And Lévinas does in fact explicitly characterize time in this connection as 'To-God (à Dieu)'.[17]

But, it may now be objected, the usual way of talking about responsibility envisages a responsibility which does not just 'emerge' now and again, but 'exists', and is today increasingly understood as 'world-wide' responsibility; and surely this view is more comprehensive and has a higher moral claim? If we look more closely, however, the claim of a responsibility spatially structured in this way proves to be deceptive. For it actually breaks down the urgency of responsibility and its radicalism. And this is so not merely because of the psychological fact that we shrink back before the immensity of the task we have set ourselves, and instead of actively taking on this responsibility, allow ourselves to be petrified by it, like a rabbit in front of a snake. It is true above all because, by defining the responsibility in universal terms, the temporal responsibility for the other person here and now is all too easily denied. Consequently talk about 'world-wide' responsibility and a concern for 'humanity' can actually lead to the withholding of the elemental means of life from one's contemporaries.

Who has time for the laborious search for social justice on the spot when the survival of the species is at stake? Because of the global problem of over-population, for example, rigid birth control programmes are promoted which withdraw responsibility from parents for the number of their children (these programmes, incidentally, being particularly favoured *for the poorer countries* by the consumer states of the northern hemisphere). In other places the 'unauthorized' birth of children is punished (in China, for example), and abortion is practised as a means of assuming world-wide responsibility. So in the name of this responsibility for the life of future generations, the right to life of people living in the present, or of those still unborn, is restricted, or even denied them altogether.[18] In view of the inner logic of this universality, it is

[17] E. Lévinas, 'Diachrony and Representation', in *idem, Entre Nous* (1998), 212.
[18] Cf. here S. Hauerwas, 'The Moral Limits of Population Control', in *idem, Truthfulness and Tragedy* (1977), 116–26.

impossible to dismiss the suspicion that 'world-wide' responsibility is a code phrase for the world-wide egoism of the industrial nations.

This is shown, for example, by the outstanding role played by expert predictions of future developments in determining this responsibility. The importance of these predictions depends less on their (in fact slender) prognostic reliability than on their moral capacity to wake people up and, by facing them with the future consequences of particular ways of behaving, to impel them to correct this behaviour. But this roundabout method—the projection of possible consequences for the future—abstracts from the immediacy of the responsibility which emerges from the needs of the other person. It is not the other's hunger which galvanizes people into responsible action; it is the prospect of a dramatic scarcity of food resources (and the then threatening stream of economic refugees). It is not the immediate damage to the health of the men, women, and children living near nuclear power stations which makes people revise their thinking; it is the vision of the far-reaching contamination resulting from reactor catastrophes. And so we might go on.

In this way 'responsibility for the world' can turn out to be a strategy in which responsibility for the other, specific person is actually dispensed with, since to range far afield over the whole world ultimately serves to bring *ourselves* (the rich nations, who still enjoy peace, food, resources, and so forth), or *our* children, into the orbit of the responsibility which ethics is supposed to motivate. 'Humanity' then becomes the ethical stimulant which elicits responsibility by way of the vision of our own dismay, instead of acting out of actual dismay over the needs of other people. So we see that the temporality of responsibility is not an absolute antithesis to its spatial definition, inasmuch as the spatial-universal definition can also be expressed in temporal categories—perhaps as solicitude for the future of humanity, which is projected when the future is supposed to be safeguarded through the manipulation of the present, either technologically or by directing its behaviour patterns.

In contrast, we may remind ourselves once more, the temporality of responsibility, as a hallmark of a sabbatical existence, has to do precisely with its non-representability. In this perspective the temporality of responsibility stands for that which cannot be defined and projected—not even in the sense of one's own consternation or dismay. Consequently the sabbath-temporal diachrony belongs, and belongs essentially, to Jewish–Christian responsibility. For its nature appears in mercy and not in solidarity, the (spatial) scope of which always points to some resolve, made in the past and represented in the present (cf. Chapters 10 and 11).

We are therefore faced with the paradox that the notion of an *existing responsibility* actually leads to a disregard of the *existing needs* of human beings. Existing responsibility always requires an object, whereas emerging responsibility comes to us from the other person, who is the real subject in the event of the transference of responsibility. To overlook this point is characteristic of Hans Jonas's stimulating suggestion about the 'imperative of responsibility', and the problem it raises. Yet Jonas's concept is certainly differentiated in its scope. Even if his 'heuristics of fear' is also guided by 'advance knowledge', he knows, for all that, that this can only be true in a modest sense which does not make the certainty of the prediction the starting-point for the ethics required. And the responsibility which is evoked through the precedence of the negative over the positive prediction (criticism of utopianism),[19] is undoubtedly intended to apply to the matter in hand or to the persons acually concerned, and not ultimately simply to ourselves. But in spite of that, the effect of his ethics is ultimately an abstraction from the other person, because, as he himself says, this ethics is 'quite different from the imperative of the previous ethics of contemporaneity'.[20] It is only the extension of responsibility to humanity as such which, according to Jonas, is enjoined today—only the 'being of the human being' as categorical imperative,[21] or the 'ontological idea of the human being' as an existent being, which gives real 'substance' to our responsibility for our fellow human beings.

This objectifying character of Jonas's concept of responsibility goes together with the way he defines the relationship between responsibility and power, where he carries on the problematical tradition of which Max Weber is a prime example. Jonas certainly recognizes that we can only ever talk about responsibility in the context of a specific power; and that is certainly a ground for recognition, for it is precisely the failure to see this connection which has led talk about responsibility into the mixture of hybris

[19] Jonas, *Imperative of Responsibility*, 160 ff.   [20] Ibid. 10.
[21] Ibid. 88 f.

and resignation which marks it so profoundly today. But it is only the person who has power to whose responsibility we can appeal— and a *particular* power at that, which circumscribes a *particular* responsibility.

It is this undoubtedly correct insight, however, which now motivates the extension to humanity as a whole in Jonas's concept of responsibility. For he believes that the expansion of human power (which is above all technologically determined) has reached a stage which brings the annihilation of the human being's own race within the bounds of possibility.[22] Now, as this passage already suggests, the concept of power applied here is essentially guided by the notion of what is practicable; power is defined by Jonas as 'causal Power',[23] which is supposed to bind together 'I will' and 'I ought' in the human being.

As a result, the human being is at once the subject of his responsibility and (by virtue of his humanity) its object, and this unification, mediated through the specific, Weber-like colouring of the concept of power, leaves no room for the other person. Max Weber stands sponsor here, even though he receives no more than a footnote, because his version of an 'ethic of responsibility' also depends on the *possibilities* of action and its *foreseeable* results. This is completely in line with Weber's understanding of power as 'that opportunity existing within a social relationship which permits one to carry out one's own will even against resistance'.[24] Just as Weber saw the connection between power and responsibility represented in the person of the professional politician, so Jonas finds his 'eminent paradigm' for the imperative of responsibility in the statesman— that is, in an individual person, and not, as it might be, in a political institution or praxis.

The criticism which can be made here from the perspective of 'temporally' structured responsibility, contrasts this concept of power with another, which does not orientate itself towards implementation of the possibilities of the (ideally conceived) individual, but instead looks towards the possibilities which are given through

---

[22] Ibid. 136 ff.   [23] Ibid. 115.

[24] M. Weber, *Soziologische Grundbegriffe*, 6th edn. (1984), 89 (see ET *Basic Concepts in Sociology* (1962)), being sections 1–8 of his *Theory of Social and Economic Organization*). By politics Weber means a social action which is directed to the acquisition of power and the use of power for the purpose of implementing the interests of one party against those of others (see also his *Wirtschaft und Gesellschaft* (1921–), 11 f. (ET *Economy and Society* (1978)).

the free co-operative action of many different people. This is the inter-subjective concept of power which Hannah Arendt developed. Here power is first formed in action, and is not implemented as the power which is already presumed to exist (in Arendt's diction 'violence'). This inter-subjective concept also sets the responsibility that is bound up with power in another light. For in the face of today's 'global' challenges, responsibility must not be seen primarily in the *limitation* of power, as a voluntary self-control. The reverse would actually be the case. The challenges of the present day would only be responsibly assumed by way of an *increase* of power—of course in this political, non-technological sense.[25] More: it is only the power emerging in and through political action that would allow a *particular* responsibility to develop, a responsibility evoked by particular needs and requirements, which could then really be implemented in particular ways—ways determined by the degree of the power acquired.

A responsibility of this kind is characterized by the capacity for accountability which, as we have stressed, is a basic element of political existence. (The spatially determined responsibility, on the other hand, which takes its bearings from its power to implement its aims, tends towards self-justification, since it is always a matter of the realization or limitation of *its own* possibilities.) In the rendering of a political account, responsibility preserves the inter-subjectivity of the way it has come into being—which is through the shared formation of power. In this way it accords with what already belongs to the concept of responsibility from the very etymology of the word: for responsibility is really a *nomen actionis*, a noun of action, which presupposes the situation of inter-subjective accountability, 'being responsible to an authority'.[26] This dialogue situation cannot be reduced to the ideational presupposition of an

---

[25] In this light, the attempts to respond to the global demands with a 'Global Ethic' sustained by the moral power of the world religions seem to me to move in the wrong direction, since these reflections are nurtured by a lack of hope in political existence, and contribute to the further suspension of that hope. The world needs good politics rather than a shared ethos; it is not agreement about shared ethical foundations (illusory enough) which are required, but the empowerment for political life which is nurtured by any given ethos. This power would tend rather to be lost if a complex ethos were to be reduced to the distillation of ethical 'basic principles'.

[26] Cf. G. Picht, 'Der Begriff Verantwortung', in *idem, Wahrheit, Vernunft, Verantwortung* (1969). Picht reminds us that 'responsibility' was originally an eschatological term, which confronts us with the situation of the Last Judgement, in which everyone has to provide an answer to the questions of the universal Judge.

'existing' responsibility. Consequently, an individual cannot, either, 'assume' political responsibility for some fact or development, as is usually demanded today if some public matter has gone wrong (where the demand is generally the equivalent of a cry for resignation). This belongs rather to the context of the political accountability of people who act responsibly *together*.

If we look again at what was said above, we can put it in a nutshell by saying: what is required is not a limitation of power through responsibility; it is the limitation of responsibility through (political) power. The popular demand for a 'voluntary limitation of power', as mirrored in the question 'Should we do what we can do?', might itself be the expression of an unrestricted, presumptuous concept of responsibility—a responsibility whose practical limits are, conversely, drawn too narrowly (as far as the other person is concerned). Jonas is of course right in saying that we must not *ourselves* limit our responsibility—that would certainly be irresponsible. But we have to ask whether our responsibility does not *find* a limitation, one which it does not lay on itself— whether it can subject itself to a salutary limitation which does not simply reflect the limits of what is practicable.

Here traditional talk about the responsibility of the human being before God can now be taken up in a way which takes into account the positive connection with the question of power. For this talk does not merely involve the idea of a divine authority to which responsibility has to render an account; taken by itself, that could still be seen as the preliminary religious form of the Kantian 'inner court of justice'. 'Responsibility before God' entails, rather, that here God himself acts by *empowering* human beings, thereby making their responsibility a responsibility that is limited and particular. The limitations of human responsibility are then not defined negatively—through the limits of their own power—but positively: through what God himself does *for* human beings.[27]

[27] In this sense of a 'salutary limitation' Hans G. Ulrich talks about a limitation 'which the human being does not come up against when he has exhausted his own possibilities, but where God forestalls him in a salutary way'. Here Ulrich also stresses the wholesome limitation of responsibility in terms of the surveyable character that it can assume when perceived in a political way: particularly the surveyability of the responsibility which can be politically assumed in this way: 'The task is then to carry over responsibility in respect of the far-reaching and by no means foreseeable consequences of technological action into an ethics of surveyable political action and judgment' ('Hoffnung und Verantwortung', *EvTh* 46 (1986), 34).

Defined positively, this implies that human beings are not just responsible for whatever God leaves over for them. It is rather that the inner space of this responsibility can only be seen and entered into at all by way of the boundaries drawn. Viewed theologically, as 'saving the world', 'the fate of the human race', and however these universal claims may be formulated, they are outside the bounds of our responsibility, and eyes can be focused on the other person in a quite specific sense. Thus people are freed for responsible creatureliness and neighbourliness. Here the works of God for human beings do not delineate the frontiers of their activity and their responsibility in a negative sense; it is precisely the experience, the contemplation, and the use of these works as gifts of grace which sets particular, temporally structured responsibility free.

The community gathered together for worship will not assent to any 'advance knowledge', however justified and sure it may be, which overlooks the immediate concerns of human beings—either in the search for a utopia or through a 'heuristics of fear'. It has no need to see what cards God has up his sleeve, because it rests in the sufficiency of his promise, the certainty of which can be tasted in worship. So it can confidently allow itself to be directed to the neighbour, whose 'demand' constitutes the law of its activity.

The empowerment which takes place in worship does not conform to the alternative of 'personal' or 'collective' responsibility either. It is true that the empowerment for responsibility clearly lies in the shared act of the *leitourgia*. Here—and especially, as we have seen, in the prayers of intercession—the specific universality of Christian responsibility can also be found, since we are explicitly told to pray 'for all'. But this universality is entirely open for 'the' other, in the specific sense. In the prayer for all human beings, the Spirit sees to it that the face of individuals too always comes before the individual petitioner. So in this sense the transpositional power of the Spirit also means both universality and particularity: responsibility for all human beings and for this particular human being must no longer be seen over against each other.

The salutary limitation of responsibility reflects the political existence of the worshipping community as God's citizenship. For responsibility presupposes the freedom to act, and therefore political life. (In the pre-Christian *oikos* there was no responsibility but at most obligation.) Since in the Church *polis* every Christian enjoys full responsibility as the consequence of his or her unrestricted rights as citizen, this responsibility is accordingly limited—limited by the responsibility that the other person assumes. Since responsibility arises through the inter-subjective assumption of different charismata, it remains a responsibility which is always particular, through the political assumption of the various functions or ministries. Every individual member has a particular responsibility; no one has responsibility for the whole, for that is God's. Consequently, in their experience of the political form of the Church's life, people are sensitized against talk about 'total responsibility' wherever such a responsibility is deemed to exert a claim. Since the empowerment for the 'good life' in the citizenship of God must again and again be sought in worship, and since this means that the inter-subjective transpositions of power call for special attention, politics cannot be understood in a tutelary sense.

We have arrived at the end of our study. Analyses of the concept of responsibility have once again emphasized that the differentiating power of an ethics springing from political worship can prove itself against a central figure of ethico-political thinking. They have again made clear what the study as a whole has tried to show: that if worship is their form of life, Christians are exemplary citizens.

BIBLIOGRAPHY

Adler, Jakob G. C., 'Jakob G. Chr. Adlers Schleswig-Holsteinische Kirchenagende 1797', in *Evangelischer Gottesdienst*, 158–165.

Adorno, Theodor W., *Against Epistemology: A Metacritique. Studies in Husserl and the Phenomenological Antinomies*, trans. W. Domingo (Oxford, 1982).

Albrecht, Christoph, *Schleiermachers Liturgik, Theorie und Praxis des Gottesdienstes bei Schleiermacher und ihre geistesgeschichtlichen Zusammenhänge*, Veröffentlichungen der evangelische Gesellschaft für Liturgieforschung 13 (Göttingen, 1963).

Alt, Franz, *Politik ist möglich* (Munich 1983).

Apel, Karl-Otto, *Diskurs und Verantwortung: Das Problem des Übergangs zur postkonventionellen Moral*, 2nd edn. (Frankfurt, 1992).

Arendt, Hannah, *Between Past and Future* (London, 1961).

—— 'The Crisis in Culture', in *Between Past and Future*, 197–226.

—— *The Human Condition* (1958); 2nd edn. (Chicago and London, 1998).

—— *On Revolution* (London, 1963; Harmondsworth, 1973, repr. 1990).

—— *On Violence* (London and New York, 1970).

—— 'Religion and Politics', *Confluence*, 2 (Sept. 1953), 105–26.

Aristotle, *Nicomachean Ethics*, trans. J. A. K. Thompson (Harmondsworth, 1955).

—— *Politics*, trans. T. A. Sinclair (Harmondsworth, 1962).

Austin, J. L., *How To Do Things with Words*, 2nd edn., ed. J. O. Urmson and M. Sbisà (Oxford, 1976).

Baldovin, John F., SJ., *The Urban Character of Christian Worship: The Origins, Development, and Meaning of Stational Liturgy*, Orientalia Christiana Analecta 222 (Rome, 1987).

Balz, Horst, 'λειτουργία', EWNT ii, 858–61.

Barth, Hans-Martin, 'Die ekklesiologische Dimension der Ethik', *KuD* 43 (1988), 42–59.

Barth, Karl, 'The Christian Community and the Civil Community', in idem., *Against the Stream: Shorter Post-War Writings 1946–1952*, ed. R. G. Smith, trans. E. M. Delacour and S. Godman (London, 1954).

—— *The Christian Life*, CD IV/4. Lecture Fragments, trans. G. Bromiley (Edinburgh, 1981).

—— *Church Dogmatics*, ed. G. W. Bromiley and T. F. Torrance, trans. G. W. Bromiley and T. F. Torrance *et al.* (Edinburgh, 1936–69, repr. 1981).

—— *The Knowledge of God and the Service of God according to the Teaching of the Reformation*, Gifford Lectures 1937–8, trans. J. L. M. Haire and I. Henderson (London, 1938).

Bayer, Oswald, *Autorität und Kritik: Zur Hermeneutik und Wissenschafts-theorie* (Tübingen, 1991).
—— *Freiheit als Antwort: Zur theologischen Ethik* (Tübingen, 1995).
—— *Leibliches Wort: Reformation und Neuzeit im Konflikt* (Tübingen, 1992).
—— *Responsive Freedom*, (forthcoming trans. of *Freiheit als Antwort*), (Oxford); see esp. pp. 13–19, 83–93, 116–46, 147–63).
—— *Theologie: Handbuch der Systematischer Theologie*, i (Gütersloh, 1994).
—— 'Theologie und Gottesdienst', in Friedrich-Otto Scharbau (ed.), *Erneuerung des Gottesdienstes*, Klausurtagung der Bischofskonferenz der VELKD 1989; Referate und Berichte; ZUR SACHE 32, Kirchliche Aspekte heute (Hanover, 1990), 19–35.
Beck, Ulrich, and Beck-Gernsheim, Elisabeth, *The Normal Chaos of Love*, trans. M. Ritter and J. Wiebel (Cambridge, 1995).
Becker, Joachim, *Wege der Psalmenexegese*, Stuttgarter Bibelstudien 78 (Stuttgart, 1975).
Die Bekenntnisschriften der evangelisch-lutherischen Kirche, hg. im Gedenkjahr *der Augsburgischen Konfession 1930*, 8th edn. (Göttingen, 1979). (See also *The Book of Concord.*)
Bellah, Robert N., *et al.*, *Habits of the Heart. Individualism and Commitment in American Life* (Berkeley and London, 1985; rev. edn. 1996).
Benhabib, Seyla, *Situating the Self: Gender, Community and Postmodernism in Contemporary Ethics* (Cambridge, 1992).
Berger, Teresa, '*Lex orandi—lex credendi—lex agendi*: zu einer ökumenisch konsensfähigen Verhältnisbestimmung von Liturgie, Theologie, Ethik', *Archiv für Liturgiewissenschaften*, 27 (1985), 425–32.
Berman, Marshall, *The Politics of Authenticity*, (New York, 1980).
Bethge, Eberhard, *Dietrich Bonhoeffer, Theologian, Christian, Contemporary*, trans. E. Mosbacher *et al.*, rev. and ed. Victoria Barnett (Minneapolis, 2000).
Bethke Elshtain, Jean, 'Christianity and Patriarchy: The Odd Alliance', *Modern Theology*, 9 (1993), 109–22.
—— *Public Man, Private Woman: Women in Social and Political Thought* (Princeton, 1981; 2nd edn. 1993).
Betz, Hans D., *Galatians: A Commentary on Paul's Letter to the Churches in Galatia*, Hermeneia (Philadelphia, 1979).
Beutel, Albrecht, *In dem Anfang war das Wort: Studien zu Luthers Sprach-verständnis* (Tübingen, 1991).
Bizer, Christoph, 'Das Evangelische Christentum und die Liturgie: zum Kirchenverständnis des neuen Agendenentwurfs', *PTh* 82 (1993), 148–59.
Boff, Leonardo, *Sacraments of Life—Life of the Sacraments*, trans. John Drury (Washington, 1987).

Bohren, Rudolf, *Predigtlehre*, Einführung in die evangelische Theologie 4 (Munich, 1971).

Bonhoeffer, Dietrich, *Discipleship*, trans. Barbara Green and R. Krause (vol. 4 of *Works*, general editor Wayne Whitson Floyd junr.) (Minneapolis, 2001).

—— *Ethics*, ed. E. Bethge, trans. N. Horton Smith (London, 1971).

—— *Letters and Papers from Prison*, 4th enlarged edn., ed. E. Bethge, trans. R. H. Fuller *et al.* (London and New York, 1971).

—— *Sanctorum Communio: A Theological Study of the Sociology of the Church*, trans. R. Krauss and Nancy Lukens (vol. 1 of *Works*, general editor Wayne Whitson Floyd junr.) (Minneapolis, 1998).

—— *Das Wesen der Kirche: Aus Hörernachschriften zusammengestellt und hg. von Otto Duzus* (Munich, 1971).

The Book of Concord: The Confessions of the Evangelical Lutheran Church, trans. and ed. T. G. Tappert in collaboration with J. Pelikan *et al.* (Philadelphia, 1959).

Bradshaw, Paul F., 'Gottesdienst IV: Alte Kirche', *TRE* 14 (1985), 39–42.

Brown, Peter, *Power and Persuasion in Late Antiquity: Towards a Christian Empire* (Madison, 1992).

Brunner, Peter, *Worship in the Name of Jesus*, trans. M. H. Bertram (St Louis, 1968).

Bultmann, Rudolf, 'Das Problem der Ethik bei Paulus', *ZNW* 23 (1924), 123–40.

Cone, James H., 'Sanctification, Liberation, and Black Worship', *ThTo* 35 (1978), 139–52.

Cornehl, Peter, 'Gottesdienst VIII: Evangelischer Gottesdienst von der Reformation bis zur Gegenwart', *TRE* 14 (1985), 54–85.

—— 'Theorie des Gottesdienstes: ein Prospekt', *ThQ* 159 (1979), 178–95.

Cox, Harvey, 'Die Inkarnation des Mammon: Warenkult und Simulation in der inszenierten Gesellschaft', *LM* 1 (1993) 4–7.

Dannowski, Hans W., *Kompendium der Predigtlehre* (Gütersloh, 1985).

Davies, Horton, *Worship and Theology in England*, vol. v: *The Ecumenical Century 1900–1965* (Princeton, 1965).

Delaruelle, Etienne, 'Le Travail dans les règles monastiques occidentales du 4ᵉ au 9ᵉ siècle', *Journal de Psychologie Normale et Pathologique*, 41/1 (1948).

Denzinger, Heinrich, and Schönmetzer, A. (eds.), *Enchiridion Symbolorum Definitionum et Declarationum de rebus fidei et morum*, 36th edn. (Freiburg/Br, 1976); also *The Sources of Catholic Dogma*, trans. R. J. Deferrari from the 13th edn. of Denzinger's *Enchiridion Symbolorum* (St Louis and London, 1955).

Diebner, Bernd-Jörg, 'Gottesdienst II: Altes Testament', *TRE* 14 (1985), 5–28.

364   *Bibliography*

Dix, Dom Gregory, *The Shape of the Liturgy* (1945); 2nd edn. (London, 2001).

Douglas, Ann, *The Feminization of American Culture* (New York, 1977).

Duchrow, Ulrich, *Christenheit und Weltverantwortung: Traditionsgeschichte und systematische Struktur der Zweireichelehre* (Stuttgart, 1970).

Erneuerte Agende: Vorentwurf, ed. VELKD und EKD (Hanover and Bielefeld, 1990).

Evangelischer Gottesdienst: Quellen zu seiner Geschichte, 2nd completely revised edition of *Quellen zur Geschichte des evangelischen Gottesdienstes*, ed. W. Herbst (Göttingen, 1992).

Everett, William J., *God's Federal Republic: Reconstructing our Governing Symbol* (New York, 1988).

Exegetisches Wörterbuch zum Neuen Testament, 2 vols., ed. H. Balz and G. Schneider; 2nd rev. edn. (Stuttgart, etc. 1992).

Feldmeier, R., *Die Christen als Fremde* (Tübingen, 1992).

Fischer, Johannes, *Leben aus dem Geist. Zur Grundlegung christlicher Ethik* (Zürich, 1994).

Forrester, Duncan B., *Beliefs, Values and Policies: Conviction Politics in a Secular Age* (Oxford, 1989).

——'Lex Orandi—Lex Credendi', in Duncan B. Forrester (ed.), *Theology and Practice* (London, 1990), 71–80.

Foucault, Michel, *Discipline and Punish: The Birth of the Prison*, trans. A. Sheridan (London, 1977; Harmondsworth, 1991).

Fowl, Stephen E., and Jones, L. Gregory, *Reading in Communion: Scripture and Ethics in Christian Life* (London, 1991).

Freiheit im Leben mit Gott: Texte zur Tradition evangelischer Ethik, ed. with intro. by Hans G. Ulrich, Theologische Bücherei: Studienbücher 86 (Gütersloh, 1993).

Friedrich, Gerhard, 'Die Fürbitte im Neuen Testament', in *idem, Auf das Wort kommt es an. Gesammelte Aufsätze zum 70. Geburtstag*, ed. Johannes H. Friedrich (Göttingen, 1978), 431–56.

Gadamer, Hans-G., *Truth and Method*, 2nd rev. edn., trans. rev. J. Weinsheimer and D. G. Marshall (London, 1989).

Georgi, Dieter, 'Die Visionen vom himmlischen Jerusalem in Apk 21 and 22', in Dieter Lührmann and Georg Strecker (eds.), *Kirche: Festschrift für Günther Bornkamm*, (Tübingen, 1980), 353–72.

Gogarten, Friedrich, *Politische Ethik: Versuch einer Grundlegung* (Jena, 1932).

——*Die Verkündigung Jesu Christi, Grundlage und Aufgabe* (Heidelberg, 1949).

'Der Gottesdienst in der politischen Welt: "Politischer Gottesdienst". Ein Hilfe zur Urteilsbildung', Kammer für Theologie der EKD, ed. Kirchenamt der EKD (Hanover, 1995).

Guroian, Vigen, *Incarnate Love: Essays in Orthodox Ethics* (Notre Dame, Ind., 1987).

—— 'Seeing Worship as Ethics', in *idem, Incarnate Love,* 51–78.

Gutiérrez, Gustavo, *A Theology of Liberation: History, Politics and Salvation,* trans. and ed. Caridad Inda and J. Eagleson (Maryknoll, NY, and London, 1973; rev. edn., Maryknoll, NY, and London, 1988).

Habermas, Jürgen, *Between Facts and Norms: Contributions to a Discourse Theory of Law and Democracy,* trans. W. Rehg (Cambridge, 1996).

—— 'Bewußtmachende oder rettende Kritik: die Aktualität Walter Benjamins', in S. Unseld (ed.), *Zuv Aktuahtät Walter Benjamins: aus Anlass des 80. Geburtstages von Walter Benjamin* (Frankfurt, 1972), 173–223.

—— *Erlaüterungen zur Diskursethik,* 2nd edn. (Frankfurt, 1992).

—— 'Hannah Arendts Begriff der Macht', in *idem, Politik, Kunst, Religion: Essays über zeitgenössische Philosophen* (Stuttgart, 1989), 103–26.

—— *Justification and Application: Remarks on Discourse Ethics,* trans. C. Cronin (Cambridge, Mass., and London, 1993) (includes three essays from *Erlaüterungen zur Diskursethik*).

—— *Moral Consciousness and Communicative Action,* trans. C. Lenhardt and S. Weber Nicholsen (Cambridge, 1990).

—— 'Öffentlichkeit', in *idem, Kultur und Kritik: Verstreute Aufsätze* (Frankfurt, 1973), 61–9.

—— *The Structural Transformation of the Public Sphere: An Inquiry into a Category of Bourgeois Society,* trans. T. Burger, with the assistance of F. Lawrence (Cambridge, 1989).

Hardy, Daniel W., and Ford, David F., *Jubilate: Theology in Praise* (London, 1984).

Harvey, Barry A., 'Insanity, Theocracy, and the Public Realm: Public Theology, the Church, and the Politics of Liberal Democracy', *Modern Theology,* 10 (1994), 27–57.

Hauerwas, Stanley, *After Christendom? How the Church is to Behave if Freedom, Justice, and a Christian Nation are Bad Ideas* (Nashville, 1991).

—— 'Children, Suffering and the Skill to Care', in *idem, Truthfulness and Tragedy,* 147–202.

—— 'The Church's One Foundation is Jesus Christ her Lord, or In a World without Foundations all We Have is the Church', in *idem, In Good Company,* 33–49.

—— *A Community of Character: Toward a Constructive Christian Social Ethic* (Notre Dame, Ind., and London, 1981).

—— *In Good Company: The Church as Polis* (Notre Dame, Ind., 1995).

—— 'The Liturgical Shape of Christian Life: Teaching Christian Ethics as Worship', in *idem, In Good Company,* 153–68.

Hauerwas, Stanley, 'The Moral Limits of Population Control', in *idem*, *Truthfulness and Tragedy*, 116–26.

—— 'What Could it Mean for the Church to be Christ's Body? A Question without a Clear Answer', in *idem*, *In Good Company*, 19–31.

—— and Baxter, Michael, 'The Kingship of Christ: Why Freedom of "Belief" is not enough', in Hauerwas, *In Good Company*, 199–216.

—— and Willimon, William H., *Resident Aliens: Life in the Christian Colony* (Nashville, 1989).

—— with Richard Bondi and David B. Burrell *Truthfulness and Tragedy: Further Investigations into Christian Ethics* (Notre Dame, Ind., and London, 1977).

Hebert, A. Gabriel, *Liturgy and Society: The Function of the Church in the Modern World* (London, 1935).

Hegel, Georg W. F., *Elements of the Philosophy of Right*, ed. Allen W. Wood, trans. H. B. Nisbet (Cambridge, 1991).

—— *Lectures on the History of Philosophy*, trans. E. S. Haldane and Frances H. Simon, vol. i (London, 1892).

—— *Lectures on the Philosophy of Religion*, ed. and trans. Peter C. Hodgson *et al.*, 3 vols. (Berkeley and Los Angeles, 1984–7).

—— 'The Spirit of Christianity and its Fate', in *idem*, *Early Theological Writings*, trans. J. M. Knox (Chicago, 1948).

Herms, Eilert, 'Überlegungen zum Wesen des Gottesdienstes: aus Anlaß des Entwurfs für eine "Erneuerte Agende"', *KuD* 40 (1994), 219–47.

Herrmann, Wilhelm D., *Ethik: Grundriß der theologischen Wissenschaften*, 5/2, 4th edn. (Tübingen, 1909).

Heschel, Abraham J., *The Sabbath: Its Meaning for Modern Man* (New York, 1951).

Hornig, Gottfried, 'Die Freiheit der christlichen Privatreligion: Semlers Begründung des religiösen Individualismus in der protestanischen Aufklärungstheologie', *NZSTh* 21 (1979), 198–211.

Huber, Wolfgang, *Kirche und Öffentlichkeit*, 2nd edn. (Munich, 1991).

—— 'Öffentliche Kirche in pluralen Öffentlichkeiten', *EvTh* 54 (1994), 157–80.

Hütter, Reinhard, 'The Church as Public: Dogma, Practice, and the Holy Spirit', *Pro Ecclesia*, 3 (1994), 334–61.

—— *Evangelische Ethik als kirchliches Zeugnis: Interpretationen zu Schlüsselfragen theologischer Ethik in der Gegenwart*, Evangelium und Ethik 1 (Neukirchen-Vluyn, 1993).

—— *Suffering Divine Things: Theology as Church Praxis*, trans. Doug Stott (Grand Rapids, Mich., and Cambridge, 2000).

Hunter, James D., *American Evangelicalism* (New Brunswick, NJ, 1983), 91–101.

Hutter, Ulrich, 'πολίτευμα; πολιτεύομαι', *EWNT*, iii. 310–12.

The Identity of Anglican Worship, ed. Kenneth Stevenson and Bryan Spinks (London, 1991).

Iwand, Hans J., *Erläuterungen zur deutschen Ausgabe von 'de servo arbitrio'* (Munich, 1954).

Jetter, Werner, *Symbol und Ritual: anthropologische Elemente im Gottesdienst*, 2nd rev. edn. (Göttingen, 1986).

John Paul II, *Veritatis Splendor: Regarding Certain Fundamental Questions of the Church's Moral Teaching*, encyclical published in English by the Catholic Truth Society (London, 1993).

Jonas, Hans, *The Imperative of Responsibility: In Search of an Ethics for the Technological Age*, trans. H. Jonas with the collaboration of D. Herr (Chicago, 1984).

Jones, L. Gregory, *Embodying Forgiveness: A Theological Analysis* (Grand Rapids, Mich., 1995).

—— *Transformed Judgment: Toward a Trinitarian Account of the Moral Life* (Notre Dame, Ind., and London, 1990).

Josuttis, Manfred, *Der Weg ins Leben: eine Einführung in den Gottesdienst auf verhaltenswissenschaftlicher Grundlage*, 2nd edn. (Gütersloh, 1993).

—— 'Das Ziel des Gottesdienstes: Aktion oder Feier?', in *idem, Praxis des Evangeliums zwischen Politik und Religion: Grundprobleme der Praktischen Theologie* (Munich, 1974), 142–63.

Jüngel, Eberhard, *Anfechtung und Gewißheit des Glaubens oder wie die Kirche wieder zu ihrer Sache kommt*, 2nd edn. (Munich, 1976).

—— 'Anrufung Gottes als Grundethos christlichen Handels: einführende Bemerkungen zu den nachgelassenen Fragmenten der Ethik der Versöhnungslehre Karl Barths' in *idem, Barth-Studien*, Ökumenische Theologie 9 (Gütersloh, 1982), 315–31.

—— 'The Church as Sacrament?', in *idem, Theological Essays*, trans. J. B. Webster (Edinburgh, 1989), 189–213.

—— 'Der evangelisch verstandene Gottesdienst', in *idem, Wertlose Wahrheit*, 283–310.

—— *Wertlose Wahrheit: zur Identität und Relevanz des christlichen Glaubens*, Theologische Erörterungen III, BevTh 107 (Munich, 1990).

Käsemann, Ernst, 'The Cry for Liberty in the Worship of the Church', in *idem, Perspectives on Paul*, trans. Margaret Kohl (London, 1971), 122–37.

—— 'Worship in Everyday Life: A Note on Romans 12', in *New Testament Questions of Today*, trans. (except for ch. 12) W. J. Montague (London, 1969), 188–95.

Kant, Immanuel, *Critique of Judgement*, trans. J. C. Meredith (Oxford, 1928).

—— *Critique of Pure Reason*, trans. and ed. Norman Kemp-Smith (London, 1929; rev. edn. 1933).

—— *Metaphysic of Morals*, trans. M. Gregor (Cambridge, 1996).

Kant, Immanuel, *Religion within the Limits of Reason Alone*, trans. T. M. Greene and H. H. Hudson (Chicago, 1934).
—— *Werke*, ed. W. Weichschedel, 10 vols., special edition (Darmstadt, 1983).
Kavanagh, Aidan, *On Liturgical Theology* (Collegeville, Minn., 1984).
Kerr, Fergus, *Theology after Wittgenstein* (Oxford, 1986).
Klauck, Hans-J., *Gemeinde zwischen Haus und Stadt: Kirche bei Paulus* (Freiburg, 1992).
—— *Hausgemeinde und Hauskirche im frühen Christentum*, Stuttgarter Bibelstudien 103 (Stuttgart, 1981).
Kohlberg, Lawrence, Levine, Charles, and Hewer, Alexandra, *Moral Stages: A Current Formulation and a Response to Critics* (Basle, etc., 1983).
Kraus, Hans-J., 'Gottesdienst im alten und neuen Bund', *EvTh* 25 (1965), 171–206.
Lange, Ernst, 'Was nützt uns der Gottesdienst?', in *idem, Predigen als Beruf: Aufsätze*, ed. Rüdiger Schloz (Stuttgart and Berlin, 1976), 83–95.
Lasch, Christopher, *The Culture of Narcissisim: American Life in an Age of Diminishing Expectations* (New York, 1978).
Lash, Nicholas, 'Performing the Scriptures', in *idem, Theology on the Way to Emmaus* (London, 1986), 37–46.
Lehmann, Paul, *Ethics in a Christian Context* (New York and Evanston, Ill., 1963).
—— *The Transfiguration of Politics: The Presence and Power of Jesus of Nazareth in and over Human Affairs* (New York and Toronto, 1975).
Leuenberger, Robert, ' "Politischer Gottesdienst" ', *ZThK* 69 (1972), 100–24.
Lévinas, Emmanuel, 'Diachrony and Representation', in *Entre Nous*, 159–77.
—— *Entre Nous: On Thinking-of-the-other*, trans. M. B. Smith and Barabara Harshav (Chichester, NY, 1998).
—— 'Is Ontology Fundamental?', in *idem, Entre Nous*, 159–77.
—— *Otherwise than Being, or Beyond Essence*, trans. A. Lingis (The Hague, Boston, and London, 1981).
Lindbeck, George A., *The Nature of Doctrine: Religion and Theology in a Postliberal Age* (Philadelphia, 1984).
Link, Christian, 'Vita passiva: Rechtfertigung als Lebensvorgang', *EvTh* 44 (1984), 315–51.
Living No Longer for Ourselves: Liturgy and Justice in the Nineties, ed. Kathleen Hughes and Mark R. Francis (Collegeville, Minn., 1991).
Löwe, Hartmut, 'Der Beitrag der Kirchen zur politischen Kultur', Vortrag zur 40-Jahr Feier des Politischen Clubs Tutzing 1994 (typescript, printed in shortened form in *Tutzinger Blätter*, 4 (1994), 3–5).

Löwith, Karl, *From Hegel to Nietzsche: The Revolution in Nineteenth-Century Thought*, trans. D. E. Green (London, 1965: repr. with a preface by H.-G. Gadamer, New York, 1991).

Luhmann, Niklas, *The Differentiation of Society*, trans. S. Holmes and C. Larmore (New York, 1982).

—— *Die Funktion der Religion*, 3rd edn. (Frankfurt, 1992).

—— 'Moderne Systemtheorien als Form gesamtgesellschaftlicher Analyse', in Jürgen Habermas and Niklas Luhmann, *Theorie der Gesellschaft oder Sozialtechnologie: was leistet die Sozialforschung* (Frankfurt, 1976), 7–24.

—— *Social Systems*, trans. J. Bednarz with D. Baecker (Stanford, Calif., 1995).

Luther, Martin, *Ausgewählte Schriften*, ed. Karin Bornkamm and Gerhard Ebeling together with Oswald Bayer *et al.*, 6 vols. (Frankfurt, 1982 (Insel edn.)).

—— 'Daß eine christliche Versammlung oder Gemeinde Recht und Macht habe, alle Lehre zu urteilen und Lehrer zu berufen, ein- und abzusetzen: Grund und Ursach aus der Schrift', WA 11, 408–16.

—— *De servo arbitrio*, WA 18, 600–787.

—— *Deutsche Messe und Ordnung des Gottesdienstes*, WA 19, 72–113.

—— 'Eine einfältige Weise zu beten für einen guten Freund', WA 38, 358–75.

—— 'Ein Sermon von den guten Werken', WA 6, 202–76.

—— 'Ein Sermon von dem heiligen hochwürdigen Sakrament der Taufe', WA 2, 724–37.

—— 'Ein Sermon von dem heiligen hochwürdigen Sakrament des heiligen wahren Leichnams Christi und von den Bruderschaften', WA 2, 742–58.

—— 'Ein Sermon von dem neuen Testament, das ist von der heiligen Messe', WA 6, 353–78.

—— *Fastenpostille*, WA 17/II, 1–237.

—— *Genesisvorlesung von 1535–1545*, WA 42–4.

—— *The Large Catechism* (1529), trans. R. H. Fischer, in *The Book of Concord*, ed. T. G. Tappert *et al.* (Philadelphia, 1959; 16th printing 1987).

—— *Luther Deutsch: Die Werke Luthers in Auswahl*, ed. Kurt Aland (Göttingen, 1991).

—— *Luthers Epistelauslegung*, vol. 1: *Der Römerbrief*, ed. Eduard Ellwein (Göttingen, 1963); vol. 4: *Der Galaterbrief*, ed. Hermann Kleinknecht, 2nd edn. (Göttingen, 1987).

—— *The Smalcald Articles* (1537), trans. T. G. Tappert, in *The Book of Concord*, ed. T. G. Tappert *et al.* (Philadelphia, 1959; 16th printing, 1987).

Luther, Martin, *The Small Catechism* (1529), trans. T. G. Tappert, in *The Book of Concord*, ed. T. G. Tappert *et al.* (Philadelphia, 1959; 16th printing, 1987).

——— *Tractatus de libertate christiana*, WA 7, 49–73; trans. K.-H. zur Mühlen in *Martin Luther: Freiheit und Lebensgestaltung: Ausgewählte Texte*, ed. and partly newly trans. by K-H. zur Mühlen (Göttingen, 1983), 37–74.

——— 'Unterschied des rechten und falschen Gottesdienstes', WA 10 I, 1, 674–7.

——— *Vom Abendmahl Christi: Bekenntnis*, WA 26, 261–509.

——— *Von den Konzilien und Kirchen*, WA 50, 509–653.

——— 'Von der Ordnung des Gottesdiensts in der Gemeinde', WA 12, 35–37.

——— 'Vorrede zu: Deutsche Messe und Ordnung des Gottesdienstes', WA 19, 72–8.

——— *Werke: Kritische Gesamtausgabe* (Weimar, 1883–).

——— *Works*, ed. Jaroslav Pelikan and Helmut T. Lehman, 54 vols. (Philadelphia and St Louis, 1955–).

——— *Die Zirkulardisputation über das Recht des Widerstandes gegen den Kaiser (Mt 19, 21)*, WA 39 II, 39–91.

Machiavelli, Niccolò, *The Prince*, trans. George Bull (Harmondsworth, 1999).

MacIntyre, Alasdair, *After Virtue: A Study in Moral Theory*, 2nd edn. (Notre Dame, Ind., 1984; London, 1985).

——— *A Short History of Ethics: A History of Moral Philosophy from the Homeric Age to the Twentieth Century* (New York, 1966).

——— *Three Rival Versions of Moral Enquiry: Encyclopaedia, Genealogy, and Tradition* (Notre Dame, Ind., 1990).

——— *Whose Justice? Which Rationality?* (Notre Dame, Ind., 1990).

Marcuse, Herbert, *Towards a Critical Theory of Society*, ed. Douglas Kellner (London, 2001).

Marx, Karl, *Capital*, ed. Friedrich Engels, vol. 3 (Moscow, 1959).

——— 'Nationalökonomie und Philosophie', in *idem, Die Frühschriften*, ed. S. Landshut (Stuttgart, 1971), 225–316.

Mascall, Eric L., *Corpus Christi: The Church and the Eucharist* (London, New York, and Toronto, 1953).

Mbuy Beya, Bernadette, 'Die Last des Schweigens abschütteln: wie schwarze Christinnen für ihre Befreiung kämpfen', German trans. by E. Tocha-Ring, *Publik Forum*, 22, (1994), 24–5.

McClendon, James W. jun., *Ethics: Systematic Theology*, i (Nashville, 1986).

Meeks, Wayne A., *The First Urban Christians: The Social World of the Apostle Paul* (New Haven and London, 1983).

Meier, C., 'Politik 1: Antike', *HWPh* 7, 1038–47.

Meister Eckhart, *Deutsche Predigten und Traktate*, trans. and ed. Josef Quint, 7th edn. (Munich, 1995).

Milbank, John, 'Can Morality be Christian?', in *idem, The Word Made Strange* (Oxford, 1997).

—— *Theology and Social Theory: Beyond Secular Reason* (Oxford, 1990).

Newbigin, Leslie, *The Gospel in a Pluralist Society* (Grand Rapids, Mich., 1989).

Nicol, Martin, *Meditation bei Luther* (Göttingen, 1984).

Nietzsche, Friedrich, *The Gay Science*, trans. J. Nacuckhoff (Cambridge, 2001). See also *Complete Works of F. Nietzsche*, authorized trans., ed. O. Levy (New York, 1974).

—— *On the Genealogy of Morals*, trans. Douglas Smith (Oxford, 1996).

O'Donovan, Oliver, *The Desire of the Nations: Rediscovering the Roots of Political Theology* (Cambridge, 1996).

—— *Liturgy and Ethics*, Grove Ethical Studies 89 (Nottingham, 1993).

—— *Resurrection and Moral Order: An Outline for Evangelical Ethics*, 2nd edn. (Leicester and Grand Rapids, Mich., 1994).

Otto, Eckhart, *Theologische Ethik des Alten Testaments*, Theologische Wissenschaft 3/2 (Stuttgart, Berlin, and Cologne, 1994).

Panikkar, Raimundo, *Worship and Secular Man. An Essay on the Liturgical Nature of Man, Considering Secularization as a Major Phenomenon of our Time and Worship as an Apparent Fact of All Times: A Study Towards an Integral Anthropology* (Maryknoll, NY, and London, 1973).

Patsch, Hermann, 'εὐχαριστία', *EWNT* ii. 221–2.

Picht, Georg, 'Der Begriff der Verantwortung', in *idem, Wahrheit, Vernunft, Verantwortung* (Stuttgart, 1969), 318–24.

Plato, *Laws*, trans. T. J. Saunders (Harmondsworth, 1970).

—— *Republic*, ed. G. R. F. Ferrari, trans. T. Griffith (Cambridge, 2000).

—— *Statesman*, trans. C. Rowe (Indianapolis and Cambridge, 1999).

—— *Complete Works*, ed. J. M. Cooper (Indianapolis and Cambridge, 1997).

Polanyi, Michael, *Personal Knowledge: Towards a Post-Critical Philosophy* (London, 1958).

Politisches Nachtgebet in Köln: Im Auftrag des ökumenischen Arbeitskreises 'Politisches Nachtgebet', ed. Dorothee Sölle and Fulbert Steffensky, 2 vols. (Berlin, etc., 1969 and 1971).

Prenter, Regin, *Spiritus Creator: Studien zu Luthers Theologie*, FGLP 10th ser., vol. 6 (Munich, 1954).

Quick, Oliver C., *The Christian Sacraments* (London, 1927; 2nd edn. 1932, repr. 1952).

Rahner, Karl, *Grundkurs des Glaubens* (Munich, 1976).

Ramsey, Michael A., *From Gore to Temple: The Development of Anglican Theology between Lux Mundi and the Second World War 1889–1939* (London, 1960).

Rasmusson, Arne, *The Church as Polis: From Political Theology to Theological Politics as Exemplified by Jürgen Moltmann and Stanley Hauerwas* (Lund, 1994).

Rathey, Markus, 'Eucharistische Ethik in Luthers Abendmahlssermon von 1519', *Luther*, 2 (1992), 66–73.

Rawls, John, *A Theory of Justice*, rev. edn. (Oxford, 1999).

Religion and American Public Life: Interpretations and Explorations, ed. Robin W. Lovin (New York, 1989).

The Religion of the Incarnation: Anglican Essays in Commemoration of Lux Mundi, ed. Robert Morgan (Bristol, 1989).

Ricoeur, Paul, 'Nommer Dieu', *Études théologiques et religieuses*, 52 (1977), 489–508.

Rieff, Philip, *The Triumph of the Therapeutic: Uses of Faith after Freud* (New York and London, 1966; with a new preface, Chicago and London, 1987).

Riesman, David, *The Lonely Crowd: Individualism Reconsidered* (New York, 1954).

Ritschl, Dietrich, *A Theology of Proclamation* (Richmond, 1960).

Robinson, John A. T., *Liturgy Coming to Life* (Philadelphia, 1960).

Roloff, Jürgen, 'ἐκκλησία', *EWNT* i. 998–1011.

——*Exegetische Verantwortung in der Kirche: Aufsätze*, ed. Martin Karrer (Göttingen, 1990).

——'Heil als Gemeinschaft: kommunikative Faktoren im urchristlichen Herrenmahl', in idem, *Exegetische Verantwortung in der Kirche*, 171–200.

——*Die Kirche im Neuen Testament*, NTD Ergänzungsreihe 10 (Göttingen, 1993).

——'Zur diakonischen Dimension und Bedeutung von Gottesdienst und Herrenmahl', in idem, *Exegetische Verantwortung in der Kirche*, 201–18.

Rorty, Richard, *Contingency, Irony and Solidarity* (Cambridge, 1989).

——'Der Vorrang der Demokratie vor der Philosophie', in Forum für Philosophie Bad Homburg (ed.), *Zerstörung des moralischen Selbstbewußtseins: Chance oder Gefährdung? Praktische Philosophie in Deutschland nach dem Nationalsozialismus*, (Frankfurt, 1988), 273–89.

Rothe, Richard, *Theologische Ethik*, III/2 (Wittenberg, 1948).

Safrai, Shmuel, *Die Wallfahrt im Zeitalter des Zweiten Tempels*, FCJD 3 (Neukirchen-Vluyn, 1981).

Sauter, Gerhard, 'Consensus', *TRE* 8 (1981), 181–9.

——*In der Freiheit des Geistes: theologische Studien* (Göttingen, 1988).

——'Die Kirche in der Krisis des Geistes', in Walter Kasper and Gerhard Sauter, *Kirche—Ort des Geistes*, Kleine ökumenische Schriften 8 (Freiburg, Basle, and Vienna, 1976), 57–106.

——'Was ist Wahrheit in der Theologie? Wahrheitsfindung und Konsens der Kirche', in idem, *In der Freiheit des Geistes*, 57–82.

Schleiermacher, Friedrich D. E., *The Christian Faith*, trans. of 2nd edn. by H. R. Mackintosh and J. S. Stewart (Edinburgh, 1928; Philadelphia, 1976).

——*Christliche Sittenlehre in Vorlesungen (Wintersemester 1822–23) aus Nachschriften*, ed. L. Jonas, 2 vols. (Gotha, 1891).

——*Hermeneutics and Criticism*, trans. and ed. A. Bowie (Cambridge, 1998).

—— *On Religion: Speeches to its Cultured Despisers*, trans. J. Oman (London, 1893, reissued New York, 1958).

—— *Die Praktische Theologie nach den Grundsätzen der evangelischen Kirche im Zusammenhange dargestellt: aus Schleiermachers handschriftlichen Nachlässen und nachgeschriebenen Vorlesungen*, ed. Jacob Frerichs (Berlin, 1850).

Schlier, Heinrich, 'Die Kirche nach dem Brief an die Epheser', in *idem, Die Zeit der Kirche*, 159–86.

——*Die Zeit der Kirche: exegetische Aufsätze und Vorträge*, 5th edn. (Freiburg, Basle, and Vienna, 1972).

Schmidt, Klaus, 'Das Politische Nachtgebet 1968', in *Evangelischer Gottesdienst*, 298–307.

Schrage, Wolfgang, *Der erste Brief an die Korinther, I/1: 1 Kor 1,1–6, 11*, EKK VII/1 (Zürich, etc. 1991).

——*Ethik des Neuen Testaments*, 5th rev. and expanded edn., NTD Ergänzungsreihe 4 (Göttingen, 1989).

Schüssler-Fiorenza, Elisabeth, *In Memory of Her: A Feminist Theological Reconstruction of Christian Origins* (New York and London, 1983).

Searle, John R., *Speech Acts: An Essay in the Philosophy of Language* (Cambridge, 1969).

Second Vatican Council, The Constitution on the Sacred Liturgy, in *Conciliar and Post-Conciliar Documents*, ed. A. Flannery, rev. edn. (Dublin, 1988).

Sedgwick, Timothy F., *Sacramental Ethics, Paschal Identity and the Christian Life* (London, 1927; 2nd edn. 1932, repr. Philadelphia, 1987).

Smallwood, Mary E., *The Jews under Roman Rule: From Pompey to Diocletian*, Studies in Judaism in Late Antiquity 20 (Leiden, 1976).

Smend, Julius, *Der evangelische Gottesdienst: Ein Liturgik nach evangelischen Grundsätzen in 14 Abhandlungen* (Göttingen, 1904).

Soden, Hans von, 'Sakrament und Ethik bei Paulus: zur Frage der traditionsgeschichtlichen und theologischen Einheitlichkeit von 1. Kor 8–10', in *idem, Urchristentum und Geschichte: gesammelte Aufsätze und Vorträge*, ed. Hans von Campenhausen, vol. i (Tübingen, 1951), 239–75.

Spaemann, Robert, 'Funktionale Religionsbegründung und Religion', in *idem, Philosophische Essays*, expanded edn. (Stuttgart, 1994), 208–31.

Spaemann, Robert, 'Überzeugungen in einer hypothetischen Zivilisation', in Oskar Schatz (ed.), *Abschied von Utopia? Anspruch und Auftrag der Intellektuellen* (Graz, etc. 1977), 311–31.

Sternberger, Dolf, *Drei Wurzeln der Politik: Schriften* II, 1; II, 2 (Frankfurt, 1978).

Stringfellow, William, *An Ethic for Christians and Other Aliens in a Strange Land*, 2nd paperback edn. (Waco, Tex., 1978).

Suggate, Alan M., *William Temple and Christian Social Ethics Today* (Edinburgh, 1987).

Sykes, Stephen W., *The Identity of Christianity: Theologians and the Essence of Christianity from Schleiermacher to Barth* (Philadelphia, 1984).

Taylor, Charles, *Sources of the Self: The Making of Modern Identity* (Cambridge, Mass., 1989).

Temple, William, *Christianity and Social Order* (1942), reissued with introduction by Ronald H. Preston (New York, 1977).

——*Nature, Man and God* (London and New York, 1956).

——'Theology Today', in *idem, Thoughts in War-Time* (London, 1940), 93–107.

Theissen, Gerd, *The Social Setting of Pauline Christianity*, trans. J. H. Schütz (Minneapolis and Edinburgh, 1982).

Theologie und funktionale Systemtheorie: Luhmanns Religionssoziologie in theologischer Diskussion, ed. Michael Welker (Frankfurt, 1985).

Theologisches Handwörterbuch zum Alten Testament, 2 vols., ed. Ernst Jenni with the co-operation of Claus Westermann, 4th rev. edn. (Munich and Zürich, 1984).

Thilo, Hans-Joachim, *Die therapeutische Funktion des Gottesdienstes* (Kassel, 1985).

Thomas Aquinas, *Summa Theologiae*, Latin text and English translation, Blackfriars edn. (London and New York, 1964–).

Tönnies, Ferdinand, *Gesellschaft und Gemeinschaft: Abhandlung des Communismus und des Sozialismus als empirischer Culturformen* (Leipzig, 1887).

Torres, Camillo, *Priest and Revolutionary*, ed. J. A. Garcia and C. R. Calle (New York, 1968).

Troeltsch, Ernst, *The Social Teaching of the Christian Churches*, trans. O. Wyon (London, 1931; with introduction by H. Richard Niebuhr, Chicago, 1981; Louisville, Ky., 1992).

Ulrich, Hans G., *Eschatologie und Ethik: die theologische Theorie der Ethik in ihrer Beziehung auf die Rede von Gott seit Friedrich Schleiermacher*, BevTh 104 (Munich, 1988).

——'Die "Freiheit der Kinder Gottes": Freiheit in der Geschöpflichkeit: zur Tradition evangelischer Ethik', in *Freiheit im Leben mit Gott*, 9–40.

——— 'Heiliger Geist und Lebensform', in Werner Brändle and Ralf Stolina (eds.), *Geist und Kirche: Festschrift für Eckhard Lessing* (Frankfurt, etc. 1995), 55–78.

——— 'Hoffnung und Verantwortung', *EvTh* 46 (1986), 26–37.

Vajta, Vilmos, *Die Theologie des Gottesdienstes bei Luther* (Göttingen, 1952).

Volp, Rainer, *Liturgik: Die Kunst, Gott zu feiern*, vol. 1: *Einführung und Geschichte*; vol. 2: *Theorien und Gestaltung* (Gütersloh, 1992, 1994).

Wadell, Paul, 'What Do All Those Masses Do for Us? Reflections on the Christian Moral Life and the Eucharist', in *Living No Longer for Ourselves*, 153–69.

Wagener, Ulrike, *Die Ordnung des 'Hauses Gottes': Der Ort von Frauen in der Ekklesiologie und Ethik der Pastoralbriefe*, WUNT 65 (Tübingen, 1995).

Wainwright, Geoffrey, *Doxology: The Praise of God in Worship, Doctrine and Life: A Systematic Theology* (New York, 1980).

——— 'Der Gottesdienst als "Locus Theologicus" oder: Der Gottesdienst als Quelle und Thema der Theologie', *KuD* 82 (1982), 248–57.

Wannenwetsch, Bernd, 'Communication as Transformation: Worship and the Media', *Studies in Christian Ethics*, 13 (2000), 93–106.

——— *Die Freiheit der Ehe: das Zusammenleben von Frau und Mann in der Wahrnehmung evangelischer Ethik*, Evangelium und Ethik 2 (Neukirchen-Vluyn, 1993), 231–54.

——— 'Die Grenzen liberaler Toleranz: wer verbindlich lebt, provoziert die offene Gesellschaft', *LM* 11 (1993), 31–2.

——— *Innen und Außen? Evangelische Praxis Pietatis als gottesdienstliche Frömmigkeit*, Themenband 'Frömmigkeit' der Wissenschaftlichen Gesellschaft für Theologie, ed. W. Sparn (Gütersloh, 2004).

——— ' "Intrinsically Evil Acts": Why Euthanasia and Abortion Cannot be Justified', in Reinhard Hütter and Theo Dieter (eds.), *Ecumenical Ventures in Ethics: Protestants Engage Pope John Paul II's Moral Encyclical* (Grand Rapids, Mich., 1997).

——— 'Der liberale Zwiespalt: politische Nebelfelder zwischen Wertkonservativen und Habitualkritikern', *LM* 3 (1994), 12–14.

——— *Liturgy*, Blackwell Companion to Political Theology, ed. W. Cavanaugh and P. Scott (Oxford, 2003).

——— 'Luther's Moral Theology', in *Cambridge Companion to Martin Luther*, ed. D. McKim (Cambridge, New York, and Melbourne, 2003), 120–35.

——— 'Members of One Another: *Charis*, Ministry and Representation: A Politico-Ecclesial Reading of Romans 12', in G. Bartholomew *et al.* (eds.), *A Royal Priesthood? The Use of the Bible Ethically and Politically* (Carlisle and Grand Rapids, Mich., 2002), 196–220.

——— 'Das "Natürliche" und die "Moral": zur neueren Diskussion um die Homosexualität in der Kirche', *ZEE* 38 (1994), 168–89.

Wannenwetsch, Bernd, 'Old Docetism—New Moralism? Questioning a New Direction in the Homosexuality Debate', *Modern Theology*, 16 (2000), 353–64.

—— 'The Political Worship of the Church: A Critical and Empowering Practice', *Modern Theology*, 12 (1996), 269–99.

Webber, Robert E., and Clapp, Rodney, *People of the Truth: The Power of the Worshipping Community in the Modern World* (San Francisco, 1988).

Weber, Max, *Basic Concepts in Sociology*, trans. H. Secker (New York, 1962) (being sections 1–8 of his *Theory of Social and Economic Organization*, trans. A. R. Henderson and T. Parsons (London and New York, 1947), 1964).

—— *Economy and Society: An Outline of Interpretative Sociology*, trans. E. Fischof *et al.*, 2 vols. (Berkeley, 1978).

—— *The Protestant Ethic and the Spirit of Capitalism*, trans. T. Parsons, with a foreword by R. H. Tawney (1930, last repr. London, 2001); new trans. by Stephen Kalberg (Chicago and London, 2001).

—— *Soziologische Grundbegriffe*, with an introduction by Johannes Wickelmann, 6th newly rev. edn. (Tübingen, 1984).

—— *Wirtschaft und Gesellschaft*, 5th rev. edn. (Tübingen, 1972).

Weder, Hans, *Neutestamentliche Hermeneutik*, Zürcher Grundrisse zur Bibel (Zürich, 1986).

Welker, Michael, *God the Spirit*, trans. J. F. Hoffmeyer (Minneapolis, 1994).

—— *Kirche im Pluralismus* (Gütersloh, 1995).

—— *Kirche ohne Kurs? Aus Anlaß der EKD-Studie 'Christsein gestalten'* (Neukirchen-Vluyn, 1987).

Wendland, Heinz-Dietrich, 'Das System funktionalen Gesellschaft und die Theologie', in *idem, Botschaft an die soziale Welt: Beiträge zur christlichen Sozialethik der Gegenwart* (Hamburg, 1959), 124–40.

Westermann, Claus, *Genesis: A Commentary*, vol. 1: *Genesis 1–11*, trans. J. J. Scullion, SJ, (Minneapolis, 1984).

Wilckens, Ulrich, 'Römer 13.1–7', in *idem, Rechtfertigung als Freiheit: Paulusstudien* (Neukirchen-Vluyn, 1974), 203–43.

Williams, Rowan D., 'The Suspicion of Suspicion: Wittgenstein and Bonhoeffer', in Richard H. Bell (ed.), *The Grammar of the Heart: New Essays in Moral Philosophy and Theology* (San Francisco, 1988), 36–53.

Willimon, William H., *The Service of God: Christian Work and Worship* (Nashville, 1983).

Wittgenstein, Ludwig, *Philosophical Grammar*, ed. Rush Rhees, trans. A. J. P. Kenny (Oxford, 1974).

—— *Philosophical Investigations*, trans. G. E. M. Anscombe (Oxford, 1967).

—— *Tractatus logico-philosophicus*, German text with trans. by D. F. Pears and B. F. McGuiness, intro. by Bertrand Russell (London, 1961).

——*Zettel*, ed. G. E. M. Anscombe and G. H. von Wright, trans. G. E. M. Anscombe (Oxford, 1967).

Worship and Ethics: Lutherans and Anglicans in Dialogue, ed. Oswald Bayer and Alan Suggate (Berlin and New York, 1996).

Yoder, John, *Body Politics: Five Practices of the Christian Community before the Watching World* (Nashville, 1992).

Zizioulas, John D., *Being as Communion: Studies in Personhood and the Church* (Crestwood, NY, and London, 1985).

INDEX OF SUBJECTS

citizenship:
  Christian 46, 106–7, 117, 137–9,
    152, 156–8, 181
  and civil religion 264–5
  in classical *polis* 118–22, 123, 159
  and conciliar consensus 298
  and politics 12–13, 64
  and resident aliens 135, 140–5,
    157–8
  and Roman Empire 135, 140–1,
    142–5
  and worship 7, 11, 279, 325,
    358–9
city, and stational liturgy 260–5,
  267
  see also *polis*
city of God 106, 252, 253–4
  Church as 12, 25–6, 207
  in Revelation 139–40
civil society 241, 266, 269, 272
  and Church and State 31,
    272–5
civitas caelestis, see city of God
civitas terrena 106, 248 n.16, 252–5
class, social, in Roman
  Empire 135–6, 142, 152–3
clericalism 36, 52, 56, 58, 161–2,
  242
commandment ethics 59–66
commonwealth:
  Church as 13, 91, 99, 145
  earthly 91, 99, 250, 252
communication:
  and agreement 319
  see also hearing; language;
    preaching
communion, see Eucharist
communion of saints 54–5, 75, 160,
  182, 198
communitarianism 3–4, 217
community:
  in Bonhoeffer 24–5
  Church as standard 111

discourse community 285, 304,
  312–13
  and morality 4, 19
  and redemption 207
  and regulation 26, 33–4
  and society 217
  see also communion of saints
community of goods 145, 146,
  326–7
  in Lord's Supper 181–5
compassion, see mercy
completeness of worship 73–5
conciliarism, and
  consensus 299–300
concordats 238, 239
Confessing Church
  (Germany) 166
conflicts:
  in the Church 155, 158 n.65
  social 243
congregation:
  as audience 23–4, 25
  and completeness of
    worship 73–4
  and consumer 8, 76
  as context for Christian ethics 54
  and different types of
    assembly 149–51
  and discipline 163–6
  early Christian 134–7, 341
  and ecumenical experience 8,
    75–6
  as *ekklesia* 138–41, 149–50, 154–5
  liturgical function 8, 36, 70 n.19,
    76–7, 159–63, 341
  as *oikos* 157 n.64
  as *polis* 9–12, 13, 54, 89, 141–4,
    154–5
  in private houses 138, 147, 150–4
  worship as public life 7, 146–54,
    235, 254, 269–72
consensus 6, 26, 99, 281, 298–304,
  307, 317–18

and prohibition of
  images 129–30
and public life 201, 240, 252
and sharing of gifts 281
and social criticism 38, 214–18,
  245–6
and trust 312–13
political theory 117–18
  in Aristotle 121–5
  classical 118–25, 131, 135,
    189–90, 253–4
  in Plato 119–21, 131, 268
  see also social theory
politics:
  in Aristotle 9–10, 26–7, 65 n.10,
    189
  and the Church 114–15, 117–18,
    250–1, 269, 310, 341
  and civil society 274
  and decision-making 298–304
  end 113–16
  ethics of 13–14, 170–2
  flight from 185–8, 191–203, 223,
    294–5
  and forgiveness 281, 307–12,
    315 n.26
  and freedom and necessity
    175–7, 188, 191
  and gender 119–21
  and hearing 282, 311
  and hermeneutics of
    suspicion 281, 286–90, 306,
    313–16
  of identity 171, 271–2
  and intercession 76, 339–41
  in Luther 61–5, 185–8
  in Milbank 104–6, 113–16, 251–2
  overfamiliarizing 171, 173
  as political action 10, 27–8, 30
  and society 208, 242–4,
    269–70
  in Temple 91–2, 96–101
  theological 28 n.19

and therapeutic culture 294–5
and trust 284, 288–9, 306,
  312–16
and two kingdoms/cities
  theory 11, 64–5, 106–7, 142,
  175–7, 252–4, 260
and violence 104–6, 115
and worship 6–13, 114, 279
see also rhetoric, political;
  totalization, political
poor, and Christian
  citizenship 145–6 n.46
postmodernism:
  and ethics 1, 125
  and identity 208, 218–34
  and Milbank 104–16
  and politics 118
  and publics 235–6
  and Rorty 218, 219–26
potentia and *potestas* 131–2
power:
  of the Church 10–11, 27, 143,
    271–2
  divine 132
  and knowledge 98
  and necessity 122–3
  political 213, 252, 258, 286
  and promise 315 n.26
  and responsibility 354–5
  and violence 10–11, 27, 113–15,
    258, 356
praise 6–7, 25, 62–3, 74, 77, 293,
  339
praxis:
  Church as 3, 114–15, 241, 272
  politics as 10, 27
  and theory 103, 107–8, 197,
    202–6
prayer:
  in Kant 45–6
  see also intercession
preaching:
  and hearing 61, 284

INDEX OF NAMES

INDEX OF BIBLICAL REFERENCES

Index compiled by Meg Davies (Registered Indexer, Society of Indexers)